mapping
postmodernism

a survey of *Christian* options

Robert C. Greer

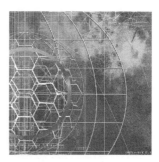

InterVarsity Press
Downers Grove, Illinois

InterVarsity Press
P.O. Box 1400, Downers Grove, IL 60515-1426
World Wide Web: www.ivpress.com
E-mail: mail@ivpress.com

InterVarsity Press® is the book-publishing division of InterVarsity Christian Fellowship/USA®, a student
movement active on campus at hundreds of universities, colleges and schools of nursing in the United States
of America, and a member movement of the International Fellowship of Evangelical Students. For
information about local and regional activities, write Public Relations Dept., InterVarsity Christian
Fellowship/USA, 6400 Schroeder Rd., P.O. Box 7895, Madison, WI 53707-7895, or visit the IVCF website at
<www.ivcf.org>.

All Scripture quotations, unless otherwise indicated, are taken from the Holy Bible, New International
Version®. NIV®. Copyright ©1973, 1978, 1984 by International Bible Society. Used by permission of
Zondervan Publishing House. All rights reserved.

Material from Joshua: A Parable for Today by Joseph Girzone, copyright. Used by permission of Doubleday, a
division of Random House, Inc.

Cover design: Kathleen Lay Burrows

Cover image: Digital Vision/Getty Images

ISBN 0-8308-2733-1

Printed in the United States of America ∞

Library of Congress Cataloging-in-Publication Data

Greer, Robert (Robert C.)
  Mapping postmodernism: a survey of Christian options / Robert
  Greer.
    p. cm.
Includes bibliographical references and index.
  ISBN 0-8308-2733-1 (pbk.: alk. paper)
  1. Postmodernism—Religious aspects—Christianity. 2. Theology,
Doctrinal—History—20th century. I. Title.
  BR115.P74G74 2003
  230'.09'05—dc21

                                              2003008231

| **P** | 17 | 16 | 15 | 14 | 13 | 12 | 11 | 10 | 9 | 8 | 7 | 6 | 5 | 4 | 3 | 2 | 1 |
| **Y** | 15 | 14 | 13 | 12 | 11 | 10 | 09 | 08 | 07 | 06 | 05 | 04 | 03 | | | | |

Dedicated to

Jesus Christ,

the author and finisher of my faith.

¡Sólo tú, más que Venus,

puedes ser

estrella mia de la tarde,

estrella mia del amanecer!

— Juan Ramón Jiménez

Contents

Acknowledgments

This book is loosely based on my Ph.D. dissertation at Marquette University. I therefore would be remiss if I did not acknowledge the enormous help patiently offered to me from my academic advisor at Marquette, D. Lyle Dabney, Ph.D. What is written shadows his thinking on a number of topics. My editor, Gary W. Deddo, Ph.D., at InterVarsity Press, came up with the original concept of this book. His constant encouragement and insights have been invaluable. John Fawcett, Greg Morrison and Maggie Noll, research librarians at the Buswell Memorial Library at Wheaton College, were more than helpful as they assisted me in the location of books, periodicals and so forth, as well as offering me helpful insights.

I also wish to give a special word of thanks to Art Baltzley, Gray Scott, Ron and Diane Brown, Bill and Joy Baxter, Elwood Chipchase, Norm Sparling, and Rob and Teri Wessels, who have helped me in personal ways, without which this book would indeed have never been written.

About This Book

Just prior to writing *Mapping Postmodernism: A Survey of Christian Options,* I was asked to teach a three-week modular course on contemporary theology at a Bible school in the southern tip of Texas. One day, after my class was finished, I got into a car and turned on a local Christian radio station as I drove down the road. The topic being discussed was postmodernism. The speaker was a woman. With much passion in her voice, she insisted that postmodernism was an enemy to the Christian faith and that what was needed in the church was a resolute reaffirmation of absolute truth. At no time during her talk did she give any attention to the problems related to absolute truth. She did not comment that absolute truth—as typically understood in Western culture—is a modernist construct and carries within it modernist baggage, much of which stands in opposition to and undermines the Christian faith. Instead, she fired all her salvos at postmodernism and shored up absolute truth as the line of defense from which the church should never retreat. How typical, I said to myself, was this woman's understanding of postmodernism in the Christian community at large.

It is my belief that to a large extent, the church—especially its Protestant evangelical and fundamentalist traditions—is unaware and essentially uncritical of its philosophical undercarriage. In regards to the question of absolute truth, the church has failed to recognize that due to its complicity with modernism, absolute truth has become a Trojan horse to the church. It was offered as a gift by Enlightenment scholars and left outside the church walls. Revered as something intrinsically good, it was later wheeled through the church's heavily guarded theological gates by its own leadership and afforded a prominent place inside the walls for all to see and admire. Within its bowels, however, was hidden a pernicious enemy to the Christian faith. This enemy has subsequently come out of hiding and, in the name of truth, conquered much of Christian theology in both its liberal and conservative traditions.

For many readers, my characterization of absolute truth as a pernicious enemy to the Christian faith will almost certainly raise many eyebrows. It could cause some to think that this book is an argument in favor of radical relativism, that it stands inside the postmodern paradigm though formally and perhaps only superficially speaking against it. A close reading of each of the chapters, however, should present a different picture.

Mapping Postmodernism has three fundamental subjects on its literary canvas. Alongside (a) a survey of four options within the church regarding postmodernism, this book presents to the reader (b) the problem of radical relativism latent within this philosophical structure and (c) insights from contemporary Christian scholars as they press for a theology that avoids the shortcomings of the postmodern oeuvre. Consequently, as the book unfolds, it gradually makes a case for absolute truth, albeit in a form that is not premodern, modern, existential or postmodern. Though moving Christian theology forward into new territory, where new problems facing the church are being confronted, I am hopeful that the reader will find the book to be faithful to Scripture.

This picture, however, is painted with a broad brush. Gary Deddo, one of the editors at InterVarsity Press, is of the opinion that a number of books have already been published that address the complicated issues related to postmodernism from the lofty perch of doctoral and postdoctoral analyses. They are highly specialized, requiring much prior knowledge. On the other end of the spectrum are a sizeable number of books written on the popular level. Still lacking, he explained, are books that are neither of the two extremes. It was this kind of book that I was asked to write.

In this respect, I am mindful of two statements, one by John Steinbeck and the other by C. S. Lewis. Steinbeck wrote:

> We have not known a single great scientist who could not discourse freely and interestingly with a child. Can it be that the haters of clarity have nothing to say, have observed nothing, have no clear picture of even their own fields?[1]

Lewis wrote:

> You must translate every bit of your Theology into the vernacular. This is very troublesome and it means you can say very little in half an hour, but it is es-

sential. It is also of the greatest service to your own thought. I have come to
the conviction that if you cannot translate your thoughts into uneducated language, then your thoughts were confused.[2]

I was not asked to write a book for children or in uneducated language.
What I was asked to write was something similar. My book was to be balanced and concise, something that moved in the direction that Steinbeck
and Lewis pointed.

I discovered, though, that writing a balanced and concise treatment of the
question of postmodernism in the church was a daunting task. Though
Shakespeare once said that brevity is the soul of wit, in theological studies
brevity runs the risk of reductionism. How does one be concise without falling victim to oversimplifications?

Answering this question was not easy, and I am not sure to what extent
the book achieves this goal. I do believe, though, that part of the answer
required the use of some philosophical and theological jargon. Those who
are engaged in the postmodern debate inside the church typically use such
specialized language. If we want to understand this debate, we must understand these terms. In my conversations with various people inside the
church I have found it remarkable that even such basic terms as *modernism*
and *postmodernism* are often misunderstood, at times even mistakenly
blended into a single, vague and confusing concept. The confusion is com-
pounded when this hybrid modernism is perceived as being synonymous
with *liberalism*—another mistake.

I have, therefore, included in the back of the book an appendix that defines five major paradigms—premodernism, modernism, existentialism,
postmodernism and post-postmodernism—and a glossary of key terms.*
Readers with a limited understanding of the postmodern worldview should
read the appendix and glossary before moving to chapter one.

Speaking of definitions, in my definitions of *modernism* and *postmodernism* I chose Eberhard Jüngel's book *God as the Mystery of the World* as my
starting point. The book is highly regarded in academia and falls within
mainstream scholarly thought. In my presentation of these two movements
I therefore identify René Descartes (with his articulation of the *Cogito*) as the
philosopher who gave birth to the modernist era, and Friedrich Nietzsche as
the transitional philosopher who dealt it its mortal blow, setting the stage in

---

*First references to words found in the glossary will be made bold in the text. Occasionally the
form of words may not be exactly the same in the glossary as in the text.

the West for the postmodern era. Alongside Nietzsche, I identify Martin Heidegger as another proto-postmodernist, a second pivotal thinker who anticipated this new philosophical era. Moreover, I identify Ludwig Wittgenstein, Michel Foucault, Richard Rorty and Jacques Derridá as representative of that cadre of scholars who matured the postmodern paradigm in the middle and latter decades of the twentieth century. All that said, I define modernism with the *Cogito* and postmodernism with efforts to move beyond the *Cogito*.

Moreover, *Mapping Postmodernism* shares Jüngel's optimism. Though many people are troubled by the death of God (absolute truth) in Western culture, Jüngel sees this seeming death as an opportunity for new reflection, pressing the church to further develop its own theological science. In the introductory pages of his book, he wrote:

> It would seem to be agreed that we are living in an age of the verbal place-lessness of God. This placelessness finds its counterpart in the increasing inability to think God and the speechlessness of theology. . . .
>
> Nevertheless, this dubiousness need not lead to a state of theological mourning. Such aporias (situations of doubt or dubiousness), if they are really thought through, are still an appropriate way to intensify not only the awareness of the problem but also the possibilities for further development of the science. Where the difficulties grow, the possibilities also increase.[3]

The possibilities also increase because, with the death of absolute truth, the church is positioned to occupy the void left by its death. It is availed an opportunity to redefine the notion of absolute truth in Christian categories (that is, be instrumental in its resurrection) and thereby offer a solution to the problem of radical relativism that is ravaging the West. This will occur, however, only as the church strips itself of its modernist and postmodernist undergarments (death rags!), adorns itself with a theology that is full of life, and preaches afresh the message of the gospel. This, then, is its momentous opportunity: to make the hearing of God's Word and the recognition of his sovereign place in our lives understandable in a fresh and new way to an increasingly confused and troubled world.

With the parameters of the modernist and postmodernist epochs so defined, the following is a sampling of the scholars of whom I am indebted in the writing of this book. I made extensive use, in addition to Jüngel, of George Lindbeck's insights, having written my Ph.D. dissertation at Marquette University on his theological thought as he grappled with the problems and possibilities of postmodernism. I have also drawn from the observations of Jürgen Moltmann, a famed colleague of Jüngel at the University of Tübingen. I made use of Moltmann's insights of temporality in relation to theology proper. They have far-reaching implications in the field of ecumenical and hermeneutical studies. Here Moltmann's *Theology of Hope* and *The Trinity and the Kingdom* have been of particular help. One of Moltmann's students, D. Lyle Dabney (an individual who also served as my academic advisor at Marquette University), provided additional insights in his pursuit of an understanding of Luther's notion of *theologia crucis* in the arena of hermeneutical theory. Specifically, his book *Die Kenosis des Geistes: Kontinuität zwischen Schöpfung und Erlösung im Werk des Heiligen Geistes* (available only in German) was invaluable as I considered the role of the Holy Spirit in this respect. He argued that prior to the turn to language (a move that typifies postmodernism) exists the turn to relationship. Paralleling Dabney's thought, Thomas Smail and Robert Jenson were helpful in their understandings of the ancient *filioque* controversy and its current implications for hermeneutical and ecumenical studies. Though I do not mention the *filioque* controversy in the text by name, it is shadowed there and mentioned in the endnotes.

In addition to an acquaintance with these scholars, our understanding of the postmodern debate occurring within the church today will be strengthened as we come to terms with five premises that explain the relationship between postmodernism and what it replaced, modernism:

1. With the advent of the Enlightenment in mid-eighteenth-century Europe, the philosophy of modernism usurped Protestant Christian theology in both its liberal and conservative expressions (Roman Catholic theology caught up with this hermeneutical move in the early to mid twentieth century). This new method was grounded in the Cartesian *Cogito*.

2. This new hermeneutical substructure altered the whole notion of absolute truth in the West, causing unalterable and static principles to become more fundamental than the living God.

3. The goals of this Enlightenment move, however, proved to be unachievable since scholarship could not arrive at a consensus as to what these unalterable principles should be. This problem manifested itself in both theological liberalism and conservatism.

4. Postmodernism emerged in the mid to late twentieth century as a corrective to the modernist dilemma. Arguing against the whole notion of consensus, postmodernism argued for individualized truths grounded in the notion of language theory. Specifically, the system of language formats our minds to receive and make sense of data. Since languages differ, the shaping of data correspondingly differs from culture to culture. With this insight, postmodernism offered validation for the notion of radical relativism.

5. Serving as a corrective to modernism, postmodernism is dependent on the modernist paradigm. It cannot exist apart from its own rebellion against the *Cogito,* nor can it articulate itself apart from the use of modernist terms and categories, causing some scholars to wonder whether postmodernism is not truly *post,* as alleged, but rather *ultra*—modernism in its final form.

These five premises serve as plumb lines (to borrow a term from Hugh of St. Victor) reflecting the transition from modernism to postmodernism. They also reflect the irony of modernism's resiliency that exists within this transition—it refuses to die, residing inside that which has allegedly replaced it. The premises provide the reader with a fundamental logic for this book, that is, they help the reader understand a debate taking place in the church. The debate is indeed complex; differing conclusions are rendered by differing scholars as they grapple with complicated questions. Some scholars are pressing for a theology that goes beyond both modernism and postmodernism, which I call post-postmodernism. These plumb lines, then, offer structure to a debate that can easily become unwieldy to the uninitiated or novice inquirer.

In addition to these five premises, I will observe three rules of thumb in this book: (a) that which defines modernism is the *turn to the subject* as the beginning of knowledge, (b) that which defines postmodernism is the *turn to language* as the beginning of knowledge and (c) that which defines post-postmodernism is the *turn to relationship* as the beginning of knowledge. I believe the "turn to relationship" as the beginning of knowledge has much in its favor, particularly the similarity of this posture with that of the Old Testament book of Proverbs, where it is stated repeatedly that the fear of the Lord is the beginning of knowledge/wisdom (e.g., Prov 1:7; 9:10; 15:33). The Hebrew word translated "fear," *yir'â,* implies relationship, a reverential trust in God. Here is where the pursuit of knowledge should begin.

It is my opinion, then, that post-postmodernism is superior to both modernism and postmodernism. Relational in orientation, it recognizes that the first move in the acquisition of knowledge comes from God, not from us. Not only is God the One revealed, he is also the One who reveals. He speaks through his written Word (verbal communication) and his actions in history (nonverbal communication). This is true not only of religious truth but of truth in all its categories. Our response, then, is to draw close to him and listen, praying that we will indeed have ears to hear (cf. Rev 2:7, 11, 17, 29; 3:6, 13, 22).

At this point, a few autobiographical remarks are in order. Since, as I will argue later in this book, we must consider the role of "the language game" (a specific historical and cultural situation and its impact on the shaping of truth) as one seeks truth, the reader has a right to know—at least to some extent—my own language game. Without such knowledge the arguments presented in this book will lack a proper grounding, inclined to float in theological air rather than be correctly situated in the real world.

I was raised in a Roman Catholic home, my mother being of that religious tradition and the one who established the spiritual direction for the children. My father had no formal religious identity and therefore offered little religious input, other than to minimize its significance. My church attendance was intermittent. I found the worship services lifeless and uninteresting, partly because of poorly understood rituals accompanied with sacerdotal words spoken in Latin. Church attendance was therefore a duty to be performed rather than an experience to be celebrated. By the time I reached my teen years I had had enough and my church attendance ended. I adopted the spiritual perspective of my father, having jettisoned formalized religion altogether.

At the age of eighteen, however, I experienced another change. A religious conversion restored me to the church, albeit one of a Protestant fundamentalist orientation. Central to my conversion experience was the gospel of Jesus Christ—understood in Protestant categories—that I found irresistibly attractive. Catalysts to my conversion were several individuals who took a special interest in me. They were biblically literate, practiced an active devotional life with God, attended worship services that they found to be interesting and stimulating, loved one another and demonstrated a similar attitude of love towards me. I accepted without question the whole fundamentalist package of theology—the verbal plenary inspiration of the Bible, the doctrine of creation and the fall, heaven and hell, the Trinity, Jesus Christ as God incarnate, born of a virgin, redemption by his blood from sin and death, his bodily resurrection, ascension and future return to establish his kingdom on this earth. What is more, I adopted a fundamentalist attitude of ecclesial separation known as *second-degree separation.* Not only did I separate from those people who were not truly "born again," I also separated from other Christians who conducted themselves in a disorderly manner (specifically, I separated from those who fellowshipped with Roman Catholics, those identified with Eastern Orthodoxy, mainline denominations tainted with theological liberalism, etc.).

After attending a fundamentalist Bible school and then marrying my wife, we moved to the Midwest where I became an assistant pastor of a large, multistaffed church. The senior pastor rejected the notion of second degree separation and introduced my wife and me to an understanding of the Christian faith that was less judgmental and which celebrated rather than disdained theological and practical differences within the church. Here, Roman Catholicism, Eastern Orthodoxy and mainline denominations were not rejected out of hand, as had been the case in my former spiritual experience.

Coinciding with this time at the church, my wife and I were members of a mission agency and spent part of our time traveling to a large number of churches raising financial and prayer support as we sought to serve the Lord on the mission field. In 1980, we left the Midwest and moved to south Texas where we learned Spanish in a concentrated one-year program.

Upon completing our language studies, we entered Mexico where we served as missionaries among the Aztec people. This proved to be a formative experience for us as we saw firsthand the negative side of religious triumphalism evidenced as each ecclesial group vied for exclusive dominance: Catholics and Protestants struggled with one another and ecclesial groups within Protestantism engaged in similar skirmishes with one another. We also observed Roman Catholicism in a pre-Vatican II stance where a version of the Marian cult was in full swing. Not only did Mary achieve (albeit unofficially) the status as coredemptrix, participating with Jesus in the role of redeemer, she also achieved a pneumatological status, usurping the role of the Holy

Spirit by being the one to whom people looked for spiritual comfort, guidance into truth and answers to prayer. We found all of this to be very troubling.

In 1986, we left Mexico and returned to the western United States where I pastored a church. At this time I pursued a master's degree in theology at Wheaton College—at first through correspondence and then with trips to the Illinois campus. We finally moved to the western Chicago suburbs where I completed my degree. At Wheaton, I was further exposed to differing ways in which theology can be shaped. Though I was not yet formerly exposed to the Wittgensteinian notion of language games, the differing perspectives on theology offered at Wheaton nudged me in that direction.

In 1995 I began a Ph.D. program in systematic theology at Marquette University in Milwaukee, Wisconsin. Marquette, being an institution founded by the Society of Jesus (the Jesuits), proved to be another significant turn in my theological pilgrimage. Clearly within the orb of post-Vatican II thought, Marquette presented a side of Roman Catholicism that I had known to exist but to which I had little direct exposure. Two of the major concerns at Marquette were (a) the development of a viable ecumenical method and (b) a way past the modernist debacle that had paralyzed Christianity without falling prey to the radical relativism of postmodern thought. It was here that the perspective of the modernist hermeneutic possessing both a liberal and a conservative expression was forcefully and convincingly presented. Reflecting back on my days at Wheaton, I began recalling that several of the more prominent professors had presented a similar case—albeit from an evangelical perspective. As I continued my studies at Marquette, I visited with these Wheaton professors privately to gain what I hoped to be a more complete picture of this theological problem that was troubling the church.

My dissertation project specifically addressed this problem. Exploring the theology of the esteemed Lutheran theologian George A. Lindbeck, I examined how he grappled with the problem of modernism and postmodernism and sought a means by which to move the church forward through an engagement with postmodern thought. In my research I encountered several problems with his methodology and suggested correctives that, I believed, enabled his system to achieve its intended objectives. My dissertation was entitled "Lindbeck on the Catholicity of the Church: The Problem of Foundationalism and Antirealism in George A. Lindbeck's *Ecumenical Methodology*." It was successfully defended at Marquette in the fall of 1999, and I graduated January 2000 with my doctorate.

Upon completion of this degree, I underwent another turn in my spiritual journey by reacquainting myself with my Protestant fundamentalist roots. Protestant fundamentalism, as this book will bear out, contains two significant problems: (a) in spite of its conservative orientation, it is grounded in a modernist hermeneutic, and (b) it lacks a viable ecumenical methodology with which to prevent fractures within its own and other ecclesial bodies. Nevertheless, with a sense of irony, I found the fellowship of a small cadre of Christians who identify themselves as fundamentalists to be personally satisfying and enriching. These people are characterized by lives surrendered to the authority of Scripture, are constant and effective in their prayer lives and are committed in their love for one another. Admirable traits indeed. Yet, having said this, I do not discount the problems with the overall fundamentalist oeuvre of which they are a part. My enriching fellowship with these individuals merely reflects the pervasive reach of language games, how each community is characterized by its own "game," so to speak, and how each needs to be examined and appreciated on its own merits. More to the point, though returning to my fundamentalist roots, I have done so not as a fundamentalist but as someone who has learned how to appreciate the sagacities of fundamentalism while avoiding its foibles (I maintain a similar posture towards Roman Catholicism, mainline Protestant denominations, Eastern Orthodoxy, etc.). To respond by discarding fundamentalist Christianity because of its penchant for triumphalistic thinking is to fall into the fundamentalist trap.

One final comment. As this book was being written, I experienced a trial in my personal life that taxed my faith to its limits, even beyond, or so I thought. I therefore found myself experiencing the irony of writing a book about the means of prioritizing faith in the systematization of theology while struggling with faith as I worked through these personal issues in my own life. Not easy, I discovered. I identified only too well with the words written by Alister McGrath in his book *The Journey: A Pilgrim in the Land of the Spirit*. Writing autobiographically, he explained that the Christian life

> seemed to be little more than just kicking ideas around. It was as if there were one part of my life that dealt with ideas, and this somehow never seemed to

come into contact with anything else. It began to seem unreal and irrelevant. As I wrestled with this, I began to realize that my faith was actually quite superficial. I had *understood* things, but had failed to *appreciate* them. I had not made the connections that would have led to the enrichment of my faith and the deepening of my spiritual life. Quite simply, I had missed out on some of the great riches of the faith. As I began to discover them, I found myself wishing that I had encountered them long before. Then I began to do some serious reading and reflection.[4]

This book was therefore born in the midst of serious devotional reading and personal reflection as I struggled to move from understanding to appreciation in the Christian life. Here in the crucible of life where people struggle, doubt and are forced—sometimes in spite of themselves—to stretch their faith, my faith was stretched. To paraphrase Steinbeck, this was a time when I discovered that though my faith was not strong, at least it was permanent.[5] And since it was permanent, I was able to incrementally build on it with a prayer life that was active and alive.

This book was also born in the context of a loving Christian community. I discovered that such a community is essential to the growth of faith since love provides the needed encouragement to press forward in faith when many outward evidences are so discouraging. This is especially true for someone like myself who has a natural propensity to try to rationally figure out solutions to problems before taking a step forward. Hence, to my chagrin I discovered that when push came to shove I was a modernist at heart. It was a combination of the Spirit of God working through the Word of God and the people of God that nudged me forward to a life of faith.

Upon completion of the first draft of *Mapping Postmodernism,* I picked up Kathleen Norris's book *Amazing Grace: A Vocabulary of Faith* and read afresh a few of the chapters. Early in the book she wrote, "Faith, of course, is not readily understandable, which makes it suspect among people who have been educated to value ideas insofar as they are comprehensible, quantifiable, consistent." Like a poem, she added, faith transcends human ideas and reaches into the realm of sublime experience. She then concluded, "Faith does not conform itself to ideology but to experience. And for the Christian this means the experience of the person of Jesus Christ, not as someone who once lived in Galilee but who lives now in all believers."[6]

These well-crafted words set the theme of this book. The person of Jesus Christ—not someone who only lived long ago in Galilee but who now lives in all believers—is the cornerstone of truth. It is this living person where truth, in its most sublime and absolute form, resides. He is not comprehensible, quantifiable or consistent. Indeed, in some respects he is opaque and mysterious. His ways are not our ways nor his thoughts our thoughts, Scripture says. He is, however, alive, and he transcends all human rationality—the one whom we are called upon to love and to whom every human being will someday bend the knee and confess as Lord (cf. Phil 2:6-11). As such, faith requires experiential engagement with Jesus Christ. He cannot be understood from afar or in the abstract.

In this respect, the final stanza of that great Reformation hymn "A Mighty Fortress Is Our God" comes to mind. Here Martin Luther wrote:

Das Wort sie sollen lassen stahn   That word above all earthly powers—
und kein Dank dazu haben.   No thanks to them—abideth;
Er ist bei uns wohl auf dem Plan   The Spirit and the gifts are ours
mit seinem Geist und Gaben.   Through him who with us sideth.
Nehmen sie den Leib,   Let goods and kindred go,
Gut, Ehr, Kind und Weib,   This mortal life also;
lass fahren dahin,   The body they may kill:
sie habens kein' Gewinn;   God's truth abideth still,
das Reich muss uns doch bleiben.   His kingdom is forever.

Indeed! Amen and Amen.

The Advent of Postmodernism

In his bestselling book *The Closing of the American Mind,* Allan Bloom wrote, "There is one thing a professor can be absolutely certain of: almost every student entering the university believes, or says he believes, that truth is relative."[1] This comment well illustrates a major paradigm shift occurring in Western culture—the transition from modernism to postmodernism. Moreover, what Bloom wrote in 1987 characterizes Western culture all the more now in the twenty-first century.

Roughly stated, modernism affirms the existence of absolute truths. Postmodernism affirms the opposite: the nonexistence of absolute truths.[2] Though similar in other respects, in this respect they are polar opposites.

Modernism has reigned in Western culture for about two hundred years. During these years it entrenched itself as the sole proprietor of Western philosophy, understood to be self-evidently true, requiring no proof for its underlying assumptions. The fact that postmodernism has succeeded in uprooting modernism within an entire culture is therefore a noteworthy achievement, a feat that no other philosophical system or religion had previously been able to accomplish. Almost everything—especially issues in the realm of moral and social values—are being reconsidered from within the postmodern rubric. Many of the conclusions now being drawn in the context of postmodernism differ widely from the previously drawn conclusions of modernism.

The results of this transition have been predictable. The new conclusions emerging from within postmodernism have shocked many people. And rather than embracing the new morality and the new social mores, these people have become the new counterculture. Like Old Testament prophets, they are foretelling an impending doom upon Western culture unless it turns back, repents from its dalliance with postmodernism and once again affirms the existence of absolute truth.[3]

It is here where conservative Christianity has been most noticeable in the public forum. A number of books have been published in the 1990s and early 2000s by Christian authors excoriating postmodernism and admonishing the Christian community to stand firm against the postmodern tide saturating the West. In the pulpits, on the radio and on television, this same message has been presented. With Bible in hand the Christian believer argues for absolute truth, often with the words "thus saith the Lord" serving as a centerpiece to his or her arguments. Hence, where polemical works had previously targeted secular modernity as one of Christianity's chief foes, the new foe is postmodernism.[4] Only by understanding and embracing that which constitutes *absolute truth,* leaders within the Christian community explained, could the battle be waged successfully.

A small cadre of other Christian scholars, however, have also joined this postmodern fray, but from a different perspective. Rather than excoriating postmodernism, these scholars have taken a more nuanced approach. Weighing postmodernism's strengths and weaknesses, along with the strengths and weaknesses of the antipostmodern crowd, they have determined that postmodernism indeed has some positive qualities that could help the church overcome some nagging problems that have appeared unsolvable in recent decades and centuries. Stanley J. Grenz and Roger E. Olson are representative of this approach to postmodernism. They explain, "Although the emerging postmodern mind may appear to put faith on the defensive, it actually marks a new day of opportunity for theology."[5] After reviewing one periodical that addressed the question of postmodernism from a biblical perspective, Edgar V. McKnight wrote:

> Instead of a simplistic condemnation or commendation of postmodernism, I found an evenhanded evaluation of what the new philosophical worldview might mean. One writer sees "a new set of challenges and temptations for biblical Christians," but he also sees that "the postmodern age . . . presents untold opportunities for recovering the historic Christian faith."[6] Another writer cites Stephen Toulmin's book *Cosmopolis* and examines four areas mentioned by Toulmin where "considering the values of postmodernism will be a worthy endeavor." The writer suggests that in these areas the shift away from modern values to postmodern values "involves returning to medieval and pre-enlightenment (read 'Reformation') values."[7]

In other words, this nuanced approach to postmodernism is not a carte blanche acceptance of postmodern ideals, nor a nostalgic insistence on the inherent rightness of absolute truth and a polemic attack against postmodernism from that posture. Rather, it is a path that avoids the dark sides of both postmodernism and absolute truth while at the same time benefiting from their strong points.

And herein lies the problem. The church, especially the two subtraditions of evangelicalism and fundamentalism within the broad Protestant tradition, tends to be well-versed on the dark side of postmodernism (e.g., radical relativity and deconstructionism). It tends to be less studied, however, on the dark side of absolute truth.

THE DARK SIDE OF ABSOLUTE TRUTH

Absolute truth, as it is typically understood in Western culture, possesses a very problematic dark side. This dark side can be divided into two broad categories.

First, there is the problem of *competing absolute truths*. People who affirm the notion of absolute truth cannot seem to agree with one another about what this absolute truth should look like.[8] Christian people often illustrate such disagreements: One Christian believer, with the Bible in hand, claims to understand and embrace absolute truth, yet has profound disagreements with other Christians similarly endowed with the Bible. The plethora of Christian denominations, most of which exist due to doctrinal disagreements with other denominations that generated splits/separations/divisions/schisms somewhere in their respective histories, gives ample evidence that the question is not so much whether one possesses absolute truth, but rather whose version of absolute truth one espouses. (Will the real absolute truth please stand up?) Is it any wonder that society at large is hesitant and/or resistant when Christians enter the public square and try to mandate a truth that they insist is inviolable and universally applicable?

Second, there is the problem of *hidden agendas*. Michel Foucault's hermeneutics of suspicion come to mind, according to which the notion of absolute truth is more correctly understood as a code word for *power and control*.[9] Foucault argues that an individual or community typically takes a debatable issue and grounds it in the underlying assumptions and limitations of their own categories and definitions—with the end result that they stack the deck, so to speak, to guarantee a desired outcome. The word *God* is a good example of this. The Christian definition of the word is widely different from a Hindu or Buddhist definition. During a debate, whoever's definition controls the conversation controls the range of conclusions permitted by that conversation, and thereby wins by default.

According to Foucault, such "stacking of decks," as one insists upon one's own definition, always occurs by those who affirm the notion of absolute truth. He therefore concludes that the whole idea of absolute truth is a phantom construct designed to prevent people from noticing the real agenda as differing communities (belief systems) debate one another. The real agenda, says Foucault, is the maintenance of one's own belief system as the solely legitimate system within a larger community. To the degree that a community is successful in this effort, it will maintain power and control over the larger community of which it is a member.

Noteworthy in this observation of the dark side of absolute truth is how little attention it has received in much of conservative Christian scholarship. Absolute truth has been defended in current apologetic writings as if the cure to the problem of radical relativism is simply a nostalgic reaffirmation of the overall paradigm of absolute truth. Yet by failing to adequately address its dark side, conservative Christian scholarship is playing into the hands of postmodernism. They are undermining themselves because the problem of the dark side of absolute truth is a major concern of contemporary scholarship, not just in the academic discipline of theology, but also in the other so-called soft sciences (e.g., philosophy, psychology, sociology, anthropology) and even in the hard sciences.[10] By failing to address the dark side of absolute truth, much of conservative scholarship is becoming increasingly out of step with the central questions and insights that drive contemporary thought. Such scholarship is therefore not to be taken seriously, as it is on its way to intellectual isolation and cultural ghettoization. As such, it has left the door wide open to alternative systems that are more engaged with the questions related to the dark side of absolute truth. Enter postmodernism.

The solution for conservative Christian scholarship, of course, is to face the problem squarely. As already noted, a minority of scholars has emerged within conservative Christian tradition that is doing just this. These scholars are arguing that the questions and concerns that the church has of postmodernism *must include a serious dialogue with the questions related to the dark side of absolute truth*. Their point is that one cannot credibly address the problems with the one without at the same time pointing out problems with the other (see Mt 7:3). Hence, by pointing out the problems related to absolute truth, these scholars are attempting to extract "the plank" from the theological eyes of those inside the faith so that the questions related to postmodernism can be more correctly assessed. Nevertheless, like many of the prophets from the Old Testament, this cadre of scholars is neither welcomed nor understood by many of their own colleagues and ecclesial leaders. As one might expect, theological eye-surgery is seldom pleasant.

This is not to suggest, however, that the cadre of Christian scholars mentioned above are closet postmodernists. They are not attempting to subtly maneuver the church theologically so that it will, perhaps unwittingly, jettison the whole notion of absolute truth and begin to think as postmodernists. As John R. W. Stott has rightly explained, within the Christian faith there is an absoluteness that cannot be surrendered, an absoluteness that should give us a sense of certainty and confidence to that which we know to be true. "In those things which are clearly revealed in Scripture," he has written, "Christians should not be doubtful or apologetic. The corridors of the New Testament reverberate with dogmatic affirmations beginning 'We know,' 'We are sure,' 'We are confident.'"[11] Similarly, C. S. Lewis wrote several decades earlier:

> The thing which I have called for convenience the *Tao,* and which others may call Natural Law or Traditional Morality, . . . is not one among a series of possible systems of value. It is the sole source of all value judgements. If it is rejected, all value is rejected. If any value is retained, it is retained. . . . The rebellion of new ideologies [e.g., postmodernism] against the *Tao* is a rebellion of the branches against the tree: if the rebels could succeed they would find that they had destroyed themselves. The human mind has no more power of inventing a new value than of imagining a new primary colour, or, indeed, of creating a new sun and a new sky for it to move in.[12]

Hence, this cadre of Christian scholars insists that absolute truth *does* exist. Nevertheless, what is needed is some serious rethinking in our understanding of it. We need to grapple with its dark side and offer a response to our postmodern friend whereby our sense of certainty in what we know to be true (the gospel) is able to circumvent problems often associated with its dark side.[13]

THE ROLE OF POSTLIBERALISM

One of the major efforts to grapple with the dark side of absolute truth and achieve a nuanced assessment of postmodernism has been the postliberal project. *The Nature of Doctrine: Religion and Theology in a Postliberal Age,* written by George A. Lindbeck in 1984, is a major effort to integrate post-modern categories into the Christian faith with the goal of overcoming its modernist mindset and restoring it to some facsimile of its historic premodern form. This project has apparently struck an important nerve within the church, evidenced by the wide attention it has received and debate it has generated within the religious community.

Because of this, any effort to study the question of postmodernism apart from a prior understanding of postliberalism will likely generate myopic and simplistic conclusions. In this book, I will therefore give postliberalism a wide berth as I discuss the challenges and claims of postmodernism. Understanding the postliberal project, however, requires much more than an assessment of the modern-postmodern debate. One must also think through this debate in the context of the ecumenical agenda, since it was the lack of success in the arena of ecumenism that generated the questions and proposed solutions that ultimately gave birth to postliberalism.

THE QUESTION OF ECUMENISM

At this point, however, the typical Protestant evangelical Christian is at a disadvantage. The numerous ecclesial bodies that make up this tradition often understand the Bible as possessing an exactitude that leaves little room for varying interpretations, ambiguity or mystery. Alister E. McGrath made a similar observation when he bemoaned Protestant evangelicalism as often possessing a "military precision," where every last detail has been sorted out and provision been made for every contingency. Fed up with the Christian faith so defined, he confessed his fatigue of "trite and shallow answers to the big problems of Christian living by well-meaning pastors and friends."[14]

Such an environment, which requires a military precision in doctrine, invariably breeds attitudes of **triumphalism** that spark condemnations and ecclesial separations, because military precision gives little tolerance to variances in doctrine by well-meaning Christians. According to this logic, the tolerance of doctrinal and theological differences—whether great or small—is a sign of spiritual compromise and must therefore be wholly avoided.

Illustrations of this phenomenon within the church are legion. To cite one example, in the final decade of the twentieth century the IFCA-International[15]—an ecclesial body renown for its firm stance against false doctrine—experienced its own divisions and separations. Certain regional fellowships and specific churches within this body determined that variances on specific doctrinal issues existed between themselves and the national body. With a spirit of military precision, they therefore separated and either formed their own or joined other ecclesial bodies. It mattered not that the doctrinal variances in question did not address the major theological questions that have traditionally divided orthodoxy from heterodoxy in the church. Error was error. Hence, an ecclesial body famous for its separated stance against false doctrine ironically found itself fragmenting based upon the application of a similar rationale by those in its own membership.

This illustration, and many others that could be cited, makes the case that Protestant evangelicalism lacks a viable ecumenical methodology. In its desire to remain doctrinally pure and therefore separated from apostasy, Protestant evangelicalism has fallen victim to its own principles and priorities—committed to doctrinal purity, it has not been able to prevent a chain reaction of additional separations from occurring within itself. That is to say, Protestant evangelicalism has a natural tendency to take ecclesial separation too far. Yet when juxtaposed with Jesus' own words about love and unity (e.g., Jn 13:34-35; 17:20-23) something seems to be seriously wrong with the "military precision" of Protestant evangelicalism that has resulted in so much fragmentation and disunity.

Accordingly, Protestant evangelicalism's penchant to separate, what John R. W. Stott describes as "our pathological tendency to fragment,"[16] needs to be seriously reconsidered. We need a renewed ecumenical vision and priorities while at the same time maintaining fidelity to the canonical Scriptures. This vision includes a conviction commensurate with that of the first-generation Protestant Reformers who hoped that their excommunication from Rome would be short-lived and that a return to the mother church would occur once Rome ceased from its "ragings against the gospel."[17] This, for example, was the hope of Philipp Melanchthon, Luther's close colleague, who maintained that if the pope "would allow the gospel, we might allow him his superiority over the bishops which he has by 'human right.' We could make this concession for the sake of the peace and general unity among those Christians who are now under him and might be in the future."[18] A contemporary evangelical scholar has written something similar:

> The loss of Christian unity at any point is tragic and destructive. When that loss threatens our unity in the gospel itself, it is catastrophic. To work toward unity in the gospel is not a matter of ecclesiastical politics; it is a matter that touches the soul of the church itself and the souls of all its members. To seek

unity in the gospel is neither a quixotic crusade nor a frivolous search; it is a
matter of the most urgent priority for the Christian. All who embrace the gospel and love its content are visited by a divine mandate to preserve that unity
and to defend it together.[19]

In other words, the mission of ecumenism—in spite of its problems located in the current scholastic conversation within Christendom—is not only
correct in principle, it is also the will of God.

THE PURPOSE OF THIS BOOK

The purpose of this book is to introduce the reader to the current debate
within the church regarding postmodernism. It stands apart from those
books that are either highly condemnatory or laudatory of postmodernism.
It takes the position that postmodernism has both strengths and weaknesses
and, therefore, should be considered within that context. In the final analysis, this book argues that Christian theology move past postmodernism and
seek a new system that is more agreeable with the Word of God so that we
can be better positioned to hear God speak.

This book is intended for undergraduate and master's level students.
While this is the target audience, some readers who have not formally attended college level institutions yet are academically studious (including, of
course, many pastors) may also benefit from this book.

This book is not intended to be innovative. Rather, it is meant to be a survey of sorts. In the final chapters I offer my assessment of where this debate
is going, yet even here I make no attempt to pioneer new theological
ground. What I have written in these final chapters is being and has been
said by others. In certain cases, it has been said by others long ago. Yet it is
possible that, having been said long ago, it did not have as strong an impact
on academia and the church as it could have had—typically, different epochs are concerned with different questions. By bringing these voices to the
present, I am merely attempting to show a cohesiveness of the past with the
present in a book that is a concise treatment of the subject matter, and suggest its future movement based on this trajectory.

Though not innovative, this book will nevertheless attempt to shine light
on a significant disparity that exists within the church today. Because of its
complicity with modernism, systematic theology—in both its liberal and
conservative traditions—reduced our ability to hear the voice of God. This
being the case, the ministry of the Holy Spirit has been marginalized in much

of its formalized theology. Not willing to be left on the sidelines, however, the Holy Spirit has continued to speak, albeit with people not formally trained in theology as his primary audience. This, of course, has generated a regrettable dichotomy within the church: systematic theology and pietism have little to do with one another. It is upon this issue, then, that *Mapping Postmodernism: A Survey of Christian Options* attempts to shine light.

Helmut Thielicke, pastor to the German people during the Second World War and post-war years, has commented upon this dichotomy. Writing to the German people shortly after the conclusion of the Second World War when their lives had been shattered in every conceivable way (economically, socially, physically, personally, morally), he said:

> Many people today hesitate to go to a pastor because they think that he will simply apply to their problem some ready-made dogmatic formula in which he does not express himself (as they are doing) and which he does not basically share. They thus prefer to go to other men and women whom they meet in the office or on the train or in the street. It is not that these people can give them a patent remedy for the problem which bothers them. The only answer they want is a little sympathy and understanding. They do not want an answer in the strict sense. They certainly do not want anything ready-made and therefore alien. . . . What we desire is not a voice from beyond, but a voice which comes from this world, the voice of brother men in solidarity with us, the voice which chimes in with the chorus of the struggling and oppressed.[20]

Disgusted with the patent ready-made remedies that had typified German theology, the German people were no longer interested in hearing "a voice from beyond." Instead, they yearned for words that spoke to their existential now, "from within this world," in the midst of their specific doubts, fears and horrendous pain. Because of its complicity with modernism, systematic theology had somehow lost its ability to speak thus. It was in this context that Thielicke sought to draw the German people back to God, to help them understand God in their specific and very difficult now.

It is my conviction that if theology cannot speak to people who are broken, it cannot speak at all. More than other people, broken people yearn to understand how that which they know to be true can make sense with how they live at a practical level. This book attempts to restore the link between systematic theology (how people think) and practical piety (how people live). It will do so by demonstrating the problems of modernism in theology and suggest a way to move beyond it.

The next step. In 1996 Donald Carson wrote that certain avant-garde intellectuals "have passed through postmodernity and emerged on the other side"[21] and are now announcing its impending death. He added, however, that "they are casting about gamely for another worldview," but at the moment "there is no pattern on the horizon to replace postmodernism."[22] Whether or not that assertion was true in 1996, it is certainly not true now. In this book, I will give voice to a number of theologians who are in hot pursuit of an epistemology with which to repudiate both modernism and postmodernism. Collectively, their voices are giving shape to a new paradigmatic structure from which to philosophize and theologize. I call this newly forming paradigm post-postmodernism.

The implication, then, is that the next step is not a turn backwards towards a premodernism. Many Christians would prefer a backward move, since the highly venerated apostolic age is located in the distant past. Such a step backwards in time is wrought with much difficulty, though, because we cannot ignore the history that has transpired between then and now. The Christian religion is a historical religion precisely because we believe that God acts in history. To imagine that we can think through the Christian faith "purely spiritually" (ahistorically), then, is to do damage to the very faith revealed in Scripture that we affirm. Because the Christian religion is a historical religion, we therefore must embrace our past *and* present, and from that posture move forward into the future.

An analogy may be helpful here. If I were somehow capable of transporting myself back in time to first-century Palestine, I could not truly adopt a first-century worldview and think from that posture. My knowledge of airplanes, electricity, the Copernican revolution on astronomy, the theological and philosophical trajectories that have emerged since the first century, the history of the succeeding centuries and so on would cause me to always think as a twentieth/twenty-first-century person in spite of the fact that I am now a bona fide member of the first-century world. To be sure, my presence in the first century would add nuances and perspectives of the first century world not otherwise available to me in the twenty-first century. Still, I could never fully enter that worldview. I am forever a twentieth/twenty-first-century person. Stated otherwise, I cannot *unthink* what I know and have experienced. In reference to questions related to modernism and postmodernism, this is equally true. I cannot *unthink* modernism and postmodernism. It is therefore impossible to think as a premodern in the truest sense of the word. All one can do is move forward.[23]

Moving forward in a direction that is post-postmodern, however, does not require that we set aside the premodern worldview in its entirety as something not worthy of examination and consideration. It *can* and *should* be examined and considered, provided that we do not attempt to wholly replicate it in our theologies. That is, the context of our articulations cannot be presented with a philosophical or theological naiveté, as if modernism and postmodernism never existed. Any attempt to do so will not only betray our own worldview but also lack relevance to the worldview of our audience. It will cause us to drift into an intellectual ghetto. Hence, premodernism can be examined but must also be recast in our current twenty-first-century context.

In this book, I will attempt to do just that. I will draw from premodern values but will also use the modernist notion of **foundationalism** as a point of reference, observing how the differing positions in the postmodern debate respond to it. What we will therefore construct is a facsimile of premodernism—similar yet maintaining important distinctions.

The overall outline. The overall outline of this book runs as follows: We will set the stage to this debate by first examining the dark side of absolute truth and the theology of ecumenism (chapters 1-2). We will then look at the four positions in the debate (chapters 3-6). Each of these chapters will highlight a theologian who is a major player articulating one of the four positions: Francis A. Schaeffer, Karl Barth, John H. Hick and George A. Lindbeck. Each one has distinguished himself in the postmodern debate by examining the issues at hand from a decisively different perspective. Two are now dead (Schaeffer and Barth) and two are still alive (Hick and Lindbeck). Though it would have been more consistent for me to choose four scholars who are alive, in my estimation no singular living theologian has emerged who has filled the shoes left by either Schaeffer or Barth.

After completing this review of the four positions, we will consider how this debate is being advanced in a post-postmodern direction. The chapter entitled "Absolute Truth Revisited" (chapter 7) will consider a paradigm that differs from that in which the modernist-postmodernist debate is being cast. Then the chapter entitled "What Now?" (chapter 8), will then examine how this newly forming paradigm is playing itself out pragmatically in the real world.

In short, the purpose of this book is to enter the conversation of Christian scholars as they debate the phenomenon of postmodernism inside the church. With this debate better understood, insights should emerge that will point us in a direction this conversation is moving, a trajectory that may be opening the door to a viable post-postmodernism.

QUESTIONS

Basic Concepts

1. Generally speaking, what is the distinction between modernism and postmodernism?

2. In the postmodern world, who constitutes the new counterculture, and what is their essential concern?

3. Briefly stated, what are the dark sides of modernism and postmodernism?

4. Explain the problem of absolute truth regarding plural absolute truths and hidden agendas.

5. What is the overall agenda of the postmodern project?

6. Why is Protestant evangelicalism in need of an ecumenical methodology?

Further Thought

Read the appendix and consider the following questions.

1. Why is it difficult for people situated in the modernist worldview to think in terms of the *quid pro quo* that characterized the premodern world?

2. Modernism is identified with two principal characteristics: distanciation and the *Cogito*. These two concepts fell into disrepute toward the end of the twentieth century. Why?

3. In what respect are modernism and existentialism similar or dissimilar?

4. In what respect are existentialism and postmodernism similar or dissimilar?

5. Post-postmodernism carries within it much of the postmodern worldview, yet it does so without jettisoning the notion of absolute truth by expanding the notion of language: the *word* with the *Word*. What is meant by this expansion, and how does it modify without wholly repudiating the postmodern paradigm?

1

The Dark Side of
Absolute Truth

This chapter title, "The Dark Side of Absolute Truth," may appear oxymoronic to some readers, since in their estimation absolute truth is idyllic—the epitomization of truth in its purest form. It has no dark side. One may as well speak of the dark side of God as of the dark side of absolute truth. Admittedly, there is some truth to this claim. For example, if one cites John 14:6, where Jesus said, "I am the way and the truth and the life," and rightly concludes that Jesus Christ—the second person of the Trinity—is absolute truth par excellence, then to describe absolute truth as possessing a dark side would indeed be an oxymoronic assertion.

Yet that is not how I will be using the term *absolute truth* in this chapter. Rather than identifying absolute truth with Jesus Christ (a person), I will identify it in the fashion that has typified Western culture since the Age of the Enlightenment. That is, I will identify absolute truth as an encyclopedic collection of abstracted principles that are understood to be timelessly valid and therefore immutable—not subject to change. Existing independently from the specifics of any given culture and from any given historical moment, these principles are transcultural and ahistorical. In a sense, they are other-worldly. The person who has access to this encyclopedic collection of truths is understood to possess **God's eye,** enabled to see and assess reality with the precision and exactitude of God himself. This is where the dark side of absolute truth resides.

This chapter is necessary because it is this dark side of absolute truth that has given rise to the postmodern agenda. Unless one rightly appreciates the problem that postmodernists are attempting to solve, one cannot understand why they are dissatisfied with philosophy and theology in its current state and are seeking new answers to old problems. Without such an understanding, it is possible for (a) postmodernists and those who oppose postmodernism to talk past each other, and (b) those attempting to understand the postmodern debate to misunderstand central issues being addressed. Since the purpose of this book is to clarify the postmodern debate that currently exists within the church, understanding the dark side of absolute truth is therefore a crucial first step.

Our outline will be the following. We will first glean an understanding of the dark side of absolute truth by reaching back to its historical roots. This dark side of absolute truth is longstanding in Western culture—and precisely its longstanding presence allows westerners to have grown so accustomed to it as to become desensitized to it. We will therefore examine two thinkers who have profoundly influenced Western culture in regards to its understanding of absolute truth. These two individuals are Augustine of Hippo (354-430) and René Descartes (1596-1650). By examining their writings, our intent is to become sensitized to the underlying assumptions of absolute truth that drive Western culture. Second, we will consider a possible error in their writings where they confused finitude with infinitude. This error has set into motion a philosophical trajectory that still exists within Western culture. Third, we will conclude this chapter with an analysis of the impact of this understanding of absolute truth upon the church.

AUGUSTINE OF HIPPO

Augustine of Hippo is arguably the most significant single theologian within Western Christendom. Both Catholic and Protestant traditions still feel his influence—an influence that stretches more than sixteen hundred years.

A notable problem, however, exists in the interpretation of Augustine. This problem centers on the varied theological contours that can be found within his writings. Like most important thinkers, Augustine's writings reflect his own theological pilgrimage as he stretched intellectually and thought anew about complicated questions. Because of this, within his writings one does not find a flat unvaried predictable theology of thought that can be organized into a singular fixed system—rather, variations and transition points exist. Among the variations in his pilgrimage are two broad categories: he emphasized either *creation* or the *fall* as a backdrop to his hermeneutical theory. Depending on the one being emphasized, his theology took on characteristics not found in the other. In other words, over the course of his career, Augustine's theology was neither consistent nor harmonious. Rather, his thinking contains significant zigs and zags.[1]

In what follows, our interest in Augustine will be limited to his understanding of language and its relationship to truth as it corresponds to his understanding of the fall. This, of course, means that those writings of Augustine that correspond to his understanding of creation reflect a theology that differs from what we will be examining in this chapter.[2]

While pursuing a deepened understanding of the fall and its implications for us, Augustine struggled with the problem of language. The fact that language is a form of **semiotic communication** (it requires the use of symbols) posed a problem for Augustine. Semiotic communication, by definition, requires distortions due to the use of symbols that only partially represent reality and thereby imply imperfection. Because of this, Augustine asked two questions: (a) How could semiotic communication have existed in God's perfection prior to the fall, and (b) how can it exist after the completion of redemption when perfection is restored to humanity? In his book *The Fall of Interpretation: Philosophical Foundations for a Creational Hermeneutic,* James K. A. Smith addresses this problem with Augustine and makes three observations.

First, Augustine argued that language is required in order to express the soul's desires and intentions, since others "have no means of entering into my soul,"[3] which is radically interior and thus inaccessible by any other means. This is true even of infants who utter sounds that serve as external signs of internal desires. He made this point in the *Confessions* where he wrote, "Even at that time I had existence and life, and already at the last stage of my infant speechlessness I was searching out signs by which I made my thoughts known to others."[4] With God, however, it is different. Because he already knows our innermost thoughts, language and speech are unnecessary. Nevertheless, in the case of people communicating with other people, language (semiotic communication) functions as a necessary mediator.

Second, Augustine argued that words indicate the secret life of the soul, yet they do so imperfectly. This is because words are, by definition, symbols, and symbols only partially express the reality they are describing. The word *love* is a good example. The reality of love, as intended by a speaker, is never exactly understood in the same precise way by a hearer. A variance of understanding will always exist since the idea of love is communicated through a symbol (in this case, an English word conveyed by the four letters *l-o-v-e*) that merely points to the reality of love rather than embodying its reality in all its fullness. Hence, distortion is inevitable since a gap between *signa* (sign) and *res* (reality) will always exist between a word and its corresponding reality. Therefore the one hearing a word is required to interpret it in order to make sense of the reality being expressed.

Third, Augustine argued that since words inevitably result in distortion, prior to the fall communication must have been characterized by immediacy and perfection—that is, without words (i.e., a version of mental telepathy). This is because, according to the Bible, prior to the fall all creation was perfect. Moreover, once redemption is made complete at the future *eschaton,* the mediation of language will be eliminated and perfect communication (that is, communication without words) will be restored.

> Man as he labors on the earth, that is, as he has become dried up by his sins, has need of divine teaching from human words, like rain from the clouds. However, such knowledge will be destroyed. For while seeking our food, we see now in an enigma, as in a cloud, but then we will see face to face, when the whole face of our earth will be watered by the interior springs of water springing up.[5]

Augustine also believed that such wordless and signless communication is even possible now in the brief ecstatic moments when we hear deity communicate to us

> not through the tongue of the flesh, nor through the voice of an angel, nor through the sound of thunder, nor through the obscurity of a symbolic utterance. Him who in these things we love we would hear in person without their mediation. That is how it was when at that moment we extended our reach and in a flash of mental energy attained the eternal wisdom which abides beyond all things.[6]

What is restored, then, is the sense of immediacy that existed prior to the fall where language, and hence the distortions due to the inevitable interpretations of language, is absent.

In other words, according to Augustine the soul's redemption is a release from temporality (finitude) and the distortions that it generates through language and in its place an embrace of perfection and its absence of distortion. The individual's ascent and return to God climbs out of the temporality of creation and rises to the eternal "where there is no past and future, but only being, since it is eternal."[7] This redemption is only *tasted* in ecstatic moments that break through and into the current temporal world. Hence, the soul seeks redemption from finitude. The problem of finitude causes a longing for the redemption from time—an indication that time itself is somehow fallen, that the soul has somehow fallen into time.[8] While not coeternal with God, Augustine argued that at the *eschaton* the state of being of each redeemed individual will be one of "no variation and experiences no distending in the successiveness of time" precisely because such an individual now "lies outside of time."[9]

It is here where Smith disagrees with Augustine. Smith observes first that as created beings we are by nature—and will always be—finite. This means that, by definition, finite beings cannot be omnipresent nor exist in a timeless ever-present mood. Instead, they are limited to specific points of view and within the medium or horizon of time where they experience the passing of events in sequential order. In other words, to escape location and temporality is to become omnipresent, an attribute restricted to God alone. Smith also observes that finitude is not the result of the fall but rather a result of the creation that God called "very good" (Gen 1:31).

We must therefore not confuse the Pauline phrase "then I shall know fully, even as I am fully known" (1 Cor 13:12), for example, with omniscience. This verse merely refers to a knowledge no longer tainted by sin. At the *eschaton,* we will know and continue to grow in knowledge with fully redeemed minds—but our knowledge will still be restricted to the limitations of finitude.[10]

According to Smith, then, Augustine's understanding of redemption jeopardizes "the central distinction between Creator and creature."[11] He asks, "How can we be other than finite and yet not pretend to divinity? Does not the portrayal of finitude and temporality as fallen erase any distinction between 'creaturehood' and sin? Does this not push evil back to creation itself? Are we guilty for being human (*homo*)?"[12] Language implies the need for interpretation and interpretation implies a distinction between *signa* (sign) and *res* (reality). All this belonged to creation prior to the fall and will constitute the experience of the redeemed souls at the *eschaton*. It is part of what God originally declared to be "very good." Language and interpretation are therefore not behaviors to be redeemed from, but rather behaviors to be restored to their original unfallen states. Stated otherwise, there is nothing inherently wrong with semiotic communication, limited points of view, the need for interpretation and the range of differing interpretations due to the fact that individuals view reality from differing perspectives. In their unfallen states, they are all "very good."

If Smith is correct in his assessment of Augustine, then Augustine read into Scripture rather than read out of Scripture this understanding of absolute knowledge. Smith believes that Augustine acquired it from the influence of neo-Platonism upon his theological thought. Moreover, since neo-Platonism is itself rooted in Gnosticism and early and middle Platonic thought, the roots of this understanding of absolute truth is grounded in classic Hellenism—not the Bible.

RENÉ DESCARTES

One hundred and one years after the nailing of the Ninety-five Theses on a door in Wittenberg, the seemingly innocuous event that launched the Protestant Reformation, Europe found itself embroiled in the Thirty Years' War (1618-1648). In this religious war the opposing sides were Protestants and Catholics. Both sides claimed to speak for God, declared the other side heretics and infidels, and attempted to win Europe to their particular understanding of the Christian faith. Shortly after the commencement of the Thirty Years' War, a young French mathematician, René Descartes, joined the Catholic army of Maximilian and found himself stationed in the Holy Roman Empire where hostilities were soon to erupt.

In the fall of 1619, while only having been in the army a few short months, Descartes spent a night in a "stove-heated room" in a village in southern Germany. In that room he had a series of dreams that convinced him that his mission in life was to found a new scientific and philosophical system. According to these dreams, this system would yield a "certain and evident cognition" of which everyone, regardless of his or her religious predisposition, could be convinced of its accuracy. In other words, it was to be a scientific and philosophical system that promised the acquisition of truth that was absolute and readily recognizable to any impartial inquirer. Before the war's end, Descartes left the army, migrated to Holland and commenced writing this new system. Against the backdrop of the Thirty Years' War, this philosophical system clearly stood opposed to the revelational system that had so completely divided Europe and brought on this horrific war.

In 1637, Descartes wrote the famous *Cogito ergo sum* (I think, therefore I am), though it first occurred in its French form, *"Je pense donc je suis."*[13] According to some scholars, it is the most famous of all philosophical statements. The central point of the ***Cogito*** is that Descartes declared that he doubted all things except the fact that he was indeed doubting. Through this radical

doubt, Descartes attempted to clear away the rubbish of prejudices and preconceived opinions in his mind (including the influences of culture and his
historical moment) in order to lay down a reliable foundation for the acquisition of knowledge. He explained, "I realized that it was necessary, once in the
course of my life, to demolish everything and start again right from the foundations if I wanted to establish anything at all in the sciences that was stable
and likely to last."[14] This initial embrace of doubt, then, had an ironic purpose:
its role was the pursuit of truth that was secure and indubitable—that is, a system grounded in doubt was intended, in its final form, to eliminate doubt.
Again, he explained, "Since I wished to devote myself solely to the search for
truth, I thought it necessary to do the very opposite and reject as if absolutely
false everything in which I could imagine the least doubt, in order to see if I
was left believing anything that was entirely indubitable."[15] In short, doubt
was a means to an end, not the end in itself. The end was truth that was "likely
to last"[16]—that is, truth that was absolute and universal.

The *Cogito* implied the idea of a blank chalkboard (i.e., no culture and
no history) in one's mind. On this chalkboard are written a linear series of
inferences, beginning with simple observations, with the end result being
the discovery of generalized principles that are either "distinct and complete" or at least "sufficient."[17] Because this methodology operated outside
the influences of culture and history, these generalized principles were understood to be absolutely true and universally applicable—that is, they were
recognized to be true regardless of one's cultural or historical background.
Descartes explained that the reason they sometimes constitute a *sufficient*
rather than a *complete* knowledge is because "if every single thing relevant
to the question in hand were to be separately scrutinized, one lifetime
would generally be insufficient for the task."[18] He therefore recognized the
limitations of finitude upon human thought, albeit begrudgingly. Still, his
system pressed for universalized knowledge.[19]

Descartes's *Cogito* launched the Enlightenment. In *God as the Mystery of
the World,* Eberhard Jüngel positioned Descartes at the beginning of a philosophical trajectory in the West from which succeeding generations of philosophers worked out the implications of the *Cogito*.[20] Thomas Oden argues
that the influence of the *Cogito* on human thinking remained limited to that
of the small elite group of philosophers through the majority of the seventeenth century and only emerged into mainstream thought with the fall of
the Bastille during the French Revolution in 1789. At that point this method-

ology reached down and became the assumed form of rational thought for an entire culture. In short order it spread throughout the West.[21]

Descartes's attempt at acquiring absolute truth by means of the *Cogito*, however, has proved to be problematic. The problem with his system can be posed as a question: *Is it actually possible for a human being to radically doubt everything, divest oneself of the influences of culture and the historical moment where one is located, and from that intellectual posture to think?*

Alasdair MacIntyre insists that the answer is *no*. He maintains that Descartes misdescribed his own crisis and therefore set into motion a seriously flawed philosophical methodology. He writes, "Descartes' doubt is intended . . . to be a contextless doubt."[22] Yet radical doubt cannot serve as the foundation of a scientific inquiry precisely because if one doubted everything except for the fact that one is doubting, one would not know how to begin the process of settling one's doubts. In other words, too much has been set aside. If one truly entered an intellectual state of radical doubt, one would be placed in a dazed stupor with nothing certain from which to advance in knowledge. Hence, MacIntyre insists that the notion of radical doubt (i.e., the *Cogito*) is a philosophical impossibility.

Using Descartes himself as an example, MacIntyre observes that Descartes was highly selective and inconsistent in his supposed radical doubt. He did not doubt the French or Latin languages from which he was able to articulate his doubts and proceed towards settling them. These languages provided a "way of ordering both thought and the world expressed in a set of meanings."[23] Since—as is true of all people—Descartes thought with words, the implementation of radical doubt would require him to doubt the meaning of words, syntax and grammar, leaving him without a means to effectively think. Moreover, much of what he took to be spontaneous reflections that emerged from radical doubt were actually a repetition of sentences and phrases from his school textbooks. "Even the *Cogito*," MacIntyre explains, "is to be found in Saint Augustine."[24]

Rather than commencing with scientific inquiry at a virgin beginning by means of radical doubt, Descartes was "always already"[25] in the middle of knowing as he pursued further knowledge. Accordingly, he did not divest himself of the influences of culture and history, as he claimed. He merely succeeded in pushing these influences into his subconsciousness and thereby became uncritical of their influences upon his mind and philosophical thought.

AN ASSESSMENT

Augustine and Descartes sought a means to overcome their finitude and gain an understanding of truth that is infinite: timeless, ahistorical and immutable. They desired to possess a God's eye perspective that carries with it an understanding of truth that is absolute and universally applicable.

Augustine believed that prior to the fall human beings communicated with God and one another independently of language, resulting in perfect communication and knowledge. Such was a knowledge identical to God's. Augustine also believed that in brief moments in this life, during unexplainable ecstatic moments, we have access to this perfect knowledge.

Similar to Augustine, Descartes also believed that perfect knowledge is possible. Unlike Augustine, however, he argued that this knowledge is accessible provided that one follow a prescribed methodology, the *Cogito*, a system grounded in radical doubt.

In both Augustine and Descartes, the implication of their work is that finitude is *not good*, that only when human beings successfully escape the constraints of finitude and thus embrace and understand infinite truth can their knowledge be characterized as good. They believed this, in spite of the fact that God declared finitude (creation) to be *very good* (Gen 1:31). This, then, is their error. Since that which is finite cannot overcome the constraints of finitude, all such efforts are destined to fail. The fact that a pronounced lack of consensus exists within Western culture as to what constitutes absolute truth is evidence that this goal is indeed elusive and ultimately unattainable.

THE IMPACT ON THE CHURCH

The impact of Augustine's notion of pure knowledge and the Cartesian *Cogito* on the church was profound and far-reaching. In this next section I will explore their impact on the Protestant church (sixteenth to twentieth centuries), since it was here where the combination of the two first entered the church and changed its theology. Though Roman Catholicism was already indoctrinated into Augustinian theology, Catholic scholars would not combine it with the *Cogito*—that well worn and rutted road long traveled by their Protestant cousins—until the early to mid-twentieth century.

The Protestant Reformation was initially intended as a protest against Rome. As such, Reformation theologies were reactionary in nature, hoping to bring about a reformation inside rather than outside the Roman Catholic Church. With the passing of several decades, however, hope of such a reconciliation faded and the Protestant agenda shifted.

Once the break with Rome became firm, it left the heirs of the Reformation with the task of systematizing and thereby institutionalizing their new religious tradition so that their new church could stand on its own. Roughly coinciding with the advent of early Enlightenment thought, an emerging Protestant scholasticism made use of the Cartesian *Cogito* in this systematization of Reformation thought. With a sense of irony, this introduction of Enlightenment thought to the Protestant tradition reintroduced back into the church a method (the *via moderna*) that Luther had strenuously argued against.

Protestant scholasticism affected the church in a number of ways, the most basic being the division of theological liberalism from conservatism. Both shared "in the modernist cultural milieu,"[26] having adopted Enlightenment thought into their respective theological systems (see figure 1.1). As such, they clearly were strange bedfellows. George Lindbeck has commented that the two traditions were like "two foxes, snarling at each other and pulling in opposite directions, but tied together by their tails."[27]

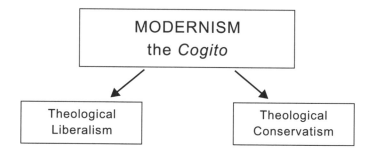

Figure 1.1

That which tied theological liberalism and conservatism together by their tails were two fundamental assumptions. First, both traditions were committed to the Cartesian *Cogito*—the notion of radical doubt and a corresponding scientific methodology—from which to construct their systems. Committed to the possibility of acquiring a God's eye perspective on human thought so that what they affirm to be true is universally true, these two traditions both embraced an understanding of truth as timeless and changeless.

Second, both traditions were committed to the principle of distanciation. Distanciation is the "onlooker" or "spectator" consciousness, "according to which we assume the real world consists in a drama on stage while we sit in the audience and watch it. We moderns have separated our subjective consciousness from the objective drama, that consciousness of what is real."[28]

This spectator consciousness generated a split between *object* and *subject* in one's critical consciousness, which enabled both theological liberals and conservatives to study from afar, without concern for the impact of one's culture or historical situation in the shaping of the inquiry and its final results.

What caused theological liberalism and conservatism to snarl at each other and pull in opposite directions turned on the question of subjectivism and objectivism. Conservative and liberal theologians asked themselves two fundamental questions:

- Is absolute truth located on an intuitive level (subjectivism) or on a cognitive level (objectivism)?

- Is the Bible to be read intuitively, with little concern as to whether the historical episodes being recounted actually took place as presented, or is it to be read cognitively, demanding that historical precision is necessary before anything is believed and embraced?

Both traditions deemed intuition and cognition necessary. The difference between the two traditions therefore turned on a third question:

- Which one—intuition or cognition—has the upper hand in one's interpretation of the Bible?

Liberalism chose intuition; conservatism chose cognition.

Theological liberalism. Since radical doubt (the *Cogito*) required the doubting of everything, the notion of supernatural manifestations through miracles, inspiration, etc. fell victim to such doubting and would only be affirmed if they could be proved through the rigors of the scientific method.[29] From the perspective of theological liberalism, they failed to be proved and thereby gave birth to the historical critical method, a method that attempts to understand the Bible in nonsupernatural categories. Consequently, liberal theologians set aside the **theologia crucis** (the theology of the cross) of Luther and the *Deus dixit* (God speaks) of Calvin as the starting point of theological thought.

In systematic theology, Friedrich D. E. Schleiermacher (1768-1834) distinguished himself as an innovative thinker, often referred to as the father of theological liberalism. He asserted that every true religion was a manifestation of an "intuition of the universe,"[30] but that the Christian religion was the highest and therefore most perfect expression of this intuition. Also, Jesus

Christ is God's chosen Redeemer, the perfect exemplar of God-consciousness for all the peoples of the world, whether they recognize this fact or not.[31]

With its emphasis on human intuition, Schleiermacher's system was a subjectively focused religious paradigm. Religious truths, however, were not individualized to specific people, as is the case in postmodern thought. Schleiermacher believed that by means of intuition all people everywhere should intuit the same reality.[32] Hence, in its pure form, such intuition pointed to the same universal conclusions about God and all of reality. The fact that many religions in the world define God and spirituality differently is merely a recognition that not all religions have advanced at the same pace in this intuitive methodology. Christianity is the most perfect and complete form, thereby serving as the measure for all religious thought. As such, the extent other world religions move towards this Christian center determines the degree of maturity each religion has advanced.

As a means of maintaining the universality of intuition—that is, a system where everyone was understood to intuit the same essential reality— Schleiermacher argued that all peoples everywhere are endowed with the same prereflective feeling. This feeling has its origin in God and guarantees the same religious trajectory as one advances in intuitive thought. Richard Crouter observes that according to Schleiermacher, "The world is viewed as having an absolute ground of unity in God, who represents neither a mere postulate nor a pure ideal, but an ontological reality *sui generis,* which is accessible in prereflective 'feeling.'"[33] His point is that there is a fixed reality and that it can be accessed through human analysis. This analysis begins at a prereflective feeling that everyone possesses and moves forward through the active use of one's own intuition. According to Schleiermacher, such a methodology leads ultimately to an encounter with the Christian God and his Son, Jesus Christ.

The weakness in the Schleiermachian system is due to a lack of consensus in scholarship as to what this intuited knowledge of God should look like. Why should we assume that the Christian God is the center of the religious universe? What should keep us from "feeling," for example, that the Islamic God is the true God and that Christian theology is correct only insofar as it corresponds to Islamic theology?

What is more, the way in which differing world religions define God does not suggest a pattern of convergence based upon differing degrees of maturity. Rather, definitions of such basic concepts as God, salvation, sin and holiness are so different as to suggest a radical divergence of meaning among the world religions. A Hindu understanding of God, for example, is radically different from a Buddhist, Islamic or Christian understanding of God. This is not only true on a cognitive level but also on an intuitive level. Though speaking the same words, the content of these words and the feelings they evoke differ radically. The differences are great enough to require an abandonment of the one and an immersion into the other before a new understanding of the term can be adequately acquired.[34]

In biblical theology, the flaw in this methodology was ultimately demonstrated by Albert Schweitzer in his landmark *The Quest of the Historical Jesus* (first published in 1910). He noted that the reconstructions of the life of Jesus by liberal scholarship were little more than projections of the scholars' own minds as they read their own worldviews back into the biblical text. This flaw reflects the essential problem with the *Cogito* itself. Since it is impossible to divest oneself of one's culture and historical moment, one's culture and history stubbornly reappear in one's theology in spite of scholarship's best efforts to hold them at bay.

Two of the more prominent standard bearers of liberal theology in the twentieth century have been Roman Catholic scholar Karl Rahner, and Evangelical Lutheran scholar Paul Tillich—Rahner with his "anonymous Christian"[35] conceptualization and Tillich with his correlational rephrasing of theological concepts in nontheological language. In both cases, these two theologians attempted to discover the absolute core upon which the Christian faith should be predicated. Rather than the biblical narrative itself being the starting point, these scholars looked for truths more basic and fundamental, truths that were universalized and the core of all true religion.

Theological conservatism. Unlike theological liberalism, theological conservativism emphasized cognitive objectivity in their attempts to secure their understanding of the Christian faith. One noteworthy trend was the use of a method called Scottish Common Sense **Realism** in its hermeneutical substructure. This system of thought began with radical doubt and the collection of hard irrefutable facts through the method of inductive reasoning. From that posture, these scholars organized the Christian faith into a seemingly airtight system, crisscrossing "the documents so as to bring together what they concluded the Bible 'teaches' about any given topic."[36] Hence, along with theological liberals, theological conservatives had also set aside the *theologia crucis* (theology of the cross) of Luther and the *Deus dixit*

(God speaks) of Calvin as the starting point for theological thought and replaced it with the *Cogito* of Descartes.

More predisposed to the possibility of the supernatural than were those committed to theological liberalism, theological conservatives sought to demonstrate the Bible's supernatural character, submitting its self-proclaimed insistence of the supernatural to the radical doubt of the *Cogito* and the corresponding scientific method. For these scholars, the result of their inquiry was affirmative: the Bible was of supernatural origin, and events specifically described in the text as supernatural (e.g., the ten plagues of Egypt, the crossing of the Red Sea on dry ground, healings, levitations, incarnation and resurrection) were accurate historical depictions.

The means by which the Bible passed this test were in two fields of inquiry: inerrancy and prophecy. Theological conservatives were impressed with (a) the historical accuracy and harmony of a book written over a span of a least one thousand years and (b) a 100 percent fulfillment rate of biblical prophecy. No other book ever written can boast such impressive credentials. Through inductive reasoning they concluded that something supernatural was at work here. The only plausible explanation was that this book was written by God. In this way the Bible passed the test of the *Cogito* and was thereby affirmed as the unique Word of God. Because of the role of prophecy and inerrancy in establishing the credentials of the Bible as the inspired Word of God, it is little wonder that for many theological conservatives these two doctrines are essential centerpieces to their faith. As such, conservative Christians are typically quite sensitive when inerrancy and issues related to prophecy are challenged by scholarship. More is at stake than the mere legitimacy of these two doctrines. Rather, the entire Christian faith is predicated on their veracity.

Church historians George M. Marsden and Mark A. Noll assert that Common Sense Realism of eighteenth-century Edinburgh, Scotland, has had a major role in the formation of Protestant evangelical thought—particularly the Protestant evangelical thought of the North American variety.[37] Common Sense Realism, say these two scholars, was a philosophy residing inside the Enlightenment, utilizing the Baconian scientific method as its essential hermeneutical model. It was later imported to the American colonies in the early eighteenth century with John Witherspoon of Princeton College functioning as a major figure. From Princeton College, this hybrid of Common Sense Realism and Protestant evangelicalism was disseminated throughout the American colonies and later across the entire continent.

Noll has added that among the various Protestant evangelical groups, Common Sense Realism "loomed large in dispensational theology."[38] Dispensationalism is a theological system that emerged in nineteenth-century Ireland and was popularized in the twentieth century, primarily in North America, by means of the *Scofield Reference Bible*. Quoting Torrey and Chafer, Noll explains:

> One of its exponents, R. A. Torrey, presented his 1898 study of *What the Bible Teaches* as "simply an attempt at a careful, unbiased, systematic, thorough-going inductive study and statement of Bible truth. . . . The methods of modern science are applied to Bible study—thorough analysis followed by careful synthesis."[39] Somewhat later the dispensationalist systematician Lewis Sperry Chafer from Dallas Theological Seminary similarly defined theology as the "collecting, scientifically arranging, comparing, exhibiting, and defending of all facts from any and every source concerning God and his works."[40] The attachment to Baconian method by evangelicals who are not dispensationalists has only been slightly less pronounced.[41]

What is noteworthy of this attachment to Baconianism (i.e., a version of modernism), however, is that Protestant evangelicals are typically unaware of this philosophical connection to their theological systems. That is, they operate "as though the process of moving from the ancient biblical text to the contemporary affirmation of doctrine and theology was self-evident."[42]

With the *Cogito* lodged within theological conservatism, it has manifested itself in at least four different expressions inside the church: (1) evidentialist apologetics, (2) triumphalism, (3) the depreciation of the historic creeds and confessions and (4) the eclipse of the biblical narrative.

1. Evidentialist apologetics. Evidentialist apologetics is a methodology that draws theological conclusions from neutral "facts." It generates inductive formulas that are believed to be universally true for anyone who faithfully follows them.

Protestant evangelicalism, especially the form that has been practiced in North America, is rife with evidentialist apologetics. One of the strongest statements of this methodology comes in the early pages of Charles Hodge's *Systematic Theology*. In this work he insisted that the "Bible is to the theologian what nature is to the man of science. It is his storehouse of facts; and his method of ascertaining what the Bible teaches is the same as that which the natural philosopher adopts to ascertain what nature teaches."[43] Charles Finney, the mass revivalist of the nineteenth century whose revivalist model

was adopted by many of the twentieth-century revivalists, understood reviv-
alism in similar terms. He explained:

> The connection between the right use of means for a revival, and a revival is
> as philosophically sure as between the right use of means to raise grain, and
> a crop of wheat. . . . Probably the law connecting cause and effect is more
> undeviating in spiritual than in natural things, and so there are fewer excep-
> tions. . . . The paramount importance of spiritual things makes it reasonable
> that it should be so.[44]

In other words, Finney argued that laws of cause and effect like those in
the natural sciences equally apply in the "science" of spiritual revival. If certain laws—or formulas—are followed, outcomes are guaranteed. More currently, television evangelist Jerry Falwell has also noted that such a method
is guaranteed to yield the same universal principles to anyone who utilizes it:

> I was studying mechanical engineering before I even became a Christian. . . .
> You come to exact, simplistic answers if you follow the proper equations, and
> the proper processes. . . . Theology, to me, is an exact science. God is God.
> The Bible is the inspired [inerrant] word of God. And if everyone accepts the
> same theses and the same equations, they will arrive at the same answer.[45]

Christian psychologist Larry Crabb Jr. has observed that for much of conservative Christianity the belief and use of formulas, with alleged guaranteed
results, has characterized a large portion of the spiritual life movement.[46] Similarly, Mark Noll asserts that evidentialist apologetics have been "the staple of
evangelicalism from the age of the [American] Revolution."[47] He points to
tracts used to refute the deistic antisupernaturalism of Thomas Paine's *Age of
Reason* of the eighteenth century,[48] and to William Paley's *View of the Evidences of Christianity* of the nineteenth century, which was often a required
text to unequivocally validate the authenticity of Christianity. Noll says that
this trend "continues into the twentieth century with considerable force as a
sub-theme in the sophisticated work of theologians like E. J. Carnell and as
the total horizon popularizers like Josh McDowell."[49] In short, Protestant evangelicalism operates under the matrix of Common Sense Realism, asserting that
when this method is consistently applied to Scripture, it yields fixed formulas
(evidentialist apologetics) that are guaranteed to work if faithfully followed.

   2. Triumphalism. In his book *Soul Survivor,* Philip Yancey captured the
spirit of triumphalism:

> One church I attended during formative years in Georgia of the 1960s pre-

sented a hermetically sealed view of the world. A sign out front proudly proclaimed our identity with words radiating from a many-pointed star: "New
Testament, Blood-bought, Born-again, Premillennial, Dispensational, fundamental. . . ." Our little group of two hundred people had a corner on the truth,
God's truth, and everyone who disagreed with us was surely teetering on the
edge of hell.[50]

Though not all triumphalists are as extreme as those in Yancey's childhood church, triumphalists do maintain the notion that they possess an exclusive corner on truth. They believe that their particular theological conclusions are absolute, reflecting the God's eye view on theology, and that all
other competing claims are false and possibly heretical.

Because of this, one can legitimately say that triumphalists see themselves
as God's self-appointed police force, guardians of truth who perceive themselves as wearing a "badge of divinity" upon their own theological systems.
They see themselves in this fashion without an adequate appreciation of the
influences of culture and history upon their own ruminations. That which
results, John D. Caputo warns, is

> someone's highly mediated Absolute: their Jealous Jahweh, their righteous Al-
> lah, their infallible church, their absolute Geist that inevitably speaks German.
> In the name of the Unmediated we are buried in an avalanche of mediations,
> and sometimes just buried, period. Somehow this absolutely absolute always
> ends up with a particular attachment to some historical, natural language, a
> particular nation, a particular religion. To disagree with someone who speaks
> in the name of God always means disagreeing with God.[51]

Such attitudes yield ecclesiastical conflicts, separations and schisms as differing theologies—all of which, according to their respective theological
communities, bear the badge of divinity—collide upon one another. In contrast to such attitudes, James K. A. Smith argues that

> everything is a matter of interpretation, including those interpretations de-
> scribed as core orthodoxy. We never have the crisp, unadorned voice of God
> because it is always heard and read through the lens of our finitude and situ-
> ationality. Even when someone purports to deliver to us the unadorned voice
> of God, or "what God meant,"[52] we always receive only someone's interpreta-
> tion, which is [falsely] wearing the badge of divinity.[53]

Some triumphalists, to their credit, try to temper their understandings of
absolute truth by making room for new insights and perspectives not previ-

ously considered. Nevertheless, the plethora of ecclesial denominations[54] suggests that a theological rigidification is common in Protestant evangelicalism (especially within those denominations characterized as fundamentalist) and that their openness to alternative perceptions is only permitted in certain limited areas of theological reflection.

3. The depreciation of the historic creeds and confessions. A rigorous implementation of radical doubt by theological conservatives also results in the doubting of the historic creeds and confessions. This naturally occurs since, according to Descartes, whatever is not doubted has the potential of prejudicing and unfairly influencing the outcome of an inquiry. Throughout Protestant evangelicalism, this depreciation of the historic creeds and confessions has had a sweeping effect. I saw this phenomenon forcefully at a seminar that I presented on postmodernism in northern California. I asked my audience—a group of people composed mostly of pastors and Christian workers—rudimentary questions related to the early ecumenical creeds and Protestant confessional statements. Most could not answer such questions.

Yet, in contrast to Protestant evangelicalism, the historic creeds and confessions were important to the sixteenth-century Reformers. Due to the abiding presence of the Holy Spirit and Jesus' promise that he would build his church (Mt 16:18)—the doctrine of **indefectability**—it was unthinkable for them to operate from the posture of radical doubt and theologize in such an individualistic and contextless fashion, a fashion independent of the historic confessions and creeds. Their knowledge of the historic creeds, however, "does not imply," Anthony Thiselton explains,

> that pre-modern thinkers [including the Reformers] did not raise critical questions; but that the basic frame of reference within which doubt or questions were expressed remained a fundamental theological one which, informed by Christology and the creeds, was perceived to deserve at least provisional trust.[55]

As such, the Reformers thought in terms of *simul justus et peccator* (simultaneously justified and sinner), a fundamental axiom that caused them to intuitively distrust their own thinking patterns. Therefore, they could not consider theologizing in such a fashion that begins with radical doubt and claims to ultimately come to a correct understanding of the Bible. They would have suspected any theological conclusion rendered by such an approach to be fraught with error.

With its singular commitment to the notion of *sola scriptura,* one of the hallmarks of the Reformation, Protestant evangelicalism has typically been defined as an anticonfessional ecclesial movement. Timothy George claims that such a stark interpretation of *sola scriptura* (Scripture alone), however, should perhaps be better described as *nuda scriptura* (naked Scripture), since it was so completely divorced from the historic development within the church.[56] In this respect, Protestant evangelicalism has distorted classic Reformation thought. It exchanged a confessional theology for one committed to the *Cogito,* albeit one dressed in conservative garb.

4. *The eclipse of the biblical narrative.* The final result of theologizing in terms of the *Cogito* is the eclipse of the biblical narrative, which is itself a form of that literary genre known as the realistic narrative. Characteristics of the realistic narrative include the following: (a) The reader is provided much information of certain characters, while other characters are barely known. (b) The plot of the narrative is understandable, yet on closer inspection the reader discovers that there seems to always exist a new dimension to consider, continually deepening relationship to explore, a sense of incompleteness in the storyline that leaves the reader frustrated yet piqued to know more. (c) It contains layers of meanings that are inexhaustible. At times, the realistic narrative offers perspectives that collide with one another, leaving the reader struggling to know how to make sense of the seeming contradictions. At other times, the presence of differing perspectives offers the possibility of intriguingly new interpretations.

In short, the realistic narrative draws the reader into a world that is never fully understood or understandable but is nevertheless irresistible and compelling, precisely because it possesses a ring of authenticity. Because of this, it generates its own life—one that draws the reader in, creating a desire to vicariously experience that life. And that is its genius: the realistic narrative sufficiently parallels the reader's own perception of the world that he or she inhabits so that placing himself or herself within the worldview that it creates becomes desirable and plausible.

The biblical narrative is a special form of the realistic narrative. Here God is included as one of the major characters—understood, of course, in biblical categories. Also, the Holy Spirit is believed to be one of the authors, understood as the One who superintended the human authors in the writing of the narrative so that the final product is indeed the Word of God. The life that resides within its pages, then, can rightly be understood as the divine life, setting it apart from all other realistic narratives.

The use of the *Cogito,* however, eclipses this understanding of the biblical narrative. With this methodology, the narrative serves as a storehouse of data from which timeless and immutable principles are drawn—principles believed to be transferable from situation to situation regardless of one's historical setting, cultural milieu and personal story. It seeks to quantify and qualify. In this respect, rather than entering into and experiencing the life that resides within the biblical narrative, life is believed to exist within static and timeless principles that are sifted and extracted from the biblical narrative. Once these principles are successfully identified, the biblical narrative is rendered superfluous and thereby becomes eclipsed.

In his book *The Eclipse of Biblical Narrative: A Study in Eighteenth and Nineteenth Century Hermeneutics,* Hans W. Frei argues that by pursuing an impersonal and impartial "absolute truth" *behind* the biblical narrative, Western Christianity co-opted the the biblical text with Enlightenment ideals. In each case, he insists, a philosophical schema independent of the biblical narrative is imposed on the text from which absolute principles were extracted. These principles were not ahistorical and acultural, as alleged, but rather grounded in the Enlightenment worldview. Though Frei emphasizes this problem within theological liberalism, in other writings he comments on this same problem in theological conservatism, due to the prevailing influences of Scottish Common Sense realism.[57]

The method of the *Cogito,* therefore, short-circuits the genius of the biblical (realistic) narrative. As we attempt to think aculturally or ahistorically, all we effectively accomplish is masking (or downplaying) the influence of our culture and history in our thoughts. As a result, the *Cogito* keeps us entrapped to our own worldview, causing us to hear our own thoughts echoed back through the influence of our own culture and historical setting that we mistakenly thought we had effectively set aside.

SUMMARY

In this chapter, we examined the dark side of absolute truth. Our purpose in doing so was to gain a greater understanding of that aspect of the modernist paradigm that has proved to be so troubling to contemporary scholarship and why there now exists an effort to move beyond modernism to something that is truly post. Scholars pressing for a new paradigm shift are emerging from the conservative right to the liberal left.

Much of Protestant evangelical theology has typically bypassed such concerns and has naively continued in these old paradigmatic structures as if nothing has changed or is in need of changing. As Grenz and Franke state, "To the task of making theological assertions and constructing theological systems, as though the process of moving from the ancient biblical text to the contemporary affirmation of doctrine and theology was self-evident."[58] Yet, as noted in this chapter, it is *not* self-evident. It is therefore prudent that we pause and reflect on this dark side of absolute truth, considering its impact in both liberal and conservative theology.

We observed that a fundamental problem with hermeneutics in its current state is the error of confusing finitude with infinitude. We noticed this error in the writings of both Augustine and Descartes, two ancient writers whose influence on the West has been enormous. Yet we, as creatures, are and will always be finite. When this fundamental insight is obfuscated in our theologies and theological reflections, we open the door to modernism and begin moving on a trajectory that takes us away from the very God who described our creaturehood as "very good" (Gen 1:31). Understanding the challenge of postmodernism within the church today therefore requires that we first pause and seriously consider this problem within the science of hermeneutics.

We will now turn our attention to a second concern that is driving the postmodern agenda: the question of ecumenism.

QUESTIONS

Basic Concepts

1. What role does the dark side of absolute truth have in the formation of the postmodern agenda?

2. What is the difference between semiotic and nonsemiotic communication?

3. Why did Augustine insist that semiotic communication characterized human relations prior to the fall and will characterize human relations at the *eschaton?*

4. Why did James K. A. Smith insist that nonsemiotic communication is an impossibility for human beings?

5. Why did Descartes pursue a form of knowledge that was not dependent upon religious beliefs?

6. According to Descartes, what role did radical doubt have in the pursuit of absolute knowledge?

7. Why did Alasdair MacIntyre insist that the notion of radical doubt was an impossibility for the human being?

8. How did theological liberalism make use of the *Cogito?*

9. How did theological conservatism make use of the *Cogito?*

10. How is the *Cogito* manifested in evidential apologetics in theological conservatism?

11. How is the *Cogito* manifested in the attitude of triumphalism in theological conservatism?

12. How is the *Cogito* manifested in the deprecation of the historic creeds and confessions in theological conservatism?

13. How is the *Cogito* manifested in the eclipsing of the biblical narrative in theological conservatism?

Further Thought

1. The *Cogito* is a shortened form of *Cogito ergo sum* (I think, therefore I am). It launched a methodology of scientific inquiry in Western culture that has lasted until the present time. What are its strengths and weaknesses in the work of theology?

2. What is the meaning of *distanciation,* and how does it impact theology in the church today?

3. What did Lindbeck mean when he said that theological conservatism and liberalism are like "two foxes, snarling at each other and pulling in opposite directions, but tied together by their tails"?

4. If we will still be limited to finite points of view at the *eschaton* and if our existence in heaven will be a montage of a multiplicity of finite points of view, how should that reality be translated in the church today prior to the *eschaton?*

The Ecumenical Imperative

Having examined the problem of the dark side of absolute truth within the church, we are now ready to take our next step. A second problem within the church, one that has existed since the schism of the eleventh century and, more recently, since the advent of Protestantism, is the lack of ecclesial unity within the church. How can the church move past the obstacles that have impeded progress toward an ecclesial reunification of the church? More to the point, in answering this question does postmodernism help or hurt?

The purpose of this chapter is to assist us in acquiring both a basic understanding and an appreciation of how scholarship has struggled to find answers to these two questions. Like the previous chapter, this chapter is preparatory but necessary, since postmodernism is aimed at overcoming not only the dark side of absolute truth but also the problem of disharmony and disunity between individuals and people-groups. In respect to the church, postmodernism plays itself out in the arena of ecumenism.

I will begin by looking at the theology of ecumenism itself. I will then examine how the science of hermeneutics affects this concern. Finally, I will look briefly at the theological pilgrimage of George Lindbeck, noting how he made use of postmodern theory with the hope of advancing the ecumenical agenda.

A THEOLOGY OF ECUMENISM

Ecumenism finds its ultimate grounding and source of authority in the words of Jesus. In the upper room, just prior to his arrest and crucifixion, he said to his disciples, "A new command I give you: Love one another. As I have loved you, so you must love one another. All men will know that you are my disciples if you love one another" (Jn 13:34-35). Later that same evening, in his high priestly prayer Jesus said to the Father:

> My prayer is not for them alone. I pray also for those who will believe in me through their message, that all of them may be one, Father, just as you are in me and I am in you. May they also be in us so that the world may believe that you have sent me. I have given them the glory that you gave me: that they may be one as we are one. I in them and you in me. May they be brought to complete unity to let the world know that you sent me. (Jn 17:20-23)

Two observations emerge from these remarks from Jesus. First, the unity that Jesus sought for the church was to be somehow patterned after the Trinity. Jesus asked, "that they [the church] may be one as we [the Trinity] are one." This, of course, suggests a complex unity for the church. The church is not to be characterized by a rigid uniformity typified by a straightforward monotheism but rather one characterized by a paradoxical tension typified by the Trinity. That is, ecclesial oneness should be a unity with variety.[1] Second, these words from Jesus demonstrate that ecclesial oneness and evangelism are inseparably linked and that it is the will of God that both be accomplished.

Reflecting on this two-dimensional response by Jesus in one of his epistles, the apostle John made it clear that their inseparableness was indeed Jesus' intention. He wrote, "If anyone says, 'I love God,' yet hates his brother, he is a liar. For anyone who does not love his brother, whom he has seen, cannot love God, whom he has not seen. And he [Jesus] has given us this command: Whoever loves God must also love his brother" (1 Jn 4:20-21). This command that Jesus "has given us" is a loose paraphrase of his two great commandments to love God and love one's neighbor. The apostle John's paraphrase of Jesus' words is a divinely authoritative interpretation to which the contemporary church must adhere if it is to remain faithful to apostolic teaching. Loving God requires us to also love one another. A viable ecumenism is therefore a divine imperative for the church.

In 1970, evangelical scholar John R. W. Stott wrote of this concern. He observed that the visible unity of the church "is both biblically right and practically desirable, and we should be actively seeking it."[2] Yet, in counterbalance, he wondered, if we were "to meet the enemies of Christ with a united Christian front,"[3] with what kind of Christianity would we face them? The only weapon with which to overthrow the opponents of the gospel is the gospel itself. Stott was concerned that if in our efforts to bring unity to the church we found ourselves required to compromise the integrity of the gospel, all such ecumenical unity would be for naught. "It would be a tragedy," he explained, "if, in our desire for their overthrow, the only effective weapon in our armoury were to drop from our hands."[4]

Stott's point reflects an abiding concern within Protestant evangelicalism. An ecumenical unity at the expense of the gospel would be a Pyrrhic victory for the church. It would be a success gained at too great a cost—a success requiring the gospel to be sufficiently watered down as to lose its salvific qualities. In doing so, Christianity would cease to exist, at least as it has been historically understood.

Other scholars, however, look at this problem of the gospel from a different perspective. Thinking in terms of Marshall McLuhan's famous dictum "The medium is the message,"[5] they insist that the gospel presented from a fragmented church generates a profound and far-reaching distortion of its definition. Hence, to preserve the definition of the gospel through ecclesial separation is of little help since such separation itself results in its distortion. Citing such passages as John 13:34-35 and 17:20-22 that we've already considered, they argue that the notion of reconciliation lies at the center of the gospel. If such reconciliation does not exist within the medium (i.e., the church) neither will it be properly manifested in the message (i.e., the gospel). Otherwise stated, if the notion of reconciliation lies at the core of the gospel message, a visibly fragmented church argues against the very message that it affirms and proclaims. At the very least, the gospel is distorted. In this sense, the reconciliation being offered is wholly other-worldly and has no practical bearing in this present world. Yet when asked what was the greatest commandment, Jesus answered with an other-worldly (loving God) *and* a this-worldly (loving one's neighbor) response (Mt 22:37-40).

Based on this line of reasoning, ecumenicists draw the following inference: *to the degree that the followers of Jesus do not reflect the love of God and his reconciliation in their relationships inside the church, they diminish the credibility of the gospel that they are proclaiming to those outside the church.* Lindbeck comments, "Now as in the first centuries, men are not likely to hear the gospel except to the degree that they find themselves compelled to say, 'see how these Christians love one another' (and God and the world)."[6]

In short, both sides of the debate on ecumenism offer compelling rationales for the rightness of their particular perspectives. In the one, doctrinal purity is paramount. In the other, active reconciliation is paramount. Though overlap exists between the two positions (ecumenicists are concerned about the integrity of the gospel and antiecumenicists are concerned about the unity of the church), emphases and the prioritizing of the doctrinal issues in question generate differing paradigms. Hence, it is to this fundamental question of paradigms that we must turn if we are to make sense of the church's differences in regard to ecumenism.

In the following, we will observe two paradigms at work in contemporary theology that have a bearing on the question of ecumenism. Both are centered on an understanding of the nature of God. The first is grounded in an understanding of God that believes him to exist *outside* of time (in a timeless ever-present mood). It is called the *epiphanic model*. The second is grounded in an understanding of God that believes him to exist *inside* of time. It is called the *eschatological model*. These two paradigms are still being debated by theologians. As we will see, they correspond to the two sides of the ecumenical debate. In the first model, doctrinal purity dominates. In the second, active reconciliation dominates.[7]

The gospel. Invariably, when the subject of ecumenism arises within the church, theological debate quickly drifts to questions related to the gospel. The central question asks, how would an ecumenical union between two differing ecclesial bodies affect the integrity of the gospel?

The epiphanic model: an other-worldly gospel. The epiphanic model sees the mission of the church primarily as proclaiming or mediating grace to individuals. Hence, the gospel is a matter between the individual and God with the church only serving as the vehicle that brings the two together. It is epiphanic in the sense that God draws the sinner away from the temporal world to issues that are timeless and other-worldly. *The Four Spiritual Laws* (now called *The Four Spiritual Principles*), developed by Campus Crusade for Christ International as an evangelistic tool, is one of many methods that typify the epiphanic model. Each of the four laws/principles draws the individual away from the temporal world and to an encounter with God who exists outside the temporal world in a timeless and other-worldly dimension.

In its pure form, Christians who affirm this understanding of the gospel insist that a person can receive Christ as Savior and yet maintain a decisively anti-Christian lifestyle for a lengthy period of time, in extreme cases lasting for the remainder of his or her life. In his book *The Gospel According to Jesus,* John MacArthur Jr. described an encounter he had with a Christian minister who affirmed such an understanding of the gospel.

> I spent some time once with a fellow minister who drove me through his city. We passed a large liquor store, and I happened to mention that it was an unusual-looking place.
>
> "Yes," he said. "There is a whole chain of those stores around the city, all owned by one man. He is a member of my Sunday School class."
>
> I wondered aloud what the man was like, and the minister replied, "Oh, he's quite faithful. He is in class every week."
>
> "Does it bother him that he owns all those liquor stores?" I asked.
>
> "We've talked about it some," he said. "But he feels people are going to buy liquor anyway, so why not buy it from him?"
>
> I asked, "What is his life like?"
>
> "Well, he did leave his wife and has been living with a young girl," the minister replied. Then after several minutes of my bewildered and uncomfortable silence, he added, "You know, sometimes it's hard for me to understand how a Christian can live like that."[8]

Understanding how a Christian can live like that requires that we go back to our understanding of the nature of God and how it shapes the nature of the gospel.

If God exists "in outer space or beyond,"[9] the gospel will also exist in outer space or beyond. It will be wholly other-worldly, a transaction between the sinner and God that occurs in an epiphanic (timeless) moment when the mind of the sinner is torn away from this world to contemplate eternal truths. Jürgen Moltmann comments that in an epiphanic gospel, faith becomes "transformed into an immediate contemplation of eternal truths of reason" that involves both "a negation and a break-away from history" in order to rightly grasp them.[10] Here the sinner makes a deal with God by affirming certain biblical assertions as true. As such, the gospel requires no psychological or behavioral changes other than to affirm a specific theory of the atonement. It is therefore not unthinkable for a man to embrace the gospel and yet leave his wife, live outside of wedlock with another woman and be the owner of a morally questionable business.

According to MacArthur, this model of the gospel has a large following in the church today: "The gospel in vogue today promises them that they can have eternal life yet continue to live in rebellion against God. Indeed, it *encourages* people to claim Jesus as Savior yet defer until later the commitment to obey Him as Lord."[11] Dallas Willard has argued similarly:

The sensed irrelevance of what God is doing to what makes up our lives is the foundational flaw in the existence of multitudes of professing Christians today. They have been led to believe that God, for some unfathomable reason, just thinks it's appropriate to transfer credit from Christ's merit account to ours, and to wipe out our sin debt, upon inspecting our mind and finding that we believe a particular theory of the atonement to be true—even if we trust everything but God in all other matters that concern us.[12]

Though many of these Christians do not conduct themselves in such an ungodly fashion as that illustrated by MacArthur, it is clear that a godly lifestyle is not required by this understanding of the gospel.

What is more, though ecclesial unity between believers of differing ecclesial traditions is deemed desirable, according to this model, the gospel can nevertheless maintain its own integrity even in the absence of ecclesial unity. It can do so because the question at hand is the relationship of the sinner to a holy God who exists outside of time and culture. Questions related to this-worldly concerns are therefore set apart from the essence of the gospel, placed at secondary or tertiary levels. Hence, the need for unity is not built into the core of the gospel—it does not require the visible unity of the church in order to be correctly understood and embraced.

With this in mind, this epiphanic or other-worldly model characterizes the gospel by the following four points:

1. Behind the passion of Jesus Christ—along with the other narratives presented in the biblical text—are timeless and changeless truths that each and every person is responsible to learn and embrace.

2. The gospel message is limited to a contemplation and acceptance of the reasonableness of these truths related to the passion of Jesus Christ—that is, the gospel is essentially a message that is to be cognitively understood and embraced.

3. Because these truths are understood to be timeless and changeless (independent of culture and history), one's salvation is limited to an awareness and acceptance of them without their required outworking in the temporal world.

4. The primary concern of the gospel is therefore between God and the individual—in comparison, all other relationships are set aside and deemed irrelevant.

The eschatological model: a this-worldly gospel. The second model high-lights God's "eschatologically triumphant mercy"[13]—where he brings "all things in heaven and on earth together under one head, even Christ" (Eph 1:10; cf. Col 1:19-20). Central to this definition of the gospel is the notion of reconcilia-tion. This includes not only the reconciliation of individuals to God, but also the reconciliation of people to people (renewed sociological sensitivities) and people to creation (renewed ecological sensitivities). As such, the gospel is de-fined as the hope-giving word of promise that is worked out in history between individuals who have been estranged and in need of reconciliation.[14] Rather than striking a deal with God that grants salvation to the individual, provided that a specific other-worldly understanding of the atonement is believed, this model requires a this-worldly engagement of the gospel by the individual. Here, God is understood to exist inside of time and the gospel, and in turn, is understood to require a working out in the give-and-take of real time.

Because God is understood to exist inside of time, he takes on more of the attributes of a person than is the case with the other model. In his critique of the first model, Moltmann comments:

> Before the unchangeable God [i.e., the God of the eternal present], everything
> is equal and equally indifferent. For the loving God [i.e., the God inside time],
> nothing is a matter of indifference. . . . We may not assume anything as existing
> in God himself which contradicts the history of salvation; and, conversely, may
> not assume anything in the experience of salvation which does not have its
> foundation in God.[15]

In this second model, the two great commandments that dominate Mat-thew's Gospel account—loving God and loving people—becomes a central component to the gospel. This is because it would be unthinkable that a per-sonal God characterized by love would offer a gospel that is not also char-acterized by love. Responding to the gospel, then, becomes more a question of relationship than of the adherence to formulas or principles.

In this model, forgiveness is essential, just as in the previous model we considered. The difference lies in the fact that in this model such forgiveness is not understood in terms of a cognitive grasp of timeless truths. Rather, in this model the gospel cannot be quantified by cognitive analysis and mathe-matical precision. The real question turns on relational themes: has a genuine reconciliation between estranged individuals taken place? Though we cannot assess whether a person is genuinely saved via a formula or shorthand de-scription, we nevertheless "know it when we see it."[16] Our spirit bears witness with the other's spirit, assessing on a noncognitive level whether he or she is a genuine believer in Jesus Christ.

The weakness of this model, however, is centered precisely on what it has marginalized. The notion of imputed righteousness, a theme that dominates the Pauline depiction of the gospel (cf. Rom 5:21), is decentralized in the eschatological model. If the alleged believer is not satisfactorily loving God or loving people, he or she is left in a state of disorientation—not knowing whether he or she is truly inside the faith. Belief is measured by the quality of love, an assessment that is subjective in orientation and thereby susceptible to error. With the notion of imputed righteousness, measuring belief is a more objective process and thus less susceptible to error: whether a person is inside the faith is determined by his or her delcaration of faith and a corresponding declaration of eternal life by God (cf. Rom 10:9-10).

According to the eschatological model, ecumenical unification of the church is integral to the gospel witness because an essential part of the gospel is the notion of reconciliation. As such, the church must be reconciled to itself if it is to be a credible and persuasive witness of the gospel. That is to say, if the promises of God cannot be seen in those who already are followers of the Christian God, there is no compelling reason for an unbeliever to trust that these same promises can be fulfilled in his or her own life. Hence, a failure to achieve a visible ecumenical unification of all Christians causes a fundamental flaw in the church's role as a sign and instrument of eschatological reconciliation in a divided world.

This eschatological or this-worldly model, then, characterizes the gospel by the following four points:

1. Because God is understood to exist in space and time, the redemption wrought by Jesus Christ affects space and time, providing an ultimate reconciliation of all things under his headship.

2. The Christian experience is essentially communal, in a time-conditioned orientation, not individualistic, in a timeless (eternal present) orientation. The emphasis not only involves one's own individual reconciliation to God through Christ, but also reconciliation to one's neighbors through Jesus Christ (cf. 1 Jn 4:20-21).

3. The spiritual truths that emerge from the Christ-event confront and challenge culture, yet always require their own cultural expression. This premise stands in opposition to the notion of abstracted spiritual princi-

ples that are timeless, changeless and transculturally and ahistorically applicable.

4. The historicalness of the gospel message (e.g., the incarnation and passion of Jesus Christ) requires an outworking of the gospel in history and culture in the life of each individual believer.

The church. A second issue integrally related to ecumenism is the doctrine of the church. The question is, if ecumenism were effectively implemented, how would it change the complexion of the church? In the following, we will examine the doctrine of the church from two perspectives: (a) the church as guardian of doctrinal purity and (b) the church as guardian of its sacramentality.

The epiphanic model: guardian of doctrinal purity. In the epiphanic model God exists outside of time and relates to us in that context. Because of this, the gospel—and all aspects of truth, for that matter—is understood in acultural and ahistorical categories, applicable crossculturally and transhistorically. The foremost responsibility of the church, then, is the guardianship of doctrinal purity, since if that were to be compromised the church would forfeit the reason for its existence. Ecclesial schisms, splits, divisions and separations are therefore considered *necessary evils* to be administered for the greater good of guarding against doctrinal error.

We should not infer from this, however, that doctrinal purity is important only when God is understood in epiphanic categories. Clearly, the church has always been concerned with doctrinal purity. We see this concern in the early ecumenical councils, the anathemas pronounced against heretics, the Inquisition and the countless theological debates conducted throughout church history. Nevertheless, with the one exception being the Great Schism of the eleventh century, which divided Catholicism from Eastern Orthodoxy, the church remained unified—until the sixteenth century.

Since the Protestant Reformation of the sixteenth century, the quest for doctrinal purity took on a new shape. At an unprecedented rate, the integrity of ecclesial unity has been sacrificed on the altar of doctrinal purity, witnessed by the almost endless number of denominational separations.

Yet the irony of this legacy is that initially the sixteenth-century Protestant Reformers had no intention of separating from the Roman Catholic Church and founding a new ecclesial tradition. Their interest was simply to bring about a spiritual renewal *within* the Roman Catholic Church. However, this was rendered an impossibility when the mother church rejected their criticisms and alternative perspectives and instead anathematized and excommunicated them. Because of the lack of ordained clergy, the Reformers and their followers deemed it necessary to ordain ministers outside the traditional episcopal succession within the Roman Catholic Church. They justified this decision on the grounds of theological expediency, hoping that their separation from the mother church would not be prolonged and that ecclesial unity would someday be restored.

Over the course of time, however, the Reformers and their followers stopped thinking of the Roman Catholic Church as the mother church to which they hoped to return someday. Instead, "Catholicism became the country of Egypt, and they thought of their own churches as the promised land."[17] The Protestant exiles had become "so thoroughly acclimatized in their new ecclesiastical homes"[18] that they viewed themselves superior in morality, spirituality and theology to the mother church that had previously cast them out. From their perspective, then, returning to the mother church violated simple logic—they had much to lose and little to gain.

This ecclesial attitude toward the mother church set a precedent within Protestantism that has been passed down through the centuries as Protestant ecclesial bodies experienced their own schisms and brought into existence new ecclesial traditions. Rather than seeking a reconciliation to mother churches, these new ecclesial bodies have understood themselves as first and foremost defenders of doctrinal purity. Loyalty to mother churches was therefore of little importance.

It is here where the epiphanic model of the church has played such an important role. The beginning of ecclesial divisions within Protestantism occurred at approximately the same time that Enlightenment ideals entered this ecclesial tradition. Thinking in terms of timeless truths devoid of cultural and historical influences, Protestantism adopted an attitude where relationships and holistic integration (this-worldly concerns) were de-emphasized in favor of the pursuit of doctrinal purity.

Francis A. Schaeffer is representative of this model. He insisted that the primary responsibility of the church is the maintenance of doctrinal purity. This, he explained, requires a steadfast commitment to specific doctrines as absolute and therefore nonnegotiable. If these doctrines are violated and repudiated by any ecclesial body, separation becomes a mandatory response. If separation does not occur, he added, "the tendency is to go from *ecclesi-*

astical latitudinarianism [toleration of false doctrine] to *cooperative comprehensiveness* [active participation in false doctrine]. Thus Christians may still talk about truth but tend less and less to practice truth."[19] Once this occurs, he added, it fatally compromises a believer's effectiveness as a witness to the gospel before a watching world.

One important means by which Schaeffer believed that doctrinal purity could be achieved was by an "analysis of concepts." This, he explained, required a careful study of the Bible with the intent of establishing the limits of orthodoxy. He insisted, "The bounds are set not by any 'method' but by the truth God has given us in propositional form in the Bible."[20] Moreover, these propositions are timeless and acultural since they come to us from a God who exists outside of time yet has chosen to break into our world and reveal them to us. They therefore possess a universal applicability.

The concern for doctrinal purity—central to this first model—has made ecumenism an almost impossible task. In their attempt to define a singular doctrinal stance among differing ecclesial traditions, theologians of various traditions have found it exceedingly difficult to form a consensus regarding the limits of orthodoxy. Commenting on the problems of interdenominational dialogue, Robert Jenson writes:

> On each traditionally disputed item, the dialogues have sought what has come to be called convergence, a narrowing of the distance between differing positions to the point where a particular dispute can no longer be incompatible with fellowship inside one churchly communion. And such convergence has, with almost monotonous consistency, been regularly achieved. But from each remaining small and apparently tolerable divergence, an urgent reference has emerged to some other topic on the agenda, causing a newly virulent division with that topic. And with that topic it has gone the same way, and so on, finally to the beginning.[21]

Hence, with few exceptions, the great divides in church fellowship "have come no nearer."[22]

In this epiphanic model of the church, then, the very nature of maintaining doctrinal purity contradicts the possibility of ecumenical unification. To have the one requires the repudiation of the other.

The eschatological model: the church as sacrament. In the second model, the church is more concerned with time-related issues. Understood as a sacrament, divine grace is channeled through the church to the world as the church serves as the custodian of holy writ, orthodoxy (as clarified by the early church councils), liturgical worship and the channel for the preaching of the Word of God. Just as the other two sacraments in the church—baptism and the Lord's Supper—point backward and forward, so does the church. As sacrament, the church points back to the actual accomplishment of God's victory in our Lord's incarnation and passion, and points forward to the complete manifestation of that victory when "humanity and all creation will become full and visible participants in the redemption which has already been accomplished."[23] Endowed with grace, the church is therefore chosen by God so that it "effects the reality which it signifies."[24]

Understood as a sacrament, then, the church becomes grounded in time-related issues. It points to the past and the future. Moreover, it possesses a present-tense quality since it must be experienced in the here and now in order to be efficacious.[25]

In this respect, when one enters a local assembly of believers where the risen Lord Jesus is worshiped and his Word is preached, that individual engages in a sacramental rite. The grace of God is present in that assembly in a manner not present anywhere else. This does not mean that the grace of God cannot be spurned by a person with an unrepentant heart. What it does mean is that the church itself is a vehicle or channel of grace and that all who enter through its doors are exposed to, and encouraged to draw from, that grace. There are four arguments in favor of this model.

First, according to the Bible, God has chosen to attach eschatological signs to his chosen people. This understanding of signs reaches back to the Old Testament and forward into the New. The essential role of the nation of Israel as the chosen people centered on their being an eschatological sign of God's unfailing promises. Though subject to the vicissitudes and corruptions of the surrounding nations, Israel remained the object of God's grace, and in the *eschaton* it will exemplify the holiness of God. The prophetic protests against the nation of Israel, as attested in the Old Testament, were intended "to purify, not subvert, traditional institutional orders."[26] Even Jesus recognized the legitimacy of the institutions among the Jewish people of his day and, accordingly, lived and worked within those structures. He did this in spite of the fact that those institutions had become corrupted by false doctrine and sinful leadership.

Based on this Old Testament precedent, God established his chosen people in the New Testament. The essential role of the church to serve as a chosen people centered on their being an eschatological sign of God's unfailing promises. Similar to the Old Testament precedent, prophetic protests in the

Church Age should be to purify—not subvert by means of ecclesial separation—traditional institutional orders.

Second, the eschatological signs of a chosen people are meaningless unless they are visible sociologically and historically. In an eschatological framework, the church is to be a sign among the nations of God's eschatologically triumphant mercy. The church is to show that grace in the reconciliation and unification of all things in Christ (see Eph 1:9-10; Col 1:19-20). Thus, Christians must be reconciled among themselves and also be reconcilers in the world if they are to be credible and persuasive witnesses. According to the Bible, God desires both an internalized and an externalized faith. Moreover, these two dimensions are necessarily interconnected (cf. 1 Jn 4:19-21).

Third, the **catholicity** (universality) of such an eschatologically defined community would necessarily include a mixture of unbelief and faithfulness. In this respect, the Protestant principle of *simul justus et peccator* (simultaneously just and sinner) would apply not only to individual believers but also to the community of believers. The negative description of the churches at Sardis and Laodicea in the third chapter of Revelation provide examples of this concept. These churches indicate "at least the possibility of making out a scriptural case for the view that a church, even while losing none of its character as a church, can be in some respects substantially unfaithful to its Lord."[27] The apartheid churches of South Africa offer a contemporary illustration. Lindbeck writes, "The apartheid churches . . . are no less churches than the black ones that they oppress, just as the sixteenth-century Catholics and Protestants were part of the same elect people as the Anabaptists whom they jointly slaughtered."[28] Though falling short of the model of love and holiness that should characterize all churches, they nonetheless were still churches and should be recognized as such.

From this understanding of the church as a sacrament, the church is best understood by what it points toward, not by what it fully possesses now. The implications of this insight cuts in two directions. On the one hand, though a sacrament, the church does not work efficaciously upon a person who is unrepentant towards God. It "does not guarantee the reality which it symbolizes. . . . It does not work automatically, i.e., magically."[29] Its sacramental character can be thwarted just as any sacramental sign can be thwarted by an unrepentant sinner. On the other hand, the church's eschatological horizon and promised blessings cannot be thwarted. It is still the channel by which God has chosen to bless his people. It remains God's channel in spite of the sinfulness of its people or leadership.

The essential character of churches, then, is paradoxical. Like individual believers, churches fall short of God's standard of holiness yet are still sustained by his gracious hand. Moreover, this paradox is not easily overcome. Stott comments on this difficulty:

> Fundamentalists have tended to hold a separatist ecclesiology and to withdraw from any community which does not agree in every particular with their own doctrinal position. They forget that Luther and Calvin were very reluctant schismatics who dreamed of a reformed Catholicism. Most evangelicals, however, while believing it right to seek the doctrinal and ethical purity of the church, also believe that perfect purity cannot be attained in this world. The balance between discipline and tolerance is not easy to find.[30]

Stott's point is that the perfect church does not exist in the world and that attempts to make it so are unrealistic. We must seek a balance between discipline and tolerance if the church is to survive.

Fourth, a singularly unified church best reflects its sacramentality since a fragmented church fails to give adequate witness to the victorious grace and eschatological redemption achieved at the cross. Typically, the Protestant position has argued for an existentialized understanding of the church according to which it possesses a spiritualized unity. Such spiritual unity exists in the invisible and spiritualized celestial city, a oneness in a strictly otherworldly dimension. Yet if the church is to be understood as a sacrament (a dispenser of grace to all those who enter into its orbit), its sense of unity must occupy both realms (this-world and other-world). A sacrament, by definition, is a channel of grace. Thus, if it fails to occupy both realms, it ceases to be a channel.

The notion of the church as sacrament therefore requires it to be ecumenically unified. A united church is therefore essential since spiritual truth cannot be understood in the abstract and, instead, can only be seen as it is worked out historically and culturally. In this respect, Moltmann argues that the epiphanic understanding of God follows "the thought forms of the Greek mind, which sees the *logos* of the epiphany of the eternal present of being"[31] as truth, and thus constructs doctrines from that perspective. He adds, however, that "the real language of Christian eschatology . . . is not the Greek *logos,* but the promise which has stamped the language, the hope and the experience of Israel. It was not the *logos* of the epiphany of the eternal present, but in the hope-giving word of promise that Israel found God's truth."[32] It reflects "a knowledge of history and of the historic character of truth."[33] An ecumenical unification is therefore necessary since the absence of unity leaves the impression that there is no historic (this-worldly) character of truth to the gospel.

THE RELEVANCE OF ECUMENISM TO THE POSTMODERN DEBATE

Having considered how our understanding of the nature of God (theology proper) generates a domino effect that ultimately acts upon our understanding of ecumenism, we will now examine how our understanding of hermeneutics has a similar effect upon ecumenism.

Modernism and ecumenism. The modernist paradigm and ecumenism have historically been a poor match. Under modernism, differing religious systems with triumphalistic attitudes have vied for universal recognition and acceptance. The modernist epistemology generated two responses within the church in the twentieth century, both of which worked against the ecumenical agenda.

The first response, *the tribalization of theology,* does theology "only in, for and with one's own kind."[34] Modernism set afoot within the church a trend of massive retreat from ecumenism. The doing of theology was "only from one's own ecclesial traditions—Lutheran, Reformed, Baptist, Anabaptist, Anglican, Methodist, Roman Catholic, Eastern Orthodox, Pentecostal, whatever."[35] This doing of theology was also characterized by specific theological camps: process, liberation, dispensational, covenant, existential, Jesus Seminar, and so on; or as an ethnic or gender subcommunity, such as feminist, gay and lesbian, African-American or Hispanic. An antiecumenical spirit has been dominant where theologians were content to work within tightly fixed ecclesial, perspectival and ethnic parameters with little interest in integrating their insights with those of the broader Christian faith.

The second response was the opposite: a movement characterized by the *universalization of theology.* This response attempted to advance the mission of ecumenism by erasing all theological particularities. This erasure was so complete as to eliminate not only such distinctions as "ethnic, ecclesial and perspectival but also any basic distinction between Christian faith and other world religions and all people of good will—hence the growth of the universalizing of theology based on some common core of truth or holiness."[36] As noted earlier, here Karl Rahner and Paul Tillich have been two of the more prominent standard bearers, Rahner with his "anonymous Christian"[37] conceptualization and Tillich with his correlational theology.

Nevertheless, both trends represent different ways in which modernism log-jammed the work of ecumenism. With the first trend, "fundamental Christian identity was associated with the loyalty to the subcommunity of common stock with its attendant customs and traditions."[38] That is, it equated absolute truth with a specific Christian subtradition that de facto was understood to be a universalized paradigm. This understanding of absolute truth was true in both liberal and conservative denominations. Those who held to this view were not able to advance the mission of ecumenism and, arguably, were not even interested in doing so. The second trend, however, was equally problematic. The conceptualization of a "common core of truth or holiness" tended to favor one paradigm of truth or holiness while trivializing or falsely representing other paradigms. It also had the tendency to be predicated upon the moods and moralisms of some prevailing culture, which determined the definition of this common core. Such favoritism doomed ecumenism since it forced capitulation of rather than fostering respect for differing theological positions.

Postmodernism and ecumenism. In contrast to its mismatch with modernism, ecumenism has found a more kindred spirit in postmodernism. This is because they both abhor fragmentation, both strive for holistic thinking, and neither requires the universal recognition of a given system and therefore is capable of avoiding the problem of triumphalism. Individual theologians are permitted to maintain the integrity of their particular theologies since they are not forced into a singular system deemed universal and absolute. Hence, in the eyes of some scholars, postmodernism is a superior epistemology to modernism in that it offers a way around the need for universals and, in its place, offers the legitimization of diversity that is less condemnatory than was previously the case.

Three of the characteristics of postmodernism that are advantageous to the work of ecumenism are the following. First, postmodernism is characterized by *plurality*. It denies that there is any one singular legitimizing system of thought on which all cultures and all historical settings depend. As Jean-François Lyotard explains, postmodernism demands a "war on totality."[39] In its place, it affirms the plurality of conflicting systems, systems that are more local and regional in scope. Stanley Grenz explains, "Each of us experiences a world within the context of the societies in which we live, and postmoderns continue to construct models . . . to illumine their experiences in such contexts."[40] These models give the impression that those who live inside their assumptions and work out their implications have a hold on reality that is universal in scope. Such impressions, however, are nothing more than "useful fictions" that one eventually abandons as he or she encounters the larger world from which reality is ordered.

Second, postmodernism is characterized by *centerlessness*. No shared focus unites the divergent elements to common standards from which people can appeal in their efforts to measure the rightness or wrongness of a given issue. As Steven Conner explains, "The postmodern condition . . . manifests itself in the multiplication of centres of power and activity and the dissolution of every kind of totalizing narrative which claims to govern the whole complex field of social activity and representation."[41] This legitimizes the understanding of society as a collage, where seemingly incompatible systems are placed side by side and recognized as possessing a rightful place within the overall picture. Or, to change metaphors, society is likened to a stew in which vegetables, onions, potatoes, meat and so on maintain their distinctive character and wholeness, yet together create a delicious meal of competing flavors and textures all in the same bowl. To blend all the ingredients into a purée (a singular flavor and texture) drastically alters the meal and, as many would agree, ruins its flavor. In this respect, modernism is likened to the purée; postmodernism to the stew.

Third, postmodernism is characterized by *subjectivism*. Postmodernists insist that all peoples view reality from finite points of view and are influenced by the cultures and historical situations from which they are located. John Hick, for example, argues that where people are born in the world, to a large extent, determines how they will understand a host of issues, including religious ones: people born into Hindu families will likely be Hindu, people born into Catholic families will likely be Catholic, people born into Pentecostal families will likely be Pentecostal. He explains, "We can refer to this manifest dependence of spiritual allegiance upon the circumstances of birth and upbringing as the genetic and environmental relativity of religious perception and commitment."[42] Grenz adds that according to postmodernism, "we do not simply encounter the world that is 'out there' but rather . . . we construct the world using the concepts we bring to it." Moreover, "We have no fixed vantage point beyond our own structuring of the world from which to gain a purely objective view of whatever reality may be out there."[43] Pure objective knowledge—a knowledge characterized as possessing the exactitude of God's eye—is therefore rendered an impossibility. We can no more stand outside of these influences and think than we can, so to speak, jump over our own shadows. Whatever we do or think, cultural and historical influences leave an indelible mark.

These three characteristics—pluralism, centerlessness and subjectivism—collectively provide a vehicle from which many scholars believe ecumenism can move beyond its modernist past. Since it sidesteps the notion of universal truth, it gives competing theologies the freedom to exist side by side without being overpowered by one or another.

Such a perspective, however, is not without its critics. They identify three problems with such thinking: (1) What if a universal truth indeed exists (e.g., Jesus is Lord)? (2) What is to prevent one of the competing theologies from insisting that it is the center and attempting to overpower the rest? (3) Is an overarching system where competing theologies are balanced together and therefore possess a sense of healthy respect for one another even feasible?

So which paradigm is more in keeping with the Christian faith? At this point in the book, we will not attempt to resolve these challenges. We only wish to bring to the reader's attention three observations. First, more than one paradigm exists that is promoted within Christian scholarship, and thus needs to be honestly considered. This is true not only in the arena of hermeneutics that we considered in this section but also in the arena of theology proper that we considered in the previous section. A failure to do so results in an ostrich head-in-the-sand mentality that does damage to one's credibility by those on the outside looking in. Second, there exists a greater compatibility of postmodernism with ecumenism than that of modernism. Third, postmodernism, though more compatible to ecumenism than modernism, still has important questions to answer.

As this book unfolds I will show that the Enlightenment, which corresponds to an understanding of God existing outside of time and to the modernist hermeneutic, has affected theology in the West. It has also stymied the work of ecumenism. New paradigms need to be considered that can move the ecumenical agenda forward without violating the integrity of the Christian faith.

LINDBECK'S THEOLOGICAL PILGRIMAGE

The presence of triumphalism in the modernist epistemology has indeed proved a major impediment to the development of a viable ecumenism for the church. Letting go of triumphalism, however, and thinking from an antitriumphalistic perspective is itself a highly problematic move. This is because at its essence the Christian faith is triumphalistic. It insists that it is right and all opposing religions are wrong. How, then, are we to move toward a viable ecumenism when triumphalism lies at the roots of the Christian faith and therefore cannot be wholly repudiated?

In this final section, we will focus on the theological pilgrimage of George Lindbeck, noting how he grappled with this problem. He observed, as have many other theologians, that the repudiation of objective truth (a move consistent with postmodern ideals) is problematic since it opens the door to the legitimization of all religious perspectives. This would result in the collapse of the distinctive character of the Christian faith. As Lindbeck was fond of quoting Luther: *"tolle assertiones et Christianismum tulisti"* (take away assertions [propositions] and you take away Christianity).[44] Lindbeck's embrace of postmodernism, then, was highly nuanced and qualified.

Being an early pioneer in the use of postmodernism within the church, Lindbeck's methodology and findings have been discussed at length in academia. A brief review of his dealings with this issue is therefore worthwhile for any serious examination of postmodernism within the church.

Lindbeck's first phase. Lindbeck was born in a remote interior province in China in 1924 where his parents served as missionaries. Distinctly non-Western in orientation, he was later to describe the Honan province as far removed from the "displays of Western power" that were more prominent in the port cities. As he put it, "The ways in which our neighbors lived and thought were as unmodern as those of the Han dynasty 2,000 years before." The Honan province also affected his understanding of the church. He added, "China laid the groundwork for a disenchantment with Christendom that led me 30 years later to hope for the end of cultural Christianity as the enabling condition for the development of a diaspora Christianity."[45] This tacit influence, then, set into motion a fundamental drive within Lindbeck to reject the *Cogito* (a Western philosophical system) and work toward a distinctly non-Western, non-*Cogito* Christian theology. Such a drive characterized his theological research ever since his early days at Yale.

Initially, Lindbeck believed that *Heilsgeschichte* (salvation history) correctly reflected the theology of the early fathers and that catholicity must be grounded in such a paradigm if it were to be an accurate reflection of the Christian faith. In contrast to *Heilsgeschichte* was the Roman Catholic two-source theory (Scripture plus church tradition). Lindbeck argued that *Heils-*

geschichte was superior since it successfully kept in check extrabiblical theological developments, such as Mariology and papal infallibility.[46]

In 1972, Lindbeck altered his thinking on this matter. In a lecture at Marquette University he asserted that papal infallibility was not necessarily incompatible with the notion of catholicity. This is because (a) Catholics no less than Protestants affirm that God alone is absolutely infallible, (b) both Catholics and Protestants have spoken of the Bible as infallible and inerrant, yet now both regard this as a misleading expression and that while there are errors, they are not the kind that compromise the witness of revelation, and (c) both Catholics and Protestants affirm infallible dogma which are stated propositionally within their respective statements of faith. As such, with the Protestant Reformation the notion of a singular infallible dogma within Catholic tradition was replaced by thousands of infallible dogma within the statements of faith of the many ecclesial bodies that make up Protestantism. That is to say, the Protestant Reformation combated the notion of the papacy by replacing one pope with thousands of popes—a highly questionable improvement.

The problem impeding the development of an operative catholicity was therefore not the doctrine of papal infallibility (in both systems there existed popes and infallible dogma). The problem resided elsewhere, specifically in the notion of propositionalism.

How can the church maintain the notion of propositionalism yet avoid propositionalism's propensity towards triumphalistic exclusivism? On the one hand, Lindbeck argued that propositionalism must be maintained because without it fundamental and nonnegotiable propositional statements such as "Jesus is Lord" will be set aside. On the other hand, he argued that propositionalism gives rise to triumphalistic thinking causing individual ecclesial traditions to become tunnel-visioned as they assert doctrinal superiority over all others. As such, triumphalism works against the notion of catholicity and, more importantly, against Jesus' prayer for the church: "that they may be one" (Jn 17:22).

Hence, Lindbeck found himself on the horns of a dilemma—the church cannot live without an objective propositionalism, yet, at the same time, cannot live with it. By agreeing to the role of authoritative propositional interpretations in ecclesial dogma, Lindbeck found himself agreeing to the latent presence of triumphalism within such dogma. Since it was the presence of triumphalism in ecclesial dogma that worked against an effective ecumenism for the church, an ecumenical unification of the church appeared to be beyond the church's reach.

Lindbeck's second phase. In the years immediately following his Marquette University lecture, Lindbeck transitioned into a postmodern direction. This transition contained three essential moves.

First, he noted that the modernist paradigm in theology has failed to generate a universally recognized theology and that theologians have not come to terms with this failure. Instead of driving theology forward past modernism, they spend a disproportionate amount of time discussing the problems posed by modernism in hopes of finding a solution still in keeping with essential modernist assumptions.

Second, he noted that in the science of theology, paradigms and content are interconnected. That is to say, the paradigm from which a person theologizes determines what is seen and organized (i.e., the content). This means that if the interpretation of the content differs between theologians, the problem may not be one of eisegesis (reading into a text what is not there) but rather one of theologizing from the posture of differing paradigms. In this sense, paradigms function a priori "as lenses from which everything else is seen."[47] Thus, if one were to change the lenses, the content would correspondingly change. Or, to switch metaphors, if a theologian from one theological community were to criticize or anathematize a specific content generated by a theologian from another religious community, his criticism or anathematization may reflect the classic apples-and-oranges fallacy.

Lindbeck observed that when, for example, "the paradigm is didactical in character, then attention is concentrated on principles and doctrines." Yet "when the paradigm, as in the work of Tillich, is a definite phenomenological description of religion understood essentially as the experience of spirituality, then the cogent theological writings will express such experiences."[48] The same could be said for other paradigms, such as those present in liberation theology. Lindbeck's essential point was this: no specific paradigm can be absolutized and thereby determined to be universally valid and the basis on which all other paradigms depend since "there is no neutral language or position . . . which can lead to an unambiguous formulation."[49]

Lindbeck also observed that this has been the fundamental problem of theology, dating back to Descartes, throughout the modern period. Theologians have privileged one paradigm over all others in order to conclusively establish the essential character of theology, yet each has failed to convincingly demonstrate why his or her paradigm should function as the privileged pair of glasses from which everything else should be seen.

Third, Lindbeck believed that the insights in language philosophy that are transforming the natural and social sciences should have a similar impact on theology. Specifically, he saw in Wittgenstein philosophical insights (which he called **"language games"**) that could bring about a new hermeneutical setting in theology: "Each area of speech in natural languages, each intellectual discipline, and each paradigmatic development within each discipline possesses its own unique logic and grammar."[50] There are similarities or family resemblances in the forms of rationality that characterize different paradigms, yet there are no methods, no subtleties and no formal logic that are universally applicable.

Accordingly, Lindbeck observed that there is no such thing as raw prelinguistic experience where reality is observed and understood. Rather, all theologies are shaped by linguistic and symbolic forms whose origin and meaning emerge from differing communities. Thus, the basic methodological assumption of much contemporary study of religion and theology is wrong: *there exists no identifiable experience of the divine, common to all human beings, though expressed in diverse ways in different religions.*

This conclusion, however, left Lindbeck with a new problem. If there is no universal system of truths, does not that eliminate the possibility of orthodoxy? His answer was *no.* Emphasizing a confessional Christianity as his starting point, he argued against specific propositions (via the *Cogito*) being universally valid. Instead, the starting point was God speaking through Scripture and through the creeds. He insisted that Barth, the Reformers and even Thomas Aquinas would assent to this move.

Differing paradigms from differing traditions arrange the grammar of belief differently, and from there distinct contents emerge, much like the family resemblances apparent within individuals who share the same parents. The confessional creeds generate the family resemblance within Christendom. None of the family members (differing ecclesial bodies within Christianity) can argue for the superiority of its particular appearance and expression, nor should the family members collectively seek to homogenize all differences into a singular expression; brought about by the compromise of all distinctions. Rather, like a family, differences are to be appreciated as the unity generated by the ecumenical creeds is maintained. Ecumenism, Lindbeck concluded, should be built upon this foundation.

SUMMARY

In addition to the concern of the dark side of absolute truth, a second concern among many scholars has been to overcome obstacles that have logjammed the ecumenical agenda. They understand modernism as one of the major impediments to this agenda and are therefore intrigued with the possibilities of postmodernism.

In this chapter, we have examined the theology of ecumenism with a special interest in how modernism and postmodernism play a role in shaping our understanding of it. Specifically, we have observed that a central question we must address goes back to the fundamental issue of the nature of God: does God exist *inside* or *outside* of time? The notion that he exists inside of time favors the postmodern agenda, whereas the notion that he exists outside of time favors the modernist agenda. Lindbeck's theological pilgrimage is significant in that it was an early attempt among Christian theologians to integrate postmodern ideals into the Christian faith without collapsing the faith into a version of radical relativism. That which drove Lindbeck was the ecumenical concern to bring unity to the church without sacrificing orthodoxy in the process.

In the next four chapters, we will begin our examination of postmodernism with a review of the four postures that currently exist within the church. In each of these postures, the presence of the dark side of absolute truth (chapter one) and the possibilities of advancing the ecumenical agenda (chapter two) cast their shadows as the arguments of each posture unfold.

QUESTIONS

Basic Concepts

1. According to the words of Jesus (Jn 13:34-35; 17:20-23), what is the connection between ecumenism and evangelism?

2. John R. W. Stott said that it would be a tragedy if in our confrontation with non-Christian arguments, "the only effective weapon in our armoury were to drop from our hands." What did he mean by this statement?

3. Thinking in terms of Marshall McLuhan's famous dictum "The medium is the message," how does a divided church affect the message of the gospel?

4. What is the epiphanic understanding of God?

5. What is the eschatological understanding of God?

6. How does an epiphanic understanding of God affect one's understanding of the gospel? Of the church?

7. How does an eschatological understanding of God affect one's understanding of the gospel? Of the church?

8. Based on the modernist paradigm, what are the two responses to ecumenism?

9. What are the three characteristics of the postmodernist paradigm that make it a better fit with ecumenism?

10. In George Lindbeck's effort to find a way to advance the ecumenical agenda, what characterized his first theological phase? What characterized his second theological phase?

Further Thought

1. The term *Pyrrhic victory* has its origin in ancient Greek history, where the Epirian army defeated a Roman army near the Pyrrhic River at Asculum in 279 B.C. The Epirian army was so badly weakened in the process of achieving the victory that the army was unable to continue fighting the war. Hence, though victorious in the battle, the army had sown the seeds for its ultimate defeat. In what respect does ecumenism run the risk of a Pyrrhic victory for the church? Thinking in terms of a strategic withdrawal, what could the church do that would be more effective where it comes to ecumenism?

2. How do the epiphanic and eschatological understandings of God affect one's understanding of ecumenism?

3. Lindbeck found himself on the horns of a dilemma when it came to foundationalist thinking: one cannot live with it and cannot live without it. What did he mean by this and how did he solve this problem?

Foundational
Realism

The first of the four positions in the postmodern debate that we will examine is that of foundational realism. This is the position most closely associated with the Cartesian *Cogito*. As we observed in chapter one, in the last two centuries both theological liberalism and conservatism have embodied the *Cogito,* though from different points of view. To a large extent, however, in the latter decades of the twentieth century theological liberalism has faded, while being replaced by a series of theologies characterized by post-*Cogito* (i.e., post-Enlightenment or postmodern) thinking.[1] Theological conservatism, however, still exists. This chapter focuses attention on that aspect of conservatism still characterized by the *Cogito*.

An early participant in the postmodern debate from within theological conservatism was Francis A. Schaeffer. His participation was somewhat unique in that many of his writings argued against existentialism (a forerunner to postmodernism). Though existentialism differs from postmodernism,[2] they are both post-*Cogito* in orientation in that they both abhor the notion of absolute truth. As such, both systems of thought share a distinct family resemblance. Millard Erickson is therefore generally accurate in his description of Schaeffer. He writes, "Schaeffer did his major work in the 1960s and 1970s before the word postmodernism was even invented, and before the demise of modernity had become evident."[3] His work was therefore remarkable in that it correctly assessed the dominant trajectory of philosophy in the latter decades of the twentieth century as transitioning away from modernism. "What he was reacting to," Erickson continues, "was postmodernism, but before anyone, including the adherents themselves, knew what it was. . . . Thus, in many ways, Schaeffer was ahead of his time."[4]

Schaeffer therefore serves as a forerunner to the debate, attempting to prepare the Protestant evangelical church to face the new hermeneutical challenge. His writings have provided the sector of the church characterized by foundational realism with its general outline and main points in the debate. If we are to understand the overall parameters of the debate from the perspective of foundational realism, we must understand Schaeffer's theological and philosophical contributions. This is necessary for historical as well as practical reasons. Current participants in the debate from the foundational realist perspective still appeal to his writings and logic to buttress their positions.[5]

In this chapter, we will begin with a look at Schaeffer's understanding of existentialism/postmodernism and why and how he opposed it. We will then examine the way in which the current expression of foundational realism uses the *Cogito* to ground truth and from that perspective condemns those who affirm postmodernism. In closing, we will examine the link between foundational realism and pietism.

FRANCIS A. SCHAEFFER

Francis August Schaeffer (1912-1984), the author of twenty-three books with more than three million copies in print, stands out as one of the more influential Christian thinkers in conservative Christianity in the latter decades of the twentieth century. He was a member of the Bible Presbyterian Church and, with his wife Edith, founded the L'Abri Fellowship, an international study center and Christian community. Though his books address a wide range of topics, his dominant theme, to which he consistently returns, is the question of existentialism. Schaeffer's thinking can be characterized by the following three points.

1. The belief in absolutes. Schaeffer argued that the West, in both its Christian and non-Christian worldviews, was committed to the notion of absolutes until the early twentieth century. In Europe, the transition away from absolutes occurred in about 1890. In the United States, it occurred in about 1935.[6] Prior to these dates, people accepted the possibility of absolutes, reasoning together on the classical basis of thesis/antithesis. They took it for granted, he explained, that if anything was true, the opposite was false. He used the formula "A is A" and "if you have A it is not non-A"[7] to illustrate this point. Thus, it was possible to discuss what was right and wrong, what was true and false. He explained, "One could tell a non-Christian to 'be a good girl,' and, while she might not have followed your advice, at least she would have understood what you were talking about."[8] He described this as living above the line of despair.

Yet a problem developed as people attempted to live out the implications of this understanding of absolute truth. As noted in chapter one where we examined the dark side of absolute truth, people were not able to arrive at a consensus as to what was and what was not absolute.

> They believed they could begin with themselves and draw a circle which would encompass all thoughts of life, and life itself, without having to depart from the logic of antithesis. They thought that on their own, rationalistically, finite people could find a unity within the total diversity—an adequate explanation for the whole of reality. This is where philosophy stood, prior to our own era [i.e., existentialism/postmodernism]. The only real arguments between these rationalistic optimists concerned what circle should be drawn. One person would draw a circle and say, "You can live within this circle." The next person would cross it out and would draw a different circle. The next person would come along and, crossing out the previous circle, draw his own—*ad infinitum*. So if you start to study philosophy by pursuing the *history* of philosophy, by the time you are through with all these circles, each one of which has been destroyed by the next, you may feel like jumping off London Bridge![9]

In other words, though absolute truth is necessary, the finite rational person is incapable of determining what it is. The result is a plurality of absolute truths, all of which oppose one another and, hence, generate a logical contradiction—truth that is universal and changeless (i.e., absolute) cannot disagree with other truths that are equally universal and changeless. Such a plurality of truths ultimately leaves people unable to know what is and what is not the correct system of truth. Yet, because (a) they are committed to the notion of absolute truth, and (b) they are unable to determine what is the correct system, (c) they experience a sense of despair since that which is essential to life is beyond their reach.

Such an understanding of absolute truth has characterized the West since early Hellenism (e.g., Plato and Aristotle).[10] It is an understanding of truth that is absolute and universal and therefore not subject to plurality where opposing systems can be deemed equally true. Descartes's *Cogito* (early seventeenth century) crystallized such thinking by providing the methodology of radical doubt as the starting point whereby absolute truth could be ascertained. In short, Schaeffer was reacting to an Enlightenment understanding of truth that was rooted in early Hellenist thought.

2. The disbelief in absolutes. Schaeffer then argued that since absolute truth was beyond the reach of people in Western culture, this brought about a philosophical tension that ultimately resulted in the West's giving up altogether on the possibility of ever acquiring absolute truth. Once this occurred, he explained, Western culture crossed over the line of despair. Georg W. F. Hegel (1770-1831) was the first major thinker to cross over this line and articulate a theology characterized by an absence of absolutes. He replaced the hermeneutical straight line of cause and effect with the triangle. That is, instead of operating on the premise of thesis and antithesis, he added the notion of synthesis. The notion of synthesis generated a spiral effect where truth routinely transitioned from thesis, antithesis, to synthesis. Synthesis then became the new thesis and started the process again. Such a dynamic changed the character of absolute truth. It was now understood in terms of **Zeitgeist** (spirit of the times), the overall mood (dominant thesis) of a culture or historical period. It was also understood in terms of *Zeitgeister* (spirits of the times), the overall trajectory of succeeding theses/antitheses/syntheses as they interact with one another and collectively move toward the *eschaton*. Such thinking, however, rendered an understanding of absolute truth as abiding principles a logical impossibility.

Søren Kierkegaard (1813-1855) carried this trajectory forward to the next level. He concluded that we cannot arrive at synthesis by reason. What was needed, he insisted, was a *leap of faith*. Kierkegaard used Abraham's sacrifice of Isaac as justification for this radical notion. He argued that Abraham's obedience was not based upon rational analysis since the sacrificing of one's son was a wholly irrational act. Nevertheless, it was still an act of faith. Kierkegaard's writings introduced intuition to the Hegelian system and gradually led to the separation of rationality from faith. Each was understood to exist in wholly distinct realms.

According to Schaeffer, Kierkegaard therefore became "the father of all modern existential thought, both secular and theological."[11] One's system of faith from which ultimate values are determined was no longer grounded in rational analysis open to critique by opposing perspectives. One believed what one believed without the necessity of logically defending it with rational arguments. This, in turn, legitimized the multiplicity of systems since, not grounded in rational analysis, the fact that differing systems were not in fundamental agreement with one another was no longer of any serious consequence. Hence, "there is one basic agreement in almost all of the chairs of philosophy today, and that is a radical denial of the possibility of drawing a circle which will encompass all. In this sense, the philosophies of today can be called in all seriousness antiphilosophies."[12]

From this leap of faith emerged three schools of existential thought: Swiss, French and German. The primary spokesperson for the Swiss school was Karl Jaspers (1883-1969), a German professor who taught at the University of Basel. He argued for the nonrational "final experience" that cannot be rationally articulated yet nonetheless gives meaning to life. The primary spokesperson for the French school was Jean-Paul Sartre (1905-1980). Sartre argued that self-authentication occurs by an act of the will. In this respect, it does not matter in which direction one acts as long as one acts. The primary spokesperson for the German school was Martin Heidegger (1889-1976). His second phase (after age 70) was what most interested Schaeffer. In this phase, Heidegger made three points: (a) a Being exists, (b) this Being is capable of making itself known, and (c) language is one with Being, and therefore Being reveals itself through language. Schaeffer explained, "We can never know rationally about what is there (brute fact), but language does reveal that something is there."[13] This, of course, is a pursuit of knowledge through a mystical use of language. In his book *What Is Philosophy?* Heidegger said that this use of language is located particularly in the poet. This means that the content of the poet's writings are less important than that of the Being that is *mystically speaking* behind the poet's words.

Theology followed this same post-*Cogito* trajectory. Following Kierkegaard's notion of the leap of faith, neo-orthodoxy was born, a system that minimized the need for a rational theological system from which to theologize, emphasizing instead the role of faith. Schaeffer wrote, "What existential [and by inference postmodern] philosophy had already said in secular language, it now said in theological language."[14] Schaeffer pointed to Karl Barth as "the doorway" into this new theology. In the introduction of his watershed commentary on the apostle Paul's epistle to the Romans, entitled *Der Römerbrief,* Barth acknowledged his debt to Kierkegaard, and throughout his career his theology consistently followed the overall scheme of the Kierkegaardian leap of faith. According to Barth, even when examined rationally through the lens of higher criticism where the Bible is seen to possess numerous errors, we can still maintain our faith through a nonrational and nonlogical leap of faith. Table 3.1 expresses Schaeffer's understanding of neo-orthodoxy.

Table 3.1

The nonrational and nonlogical	A crisis first-order experience. Faith as optimistic leap without verification or communicable content.
The rational and logical	The Scripture full of mistakes—pessimism.

According to Schaeffer, the implications of existentialism (and, again, by inference postmodernism) are forcefully presented in the arts. The American novelist Henry Miller (1891-1980) wrote pornographically, yet his writings were more than mere pornography. Miller was an antilaw writer, opposing all attempts at forming a universal moral code. "He smashed everything to pieces so that there is nothing left. Even sex is smashed."[15] Truman Capote's *In Cold Blood* follows in this same genre; the book described the cold-blooded murder of a Kansas family "without any comment as to meaning or morals."[16] In the arena of pop music, the Beatles offered a sterling example of this philosophy set to music—a form of music marked by moral relativism and ultimate meaninglessness. The music of John Cage (1912-1992) demonstrated the implications of existentialism/postmodernism even more forcefully. Cage composed his music by tossing coins, each note being determined by how each coin landed. His music was pure chance, refusing to conform to any of the metric standards and theories generally followed to create music. "In Cage's universe nothing comes through in the music except noise and confusion or total silence."[17]

Schaeffer added that he believed that much of modern homosexuality today can be traced to this new philosophy. It is a denial of antithesis that has led to an obliteration of the distinction between man and woman.

So male and female as complementary partners are finished. This is a form of homosexuality which is part of the movement below the line of despair. In much of [post]modern thinking, all antithesis and all the order of God's creation is to be fought against—including male-female distinctions. The pressure towards unisex is largely rooted here. But this is not an isolated problem; it is part of the world-spirit of the generation which surrounds us.[18]

Still, Schaeffer insisted that the problem with the typical existential/postmodern person is that he or she has not taken the implications of existentialism/postmodernism to their logical conclusion. Such a conclusion, Schaeffer insisted, is nihilism—the breakdown of all truth. In fact, even those who espouse a nihilistic system of thought cannot consistently live in their own system.

Ravi Zacharias offers a telling illustration of the problems such thinking generates. During one of his visits to California, he met a philosophy professor. Learning that this professor rejected the notion of a universally regnant absolute truth and instead argued for a pluralistic understanding of truth, he invited the man to lunch where they could have a private meeting to discuss this matter in detail. The professor accepted Zacharias's invitation.

> When we met, he wasted no time. He began with, "Your biggest problem is that you do not understand Eastern logic." I concluded it would be best to let him explain Eastern logic to me. His argument expounded on two kinds of logic, one the either/or logic and the other, the both/and logic. "The either/or logic," he said, "is built on the law of noncontradiction, meaning that if a statement is true, its opposite has to be false. . . . This is a Western way of looking at reality." I disagreed with that conclusion and asked him to cross it off his placemat where he had delineated his syllogisms. He refused, and I allowed him to proceed, knowing that sooner or later he would have to reject his conclusion. . . .
>
> After he belabored these two ideas of either/or and both/and for some time and carried on his tirade that we ought not to study truth from a Western point of view but rather from an Eastern viewpoint, I finally asked if I could interrupt his unpunctuated train of thought and raise one question. He agreed and put down his pencil.
>
> I said, "Sir, are you telling me that when I am studying Hinduism I *either* use the both/and system of logic *or* nothing else?"
>
> There was a pin-drop silence for what seemed an eternity. I repeated my question: "Are you telling me that when I am studying Hinduism I *either* use the both/and logic *or* nothing else? Have I got that right?"
>
> He threw his head back and said, "The either/or does seem to emerge, doesn't it?"[19]

Indeed it does, Zacharias answered back. Zacharias's point is that before one can share the gospel with those who have rejected the notion of universally applicable absolute truth, one must first locate that person's point of tension.

And this is precisely Schaeffer's point. According to Schaeffer, one must first learn where an individual has chosen to stop on the trajectory to nihilism and now lives, albeit inconsistently, with a facsimile of absolutes. The next step is to push him or her toward the logical conclusion of these existential/ postmodern presuppositions: a worldview that is consistently nihilistic. The way Schaeffer put it, we should push "him towards the place where he ought to be, had he not stopped short."[20] This, he insisted, is a necessary preevangelism to people living in an existential/postmodern world.[21]

3. A restoration of absolutes. According to Schaeffer, the solution to the problem of nihilism posed by existentialism/postmodernism is the authentic Christian faith, which includes the notion of faith understood in terms of absolutes and antitheses (A is not non-A). What is striking about this move is that the method by which Schaeffer attempted to solve the dilemma posed by existentialism/postmodernism was by reintroducing the methodology of radical doubt prescribed by the *Cogito*. In other words, Schaeffer attempted to solve the problem created by the Enlightenment by a more rigorous and consistent use of the Enlightenment.

With this methodology, Schaeffer's first move addressed the question of *personality*. He assumed that the human being indeed possesses personality since all empirical evidence points in that direction. That led him to ask the question of whether or not God possesses personality. He insisted that the answer must be yes since a created being (the human being) cannot rise higher than the creator (God).

He used the illustration of the formation of a new lake to illustrate his point. In the Swiss Alps, occasionally a lake would form an underground stream that would eventually break to the surface and give birth to a new lake. The original lake would lower its waterline as the new lake increased its waterline until the two waterlines were the same. This equilibrium was evidence that the two lakes were indeed connected by an underground stream. But if the second lake rose higher than the first lake, that would indicate that the two lakes were not connected and some third lake was the genuine source. Schaeffer's point was that a *result* cannot rise higher than a *source*. "Personality is like that," he explained. "No one has ever thought of a way of deriving personality from nonpersonal sources."[22] If God did not possess personality, logically neither can the human being. Since the human being does, so must God.

Schaeffer's second move postulated that a personal God would *desire to communicate* with other creatures similarly endowed with personality. This communication, he maintained, would include propositional truth that was timeless and changeless. He asked:

> Why should God not communicate *propositionally* to the man, the verbalized being, whom He made in such a way that we communicate propositionally with each other? Therefore, in the biblical position there is the possibility of verifiable facts involved: a personal God communicating in verbalized form propositionally to man—not only concerning those things man would call in our generation "religious truths," but also down into the areas of history and science.[23]

Such communication would necessarily be inerrant since it is inherently illogical for a perfect God to communicate truth imperfectly. A failure to recognize the existence of such a divine revelation has given rise to humanistic rationalism, which sets aside divine revelation as either inconsequential or impossible.

Schaeffer's third move was to conclude that if a personal God were to communicate with the human being, he would be required to address *the question of sin* in his communication. From the posture of absolute truths and antitheses, sin is the antithesis of holiness and must be squarely addressed and settled. "Rightly understood, Christianity as a system has the answers to the basic needs of [post]modern man. . . . The first basic need is caused by the lack of certainty regarding the reality of individual personality. Every man is in tension until he finds a satisfactory answer to the problem of who he himself is."[24] This is where Schaeffer introduces the incarnation, crucifixion and resurrection of Jesus Christ in an understandable way in which holiness and its antithesis, sin, is resolved.

The historic Christian answer concerning the reality of sin and its remedy is superior to the answers of the other religions in the world and thereby stands apart from them. "There is no other god like this [Christian] God. It is ridiculous to say that all religions teach the same things when they disagree at the fundamental point as to what God is like." The gods of the East, Schaeffer explained, are infinite to the point of being pantheistic. The gods of the West have tended to be personal but limited, such were the gods of the Greeks, Romans and Germans. "But the God of the Bible, Old and New Testaments alike, is the infinite-personal God."[25]

Summary of Schaeffer's strategy. We can draw three observations about Schaeffer's strategy against existentialism/postmodernism:

Existentialism/postmodernism. With his audience being primarily the lay

Christian and undergraduate reader, Schaeffer's arguments tended to be presented in general terms.[26] Specifically, he argued against existentialism,
though the trajectory of this movement eventually gave rise to the postmodern paradigm. (With the advent of postmodernism in the late twentieth century, existentialism has faded.) Painting with a broad brush, his writings tend
to reflect only two positions within the postmodern debate: those who are
in favor of postmodernism and those who oppose it. In addition, since the
word *postmodernism* had not yet entered the vernacular within academia as
the term to describe this new philosophical system, Schaeffer tended to call
this new system *modernism*—albeit an extreme form of modernism. In reading Schaeffer, care must be taken not to confuse what he described as modernism with classic modernism. They are clearly two separate systems.

Absolute truth. Though Schaeffer recognized the problem of plural absolute truths and the logical contradiction that they generate, his solution was
a return to the methodology dictated by the *Cogito*. Hence, he attempted to
solve the dilemma created by the *Cogito* by a more rigorous and, in his estimation, more correct use of the *Cogito*. This fits Kevin J. Vanhoozer's characterization of Protestant evangelicalism. He writes, "For the past forty or so
years, evangelicals have been busy trying to defend the faith against modernity, largely with the tools of modernity. In exegesis, theology, and apologetics alike, many evangelicals accepted a Cartesian view of rationality [i.e.,
the *Cogito*]."[27] Alister McGrath adds, "There is a need for us to ask whether
evangelicalism itself has become at least in some ways a secret prisoner of
the Enlightenment. . . . I sense evangelicals feeling that it was perhaps easier
to live in the Enlightenment environment."[28]

Inerrancy. The notion of the Scriptures being without error was central
to Schaeffer's understanding of absolute truth. Only in the context of inerrancy could the gospel (the incarnation, resurrection, forgiveness of sins,
etc.) be credibly presented. Central to his criticism of Barth was that Barth
devised a theological system of faith that made allowances for errors in
Scripture. Though this put Barth in good stead with those scholars characterized by higher criticism, it was an irrational move that, according to
Schaeffer, ultimately torpedoed the very substructure designed to sustain his
system of faith. In the Schaefferean system, the methodology of the *Cogito*
could only advance toward truth that was "entirely indubitable"[29] and "likely
to last,"[30] provided that the data being considered was reliable. Anything less
than an inerrant Scripture was not reliable.

These three observations deserve notice because Protestant evangelicalism has tended to follow Schaeffer's methodology in combating postmodernism. In the following, we will examine how foundational realism has addressed these three observations mentioned above. We will do so, however, in reverse order.

INERRANCY

The doctrine of inerrancy teaches that in the original autographs the Bible was written without error. The Gordon-Conwell Basis of Faith states, "The sixty-six canonical books of the Bible, as originally written, were inspired of God, hence free from error. They constitute the only infallible guide in life and practice."[31]

This definition gives room for two views that have collided upon one another within conservative Christianity today: (1) Scripture is inerrant in all that it teaches, and (2) Scripture is inerrant in matters of faith and practice only—leaving room for errors in archeology, historical references, science and so forth.[32] A great deal of writing has tried to settle the controversy generated by these two views. This book will not engage in that debate, other than to acknowledge that the two views exist. Nevertheless, the statements below about inerrancy and its relationship to foundational realism more directly reflects the first view of inerrancy than the second.

The third rail. The doctrine of inerrancy is the proverbial third rail in conservative Christianity—to tamper with it is to suffer serious consequences. Many denominations, ecclesial fellowships, parachurch organizations, Christian colleges and universities insist that the doctrine of inerrancy not be questioned. Those who do so tend to have their evangelical credentials challenged and are subjected to various forms of censure or discipline. In other words, in these ecclesial organizations, the doctrine of inerrancy is not open to debate or discussion. Rather, being one of its central tenets, it is stated prominently in their doctrinal statements and expected to be affirmed by all members without reservation. Its untouchableness is due to the critical role it plays in their hermeneutical theory.

Ecclesial organizations characterized by the doctrine of inerrancy operate on the following premise: by using the methodology of radical doubt prescribed by the *Cogito,* an individual can build a bridge through inductive reasoning to an accurate understanding of God, provided that the data being considered by such inductive reasoning is wholly reliable. This implies the need for an inerrant Scripture for the process to work.

As we observed in our examination of Schaeffer, the finite human being has historically been incapable of establishing a consensus on what an absolute system of truth should look like. One individual would draw a circle and say that all within the circle is true, only to have his circle crossed out by the next individual who had his or her own system, and so on. Schaeffer's solution was not the abandonment of this methodology—a move which Schaeffer believed would have required a reluctant acquiescence to existentialism/postmodernism—but rather the introduction of a divinely inspired text. This text constitutes a comprehensive body of data that, when correctly systematized, provide a singular and final circle of truth. It would have to be error-free, otherwise it too would generate a series of conflicting circles as scholars struggled in deciding what aspects of the text to consider errant and inerrant. Hence, the problem that had generated conflicting circles was not the method (i.e., the *Cogito*) but rather the range and quality of the evidence being examined by the method. For Schaeffer, the range and quality of evidence must be an inerrant Scripture if we are to have absolute confidence in the conclusions of this rational analysis.

Therefore, according to that sector within the church committed to foundational realism, the alternative to postmodernism is absolute truth, and the only legitimate means by which absolute truth can be discerned is through an inerrant Bible. Stated otherwise, without an inerrant Bible, absolute truth becomes an elusive goal since our final source of authority cannot be trusted as accurate—cultural relativism therefore becomes the only legitimate game in town, so to speak.[33] This sector in the church does not wish to "surrender the objectified world of nature to the secular worldview, nor do they want faith directed towards a nonobjectifiable God."[34] They insist upon an objectifiable world and understand inerrancy as the touchstone upon which it can be objectified. Foundational realists within the church therefore understand the doctrine of inerrancy as the veritable *facteur* (the most perfect and final messenger) from which to combat the challenge of postmodernism.[35]

The methodology in determining inerrancy. There are two means for establishing the Bible's credentials as an inerrant document. The first compares the archeological record—both historical and geological—with the biblical record. The second method compares the prophecies stated in Scripture with their historical fulfillment. The purpose of both systems of analysis, of course, is to establish inerrancy through independent and objective verification.

In these two methodologies, however, a problem emerges. Many passages of Scripture, some of which are central to the Christian *kerygma* (lit. "proclamation," i.e., the apostles' preaching of the gospel), are not open to such independent and objective analysis and verification. Passages of Scripture that address the incarnation, resurrection and ascension of Jesus, for example, fall into this category.

The Shroud of Turin has been rigorously studied with the hope of providing the church with independent verification of the resurrection of Jesus. It has been alleged that this shroud possesses distinctive discolored markings of a crucified man. Some scholars therefore suggest that the shroud was placed on a crucified victim of the first century at the time of his interment and his body somehow left an outline on its fibers. Moreover, these scholars have alleged that characteristics of the shroud's markings show that an energy field (such as that of a resurrected spirit) passed through its fibers. This theory, these scholars continue, accounts for the discolored markings on the shroud. The shroud has been analyzed with computerized techniques and other sophisticated tests of modern science with the hope of determining whether this shroud was the very one placed upon the deceased Jesus during his brief stay in the tomb and whether the discolored markings are the result of a burst of energy at the moment of resurrection. The shroud has been venerated by the Roman Catholic Church as a holy relic since at least the Middle Ages. Thus, its identification as the shroud of the crucified Jesus is a longstanding tradition within the church.

The scientific analysis of the evidence related to the Shroud of Turin, however, has yielded inconclusive results. All that scientific analysis has been able to confirm is that the fabric of the shroud does date to the first century and its markings are those of a crucified man. Yet questions related to the alleged energy field passing through the fabric that created its distinctive markings are left unanswered. Since no other purported external evidence to the resurrection of Jesus exists within the scientific community, the lack of certainty regarding the Shroud of Turin has eliminated the possibility of scientifically proving the resurrection of Jesus.

This lack draws attention to the fact that the New Testament Scriptures that recount the resurrection of Jesus cannot be independently validated as inerrant, as error-free. Hence, the Bible does not provide the church with a

verifiable objective witness from which a rational and logical faith (to use
Schaeffer's terms) can be grounded. To some degree at least, it lacks an aura
of objectivity.

Evangelical scholar R. C. Sproul agrees, recognizing that inerrancy is essentially a statement *of* faith rather than a grounding *for* faith. He describes
three general approaches to inerrancy. First, he cites the confessional
method, by which the Bible is confessed to be inerrant by faith alone. Second, he cites the presuppositional method, which defends the authority and
inerrancy of the Bible as a foundational premise. Third, he cites the classical
method as a combination of inductive (presuppositional) methods and de-
ductive approaches (scientific analysis) as evidence.[36] In the three approaches, the *Cogito* is either ignored (the first approach) or only partially
followed (the second and third approaches). None of the approaches arrive
at inerrancy by using the scientific method (via the *Cogito*) and then ground
the Christian faith on that basis.

Since the doctrine of inerrancy itself requires faith in order to be believed,
it too must be doubted if one is to consistently follow the methodology of the
Cogito. Yet since key elements of the Christian faith lie outside the realm of
scientific inquiry (e.g., the incarnation, resurrection and ascension) due to the
fact that they cannot be proved beyond a reasonable doubt, one can never
move past radical doubt when addressing the question of an inerrant Scripture. Instead of serving as the hermeneutical substructure or foundation on
which all other doctrines of the Christian faith are placed as the superstructure,
the doctrine of inerrancy is itself part of the superstructure. The Christian faith
therefore has no rationally or scientifically grounded foundation.[37]

The challenge of inerrancy from George Lindbeck. The underlying
premise of inerrancy says that one can believe that a document has a divine
origin and therefore is absolute truth only if the human mind can independently validate its claim. George Lindbeck argues that this premise is "man-
ifestly foolish." Not only is the doctrine unfalsifiable, causing it to be a form
of meaningless jargon, it also tries "to ground acceptance of Scripture by theories of revelation or inspiration." Nevertheless, its result is that the doctrine
"actually *weakens* its authority. It makes what needs no apologetics depend
on questionable ones."[38] The emphasis on the question of the factualness of
Scripture and the attempt to ground its factuality by rational analysis de-cen-
ters the role of faith and the Holy Spirit speaking through the biblical worldview. As Lindbeck puts it, "The story [of the biblical worldview] is logically

prior. It determines the meaning, images, concepts, doctrine, and theories of the church rather than being determined by them."[39] In other words, the doctrine of inerrancy sets aside the biblical worldview. Moreover, such reasoning reverses the Anselmian dictum of *fides quaerens intellectum* (faith seeking knowledge) by grounding faith in independently validated scientific research (rational analysis). Lindbeck argues that this approach illustrates walking by sight rather than by faith.

ABSOLUTE TRUTH

According to foundational realists, the solution to the dilemma created by modernism was a return to the *Cogito*. The irony in this move is that it returned to an epistemological system already believed to be flawed.

As we noted in our review of Schaeffer, modernism was flawed because of its spawning of a plurality of circles, each one asserting that it alone constituted absolute truth. The return to the *Cogito* by foundational realists within the church, however, was thought to be different in that it insisted upon an error-free Bible serving as the foundation on which to build in the pursuit of truth. With this hermeneutical adjustment, Schaeffer and those from his theological perspective believe that a singular circle could be drawn that would be immune to the erasure and redrawing of new circles (i.e., the problem of the contradictory plurality of absolute truths). In other words, foundational realists believe that a fixed body of absolute truths can be obtained provided that an inerrant Bible serves as the hermeneutical foundation from which to undertake the pursuit of truth.

This adjustment, however, has not proved as successful as hoped. When juxtaposed against the voluminous number of systematic theologies existing in the church, clearly a plurality of circles still exists. In spite of the fact that many of these systematic theologies affirm biblical inerrancy, we are no closer to that quintessential circle from which to understand absolute truth than are those who do not believe in an inerrant Bible. That is to say, we are still all over the map, so to speak, when it comes to drawing the circle from which to understand absolute truth. Hence, Christian theology still has the following problem: (a) by following the methodology prescribed by the *Cogito* (thinking aculturally and ahistorically with the starting point of radical doubt) and (b) from there building a theological system, (c) numerous circles are still being drawn.

Two responses to the plurality of circles. Those in the church who espouse foundational realism respond to this problem in two ways. First, some argue that though they believe the quintessential circle that defines absolute truth does exist, it is ultimately unknowable and hence an ever-elusive goal. This generates the paradox of aspiring to draw the circle while knowing that it will always lie beyond one's reach. Douglas Groothuis is representative of this response, writing that no one "has mastered these objective, absolute and universal truths or that one has nothing more to learn and is in no need of correction."[40] Nevertheless, he believes that "a reasonable certainty through dialogue"[41] is possible provided that those pursuing this knowledge are characterized by intellectual humility. That is, though the quintessential circle cannot be drawn, Groothuis claims that through dialogue with honest and humble scholars we can essentially approximate the lines of this circle, knowing that minor adjustments will always be required.

The second response argues that the quintessential circle is indeed accessible, provided that scholars engage in rigorous and honest scholarship. Rather than questioning the method, these people assume that *their circle* is the quintessential circle. Consequently, according to this view, all opposing circles are flawed. Schaeffer was aware of this second response and cautioned against it. He wrote that some Christians "tend to become absolutists even in the lesser points of doctrine. One must realize that there is a great difference between believing in absolutes and having an absolutist mentality about everything."[42] Nevertheless, he failed to explain how to avoid this problem of having "an absolutist mentality about everything" since not everyone agrees about what constitutes "lesser points of doctrine." A lesser point of doctrine for one Christian is sometimes the other person's major point.

Though the second response is clearly problematic in that those who espouse this view tend toward an absolutist mentality about everything, the first response is also problematic. The systematic theology of Rex Koivisto illustrates the problem within the first response.

The "circle" of Rex Koivisto. In his book *One Lord, One Faith,* Koivisto argued for a "theology for cross-denominational renewal" (the subtitle of the book) that would give rise to a renewed catholicity that, in turn, would foster a credible ecumenism. It was an attempt to draw a circle that he believed the entire church could agree upon.

Koivisto's proposal contained three moves. First, he identified denominational distinctives as the main barrier to the formation of the quintessential circle. Second, to overcome this problem, he insisted that Christians must be able to distinguish between "core orthodoxy which they warmly share with other believers and their own peculiar distinctives."[43] Koivisto described these denominational distinctives as "tradition," or more specifically, "microtradition." By making this distinction, he attempted to point out to Protestant evangelicals that much of what they consider "explicit biblical teaching" is only "tradition"—that is, an interpretation that cannot be divorced from the cultural lenses shaping a theologian's view. "None of us," he argued, "interprets the Bible in a vacuum. We interpret out of a cultural, historical context, through an ecclesiastical context, *looking for* the Bible's relevance to cultural problems."[44] Third, Koivisto nevertheless believed that it is possible to distinguish our microtraditions mediated through culture from "the clear teachings of Scripture." Such clear teachings comprise his "core orthodoxy," that which all true Christians share in common.

In these three moves there lies an inherent contradiction. Koivisto insisted that in order to construct a crossdenominational theology, it is essential to distinguish the microtraditions of individual denominations from the macrotradition that defines the core of the Christian faith. "Only when we have separated out what is traditional," Koivisto explained, "can we be allowed to hear the crisp, unadorned voice of God ringing out from Scripture alone."[45] Yet it is precisely here where Koivisto stumbles. James K. A. Smith asks:

> May we not legitimately ask, at this juncture, whether Koivisto's core orthodoxy—the clear teachings of Scripture—is not also influenced by tradition? Does not Koivisto himself concede such when he describes this core orthodoxy as macro*tradition*? As macrotradition, can it ever deliver the crisp, unadorned voice of God?[46]

Smith answers with a resounding no. He insists that Koivisto has failed to recognize that interpretative glasses are, as Abraham Kuyper once said, "cemented to our face." Koivisto somehow holds out the possibility that a group of teachings are the *clear teachings of Scripture* delivered immediately, unhampered by the cultural and historical space-and-time of hermeneutics. Smith counters, arguing that

> after rejecting earlier options such as the *Fundamentals* of the early twenties, the creeds of the undivided church and the Vincentian view ("what all men have at all times believed"), Koivisto finally delivers to us that which unites all Christians—*the gospel message,* which he then specifies: *"God sent His Son into the world to die as an atonement for sin, and God raised Him from the dead, so that anyone who places faith in Him receives the free gift of salvation."*[47]

Though Christians may generally agree with Koivisto in this broadly articulated definition of the gospel message, even here Smith is uncomfortable. Koivisto uses language that is partial to an imputation model and thus unfavorable to an infusion model. Smith concludes that what Koivisto presents as *the* gospel message is in fact heavily indebted to a historic Presbyterian interpretation with little or no acknowledgment of Catholic, Eastern Orthodox, Pentecostal and mainline Protestant interpretations. Hence, with the stroke of a pen Koivisto proclaims the Presbyterian interpretation of the gospel message normative and discounts all competing versions.

Clearly such provisionalism was not Koivisto's intent, and Smith may be overreaching in his assessment. Nevertheless, Smith's comments demonstrate a pervasive problem in theology today. Standing outside one's own tradition and speaking on behalf of other traditions to articulate absolute truth, a growing consensus within academia suggests, is not only difficult but impossible. The recipients of such efforts react instinctively with suspicion, looking for evidence of the speaker's tradition present in the purported absolute truth. This reaction corresponds to Foucault's hermeneutics of suspicion, which was discussed earlier.

POSTMODERNISM

In addition to their arguments regarding inerrancy and absolute truth, foundational realists oppose postmodernists, insisting that if there are no absolute standards, then the whole notion of right and wrong collapses. As Schaeffer explained, "There must be an absolute if there are to be morals, and there must be an absolute if there are to be real values. If there is no absolute beyond man's ideas, then there is no final appeal to judge between individuals and groups whose moral judgments conflict."[48] Without such a "final appeal," Schaeffer concludes, we are merely left with conflicting opinions. Among foundational realists, two perspectives critical of postmodernism have emerged.

The first perspective. The first perspective among foundational realists holds that postmodernism is a relativistic system that jeopardizes the coherence of culture. When postmodernism insists that no singular system of truth should be allowed to masquerade as the dominant system from which all other "truths" must conform, standards of morality collapse, ultimately reduced to those espoused by an individual. With such a pluralism of truth, society begins to do what is right in their own eyes (cf. Judg 17:6; 21:25), a recipe condemned in Scripture and subject to divine judgment.

Josh McDowell and Bob Hostetler typify this attitude toward postmodernism. In their book *The New Tolerance* they identify postmodernism with Satan's lie in the Garden of Eden. Paraphrasing Genesis 3:6, they write, "I will be my own god. I will determine what is right or wrong, what is true or false, what is good or evil."[49] Within the postmodern rubric, then, tolerance is the new standard, the new moral code. The only moral value not tolerated is intolerance itself. McDowell and Hostetler describe this as "an ominous cultural change in human history."[50] It jeopardizes the Judeo-Christian tradition that has historically insisted upon absolute standards of right and wrong (e.g., the Ten Commandments) from which to order society.

McDowell and Hostetler identify ten problematic implications of the new tolerance typified by postmodernism:

a. the death of truth
b. the disappearance of virtue
c. the demise of justice
d. the loss of conviction
e. the privatization of faith
f. the tyranny of the individual
g. the disintegration of human rights
h. the dominance of feeling
i. the exaltation of nature
j. the descent into extremes[51]

The first item on this list is the *death of truth*. In the postmodern rubric, truth—that is, truth that possesses a universal and timeless relevance—dies. In its place is born a cultural relativism where anything goes—provided that mutually agreed-upon cultural or individual norms are not violated. The final item on this list is the *descent into extremes*. Without the recognition of universal and timeless truth to provide a standard for morality, individuals and communities tend to frame truth in individualized and unbalanced perspectives that ultimately result in extremes that grant legitimacy to bizarre behavior.[52] The eight items in between the two end points connect the dots in a downward spiral, the inevitable steps that a culture will take once absolute truth dies.

The second perspective. The second perspective of foundational realists holds that postmodernism, in spite of its so-called tolerance of competing "truths," is itself a metanarrative and therefore has never truly moved beyond modernism. Rather than standing in contradistinction to modernism with differing starting points and assumptions, postmodernism has merely offered a major corrective to the paradigm by incorporating recently developed language theories. It is nothing more than modernism in its most intensified, extreme or final form.

According to this perspective, then, it would be more accurate to strike *post* from the term and insert *ultra.* Thomas Oden writes, "What is named post is actually a desperate extension of despairing modernity which imagines by calling itself another name (postmodern), it can extend ideology of modernity into the period following modernity. But in this semantical switch, simply by naming itself post it does not cease being ultra."[53] In other words, says Oden, there is nothing *post* about postmodernism and, accordingly, its name is misleading—"not yet grasped or rightly appraised by those in it."[54]

In a similar vein, Donald Carson has written that postmodernism can be divided into two broad subcategories—deconstructionism and constructionism—both of which are problematic. Deconstructionism is not compatible with Christian theology due to its propensity to nihilism. It, however, cannot be embraced consistently. Constructionism is also problematic due to a major flaw reflected in an internal inconsistency. He explains that advocates of constructionism are "unwilling to succumb to its most frightening implications [nihilism], and insist that humanity does share some values and truths, in practice if not in theory, and *mirabile dictu,* they turn out to support various 'green' theories: pacifism, radical feminism, and Whiteheadian metaphysics."[55] Accordingly, Carson argued that the old agendas of modernism remain but are now altered in how they are presented. Less strident because they "are cast not in terms of truth but in terms of equality, relationships, and tolerance, they resurface as politically correct items meeting all the demands of pluralism."[56] Nevertheless, by adopting these values and truths and arguing for their transcendent universality, postmodernism, in its constructionist version, has stepped back into its modernist past. It is, according to Carson, an admission that "the emperor has finally discovered that he has no clothes"[57] and is desperately searching for anything with which to cover itself, even if that means contradicting itself with the adoption of modernist values that had previously been openly repudiated.

Carson further notes that some avant-garde intellectuals are sufficiently uneasy with this inherent inconsistency within constructive postmodernism and are beginning to announce its impending death.[58]

THE QUESTION OF PIETISM

Having noted that Protestant evangelicalism is closely identified with foundational realism (a system grounded in the radical doubt of the Cartesian *Cogito*), an internal contradiction exists. On the one hand, many of the people associated with this tradition are characterized not by doubt but by vibrant lives of faith. Alister McGrath has noted this positive dimension of Protestant evangelicalism, commenting:

> Evangelicalism is one of the powerhouses of the modern Christian church in the Western world. Time and again, people—especially young people—put their discovery of the vitality and excitement of the gospel down to the witness of evangelicalism. . . . Evangelicalism, once regarded as marginal, has now become mainline, and it can no longer be dismissed as an insignificant sideshow, sectarian tendency or irrelevance. It has moved from the wings to center stage, displacing others once regarded as mainline, who consequently feel deeply threatened and alienated. Its commitment to evangelism has resulted in numerical growth, where some other variants of Christianity are suffering from severe contraction.[59]

This spiritual vibrancy, McGrath continues, is characterized by the following eight distinctives: (1) controlling convictions, (2) a devotional ethos, (3) a recognition of the supreme authority of Scripture, (4) a recognition of the majesty of Jesus Christ, (5) a recognition of the lordship of the Holy Spirit, (6) a recognition of the need for personal conversion, (7) the priority of evangelism and (8) the importance of the Christian community.[60] McGrath asserts that both Christian and secular scholarship have widely noted these trends.[61]

On the other hand, doubt (the lack of faith) and the prioritization of one's cultural worldview (as opposed to the prioritization of the biblical worldview) are endemic within this tradition. McGrath is on record criticizing Protestant evangelicalism with such a sweeping opposite observation: this movement, he explains, is "a secret prisoner of the Enlightenment."[62] He adds that Protestant evangelicals

> are liberated from captivity but as they progress they begin to hanker after the old days when though in captivity, at least they knew where they were. I sense

evangelicals feeling that it was perhaps easier to live in the Enlightenment environment.[63]

Paralleling McGrath's concerns, Timothy Phillips and Dennis Okholm comment on evangelical captivity to contemporary culture, resulting in spiritual deadness:

> Popular indicators suggest that [Protestant] evangelicalism's unique moral and theological inheritance has been traded for a bowlful of spiritual junk food that feeds the contemporary appetite. American culture now carries more weight than revelation on a broad range of issues from ethics to beliefs. The prevalence of adultery and divorce—even among nationally known figures—no longer startles. Consumer research and related techniques increasingly supplant Scripture's analysis of the church's and believer's responsibilities.[64]

They add:

> Therapy is confused with salvation. The politics of the New Right are identified as the "Christian" coalition. Certainly evangelicals remain "people of the book." But the displays that greet customers entering a religious bookstore often indicate that the focus has shifted away from the gospel narrative to exotic dimensions that assume their own autonomy or sustain these American ideologies. For evangelicals on both the right and the left of the spectrum, American culture has dissipated the central benchmark of the faith, the christological center of Scripture.[65]

How, then, are we to account for this contradiction, the characterization of Protestant evangelicalism by both spiritual vibrancy *and* deadness?

The contradiction may be due to the presence of cognitive dissonance within this religious tradition. Those Christians characterized by a vibrancy of faith, though grounded in fundamental realism (i.e., the *Cogito*), may perhaps, on a practical level, be migrating away from it toward another paradigm by which to order their own spiritual lives. Hence, the theology they formally embrace may be disconnected from the pietism they informally practice. That is to say, their piety may be grounded on other bases than that of Enlightenment modernism.

In his book *The Myth of Certainty,* Daniel Taylor describes the nature of this migration. He begins the book by asking sixteen questions designed to spark a desire to move past problems related with the mindset of the Cartesian *Cogito*. Four of the more intriguing questions are the following:

* Are you, even after years of being a Christian, ever struck by the un-

likelihood of the whole thing? Does one minute it seem perfectly natural and unquestionable that God exists and cares for the world, and the next moment uncommonly naïve?

* Do you ever think, "Those close to me would be shocked if they knew some of the doubts I have about my faith?" Do you ever scare even yourself with your doubts?

* Do you ever feel somewhat schizophrenic about the relationship of your faith to the rest of your life? Do you find yourself compartmentalizing different aspects so that tensions between them are minimized?

* Someone at work says, "Christians check their brains at the door of the church every Sunday, and most of them don't even bother to pick them up on the way out." Do you find yourself objecting or agreeing?[66]

Jarred into reflective thinking, such Christians are encouraged to develop a thirst for something better, something more spiritually alive.

Taylor then examines the hyperfundamentalism characteristic of a large segment within Protestant evangelicalism, reflecting upon its authoritarianism, narrowness, hypocrisy and intolerance. Hyperfundamentalism, he asserts, has embraced "the myth of certainty" to such an extent that it has become enormously triumphalist in attitude, having fallen victim to the dark side of absolute truth that we considered in chapter one.

Taylor's answer to this dilemma is a repudiation of the myth of certainty (i.e., the *Cogito*) and a migration towards something distinctively post. Drawing on the insights of Søren Kierkegaard, Taylor exchanges the rationalism of the *Cogito* for the suprarational, a knowledge grounded in intuition and relationship. Describing how to lead someone from error to truth, for example, Kierkegaard explains:

> First and foremost, no impatience. . . . A direct attack only strengthens a person in his illusion, and at the same time embitters him. There is nothing that requires such gentle handling as an illusion, if one wishes to dispel it. If anything prompts the prospective captive to set his will in opposition, all is lost. . . . [T]he indirect method, . . . loving and serving the truth, arranges everything, . . . and then shyly withdraws (for love is always shy), so as not to witness the admission which he makes to himself alone before God—that he has lived hitherto in an illusion.[67]

Note how much this approach differs from the one Schaeffer advocated, one that admonishes the Christian to aggressively push an individual "to-wards the place where he ought to be [i.e., nihilism], had he not stopped short."[68] Taylor then adds, "Only those with great confidence in the truth they hold can risk Kierkegaard's approach. The less secure must annihilate the opposition."[69]

Taylor's point is that faith-based pietism grows as one understands the Christian faith primarily in terms of relationship—not cognition. This rela-tionship is person-to-person and person-to-God. Spiritual truth, then, be-comes an inquiry into personhood (the divine and the human). Again, Tay-lor explains that reason

> should not be the primary tool by which one evaluates a relationship with God—not because faith can't stand up to reason, as the secularist contends, but because reason is simply inadequate for the task. It has at best certain pre-liminary contributions to make in an area where its methodology, especially when operating alone, yields meager results. Making reason the primary arbi-ter in matters of faith ignores both the nature of the message (which is a per-son and a relationship, not an argument) and the nature of the recipient (who is also a person, not a computer).[70]

In this respect, the essence of spiritual truth is grounded in the relationship of a God who is actively pursuing us.

It is the argument of this book that such a faith-based pietism has much in common with other strands of the Christian faith that are consciously pushing away from the *Cogito* and towards that which is clearly post. More will be said of this understanding of faith in the latter chapters of this book.

SUMMARY

Heir to both the Protestant Reformation and the Enlightenment, founda-tional realism is an attempt to wed the teachings of Scripture with the meth-odology of the *Cogito*. Francis A. Schaeffer is noteworthy in that, seeing Western culture move beyond the *Cogito* into what he deemed to be irrational antiphilosophy, he sought to move the church back to the *Cogito,* albeit in a more pure form. He insisted that with a purely inspired and inerrant Scrip-ture as the database from which to theologize/philosophize, one can indeed locate absolute truth that is universal and timeless—not subject to cultural and historical influences.

Though Schaeffer identified existentialism as the philosophical expres-sion that was post-*Cogito* and spoke against that, from the mid-1970s into the present, postmodernism has been the more dominant post-*Cogito* philosophy in Western culture. Scholars standing in Schaeffer's shadow, then, have applied the methodology he intended as a polemical attack against existentialism to the challenges of postmodernism.

The problem with this methodology, however, is that it has paid little attention to the dark side of absolute truth. As noted in chapter one, the church has hardly noticed the dark side of absolute truth. This failure is especially true of those identified with foundational realism. Problems related to absolute truth, then, have typically gone unchecked within the church. This is generating a curious migration within this sector of the church. Though formally still identified with theology that is foundationalist in orientation, at an informal level individual Christians are finding a more vibrant faith (i.e., one not grounded in the radical doubt of the *Cogito*) as they explore post-*Cogito* options. As such, they are reading Christian literature designed to enhance personal piety that stands opposed to the rationalism grounded in doubt and that, on the other hand, is more in keeping with the Anselmian formula of "faith seeking knowledge."

QUESTIONS

Basic Concepts

1. In what respect was Francis A. Schaeffer ahead of his time?

2. What were the three moves in Schaeffer's response to postmodernism?

3. In respect to the modernist paradigm, Schaeffer wrote, "So if you start to study philosophy by pursuing the *history* of philosophy, by the time you are through with all these circles, each one of which has been destroyed by the next, you may feel like jumping off London Bridge!" What did he mean by this?

4. According to Schaeffer, what are the characteristics of living under the line of despair?

5. Schaeffer explained that helping a person overcome the problem of living under the line of despair requires that we push the person "towards the place where he ought to be, had he not stopped short." What did he mean by this?

6. According to Schaeffer, why is an inerrant Scripture necessary for a per-

son to overcome the problem of living under the line of despair?

7. In what respect is the doctrine of inerrancy "the third rail" in conservative Christianity?

8. In the contemporary church, differing theologians and ecclesial bodies continue to articulate a multiplicity of absolute truths. What are conservative theologians' two responses to this problem?

9. Among foundational realists, what are the two responses to postmodernism?

Further Thought

1. For many conservative Christians, the doctrine of inerrancy is understood as the grounding from which Scripture can be trusted. What are the strengths and weaknesses to this approach to Scripture?

2. George Lindbeck wrote that when one attempts to ground acceptance of Scripture by theories of revelation or inspiration, the method "actually *weakens* its authority." What did he mean by this?

3. Since the Shroud of Turin does not provide conclusive evidence for the resurrection of Jesus, what effects does this inconclusiveness have upon the doctrine of inerrancy?

4. McGrath has noted positive and negative characteristics of Protestant evangelicalism. Comment on these characteristics from your own life or the lives of people you know. Also, what problems can develop in one's relationship with God when cognition is prioritized over relationship?

5. In his book *The Myth of Certainty,* Daniel Taylor argues against the notion of certainty in the Christian faith and replaces it with the dual notions of intuition and relationship. What are the strengths and weaknesses of this move? Is your Christian experience grounded in certainty or intuition/relationship? Explain.

4

Post-Foundational
Realism

The second of the four positions in the postmodern debate that we will examine is post-foundational realism. Being post-foundational, this theological position attempts to move past Enlightenment ideals, specifically the methodology of the *Cogito*. Being an epistemology characterized by realism, it retains the idea of ontological referents; that is, it insists that theology be anchored to the real world and specifically to God who has revealed himself in this world. Proponents of this position therefore find themselves agreeing with postmodern ideals in that they too are searching for a system that effectively moves past the *Cogito,* yet at the same time disagreeing with the postmodern propensity toward **antirealism.**

An early proponent of this position was Karl Barth (1886-1968). Disillusioned with the theological liberalism under which he was trained and unwilling to accept the theological conservatism of his father, Barth sought a system that effectively moved beyond the Cartesian *Cogito.* The theological system that he was instrumental in founding is called neo-orthodoxy. This Barthian approach to theology still has many followers, albeit their specific emphases modify their individual theologies—some of which reject the Barthian notion that the Bible contains the Word of God but is not in an objective sense the Word of God.[1] Accordingly, Barth's influence in twentieth-century theology has been enormous, and will likely continue well into the twenty-first century.

The logical place to begin this chapter, then, is with Barth. We will observe how his break with theological liberalism and the birth of neo-orthodoxy anticipated postmodernism without wholly entering into it. We will then fast-forward to the last decade of the twentieth century, demonstrating how Barthian theology is reflected in the postmodern debate through the specific contributions of theologians who, generally speaking, stand inside Barth's long shadow and argue from within that theological posture.

KARL BARTH

Karl Barth was born in Basel, Switzerland, in 1886. His father was a lecturer at a college for preachers and a member of a fairly conservative group within the Reformed Church of Switzerland. When Karl was two years of age, his father accepted a post as assistant lecturer at the University of Bern. Years later, following in his father's footsteps Karl also pursued a career in religion. He studied theology at the universities in Bern, Berlin, Tübingen and Marburg and, in contrast to his father's conservative theology, identified himself with the classic liberal theology of Albrecht Ritschl, in large part due to the influence of the great Ritschlian scholar Wilhelm Herrmann, professor at Marburg. In 1908 he was ordained to the ministry of the Reformed Church and accepted a position as assistant pastor in a church in Geneva. In 1911 he moved to a small parish in Safenwil, a Swiss village near the border of Germany, where he served as pastor. In 1925, he became professor of theology at the University of Münster. He later taught at the University of Bonn and finally at the University of Basel, where he lectured and finally died.

Yet it was in Safenwil, during the First World War and prior to his years as a university professor, where Barth made theological history. He wrote a commentary on Paul's epistle to the Romans, a book titled *Der Römerbrief,* first published in 1918. In this book he made his break with liberal theology and introduced the world to neo-orthodoxy. Generally speaking, it was an attempt to articulate theology in post-*Cogito* categories. The book shook the theological world.

***Barth's rejection of the* Cogito.** Barth's disillusionment with liberal theology (specifically, the *Cogito*) was due to two problems that came to his attention while at Safenwil.

First, Barth discovered that theology grounded in human thought was useless in the task of preaching to his congregation. He observed that the human soul craved a theology whose source was God above. He later wrote, "It is not the right human thoughts about God which form the content of the Bible, but the right divine thoughts about men."[2] Only when people heard God speak to their hearts did their souls experience a level of satisfaction.

Second, in August of 1914 Barth read a published statement endorsed by ninety-three German intellectuals supporting Kaiser Wilhelm's war policy. Among them were almost all of the theological teachers whom he had esteemed, some of whom he studied under. Their support of German imperialism led Barth to believe that something had to be seriously wrong in their theology for them to support such a wrong-headed non-Christian policy. He concluded that the problem was that their theology was incapable of separation from human rationality and was therefore entrapped by its own aberrant logic.

The solution, Barth reasoned, was not a return to the theology of his father, since that too was grounded in the *Cogito,* albeit from a conservative perspective. Instead, in a provocative move Barth broke with the *Cogito* by affirming *both* the validity of the higher-critical method *and* the doctrine of verbal inspiration. Early in the introduction to *Der Römerbrief,* he wrote:

> The historical-critical method of Biblical investigation has its rightful place: it is concerned with the preparation of the intelligence—and this can never be superfluous. But, were I driven to choose between it and the venerable doctrine of Inspiration, I should without hesitation adopt the latter, which has a broader, deeper, more important justification. The doctrine of Inspiration is concerned with the labour of apprehending, without which no technical equipment, however complete, is of any use whatever. Fortunately, I am not compelled to choose between the two. Nevertheless, my whole energy of interpreting has been expended in an endeavor to see through and beyond history into the spirit of the Bible, which is the Eternal Spirit.[3]

By refusing "to choose between the two," Barth made his move in a post-*Cogito* direction.

This theological move is significant for the following three reasons. First, Barth recognized the rational consistency of a system that dictated the alignment of higher criticism with theological liberalism and that of verbal inspiration with theological conservatism (see figure 4.1). Higher criticism mitigated against the notion of the verbal inspiration of the Bible (rationally speaking, how could a book full of historical inaccuracies be the product of verbal inspiration?). Hence, a logical barrier separated the notions of higher criticism and verbal inspiration. That is, the notion of historical inaccuracies in a document verbally inspired by God made no rational sense.

Second, Barth combined higher criticism with divine inspiration. The purpose of creating this hybrid was not to produce an irrational faith, but rather to break away from the seemingly all-powerful *Cogito* as a means of finding a way in which to hear God speak. As has already been discussed, the *Cogito* was an epistemology predicated on radical doubt; it set the limits of human knowledge at what could be attained through inductive reasoning. This made human rationality the final arbitrator in the work of theologizing, meaning that the human mind was in control of the entire process. Barth wanted to reach beyond the limits of human rationality and find a way across the transcendental gulf that Immanuel Kant emphasized in his writings. Only then could the individual stop hearing human words controlled by human logic and, in its place, begin to hear God.

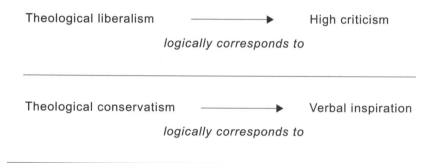

Figure 4.1

By combining higher criticism with divine inspiration, then, Barth believed that the Cartesian inductive method would be suspended, enabling the reader to become open to an alternate way of processing information. As such, the reader is positioned to hear God speak through Scripture on a level that is suprarational—that is, directly to the reader's heart. For Barth, rational analysis has a role, but one always second to the more dominant role of faith. Similar to what Schleiermacher had previously explained about a divinely guided intuition, the reader would not only hear the words of Scripture but sense the reality of a Being who exists behind the words (i.e., the Spirit of the Bible, the Eternal Spirit). The fact that some of the findings of higher criticism had widespread scholastic support helped validate this move by Barth.

Third, Barth was concerned to not give higher criticism too much emphasis since that would result in re-creating a facsimile of the liberal model and thereby reintroduce the *Cogito* to his system. He therefore deemphasized it, noting that if he were driven to choose between higher criticism and divine inspiration, he would "without hesitation adopt the latter."[4]

Distancing himself from the *Cogito,* then, is what drove Barth in this new theological direction. In the preface to the second edition of *Der Römerbrief* (1921), Barth admitted his indebtedness to Kierkegaard, a theologian/philosopher who also sought a means to hear God speak rather than the words of human rationality:

> If I have a system, it is limited to a recognition of what Kierkegaard called the "infinite qualitative distinction" between time and eternity, and to my regarding this as possessing negative as well as positive significance: "God is in heaven, and thou art on earth." The relation between such a God and such a man, and the relation between such a man and such a God, is for me the theme of the Bible and the essence of philosophy.[5]

Since Kierkegaard argued for an infinite qualitative distinction between time and eternity, a leap of faith is needed for one to hear God. Yet, rather than being characterized as an irrational faith (as we observed Schaeffer asserting in chapter three), for Barth this leap is an attempt to demonstrate that due to human sinfulness and the wholly otherness of God, human rationality cannot produce a smooth inductively structured movement from radical doubt (the *Cogito*) to religious faith.[6] Instead, as Grenz notes, "the paradoxical truths of God's self-revelation [e.g., the Trinity, the hypostatic union of Christ] must be embraced in a leap of faith by the finite human mind."[7] Only such a leap puts one in a spiritual state to hear God speak.

For Barth, this leap of faith is not to be confused with fideistic thinking, where one merely placed one's faith in faith—wishful thinking, so to speak. Rather, Barth insisted on a rigorous engagement of the human mind as God spoke to one's spirit from his wholly otherness. An exposure to and knowledge of sacred Scripture was indispensable, since that was the principal channel by which God reveals himself.

Barth's prolegomena. By putting the doctrine of the Trinity at the beginning of his *Church Dogmatics,* Barth adopted a prolegomena (preliminary discussion) in which God himself makes the first move in our knowing God. In other words, the first step in knowing God is not a certain mindset of the individual as he or she endeavors to understand God or spirituality. Rather, the first move consists of God's sovereign choice to disclose himself to the individual. The way Barth put it, "Prolegomena to dogmatics are possible only as part of dogmatics itself."[8] In a sense, Barth's prolegomena is an antiprolegomena; the "first words" (pro-legein, "to say beforehand") come not from the theologian but from God—who chooses to reveal truth, who is the subject of what is being revealed and who makes it possible for the human being to hear and grasp that revelation. The theologian is rendered passive, impacted by God's "first words."

Unbelievers (those who do not hear this revelation) can enter into constructive conversation with believers regarding this revelation and its corresponding assertions and philosophical worldview, provided that they acknowledge the proper norms of the church and are willing to work within those norms. Nevertheless, the effectiveness of such conversation is limited by the fact that unbelievers have not been personally persuaded by God's revelation.

Conversations between believers and unbelievers, then, should not be understood as a form of pre-evangelism similar to what was shown in Francis Schaeffer (see chapter three). With Barth, pre-evangelism has no essential role because pre-evangelism (Christian philosophy presented in an apologetical and polemical context) implies that by means of rational analysis the stage is set, so to speak, for the budding of a legitimate Christian faith. Barth insisted that if God is truly the wholly other, no amount of rational analysis will bring an unbeliever to an accurate understanding of God. Instead, the unbeliever is wholly dependent on God to take the first step in the awakening of such divine awareness. The Holy Spirit reveals the reality of God not in philosophical/apologetical/polemical conversations but by exposing unbelievers to the Word of God itself—the sacred text and preaching that reveal a sacred Person: Jesus Christ.

This move points back to Calvin's notion of a self-authenticating Scripture.[9] Barth explained, "It is difficult to see how in regard to Holy Scripture we can tell what is significant for the holiness of this very Scripture, unless previously it has been made clear—naturally from the Holy Scripture itself— who that God is whose revelation makes Scripture holy."[10] He insisted that we cannot begin with the created order and reason our way back to an understanding of God (apologetic analyses). This would dilute Scripture and elevate human reason. Such a move would require us to support, strengthen and confirm the witness of Scripture from some source other than Scripture itself. This, Barth insisted, is a form of idolatry: "Has not unbelief already taken place there? Does not the transition from interpretation to illustration as such already come under the interdict, Thou shalt not make unto thee any likeness?"[11] Instead, Barth maintained that God takes the initiative in self-revelation.

What is more, this self-revelation occurs in a trinitarian fashion. The Father is the creator who has willed that we know him. The primary role of the Son is to reveal the Father and to bring about a reconciliation between the two. The Holy Spirit gives us the instruction and guidance we cannot give ourselves. In this respect, the Holy Spirit is the *Yes* to God's Word. He not only speaks *to us* but also *in us*. Both directions of this speech come through God himself.

Barth's point is that a correct Christian prolegomena is a self-enclosed circle. That which is being revealed is God who reveals (the revelation and the revealer are one and the same). He is forever the subject and we are the object: "Communion with God means for man, strictly and exclusively, communion with Him who reveals Himself, who is Subject in His revelation, and indissolubly Subject at that."[12] Barth added, "Who can reveal God but God Himself?"[13]

Such a prolegomena reverses the order found in the theologies grounded in the *Cogito*. In the *Cogito,* we begin with radical doubt and inductively reason our way to God. We are the subject and God is the object. In Barth's system, God takes the first step. He is the subject and we are the object. He is the initiator who opens our minds to know him and then enables us to know him through a self-authenticating Scripture wherein the Son reveals the Father by means of the Holy Spirit. Hence, Barth's system moved in a post-*Cogito* direction reminiscent of Calvin's writings.

Barth's understanding of eschatology. In the second edition of *Der Römerbrief,* Barth wrote of the indispensability of eschatology. "If Christianity be not altogether thoroughgoing eschatology," he wrote, "there remains in it no relationship whatever with Christ."[14]

Barth's understanding of eschatology, however, should not be confused with classic premillennial or postmillennial eschatology, two systems that look to a future fulfillment of biblical prophecy. Barth's understanding is not preoccupied with future fulfillment. In his system, the *eschaton* is breaking transcendentally into history in the here-and-now. That is, eschatology involves an existentialized experience that draws us from this world to experience the wholly other-worldliness of God in a timeless ever-present now.[15] Moltmann explains, "This . . . makes the *eschaton* into a transcendental eternity, the transcendental meaning of all ages, equally near to all the ages of history and equally far from all of them."[16]

In other words, Barth's system rejects the notion that history and culture have a central and controlling place in Christian theology. From his wholly otherness, God breaks into the world and challenges and confronts us with his Word that comes from outside of time and is therefore timeless and changeless. It is therefore largely a version of the theology of epiphany that we briefly looked at in chapter two.

Summary of Barth's post-Cogito system. With the publication of *Der Römerbrief* in 1918, Barth abandoned his theological liberalism, seeking a new system by which he could overcome the *Cogito.* Because it looks beyond the *Cogito,* his new theology can correctly be understood as an anticipation of postmodernism. It has profoundly changed the shape of Christian theology across confessional boundaries and, as Eberhard Jüngel has noted, "significantly altered the direction of the Protestant church."[17]

Barth's system fell short of postmodernism, however, for two reasons. First, he argued in favor of ontological referents—that is, he insisted that the Christian faith be anchored in reality. Unlike theologians committed to the *Cogito,* this ontological referent was not understood as the product of rationalistic inductive reasoning initiated by radical doubt. Rather, it came from the opposite direction—God crossing the transcendent barrier and presenting his Word to the human being. The ontological referent, therefore, is self-authenticating. It cannot be independently confirmed through rational analysis. Second, Barth argued in favor of an epiphanic understanding of eschatology. Unlike postmodernists committed to the role of culture and history in human thought, Barth's system is decisively otherworldly (acultural and ahistorical).

Having finished this brief review of Barth, we will now turn our attention to three theologians who have written in the latter decades of the twentieth century and who stand inside Barth's long shadow. Broadly speaking, they are Barthian. Peculiarities in their writings, however, separate them from classic neo-orthodoxy. Our interest in them owes to their significance to the current postmodern debate within the church.

MIROSLAV VOLF

The first contemporary theologian characterized by post-foundational realism that we will look at is Miroslav Volf (1956-). A graduate of the University of Tübingen, where he received his doctorate in theology in 1993, Volf has served as a professor of theology at the Evangelical Theological Faculty of Osijek, Croatia, professor of theology at Fuller Theological Seminary, and is now a professor of theology at Yale Divinity School. In his early childhood and theologically formative years in Croatia, Volf attended the Free Church, a subtradition underneath the Protestant evangelical umbrella.[18] More specifically, he and his family identify themselves as Pentecostals.[19] In what follows, we will observe two insights from Volf that pertain to the postmodern debate.

Semiotic and nonsemiotic communication. Discussion of semiotic and nonsemiotic communication addresses the question of signs. Semiotic communication is a transfer of knowledge that occurs by means of signs, whereas nonsemiotic communication is a more direct, signless form of communication. Volf argues that we need both semiotic and nonsemiotic communication for religious knowledge. By insisting on the role of nonsemiotic communication in our pursuit of truth he distanced himself from classic postmodern ideals.

Volf maintains that the New Testament teaches both semiotic and non-semiotic communication. The epistle to the Colossians, for example, teaches that the "word of Christ" should "dwell in you richly" (Col 3:16). As we dwell in God, he explains, God touches us not simply through language and behavioral patterns we learn in community (i.e., semiotic truth), but also at an inarticulate (nonsemiotic) mystical level. God touches us "at the depths of our souls . . . before we inhabit the Christian cultural-linguistic system, and God continues to embrace us even if we choose to move out of it."[20] Other passages in the New Testament also affirm the role of nonsemiotic communication: "All that the Father gives me will come to me" (Jn 6:37); "The Spirit himself testifies with our spirit that we are God's children" (Rom 8:16).

In other words, Volf asserts that the Christian is spiritually influenced at a nonsemiotic level prior to the impact of the language of a given religious community. This influence occurs as God initiates contact between the Christian and transcendent reality. Once that contact is made, it is validated and supplemented with the semiotic communication emerging from within the faith community. Therefore, when the New Testament speaks, for example, of a Christian living "in Corinth" and also "in God," it is describing reality on two different planes: one located in culture (the plane where semiotic truth exists) and the other located beyond culture (a plane distinct from the realm of semiotic truth). Both forms of communication occur and work together in the communication of truth to the individual.

Volf uses the illustration of a mother communicating to a newborn child to make this point:

> It seems to me, for example, beyond doubt that a person becomes a human being not only by learning her mother's language but also by feeling her mother's touch and hearing the sound of her voice. Similarly we become Christians not simply by learning the language of faith but also by being "touched" by other Christians and ultimately by God on a nonsemiotic level. The Christian semiotic system lives in the lives of the people of God through the interplay of nonsemiotic dimensions of church life (which are meaningless without the semiotic) and semiotic dimensions of church life (which are powerless without the nonsemiotic).[21]

Consequently, Volf continues, the Christian faith is a living faith. People from around the world who inhabit their own respective cultures not only (a) embrace ethical standards of Christianity through semiotic communication and (b) learn the language of the Christian faith from their respective communities also through semiotic communication, but also (c) more fundamentally are drawn in multiple ways "to follow (right where they are) the One who was crucified and resurrected for their salvation"[22] through the mystical impact of nonsemiotic communication whose origin is God himself.

This interplay of the nonsemiotic and semiotic dimensions of the Christian faith, then, locates the ontological referent. Each is powerless without the other, yet when combined they provide a grounding for the Christian faith in God. The problem with postmodernism, Volf explains, is that it is limited to only the semiotic dimension. By limiting religious knowledge to language (that is, semiotic truth), postmodernism generates systems that may be consistent with themselves yet have no actual contact with the real world. Such a system is limited to the language of faith of a religious community that may contain many religious errors. Without the nonsemiotic dimension, a postmodern religion is nothing more than a self-contained blimp floating independently of divine reality.

Intratextuality and extratextuality. A second set of dualities that Volf emphasizes in his dealings with postmodernism is the question of intratextualities and extratextualities.

According to Volf, the problem with liberal theology is its tendency to define theology in *extratextual* categories. By this, he means a methodology that uses one's own culture as the hermeneutical control for understanding and contextualizing the Bible. He acknowledges that the initial impulse behind this methodology is good—to gain the attention of the "cultured despisers" and draw these people back to God. Nevertheless, its results have been disastrous. Framing theology in the language and concepts of one's contemporary world tends to replace Scripture rather than lead to it. It also makes the individual accommodate to the prevailing norms of culture rather than shape them. Volf explains:

> Only those religious groups that make no apologies about their "difference" will be able to survive and thrive. The strategy of conformation is socially ineffective in the short run (because you cannot shape by parroting) and self-destructive in the long run (because you conform to what you have not helped shape).[23]

Consequently, in theological liberalism Christianity has lost both its distinctive identity and its voice.

The problem with conservative theology, Volf continues, is that it attempts to define theology in *intratextual* categories. By this, Volf means that the Bible serves as the hermeneutical control. Reality is thereby interpreted in terms of the Bible. Though this initial impulse is also good—to maintain the authority of the Bible over and against the world—this methodology too is disastrous. As the biblical text makes contact with contemporary culture, it is impossible to hold at bay all the influences of one's culture upon one's exegesis. All attempts to do so will result in the influences of one's culture taking on a clandestine role in one's interpretation of Scripture. Volf insists that it is more correct to understand the interrelation between the contemporary world and the biblical text as so amazingly complex and full of nuanced subtleties. As such, it precludes the possibility of any exact identification, assessment or measurement of the direction of movement in interpretation.

Accordingly, Volf maintains that pure exegesis is an impossibility. Rather, *exegesis* and, from one degree to another, *eisegesis* are inseparable compatriots as one studies the Bible. Because one cannot firmly control the hermeneutical direction, Volf asserts that it is more plausible to conclude the inevitability of an uncontrollable crisscrossing movement. The religious world is being shaped by the nonreligious world as well as shaping it. Hence, the world of a Christian can never simply be intratextual but is always intratextual-cum-extratextual:

We can look at our culture through the lens of religious texts only as we look at these texts through the lens of culture. The notion of inhabiting the biblical story is hermeneutically naïve because it presupposes that those who are faced with the biblical story can be completely "dislodged" from their extra-textual dwelling places and "resettled" into intratextual homes. Neither dislodging nor resettling can ever quite succeed; we continue to inhabit our cultures even after the encounter with the biblical story.[24]

This, of course, produces a tension within theological reflection, causing us to conclude that ahistorical and acultural theology is impossible. Theologians will always be grappling with its presence and effects upon theology (see figure 4.2).

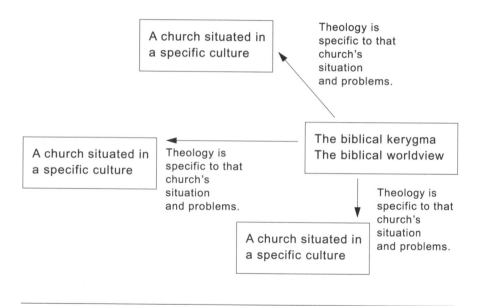

Figure 4.2

Volf identifies three consequences that follow from the notion of intratextuality-cum-extratextuality. First, we recognize that we always see the biblical story through the lens of culture. This does not mean that we are condemned to our own culture and can never make contact with the biblical culture, but rather that we must admit that everything we see is always colored by the seer. Second, we recognize that because we are "inescapably inhabitants of both worlds, laying claim to complete inhabitation of the biblical world entails almost as a rule the clandestine attempt to domesticate that world"[25] so that we can survive there. As such, this false claim of complete inhabitation of the biblical world requires us to downplay the values of the contemporary world that we are secretly and perhaps subconsciously maintaining. Third, we gain a wider perspective and new insights as we permit extratextual perspectives (along with contrasting intratextual perspectives from differing compatriots and their communities) to challenge or modify our intratextual language of faith. Otherwise, a sense of foolish arrogance naturally develops (e.g., the flat-earth society) as we insist on interpreting our social environments from only our intratextual perspectives.

Volf believes that an awareness of these three consequences preserves the integrity and strangeness of God's new world and produces the healthy paradoxical tension of struggling to live in and shape our cultures as we ourselves are shaped by our religious texts and by our cultures. He therefore insists, "There is no single correct way to relate to a given culture as a whole, or even to its dominant thrust; there are only numerous ways of accepting, transforming or replacing various aspects of a given culture from within."[26] This opens the door to pluralism in our theologies. No single theology is categorically correct.

According to Volf, then, due to the inevitable role of extratextualities upon our interpretation of the Bible, (a) the more systematic and timeless our theologies are, the less useful they will be, and (b) the more situated our theologies are in the diverse, changeable and individual cultures that the church inhabits, the more effective they will become.

JAMES K. A. SMITH

The second contemporary theologian characterized by post-foundational realism that we will look at in this chapter is James K. A. Smith. He is currently associate professor of philosophy at Calvin College in Grand Rapids, Michigan. Like Volf, he identifies himself with the Pentecostal tradition within the Protestant faith.

Smith has examined postmodernism through the lenses of both philosophy and Protestant evangelicalism. In what follows, we will examine two of Smith's contributions to the postmodern debate within the church: (a) his observation that postmodernism is not truly postmodern due to the presence of the ghost of the *Cogito;* (b) his understanding of hermeneutical theory, what he calls the hermeneutics of creationism. He asserts that a hermeneutics of creationism is a methodology that moves past the Cartesian *Cogito* in a truly post-*Cogito* direction.

***The ghost of the* Cogito.** Smith's problem with postmodernism, as generally presented by its dominant voices (e.g., Heidegger, Derridá), is that the ghost of the *Cogito* inhabits it. That is, though rejecting the *Cogito* in a formal sense, it nevertheless yearns for the *Cogito* in an informal sense—attempting to resurrect it or at least benefit from its ghost; though the *Cogito* is not seen, its presence is still felt and appreciated. In response, Smith seeks to press forward and construct an epistemology that is truly postmodern (i.e., post-*Cogito*) from which scholarship could then philosophize and theologize. His argument contains three fundamental moves.

First, though postmodernists insist that one cannot escape the influence of culture in how one thinks, they assert that this entrapment is not good. Using the *Dasein* (one's own being) of Martin Heidegger's philosophic system as a backdrop, Smith explains:

> It is because of this subjection that *Dasein* falls prey to the "dictatorship of the 'they.'" The "they" determines *Dasein*'s possibilities; and as such *Dasein* becomes bogged down in averageness, and its possibilities are "leveled down" to what everyone else is doing. *Dasein* becomes controlled by "the public" and the public's understanding of the world. The "they," moreover, makes things too easy; it "disburdens" *Dasein* of the difficulty of life and *Dasein* becomes a "nobody," "like everybody else."[27]

Smith's point is that the *Dasein* cannot escape the influences of culture, whether membership in an ethnic group, a political party, one's neighborhood, a church and so forth. This, of course, prevents the possibility of authenticity; one becomes a "nobody" in subjection to the thought patterns of one's community rather than the individualized thought-patterns of one's own self. Stated otherwise, falling prey to the dictatorial powers of culture, we thereby live "inauthentic" lives.

Second, postmodernists (in this case, Heidegger) argue that we should fight against *inauthenticity* by fighting against the "they" (culture). That is, we are encouraged to be individualistic heroes—people willing to stand up and fight, to be above average, to resist culture. This fight is a struggle for "rugged individualism, a militaristic self-affirmation that devalues and despises intersubjectivity."[28] By engaging in such a fight, we are fighting for personal authenticity.

Third, such a fight against the "they" (the pandemic influences of culture) is therefore a fight *against* postmodernism. According to Smith, this is the odd irony within postmodern thought. On the one hand, postmodernism insists that it is impossible to overcome the influences of culture upon the way we interpret the world. On the other hand, postmodernists also insist that we must at least try to free ourselves from the dominion of the "they" (culture)—otherwise, we will be doomed to live inauthentic lives.[29]

Yet is not such a fight, Smith asks, a regression back into the modernist mindset? "Have we indeed stumbled upon a vestige of the Cartesian subject, a 'tinge of Husserlian solipsism'? Is authentic Dasein actually a closet *res cogitans?*"[30] *Husserlian solipsism* is the notion that the self can know nothing but its own consciousness and that within one's consciousness exists an immediacy of knowledge—a pure knowledge that exists independently of interpretation. The term *res cogitans* indicates the existence of individual human thought—thought that exists independently of the influences of culture. Smith's point is that by arguing for authenticity, postmodernists are yearning nostalgically for modernism, to be governed by the ghost of the *Cogito*. Hence, they ironically reach for the very thing they insist is impossible to acquire.

Stated otherwise, though postmodernists argue against absolute truth and in favor of the universal influence of culture upon individual thought, they tend to reject the prevailing norms of culture and press for a form of radical individualism: truth that is ahistorical and acultural, absolutely true—albeit an absolute truth that is only absolutely true for the individual. Only then can they live authentic lives and rise above the category of nobodies.

Smith, however, disagrees with this logic. He asks, if a person learns to think from within a tradition of which he or she is a part, "why must this be portrayed as inauthentic if it is an inescapable aspect of being human?"[31] He therefore counters:

> If the world is creation—a good gift from the hand of God—and if being-with-others is a constitutive aspect of created goodness, then we may understand human relationships not necessarily as frameworks of domination (though there are certainly cases where they are) but rather as networks for connection that are as crucial to human life as the oxygen we breathe. Instead of being a violation of myself, being-with-others is to be human.[32]

As such, Smith argues that the intersubjection within culture is not necessarily bad. In many ways intersubjection offers opportunities for expressions of love and personal enrichment as people honestly engage in the give-and-take of differing perspectives, value systems and behavior. Rather than being frameworks for exploitation, the influences of one's culture can be God's chosen path for the positive development of the individual and the community, opportunities for acts of patience and love to foster peace as the space between individuals diminishes. It can also bring about personal growth and enrichment as the individual listens to points of view other than his or her own.

A creational hermeneutic. Resisting the ghost of the *Cogito* and pressing for a system that is truly post-*Cogito,* Smith argues for a hermeneutic that is, in part, more consistent with postmodern ideals. The following three points constitute a brief outline of his hermeneutical scheme.

First, Smith asserts that a creational hermeneutic is linked to a trust in the guidance of the Holy Spirit who, in turn, is the revealer of Jesus Christ. Reminiscent of what we have already seen in Barth, the Holy Spirit/Jesus Christ offers a wordless word (nonsemiotic communication) that precedes all other engagement in language, interpretation, or action. Smith explains:

> Before this Fall, and now in spite of this Fall, there is a primordial "yes": a "wordless word," a living *logos* who was "in the beginning," who tabernacles with us in flesh and whose spirit resides within us (Jn 1:1-18). It is this wordless Word, this Who, that we name "yes": "For the Son of God, Jesus Christ, whom we proclaimed among you . . . was not 'Yes and No'; but in him it is always 'Yes.'"[33]

Smith admits that a recognition of the existence of this "Yes" requires a certain kind of **fideism,** a blind faith. It is a knowledge that proceeds "from a commitment to that which is beyond seeing, the 'unbeseen' as absolute invisibility, to which one is entrusted. In this blind economy of faith, to see, in a sense, is not to see."[34] This faith, of course, draws the individual to a similar faith in the Christian Scriptures as the authentic and faithful witness to Jesus Christ. Such trust in that which cannot be seen or independently validated through human reason (i.e., the *Cogito*) is a celebration of a certain kind of madness—"the madness of faith,"[35] as he calls it. This is where knowledge begins.

Second, a creational hermeneutic allows for a plurality of interpretations within the context of the reality of Jesus Christ. It expects such a plurality because, as finite beings, our understanding of Jesus Christ will always be one from a specific point of reference, a point of reference unique to ourselves. Moreover, since the finite cannot fully absorb the infinite, our knowledge of Jesus Christ will always be partial. The combination of specific points of reference and partial knowledge necessarily yield a plurality in interpretations. Two implications emerge from this insight.

1. A plurality of interpretations permits a variety of legitimate perspectives—but not an infinite variety. There are still "good" and "bad" interpretations of Scripture. The means to adjudicate good from bad, however, is not evaluation against a master interpretation, for that would arbitrarily privilege one specific interpretation, declaring it normative (i.e., a return to modernism). Rather, Smith asserts that the means of adjudication should be based upon empirical analysis: does the interpretation in question work in the real world? Smith illustrates this point:

> The tree outside my window is, from a phenomenological perspective, transcendent to consciousness and imposes itself upon me. As "outside" of me, or transcendent, the tree is not "mine" to be manipulated. As such it imposes upon me limits for its interpretation, bad interpretations will be precisely those construals that transgress those limits. If I interpret the tree as a chimera and attempt to run through its trunk, my interpretation will quickly prove itself wrong.[36]

In other words, the pragmatic experience of reality will always place limits on legitimate interpretation. What is true of one's interpretation of a tree is also true of one's interpretation of Scripture. As with a tree, we discern good from bad interpretation through empirical testing. Does a particular interpretation of Scripture work as one reads the whole of Scripture? Does it also work in the real world? As such, Scripture imposes its own limits on legitimate interpretation.

2. The limits placed upon interpretation do not prescribe a single "correct" interpretation. Because of (a) the *situationality* of the believer to a finite perspective, (b) the *traditionality* of the believer to a specific community of faith and (c) the *undecidability* of the believer, according to which he or she cannot presume to possess the final word on any given interpretation, a plurality of interpretations will always coexist within the church. As noted above, however, the legitimate range of these interpretations should be determined empirically; that is, they should be determined by their ability to *work* with the whole of Scripture and in the real world.

A case in point, Smith explains, is the recent evangelical engagement with Catholic thought, precipitated by the document "Evangelicals and Catholics Together: The Christian Mission in the Third Millennium."[37] Smith notes that negative conservative evangelical responses to this proposal came hard and fast, implying that from the perspective of these critics there is only one correct interpretation—and it was not the Catholic version.[38] Yet, Smith continues, these conservative responses were grounded in a Reformational interpretation of the apostle Paul by Martin Luther. Hence, if we follow the critique of these conservative evangelical scholars, the gospel turns out to privilege one specific tradition (Pauline, as understood by Luther) to the exclusion of the Johannine, the Petrine and the James traditions.[39] The Pauline tradition of the gospel is highly forensic in orientation—the other traditions are not. Yet all these traditions—since they are all canonical—are de facto legitimate interpretations, different lenses from which the reality of the gospel is presented in the New Testament (see figure 4.3).[40]

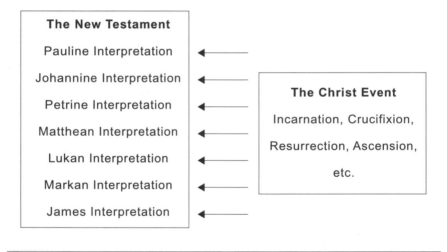

Figure 4.3

This implies, of course, that the presentation of the gospel in the New Testament by the different canonical writers (Matthew, Mark, Luke, John, Paul, James, etc.) is not a mere reiteration of the same paradigm in different words—an understanding that suggests a simple unity of thought. Rather, each canonical writer offers an interpretation of the Christ-event that is unique, not interchangeable with the interpretation of other canonical writers—an understanding that suggests a *complex* unity. For example, though many scholars have labored to whittle away at the differences between Paul and James so that they could be understood as presenting the same essential gospel paradigm, it may be more correct to see in Paul and James two distinct paradigms that are both true to the Christ event. A forensic motif dominates Paul's writings (cf. Rom 5), whereas in James a love or relational motif dominates (cf. Jas 2). The doctrine of eternal security emerges from within Paul's paradigm; in James the possibilities of apostasy and divine judgment are pressing concerns.

One may think of a floral table arrangement to illustrate this point. People sitting around the table have different views of the flowers. One person may see roses mixed with ferns, while another person may see daisies and violets with a combination of wide-bladed grasses—distinct views of the same arrangement. In order to come to a more complete appreciation of the arrangement, we would have to talk to one another—to listen to what others see. We may even consider resituating ourselves around the table and then re-examining the arrangement.

The arrangement of flowers here corresponds to the Christ-event, with the view from each seat corresponding to the perspective of one of the canonical writers. That which is seen and communicated corresponds to differing paradigms of the gospel. There is, therefore, no single paradigm of the gospel in the New Testament. Instead there exists a variety of paradigms juxtaposed against one another.

Consequently, Smith argues that these conservative responses arbitrarily established the Pauline perspective (as understood by Luther) as normative, displacing the other canonical perspectives in the process. If the other canonical perspectives were given due consideration, however, these critics would have understood that the gospel cannot be limited to a single perspective, but rather is a collage of perspectives. Each perspective can only give clarity to part of the fullness of the gospel. Because of this, ecclesial traditions—such as Protestant and Catholic—may not necessarily be in contradictory tension in their understanding of the gospel, but rather express a legitimate and biblical complex unity.[41]

Third, differences in interpretation will always exist within the church. These differences, however, should not be understood as problems to "solve" or "fight against," as modernists and classic postmodernists tend to do, but rather as opportunities for personal enrichment and growth as human beings listen to and share with one another. According to Smith, to move in a modernist direction, where differences must be solved, invariably yields a them-versus-us mentality (triumphalism) that will fragment the church. To move in a classic postmodernist direction, where intersubjectivity is deemed inauthentic and oppressive, ultimately isolates us from culture and from one another. Yet, Smith insists, to move in a creational hermeneutical direction, where intersubjectivity is affirmed, celebrates plurality while strengthening community. This hermeneutic understands the influences of a godly community upon one's thought as good. It also validates a plurality of perspectives since in our finitude we do not share the same language, possess the same vocabularies or have the same thoughts. All this is part and parcel of being finite created beings, that which God originally declared to be "very good" (Gen 1:31). This affirmation implies that our differences should be celebrated and enjoyed rather than perceived as a threat and therefore resisted. Hence, a creational hermeneutic leads us away from both triumphalism and isolationism and instead toward interdependency and community.

STANLEY GRENZ

The third contemporary theologian characterized by post-foundational realism that we will look at in this chapter is Stanley J. Grenz (1950-), professor of theology and ethics at Carey/Regent College in Vancouver, British Columbia. In our analysis of Grenz, we will limit our observations to three perspectives that he has contributed to the postmodern debate within the church: his understanding of the role of the Holy Spirit, the role of the church and the question of metanarratives.

The Holy Spirit. In a fashion reminiscent of Barth's theological move against the *Cogito,* Grenz argues that Scripture is self-authenticating and therefore needs no rational analysis to ground its authenticity. In their book *Beyond Foundationalism,* Grenz and coauthor John Franke make this point by rhetorically asking, must we "finally appeal to some court beyond the Christian faith itself, some rational 'first principle' that supposedly carries universality? In the end, must we inevitably retreat to a foundationalist epistemology?"[42] Their answer is *no.* Our final authority, they insist, is the Holy Spirit speaking in and through Scripture: "The Protestant principle means the Bible is authoritative in that it is the vehicle through which the Spirit speaks. Taking the idea a step further, the authority of the Bible is in the end the authority of the Spirit whose instrumentality it is."[43]

Grenz and Franke go on to say that the early church came to confess the authority of Scripture because the early believers experienced the power and truth of the Spirit of God working through these ancient documents. In this respect, they were convinced that these writings were animated with the Spirit of Christ. Hence, in their minds there was no further verification necessary to establish their credentials as the divinely inspired Word of God.

What is noteworthy here is that by arguing for an ontological grounding of knowledge by means of the Spirit of God speaking through the Word of God, Grenz stands opposed to a fundamental postmodern ideal. As we have already seen with Barth, Volf and Smith, by grounding knowledge in a nonsemiotic communication of truth, a central maxim of postmodernism—a maxim that insists that language (semiotic communication) must always precede knowledge—is rejected. Yet, similar to Volf, Grenz does not limit the grounding of our faith to nonsemiotic communication. The church also has a role in our grounding of faith, which it does through semiotic communication.

The church. Grenz understands the church as the second component by which the Christian's faith is grounded and nurtured. Here the Holy Spirit brings into being a new community that is centered around Jesus Christ. In turn, what the Spirit initiated through nonsemiotic communication, this community reinforces for the individual believer with semiotic communication. Such communication occurs through Scripture as it is articulated through doctrine, liturgy, music, ministry, etc. Similar to both Volf and Smith, this is where Grenz stands apart from Barth, who argued for a strict epiphanic (timeless) understanding of truth.

In Grenz's understanding of the church a key concept is that the believer is not brought to faith by means of radical doubt (the *Cogito*). Rather, the process is circular: the Holy Spirit submerges an individual within a community of faith prior to a fully developed cognitive understanding of the Christian faith. With time, a cognitive understanding develops, yet does so based upon the faith assumptions that the community instilled in the individual through observation, activity and teaching. One can say, therefore, the initial development of one's faith is *caught* rather than *taught.* One cannot learn it from afar in a state of cold objectivity; one must be first subjectively engaged in the learning process and from that insider's perspective grow in knowledge.

According to Grenz, this understanding of the church implies three things. First, *the work of the Holy Spirit in guiding the church throughout its two-thousand-year history must be respected.* "We do well," Grenz explains, "to take account of the reception of the Spirit's voice mediated to us and passed on by the faith community through the ages."[44] This, in turn, implies a healthy respect for the ecumenical creeds of the patristic age as well as the confessions that emerged in the following centuries. It also implies a rejection of the *Cogito*. By rejecting the *Cogito,* we are called on to reject (a) the radical doubt of all things, including the traditions that have served as normative interpretations for most of church history and (b) the methodology of thinking individualistically, that is, independently of the input and influences of community.

But how, Grenz asks, are we to take into account the wide diversity that characterizes the history of Christianity reflected, for example, in the many confessional statements? He answers that every interpretation of Scripture occurs within the context of a faith community. As such, each faith community provides a lens from which interpretation takes place. Moreover, a lensless interpretation is an impossibility since we all bring assumptions and a shaping of truth to every inquiry we make. Also, the Holy Spirit guides in the interpretation so that the outcome, though not fully comprehensive nor infallible, provides a fair representation of the gospel of Jesus Christ. This, of course, leads to theological diversity within the church, yet a diversity that is complementary rather than contradictory in nature.

Second, *the work of the Holy Spirit in guiding a specific local church must also be respected*. It is in the context of a specific church where we not only learn the grammar of our faith (that is, its essential interconnecting doctrines), but we also experience our faith—a move which takes us past a cognitive understanding to one that is more intuitively grasped. "I am convinced," Grenz writes, "that a personal faith commitment nurtured in a community of faith—piety—is also significant in our attempt to understand and pursue the constructive theological task."[45] Apart from a faith community where worship, discipleship and ministry intermingle, this intuitive dimension to theological knowledge cannot properly develop. Hence, we learn theology "from within," rather than as some supposedly objectivized observers who stand aloof and attempt to learn "from without."

Third, *it is in the context of a specific faith community that faith is sparked into existence and nurtured*. Grenz explains:

> Faith is by nature immediate. It arises out of the human encounter with the person of God in Christ, mediated by the community's testimony to the divine

revelation in Jesus. Personal faith, therefore, is our response to the call of God, which involves participation in the believing community.[46]

This includes our faith in the Christian Scriptures as a faithful witness to the workings of God in this world. Though there is much similarity between Grenz's prolegomena to the Christian faith and that of Karl Barth, one important difference is that Grenz insists that this faith not only is a response to the Spirit of God, but also is a response to participation with the community of God (the church) where one is exposed to truth that is propositionally articulated. This addition prevents our faith from being overly subjectivized to the individual psyche (a typical criticism of neo-orthodoxy) and grants it a level of objectivity. Grenz adds:

> In response to the neo-orthodox critique, conservatives rightly refuse to acknowledge a radical disjunction between "propositional" and "personal" revelation. In so doing they emphasize a fundamental insight encapsulated by propositionalism: Our faith is tied to a divine revelation that has been objectively disclosed. God has communicated truth—himself—to us.[47]

The faith community of which we are a member, however, clarifies this divine disclosure and maintains this objectivity with an abiding testimony to the Bible's divine authority, power to transform lives and development of a worldview that works in the real world.

The metanarrative. Grenz argues that the Holy Spirit and the church witness to the fact that the story of Jesus Christ, as presented in the canonical New Testament documents, reflects genuine events. It therefore becomes the normative criterion (metanarrative) by which all interpretations of reality are measured.

According to Grenz, by placing the metanarrative of Jesus Christ as normative, not only does it displace all other competing metanarratives (Buddhist, Hindu, Islamic, etc.), it also displaces Christian theology itself as the normative center of truth.

> Above all, it implies that, contrary to what some theologians might lead us to believe, the central purpose of the Bible is not to provide raw materials for erecting a systematic theological edifice. Rather, we engage in the theological enterprise conscious that we are servants of the Spirit and ministers within the community of those who seek to discern the Spirit's voice through the appropriated text.[48]

Echoing insights from George Lindbeck, whom we will examine in chapter six, Grenz argues that theology is second-order truth (less authoritative) and that the narrative itself is first-order truth (more authoritative). Doctrine, therefore, is not the meaning or the heart of the story. Rather, it is merely a tool to help us understand the story better. "Theology, in other words, is not the attempt to codify the 'meaning of the text' in a series of systematically arranged assertions, so that once this mission is accomplished we can then disregard, or even discard, the text."[49]

Arguing against the methodology of the *Cogito,* Grenz maintains that the search for the ultimate systematizing of theology (the all-encompassing circle that we observed Schaeffer searching for in chapter three), has preoccupied much of Protestant evangelicalism for the better part of two centuries. In this search, the biblical narrative has been eclipsed, understood as a storehouse of theological facts, and the real task of the Christian is to mine these facts so they can be codified into a logical and comprehensive system.

> Conservatives sincerely believed that in this manner they were returning the Bible to the very center of church life. What many apparently failed to see, however, is how their efforts actually could engender the opposite result. In effect, the scholastic theological agenda meant that the ongoing task of reading the Bible as text was superseded by the publication of the skilled theologian's *magnum opus* [that is, the all-encompassing circle of truth]. If the goal of theological inquiry was to extrapolate the system of propositions the divine Communicator had inscripturated in the pages of this text, it would seem that systematic theology could—and eventually would—make the Bible superfluous.[50]

Precisely on this point Grenz finds fault with Protestant evangelicalism. In much of Protestant evangelicalism, he asserts, doctrine has displaced the biblical story as more important in the formation of one's faith. What purpose would there be, he asks, to continue reading the Bible when biblical truth is more readily available in a simpler and more condensed book by a skilled theologian? Why read the Bible, except to determine whether or not that skilled theologian indeed got it right?

In agreement with postmodernists, then, Grenz insists that the story is more fundamental than the propositional statements that systematicians extract from the story. The story, especially if it is presented in the form of realistic narrative, is closer to reality, containing ever-deepening levels of meaning and nuanced implications and insights that cannot be discerned by rational analysis or codification. In contrast, propositional statements tend to be timeless, history-less, abstract, fragmented, and therefore of less practical value in understanding the real world.[51]

Moreover, when propositional statements are made subservient to the story, an interesting phenomenon develops. Differing doctrines are permitted to emerge from the story as differing perspectives of the story are examined. As noted earlier, we see this in the differing presentations of the gospel in the New Testament documents. The Pauline presentation of forensic justification, for example, differs from the Matthean presentation in which justification is better understood in relational categories (loving God and loving people). Since the story is primary and doctrine secondary, the fact that differences emerge in doctrine is not problematic. The differing presentations of the gospel, all of which are grounded in the same gospel story, are understood to complement rather than oppose one another.

SUMMARY

Standing in the shadow of neo-orthodox theologian Karl Barth, post-foundational realists are characterized as post-*Cogito* without relinquishing their commitment to epistemological realism. They insist that truth is grounded, not in a methodology of radical doubt, but instead in a more intuitive dimension: the Holy Scriptures authenticated by means of the Holy Spirit speaking through them (or, as more commonly explained, the Holy Scriptures are self-authenticating). Though these theologians stand in Barth's shadow, distinctives in their individual theologies set them apart from classic neo-orthodoxy.

Many contemporary theologians could have been chosen in his chapter to illustrate post-foundational realism. Miroslav Volf, James K. A. Smith and Stanley Grenz were chosen because they have made important contributions to the postmodern debate within the church and are therefore representative of this cadre of theologians. Each one has adopted a middle position, in some respects arguing in favor of postmodernism yet in other respects arguing against it. Specifically, (a) they insist upon the need for ontological referents to the Christian faith—a move seriously at odds with postmodern ideals—and (b) they insist that no single theological system is normative for the Christian faith and that, as a result, a plurality of theological systems is not only necessary but also advantageous. Such diversity is capable of sparking creative theological conversation within the church.

QUESTIONS

Basic Concepts

1. What do the terms *post-foundational* and *realism* mean?

2. What two problems did Karl Barth observe while in Safenwil that turned him away from theological liberalism?

3. When Barth turned away from theological liberalism, why did he not return to the conservative theology of his father?

4. What provocative theological move did Barth articulate that took his theology in a post-*Cogito* direction?

5. Barth described a correct theological prolegomena as a self-enclosed circle. What did he mean by this?

6. How did Barth characterize the doctrine of eschatology?

7. According to Miroslav Volf, what evidence does the New Testament give for both semiotic and nonsemiotic communication?

8. According to Volf, what is the problem with a theology grounded in extratextualities?

9. According to Volf, why is a pure intratextual theology an impossibility?

10. According to James. K. A. Smith, what are the three moves that characterize conventional postmodernism?

11. According to Smith, how does conventional postmodernism reintroduce a ghost of the *Cogito?*

12. What are the three moves that characterize Smith's understanding of a creational hermeneutic?

13. How does Grenz's understanding of the role of the Holy Spirit aid in advancing the church in a post-*Cogito* direction?

14. How does Grenz's understanding of the role of the church aid in advancing the church in a post-*Cogito* direction?

15. How does Grenz's understanding of Scripture aid in advancing the church in a post-*Cogito* direction?

Further Thought

1. What are the advantages and disadvantages of a intratextuality-cum-extratextuality to Christian theology and ecumenism?

2. In what respect does a pure intratextuality tend to domesticate the biblical worldview to one's own spiritual experience?

3. How does a creational hermeneutic assist in advancing the ecumenical agenda within the church?

5

Post-Foundational
Antirealism

The third of the four positions in the postmodern debate that we will examine is that of post-foundational antirealism. Being post-foundational, it stands opposed to the Cartesian *Cogito* as a means of ascertaining ultimate truth. Being antireal, it insists that the really real (the **thing-in-itself**) cannot be known in any definitive way. Instead, we only have differing lenses, made up of differing cultural and historical moments, from which we look at reality from afar.

Due to its emphasis on cultural and historical relativism, of the four positions considered in this book, this position most closely approximates conventional postmodernism. It is therefore the one position most severely criticized as a departure from historic Christianity since Christianity has historically argued against the relativization of its gospel message and for its universal applicability.

In addition, this position most closely approximates theological liberalism due to its penchant for religious pluralism and heavy dependence upon higher criticism. Its principal difference from theological liberalism involves its rejection of the *Cogito* and its affirmation of an antireal epistemology.

Among the Christian theologians characterized by post-foundational antirealism, John H. Hick (1922-) stands out as a dominant figure. "Hick is one of the most persuasive pluralists in the English-speaking world," writes Keith E. Johnson. He adds that Hick is "a careful scholar who writes with great clarity and precision. . . . [H]is hypothesis is one of the most sophisticated formulations of the pluralist position that I have encountered."[1]

In this chapter, we will examine post-foundational antirealism by beginning with Hick's contributions. Afterward, we will contrast Old Liberalism with New Liberalism, noting New Liberalism's alignment under postmodernism. Finally, we will offer a critique of this system.

JOHN H. HICK

John Harwood Hick was born in York, England, in 1922. He was baptized as an infant in the Church of England and spent his childhood and adolescent years nurtured in that church tradition. By his teen years, however, he found Christianity "utterly lifeless and uninteresting"[2] and at sixteen turned against the Christian faith, having become an avid reader and follower of such anti-Christian thinkers as Friedrich Nietzsche and Bertrand Russell.

While studying law at University College in Hull at age eighteen, Hick underwent a conversion to the Christian faith through the ministry of Inter-Varsity Fellowship. Describing this conversion experience as "irresistibly attractive,"[3] he recounts that he

> accepted as a whole and without question the entire evangelical package of theology—the verbal inspiration of the Bible; Creation and Fall; Jesus as God the Son incarnate, born of a virgin, conscious of his divine nature, and performing miracles of divine power; redemption by his blood from sin and guilt; Jesus' bodily resurrection, ascension, and future return in glory; heaven and hell.[4]

He also recounts, "I became a Christian of a strongly evangelical and indeed fundamental kind."[5] This conversion experience changed Hick's vocational direction from a career in law to ministry in the Presbyterian Church. He chose the Presbyterian Church because that was the denominational affiliation of most of his friends and mentors in the Christian Union at University College.

Having experienced a life-changing and profound religious conversion, Hick's commitment to the theology of Protestant evangelicalism was nevertheless short-lived, a commitment that lasted a mere five years. His theological pilgrimage away from conservative and fundamental Christian theology was gradual and transpired in two broadly defined phases.

The first phase (1946-1967) took place following the Second World War while Hick was studying philosophy at the University of Edinburgh and afterward while serving as a professor of philosophy and theology at several universities and seminaries.[6] It was during this time that he became increasingly impressed with the scholarship of higher criticism and correspondingly unimpressed with the doctrine of verbal plenary inspiration.[7] He also found himself unable to accept in good conscience the evangelical doctrine of eternal punishment, struggling with the problem of how a loving God could send the majority of the human race to hell for merely rejecting or not knowing of Jesus. Because of this, though still identifying himself as a conservative Christian, Hick found himself drifting away from core conservative beliefs.

The second phase (1967-1980) took place while Hick served as a professor of theology at the University of Birmingham in central England. In Birmingham, Hick was exposed to a number of non-Christian communities, including Muslim, Sikh, Hindu, Jewish and Buddhist traditions. This exposure developed within Hick an appreciation and ultimately an embrace of their theologies as legitimate expressions of religious thought. Hick explains:

> Occasionally attending worship in mosque and synagogue, temple and gurdwara, it was evident that essentially the same kind of thing is taking place in them as in a Christian church—namely, human beings opening their minds to a higher divine Reality, known as personal and good as demanding righteousness and love between man and man.[8]

As a result, Hick came to believe that there are many names of the one true God: Father-Son-Holy Spirit, Yahweh, Adonai, Allah, Vishnu, Krishna, Rama, Shiva, etc. In *God and the Universe of Faiths,* he argued that each of the world's religions should be viewed as "diverse [human] encounters with the same divine reality."[9] He articulates the fullest development of his thought in *An Interpretation of Religion,* published in 1988, where he makes his case that all religions are culturally conditioned responses to the same divine reality. With this theological move, Hick made his final break with conservative Christianity.

After his thirteen years at the University of Birmingham, in 1980 Hick moved to southern California, where he served as professor of the philosophy of religion at the Claremont Graduate School. He lectured there until his retirement.

In the following, we will look at Hick's theology in detail, noting the nature of his post-foundationalism and antirealism in three categories: (1) his use of alethic antirealism, (2) his appropriation of the term "Copernican revolution," and (3) his understanding of the historical Jesus.

Alethic antirealism. Alethic antirealism (*alētheia,* "truth") insists on the presence of lenses in front of the eyes of the seer. Because of this, one cannot understand truth independently of some lens. Hence, one's understanding always depends on the conceptual interpretations of one's culture and historical moment: "language games," as Ludwig Wittgenstein described them—paradigms that organize truth in logical systems unique to themselves. Each paradigm serves as a lens from which reality is examined and conclusions rendered. Because no direct understanding of reality is possible, no overarching, external or foundational metaparadigm exists from which to assess the individual rightness or wrongness of each paradigm. Rather, each paradigm is left to itself, assessing its own rightness and wrongness by internal consistency and pragmatic feasibility. This, of course, opens the door to theological and philosophical pluralism, since there is a multitude of differing paradigms in the world.

Drawing on the Kantian distinction between a thing-in-itself and the thing as humanly perceived, Hick argues that an impenetrable transcendent gap exists between the *ousia* of God (God's essence) and our understanding of God.[10] Citing one of the early church fathers, Gregory of Nyssa, for support of his position, Hick insists that God cannot be grasped by any term, idea or any other device of our apprehension. Rather than defining who God is, all the human mind can define is who or what God is not (that is, to think apophatically). As Gregory explained, God remains "beyond the reach not only of human but of angelic and all supramundane intelligence, unthinkable, unutterable, above all expression in words, having but one name that can represent His proper nature, the single name being 'Above Every Name.'"[11] Other theologians that Hick draws upon to support this apophatic strand running through Christianity are Augustine, Aquinas, Lactantius, Dionysius the Areopagite, John Scotus Erigena, St. John of the Cross, the writer of the *Theologia Germanica,* Martin Luther, Karl Barth, Paul Tillich and Meister Eckhart.[12]

According to Hick, this impenetrable transcendent gap renders it impossible through inductive logic to bridge our understanding of God to God himself. Rather, we are left with lenses from which to look across the gap. Moreover, these lenses are of our own making. Our location in history and the character of our particular culture are the two principal materials from which we shape and color our lenses.

In contrast to Hick, Kant would never have agreed to such an understanding of culture and the historical movement. For Kant, though the transcendental gap exists, we can nonetheless make progress to where, broadly speaking, a convergence of thought is possible.

Hick's system, of course, implies that there are many lenses and that what one seer sees is likely to be significantly different from what another sees.

Furthermore, Christianity constitutes only one of these lenses, with other world religions and philosophies constituting differing lenses. Hick explains:

> It therefore seems logical to me to conclude that not only Christianity, but also these other world faiths, are human responses to the Ultimate. They see the Divine/Sacred/Ultimate through different human conceptual "lenses," and they experience the divine/sacred/ultimate presence through their different spiritual practices in correspondingly different forms of religious experience. But they seem to constitute more or less equally authentic human awarenesses of and response to the Ultimate, the Real, the final ground and source of everything.[13]

This insistence that all religious knowledge must use lenses shaped by one's culture and historical moment is characteristic of alethic antirealism, which does not deny the actual existence of the divine/sacred/ultimate but merely insists that through inductive logic one cannot bridge the transcendent gap and make contact with he/she/it. Hick calls this a "critical realist epistemology,"[14] yet it is only "realist" in the sense that he acknowledges that the divine/sacred/ultimate truly exists. That is, he opposes *creative antirealism*. Nevertheless, because of his insistence in the use of lenses, his system is more correctly understood as an antireal epistemology.

The Copernican revolution. The sixteenth-century astronomer Nicolaus Copernicus rearranged our understanding of the solar system by replacing the earth with the sun as the center of the planets. The paradigm shift that Copernicus proposed was initially resisted by mainstream scholarship. Yet it was ultimately embraced and proved to be an enormous contribution to science, having changed the course of astronomy in the West. In his book *God Has Many Names,* Hick appropriated this concept from astronomy to describe his own theological system. He explained that the Christian religion should not be understood as the center of all religious thought. Instead, God should be located at the center and the Christian religion placed in orbit along with the many other world religions.

> It was possible to develop . . . the idea of a "Copernican revolution" in our theology of religions, consisting in a paradigm shift from a Christianity-centered or Jesus-centered model to a God-centered model of the universe of faiths. One then sees the great world religions as different human responses to the one divine Reality, embodying different perceptions which have been formed in different historical and cultural circumstances.[15]

Hick adds:

> Copernicus realized that it is the sun, and not the earth, that is at the centre, and that all the heavenly bodies, including our own earth, revolve around it. And we have to realize that the universe of faiths centres upon *God,* and not upon Christianity or upon any other religion. He is the sun, the originative source of light and life, whom all the religions reflect in their own different ways.[16]

Hence, an unknown and unknowable God lies at the center of religious thought rather than the knowable God of the Bible or any other specific religious system.

Yet by placing the Christian religion in orbit with the many other world religions, all of which circle the center (an unknowable God), Hick found himself confronted with a problem. On the one hand, he argued that no single religious paradigm can serve as the norm from which all other religions are judged right or wrong. On the other hand, he argued that not all world religions or philosophies should be understood as orbiting around the one true God. "Religious phenomena . . . can in principle be assessed and graded, and the basic criterion is the extent to which they promote or hinder the great religious aim of salvation/liberation."[17] Therefore, to some extent a universally recognized moral criteria must be invoked. But then Hick reverses himself, noting that "we cannot realistically assess and grade the great world religions, as totalities."[18]

Where, then, does Hick stand? Does he or does he not believe in some universal principles from which to assess differing religious paradigms? Though he argues against universal principles, he also affirms them.

Hick has therefore found himself on the horns of a dilemma. Though his system is grounded in alethic antirealism, he apparently cannot live consistently within this epistemological system. The manifest reality of God requires that those religions in true orbit around God must, to some extent, realistically reflect his character. This implies that someone has successfully found a way across the transcendent gap and can accurately determine God's essential character. Only then can we reasonably assess and grade the differing religious systems. Hick must either arrive at such an understanding through inductive reasoning or divine revelation. In either case, his antirealism falls since antirealism cannot accept the notion of someone successfully bridging the transcendent gap between phenomena and noumena. That successful contact would result in (a) antirealism collapsing into a form of realism and (b) the alteration of his Copernican revolution so significantly that instead of removing Christianity from the center and replacing it with an unknown God, the center is now occupied by a known God of some religious system. It is because of this contradiction in Hick's writings that Ward J. Fellows comments that Hick's "Copernican revolution is not, in intent or full force, a complete [antireal] relativism."[19]

The historical Jesus. For Hick's Copernican revolution to work, the Christian message of Jesus Christ being God incarnate (orthodox Christology) must be debunked. This is necessary because if that particular doctrine is permitted to stand, then the Christian faith moves out of its orbit with all the other world religions and is back at the center of the religious solar system. Moreover, if Jesus' words are understood to be divine, it opens the door to metaphysical realism. It does so because the transcendental gap between God and his creation—a gap that Hick insists on—would have been breached, not by means of human inductive logic, but rather by the immanent presence of a self-disclosing God. We can summarize Hick's debunking of the deity of Christ with three moves.

First, Hick argues that the earliest New Testament documents were not eyewitness accounts of the words and works of Jesus. Instead, they were written "between forty and seventy years after Jesus' death by people who were not personally present at the events they describe."[20] The very nature of the documents, Hick argues, suggests that the authors were not personally present. "All are dependent on sources in a way in which an eyewitness would not be."[21]

Second, Hick argues that the New Testament documents are all documents of faith. This means that the authors of the New Testament were not impartial or objective historians, but rather evangelists with an ulterior religious agenda in mind. As such, they stretched the truth to fit this agenda. They took a charismatic and highly effective religious leader who met an untimely death and transformed him into something he never claimed to be. At first, Jesus

> seems to have been as a Spirit-filled prophet and healer. . . . This God-inspired man seems to have understood his own role as that of the final prophet, proclaiming the immanent coming of the kingdom on earth. And the early church lived in the fervent expectation of his return as God's agent to inaugurate the kingdom.[22]

Nevertheless, Hick adds, as this expectation of the coming of God's kingdom gradually faded and faith gave way to discouragement, the church needed a renewed sense of hope to legitimize their own religious identity as Christians. The New Testament documents were written during this time to fill this need and revitalize the church's sagging faith. Hence, by means of these documents Jesus was exalted in communal memory from prophet to God incarnate.

Third, Hick argues that in the ancient world the term "son of God" was used loosely of gifted human beings: emperors, pharaohs, philosophers and religious figures. The "son of God" designation was familiar within Judaism. Israel as a whole was called God's son (Hos 11:1); angels were called "sons of God" (Job 38:7, see NIV footnote); kings were called sons of God (2 Sam 7:14; Ps 2:7). "Indeed, any outstanding pious Jew could be called a son of God, meaning one who was close to God, served God, and acted in the spirit of God. In terms of our modern distinction, this was clearly intended as metaphor."[23] Because of this, it would have been entirely natural that Jesus, as a great charismatic preacher and healer, would have been thought of as a son of God—not in terms of the second person of the Trinity, but rather as a remarkably pious and charismatically gifted Jew. However, this idea was sometimes less clearly metaphorical in the Gentile world. When Paul took the gospel into that world, this "son of God" metaphor underwent a gradual change from metaphorical, to semi-metaphorical, to semi-literal, and then finally, after several centuries, to the literal God the Son.

Summary of Hick's system. Due to its rejection of the *Cogito* and its affirmation of an antireal epistemology, Hick's system is a close approximation of conventional postmodernism in its more pure form. In regard to religious truth, God is ultimately understood apophatically—that is, we know what God *is not* rather than what he *is*. As such, he is unknowable in an absolute sense of the word. This implies three things: (1) No world religion can possess a knowledge of God accurate enough to serve as a standard from which all other world religions can be measured, since God is essentially unknowable. (2) All world religions, including Christianity, are essentially on an equal footing with one another, understanding God from the perspective of their own cultural and historical milieu. (3) All religious truth is thereby relativized to each world religion with its rightness and wrongness dependent upon internal consistency and pragmatic feasibility.

OLD LIBERALISM VERSUS NEW LIBERALISM

Post-foundational antirealism is similar to theological liberalism in that they both express and legitimize religious pluralism. Important differences exist, however, in how these two systems arrive at their understanding of religious pluralism. The differences are sufficient to split this theological system into Old and New Liberalism.[24]

Old Liberalism. Old Liberalism (sometimes referred to as Classical Liberalism) is grounded in modernist thought. More to the point, it is grounded in the Enlightenment thought of Friedrich Daniel Ernst Schleiermacher (1768-1834). Its starting point is human experience, with a deemphasis on the fallenness of human reason and passion. Schleiermacher emphasized the immanence (divine presence) rather than the transcendence (wholly otherness) of God. Because of his immanence, Schleiermacher believed that as an individual surrendered him or herself in an attitude of total dependence upon God, he or she would make genuine contact with deity. He explained, "True religion is sense and taste for the Infinite."[25] This god-consciousness—a state of mind accessed through one's intuition (rather than reason)—was a central component to Schleiermacher's understanding of Christ-centered spirituality. Nicola Hoggard Creegan explains:

> In acknowledging this relationship with God through god-consciousness there is a mystical reorientation. The world is not inert but holds the supernatural within it. Human nature is not barren but holds within it the seeds of god-consciousness, which in turn points toward the great incarnation, the full god-consciousness of Christ.[26]

Since Christ was that historic figure who most fully personified god-consciousness, Christ therefore became the great example for all humanity. This divided all humanity into two broad categories: those who recognized their mystical union with Christ and were actively pursuing a maturation of their god-consciousness and those who possessed no such recognition.

This move by Schleiermacher undercut religious pluralism by insisting upon a form of universalism that was wholly Christ-centered. He insisted that all world religions were held together by the Christian worldview. That is, non-Christian religions were imperfect expressions of the Christian faith. People identified with such religions were therefore grounded in a Christ-centered god-consciousness and were being drawn to Christ whether they knew it or not. Creegan explains, "It immediately points toward a worldview which is corporate and in which nothing has meaning unless it can be explained in relation to God and to Christ."[27]

What is more, this universalism was not the product of one's cultural orientation or the historical moment in which one lived, but rather ontologically grounded in the God who self-discloses himself to the human heart. In *The Christian Faith,* Schleiermacher made this point forcefully:

> Our whole existence does not present itself to our consciousness as having proceeded from our own spontaneous activity. . . . But the self-consciousness which accompanies all our activity, and therefore . . . accompanies our whole existence, is itself precisely a consciousness of absolute dependence; for it is the consciousness that the whole of our spontaneous activity *comes from a source outside of us.*[28]

This source from outside of us points to an objective God who has unambiguously revealed himself to the human heart.

One of the more articulate twentieth-century theologians to carry forward the Schleiermachian paradigm was Karl Rahner (1904-1984) with his "anonymous Christian" conceptualization. This theory argues that all people of all religions are Christians, albeit with differing religious nomenclatures defining the same essential divine reality or without any clear nomenclature and therefore possessing an inarticulate implicit faith. All people therefore possess a prereflective inarticulate experience of the divine, which is the heart of every religion, with the saving grace of Christ drawing them to God. Those non-Christians who respond to this inward call already share in the same justification, the same salvation that is at work in Christians, even though, unlike Christians, they have no conscious adherence or visible sacramental bond to the historical Jesus Christ.

New Liberalism. New Liberalism is grounded in postmodern thought. It denies the existence of universals and insists upon the localization of truth to specific cultures in their historical situations. Each culture, whether religious or nonreligious, networks truth in ways unique to itself. Therefore, the way truth is framed within one culture may be incommensurate with the way another culture frames truth. The differences can be so great that no equivalents of crucial terms can be found in common.

In the place of a singular worldview from which all religious truth is systematized (whether that worldview be Christian, Islamic, Jewish, Hindu, etc.), New Liberalism argues that a multitude of differing worldviews exists, all of which are looking at Ultimate Reality (God) from their individual cultural lenses. Yet since God is essentially unknowable, a theological agnosticism lies at the core of this religious system. Hick's system is a version of New Liberalism.

Hick's adoption of the term "Copernican revolution" clarifies the differences between Old and New Liberalism. Old Liberalism argues for universals and absolutes grounded in the Christian worldview. Christianity occupies the position of the sun with all the other religions orbiting around it. New Liberalism, in contrast, places the Christian religion in orbit with the other world religions and leaves the center (where God resides) essentially unknowable. It insists that there are no common or universal frameworks from which to define the most rudimentary religious conceptualizations. As such, to describe non-Christians as "anonymous Christians" is a nonsensical assertion. It makes no more sense than to describe non-Buddhists as "anonymous Buddhists."

This "revolution," of course, eliminates the whole notion of religious exclusivity. Since all religions are in orbit around an essentially unknowable God, followers of a given religious tradition cannot legitimately claim that their religion alone is the correct one. Joseph C. Hough Jr., president of Union Theological Seminary, agrees:

> A new Christian theology of religions will involve the recognition that the fomenting of religious conflict has been and still is a theological problem for Christians, because we have made our claim to God's revelation exclusively ours. Our history of internal conflict and persecution of persons of other religions is a grim reminder that we have killed each other and members of other religions in defending that exclusive claim. Ironically, by the defense of our exclusionary claim, we have often lived a contradiction of the spirit of Jesus Christ. . . . What is essential for Christian faith is that we know we have seen the face of God in the face of Jesus Christ. It is not essential to believe that no one else has seen God and experienced redemption in another place and time.[29]

Hough's point is that when we abandon religious exclusivity, singular understandings of religious doctrine that breed triumphalistic attitudes ("I'm right and you're wrong!"), which, in turn, have historically sparked pogroms, genocides, inquisitions and *jihads* must also be abandoned.

The notion of God can illustrate Hough's point. Even though differing religions use the word *God* in their systems, the meanings of the word can be so radically different as to preclude a common foundation. The Christian meaning is grounded in trinitarian thought. Islam is wholly monotheistic in orientation. Many of the Buddhist traditions understand *God* more as an idea than as a person. And so on. Hence, even though people may speak the same words, the content of these words are often radically different. The differences may be great enough to require abandoning the one definition and immersing oneself in the other before one can acquire a new understanding of the term.[30]

This point can also be illustrated in the notion of salvation. Though not a post-foundational antirealist, Peters's comments are helpful:

> If, as the Hindus or Buddhists think, salvation consists in enlightened knowing beyond ego-ness, then the Christian gratitude for forgiveness would appear irrelevant. In short, the content of salvation differs from tradition to tradition, and salvation in one case rules out salvation in other cases. . . . What rational sense would it make, then, to say that all religions are salvific? Whose definition of salvation would we use?[31]

Peters's point is that notions as basic as salvation are incommensurate between religions. Moreover, if there is no doctrine of universal salvation already within a given tradition, to force it upon such a tradition from a supraconfessional point of view violates the integrity of that tradition. Such a stance operates triumphalistically since it (a) assumes that the supraconfessionalist knows the content of the *really real* doctrine of universal salvation, (b) knows what aspects of a given tradition fit the paradigm, (c) knows what aspects require redefinition and (d) knows what aspects should be ignored. New Liberalism, then, makes no effort to demonstrate the inherent sameness of differing religions. Instead, each is permitted to stand in its own integrity juxtaposed to others in unrelieved tension.

Such differences between religions do not mean that contact or communication with one another is impossible. In New Liberalism, differing systems can communicate and learn from one another. Nevertheless, as Hough explains, there is a

> difference between an attempt to convert and an attempt to bear witness. The attempt to bear witness is the attempt to state honestly what you have discovered in faith in Jesus Christ. That is to share the things in your life that are of highest value to you, and I think this is an act of friendship.[32]

Hough adds that this attitude is different from one that states, "Now that I've told you this, you've got to believe as I do to experience this."[33] For those committed to "new liberal" thinking, what is required is the demonstration of humility and openness to conversation, not triumphalistic arrogance where one's own religious tradition is uniquely right and all others wrong.

THE QUESTION OF AGNOSTICISM

Central to post-foundational antirealism is the notion that God is ultimately
unknowable. Since all such analyses rule out inductive reasoning or divine
revelation, all we have are cultural lenses from which to think about God and
draw individual conclusions. Such radical antirealism, however, is problematic
and raises sharp responses in the postmodern debate within the church.

Clark H. Pinnock has noted that rather than being a genuine Copernican
revolution, what Hick has actually done is take Christianity out of the center
and replace it with an understanding of God commensurate with Eastern religions. He writes, "While claiming to be a view of God that transcends all
the culturally generated models of God in the world's religions, it is in fact
a truth claim familiar with Eastern monistic traditions. This means that it is a
claim every bit as *particular* as the Christian one."[34] Hick's agnosticism
about God, therefore, is disingenuous. Yet, Pinnock continues, if God is indeed unknowable, the possibility then exists that, based on our standards of
morality, God could be evil. Such a possibility makes it impossible to identify evil religions as false. Rather, such religions have just as much a right to
legitimacy as those religions that we would identify as morally upright. What
is more, Pinnock wonders how Hick arrived at this conclusion that God is
unknowable. "Has this been revealed to him?"[35] he asks. Essentially, Pinnock
concludes, Hick attempts to prove a negative assertion, an effort wrought
with much difficulty.

R. Douglas Geivett and W. Gary Phillips argue against Hick's understanding of a religiously ambiguous universe. They explain that Hick regards
competing religious perspectives as equally authentic responses to the same
reality. As such, God is perfectly undifferentiated; that is, he has no properties that human conceptualizations can access. Geivett and Phillips's problem with such agnosticism is that it leaves us with no way at all to concep-
tualize and thereby articulate God. They explain:

> This notion of the Real as undifferentiated is conceptually implausible. Hick
> has remarked that "the Buddhist concept of *sunyata* . . . provides a good sym-
> bol for the Real."[36] But if the Real is as radically undifferentiated as Hick avers,
> then there is no way even to symbolize it. Symbols are representational ob-
> jects; they carry the representational content of some object and convey that
> content to a knowing or perceiving subject. But there is no representational
> content in the Real as undifferentiated that might be conveyed by a symbol.[37]

In other words, for an entity to be manifested requires some or all of its properties to be revealed. But if God (the Real) is undifferentiated, he/she/it has no distinguishable properties. God is therefore strictly inaccessible, resulting not in the pluralism of religions but rather in their intellectual collapse. In Hick's system, religion is therefore a nonsensical concept. It causes religion to become atheistic in orientation, nothing more than social inventions that emerge in differing cultures.

THE QUESTION OF CHRIST

According to Hick, the historical Jesus and the Jesus presented in the New Testament are not the same. The New Testament portrait of Jesus is the result of layers of legendary assertions that evolved between his earthly life and the New Testament documents. Jesus' presentation as God—"I and the Father are one" (Jn 10:30)—is therefore nothing more than religious myth falsely documented as historical fact.

Such an understanding of Jesus is essential to Hick and other postmodernists of his ilk. If Jesus were God incarnate, that would debunk the Copernican revolution, and instead of arguing for cultural lenses from which to understand God, God would be challenging and confronting culture from a biblical worldview that is itself grounded in God's own words.

On two levels, Geivett and Phillips question Hick's attempt to identify the historical Jesus in terms that declassify his claim to deity. The first level addresses the New Testament witness of Christ's deity. Geivett and Phillips insist that to debunk the New Testament witness, Hick must do three things: (1) He must identify the core of Jesus' actual teachings. (2) He must rebut specific efforts to demonstrate his deity in the New Testament documents. "It will not do for him simply to assert that any argument that Jesus' words and deeds imply a claim to deity is 'highly debatable,'" they insist. "He must debate the point."[38] (3) He must show what substantive knowledge of the historical Jesus is possible on the slender basis of sayings that he is willing to authorize. Without this, it is unreasonable for Hick to affirm the saintliness of Jesus, as he has attempted to do. Geivett and Phillips counter, however, that everything known about Jesus from early documents are infused with a high Christology. He is therefore who he claimed to be or he is a liar. They conclude, then, "that Jesus did claim to be God, and we reprise the Latin refrain: *aut Deus, aut non bonus:* 'Either he was God, or he was not a good man.'"[39]

The second level addresses the Chalcedonian formulation of orthodox Christology. Hick rejects the Chalcedonian formulation on the grounds that since its affirmation of Jesus being genuinely and unambiguously God and genuinely and unambiguously human is self-contradictory, it does not make good religious sense. Hick therefore replaces a literal interpretation of the incarnation with a metaphorical interpretation.[40]

Yet Geivett and Phillips ask, is Hick's reason for repudiating the Chalcedonian formulation plausible? Since one of the two natures of Christ is deity, it only stands to reason that the relationship between the two would be mysterious and beyond the grasp of the human mind. They therefore argue that Hick's problem with the Chalcedonian formulation has more to do with his own intellectual agenda than with an honest analysis of the formulation. Hick, for example, agrees that if Jesus of Nazareth "was indeed God incarnate, Christianity is the only religion founded by God in person, and must as such be uniquely superior to all other religions."[41] Yet such cannot be the case, Hick continues, since the uniqueness of Christianity is incompatible with the enlightened awareness of other faiths in the world.[42] Therefore, since Hick assumes religious pluralism to be correct, reasoning back to the Chalcedonian formulation requires its repudiation. Geivett and Phillips conclude, "This is little more than a shrill accusation that it is bad manners for God to act in a way that we cannot explain or in a way that offends our religious predilections."[43]

THE QUESTION OF TOLERANCE

A natural consequence of the Copernican revolution mentioned earlier in this chapter is the phenomenon of moral tolerance that has emerged within the West since the advent of postmodernism. When Christianity is displaced from the center of religious thought (both conservatism and Old Liberalism) and replaced with an unknowable God (New Liberalism), moral absolutes—whether those absolutes come from abstracted principles or from a living relationship with God—are also displaced from culture and replaced with moral tolerance. Since God is unknowable, his character—and thereby morality—is equally unknowable.[44]

As we have already seen, Hick was uncomfortable with the implications of moral tolerance. He sought an ad hoc morality of salvation/liberation to serve as a universal moral code. Nevertheless, a consistent application of his system requires moral tolerance on a much wider scale. When God is understood as perfectly undifferentiated—that is, possessing no properties that the human mind can identify and understand—we do not possess a neutral objective reference point from which to construct standards of morality. Instead, we have only whatever standards a culture decides on—and even these are open to debate and adjustment. William Watkins writes:

> Cultural relativists maintain that a society's beliefs and behaviors must be understood and judged within the context of that society. Whatever a society believes is right is right within that society, whatever beliefs and behaviors it condemns as wrong are, therefore, wrong for that group. We, from our culture, cannot impose our standards on any other culture, just as other cultures cannot judge us by their standards. No culture's code of conduct has special status; it is simply one code among many, no better or worse than any other.[45]

John Leo, writing in *The Washington Times,* points out the extremes to which radical moral relativism has gone in certain quarters in the West:

> In 30 years of college teaching, Prof. Robert Simon has never met a student who denied that the Holocaust happened. What he sees increasingly, though, is worse: students who acknowledge the fact of the Holocaust but can't bring themselves to say that killing millions of people is wrong. Simon, who teaches philosophy at Hamilton College, says that 10 to 20 percent of his students are reluctant to make moral judgments—in some cases, even about the Holocaust. While these students may deplore what the Nazis did, their disapproval is expressed as a matter of taste or personal preference, not moral judgment. "Of course I dislike the Nazis," one student told him, "but who is to say they are morally wrong?"[46]

A consistent application of the Copernican revolution of post-foundational antirealism requires that nothing be defined as morally and absolutely wrong. This is because there are no universal standards of good or bad, right or wrong, normal or abnormal, that can be applied crossculturally. As a result, moral tolerance must expand to the point of nonsensical assertions that violate what most people would describe as rudimentary common sense.

SUMMARY

Of the four theological positions in the postmodern debate discussed in this book, post-foundational antirealism has the most in common with conventional postmodernism. Its insistence on the cultural and historical orientation of truth and upon the ultimately inaccessibility of "the really real," in this case God, corresponds to the philosophical moorings of Nietzsche, Heidegger, Wittgenstein and Derridá—four major postmodern thinkers of the late nineteenth and twentieth centuries.

Typical of postmodern thought, John Hick's "Copernican revolution" displaced Christianity as the center of religious thought and moved it into an orbital path along with all the other religions of the world, no more or less significant than all the rest of religious thought. With the displacement of Christianity, post-foundational antirealism has rejected orthodox Christology—that is, the combined deity and humanity of Christ (the Chalcedonian formulation). In its place, it understands God agnostically, which leaves the door wide open to the legitimacy of the many divergent world religions. With an unknowable God, a universal moral code becomes a logical impossibility, which sanctions each culture to establish its own moral system of right and wrong.

Hick's system, however, has difficulty sustaining itself in the pure form of antirealism. Since antirealism denies the possibility of moral absolutes, Hick's system has no means to legitimately reject any religion or philosophy that is clearly at odds with basic moral sensibilities, such as that of the Ku Klux Klan or neo-Nazism. Therefore, either it opens its orbit of religions to such spurious religious traditions or it recognizes the existence of some form of moral absolutes from which to assess the legitimacy of a religious tradition. If Hick chooses the former, his system collapses into moral nihilism which, from a social perspective, is pragmatically unrealistic. If Hick chooses the latter, his apophatic theology collapses along with his Copernican revolution.

This, then, is the dilemma that post-foundational antirealism faces. It has difficulty controlling its own internal propensity toward deconstructionism. It has a natural tendency to deconstruct (a) all semblances of moral rectitude to an "anything goes" permissivism and (b) all religious belief to mere social invention that can only suggest what constitutes the nature of the divine. This system of thought is therefore a version of practical atheism; though it acknowledges the existence of God, it arranges the implications of God's existence in decisively atheistic patterns.

QUESTIONS

Basic Concepts

1. Describe John Hick's conversion to the Christian faith.

2. What were the doctrinal problems and personal experiences that drew Hick away from a conservative understanding of the Christian faith?

3. In what respect is Hick's theology a form of alethic antirealism?

4. How is Hick's theology analogous to the Copernican revolution of the natural sciences?

5. The claims of Jesus as described in the New Testament render impossible Hick's Copernican revolution. What three moves does Hick make to redefine the historical Jesus?

6. What are the differences between Old and New Liberalism?

7. Clark Pinnock argues that Hick's system is not truly apophatic. According to Pinnock, how does Hick's system characterize God?

8. According to Geivett and Phillips, if God is undifferentiated (wholly unknowable), what does this imply for the work of theology?

9. Geivett and Phillips are critical of Hick's understanding of the historical Jesus on two levels. What are these two levels?

10. According to Geivett and Phillips, what does Hick fail to accomplish in the first level?

11. According to Geivett and Phillips, what does Hick fail to recognize in the second level?

12. Because of its inability to define moral standards, what are the results of moral tolerance in society?

13. Ward J. Fellows comments that Hick's "Copernican revolution is not, in intent or full force, a complete [antireal] relativism." Why?

Further Thought

1. Compare and contrast Old and New Liberalism. Which of the two systems is more compelling, and why?

2. Assuming that the version of conservative Christianity that Hick embraced in his early adulthood was foundational realism, what problems might he have encountered that would have drawn him away from it?

3. In the name of tolerance, it is popular today for people of Western culture to accept an understanding of religion that draws on the insights of John Hick. What are the long-term consequences of such a religious move?

Post-Foundational
Middle-Distance Realism

The fourth and final category within the current postmodern debate that we will examine is post-foundational middle-distance realism, a theological system more commonly known as *postliberalism.* This category differs from the other three positions presented in this book since it is a hybrid. It attempts to strike a middle distance between metaphysical realism and antirealism, preserving the positive characteristics of both. It also stands opposed to the Cartesian *Cogito.*

We will focus our attention upon the perspective of George A. Lindbeck, rather than upon other postliberal theologians such as Hans W. Frei, David H. Kelsey, William C. Placher or Ronald F. Thiemann.[1] The reason for this singular focus is that Lindbeck, more than these other thinkers, has most clearly demonstrated the hybrid character of the postliberal project, giving voice to its middle-distance quality.

GEORGE A. LINDBECK

Born in China where his parents served as missionaries, George Arthur Lindbeck is a member of the Evangelical Lutheran Church in America and a leading ecumenist and pioneer in the integration of postmodernism into the Christian faith. He has characterized himself as a "Wittgensteinian Thomistic Lutheran."[2] He is also one of the originators of postliberalism. His book *The Nature of Doctrine: Religion and Theology in a Postliberal Age,* published in 1984, was the groundbreaking work that originally framed the postliberal argument and that continues to serve as the backdrop against which postliberal dialogue is cast.

This fact was illustrated at the Wheaton College Theology Conference of 1995, a conference where evangelical and postliberal scholars dialogued together, seeking common ground from which the work of theology could be advanced. During a concluding panel discussion, Lindbeck said to the audience:

> It's understandable to me that my name should come up with numbing frequency in this conference. I happen to have introduced into the public domain the word *postliberal,* though I didn't intend to name a research program or a movement. And I happen to be, I suppose, the senior living member of the group that is willing to call itself postliberal.[3]

Following the Wheaton Conference, in 1998 the Yale Graduate School Alumni Association recognized the enormity of Lindbeck's work, noting that his "publications have shaped the agenda for an entire generation of scholars of religion and contributed indispensably to what is widely known as 'the new Yale theology'" and that he has "been more influential that most theologians of our time."[4] Similarly, James J. Buckley described Lindbeck's work as that which "effectively remaps the theological scene."[5]

Lindbeck and Derridá. Even though Lindbeck has identified himself as a *Wittgensteinian* postmodernist,[6] the comparisons and contrasts between his epistemological system and Jacques Derridá's are more useful in elucidating his understanding of metaphysical realism and antirealism than are comparisons and contrasts to Ludwig Wittgenstein. So although the general tendency in academia is to draw upon Wittgenstein to elucidate an understanding of Lindbeck, we will move in the other direction, comparing and contrasting his system to that of Derridá.

Derridá's postmodern thought is grounded in the nature of language and the individual psyche. Unlike modernist philosophers before him who argued for a *res cogitans* (human thought can exist independently of cultural influences) and the corresponding solipsism (within one's mind exists an immediacy, or a pure knowledge), Derridá insists that each person thinks with language. This is true even of infants, who think in terms of rudimentary sign language. Hence, without language thinking is impossible.

Two important implications emerge from this system. First, language precedes thought. Words and grammar serve as the building blocks from which thinking takes shape. The means by which an individual shapes questions and organizes data is therefore dependent on the peculiarities of a given language. Since each individual is also connected to a community of people, his or her thinking not only is grounded by such influences but also influences the recipients of his or her use of language. This creates a circular system: the individual influences and is influenced by the given culture that generates the language.

Second, there exists no truth that stands apart from the influences of language/culture (what Derridá calls the *transcendental signified* or the *untraceable trace*), which serves as the standard from which all other systems of truth are appraised. As a result, truth becomes relativized—deconstructed—to cultures, subcultures and ultimately the interaction of two individuals. (For a more complete understanding of the Derridean system see the glossary entries *play of the trace* and *signifiers and significations*.)

In "Scripture, Consensus and Community," an article written four years after the publication of *The Nature of Doctrine,* Lindbeck summarized his cultural-linguistic paradigm using Derridá's understanding of postmodernism as a backdrop. He made three observations.

First, Lindbeck argued that Christianity—specifically, Christianity in its premodern form—is not susceptible to the radical relativism that language theory imposes on human thought. This is because premodern Christianity is not an **ontotheologically** framed religious phenomenon (i.e., a version of Christianity grounded in the *Cogito*). Rather, it is grounded in "the Word incarnate" (Jn 1:1). As such, instead of existing in a circular system of theological reflection that has no independent grounding and is therefore subject to change, premodern Christianity is kept stable because of the other-worldly/this-worldly nature of the Word. Derridá misfired in his criticisms of the Christian religion precisely because he failed to understand it in non-ontotheological categories.

Second, having rendered invalid Derridá's attack against Christianity since he failed to consider its historically prior non-ontotheological form, Lindbeck turned the tables and finds fault with Derridá, arguing that his system is *theologically* and *philosophically* flawed.

1. Its theological flaw is centered on the *closed system* from which Derridá permits the **play of the trace** to operate. In agreement with the fundamentals of postmodernism, Derridá argues that before a person can think one must first possess language. Language opens the door to and also limits the scope of one's ability to process data into comprehensive systems of truth. Derridá argues, for example, that the reason a Latin American tends to think differently from a Japanese, a German or British person is due to the distinctives of the Spanish language. Syntax, grammar and vocabulary provide a unique ordering of his or her thought patterns. Consequently, each culture has a tendency to shape truth differently. Yet this perspective creates a destabilized system since (a) all cultures are subject to change, (b) people from one culture interact with people from other cultures, creating hybrid systems, and (c) people create their own mini-cultures due to the particularity of their own experiences and acquisition of knowledge. In a closed system, this generates an endless regress since no culture, experience or knowledge can be considered normative for all the peoples of the world.

In a closed system, there is no grounding for truth since (1) there exists no way to think independently of the influences of culture and history, and (2) a corresponding endless regress exists as truth is incessantly modified by the opinions of other individuals and cultures.

Lindbeck counters by asking, what if language is not limited to the language groups of this world? What if, instead, the possibility exists that God, from his wholly otherness, can break in and also speak in this world? Lindbeck's point is this: Derridá's system is functionally atheistic rather than theistic in orientation. He failed to consider the possibility that an unapproachable God (transcendence) is capable of approaching us by communicating and living among us (immanence). This, of course, implies an *open system* from which to think.

Hence, if the first move is God reaching down and communicating to us, rather than, through rigorous rational analysis, our constructing a religious system and reaching up to God, the dynamics of theological inquiry change. We are no longer in an endless regress where meaning cannot be fixed due to the endless modifications that a community places on the meaning of words. Instead, all understandings of truth find their ultimate grounding in the words and actions of God. What is more, we do not find this truth through inductive reasoning. Rather, through divine revelation (in both word and deed), God reveals himself.

Lindbeck therefore believed he found a way that the Derridean maxim of "language preceding knowledge" could be maintained, while preventing the resultant endless regress and cultural relativization of truth. Rather than thinking in terms of language as the word (little *w*), implying that language is the product of culture, Lindbeck thought of language in terms of the Word (big *w*). He pointed to the opening statement in the apostle

John's Gospel: "In the beginning was the Word and the Word was with God and the Word was God." Unlike human speech that is relativized to culture, God speech is capable of overcoming the problems of relativization.

If we are to correctly understand Lindbeck, this insight must not be overlooked. It creates an ontological grounding that locates Lindbeck's system within both realms of metaphysical realism and antirealism. Like Derridá, Lindbeck embraces the role of language as prior to rational thought. Unlike Derridá, though, he argues that the transcendental gulf has been breached—not by the human being but by God. Lindbeck identifies the divine *Logos*—Jesus Christ—as this grounding of all truth.

2. The philosophical flaw in Derridá's system is its inconsistent application of deconstructionism. Lindbeck turned to Euclid's *Elements* to illustrate his point. He observed that if Derridá's deconstructionism were applied to the principles of geometry presented in *Elements,* the book would be rendered unintelligible due to the presence of "an indefinite number of purposes and meanings."[7] The endless regress in the definition of words would inevitably generate a multiplicity of meanings for each and every word, with the meaning of the author no more or less authoritative than any of the other meanings. Moreover, this endless regress would eventually generate a sense of self-subversion; that is, the meaning of Euclid's own words would be modified to such an extent that they could be used as an argument against the very principles he intended to convey in his book. Clearly, then, if consistently applied to all books and all forms of communication involving words, deconstructionism would render all communication unintelligible. The way deconstructionists overcome this problem, Lindbeck continued, is through an inconsistent or arbitrary application of its methodology. Such arbitrariness, however, betrays the fallacy of its own logic. Though Lindbeck did not press further, Derridá's line of thinking inevitably leads to the self-subversion of deconstructionism itself; that is, its consistent application would naturally result in the deconstruction of deconstructionism, which is an even more profound logical fallacy.[8]

Third, Lindbeck observed that Christianity—once separated from its ontotheological counterfeit (i.e., that version of Christianity grounded in the *Cogito*)—makes room for a postmodern construct, though not in its deconstructionist mode, which he viewed as a distortion within the postmodern project. In its constructionist mode, Lindbeck claimed that Christianity points to the interpenetration of God into the world in two distinct ways.

1. God interpenetrates the world with the "Word incarnate" (i.e., the Christ-event) and his authoritative witness, which serves as "a privileged text and privileged mode of interpretation." A "privileged text and a privileged mode of interpretation," Lindbeck explains, is the canonical Bible and the canonical creeds. Since Lindbeck understands the canonical texts and creeds to be gifted to the church through the work of the Holy Spirit, rather than rationally discerned through the canons of modernity, they are not properly understood as products of the *Cogito*.[9]

2. God interpenetrates the world through existential and always-contemporaneous divine words that possess a fixed meaning only the moment they are spoken. According to Lindbeck, these are the words of the ascended Jesus, spoken to the hearts of each believer by means of the Holy Spirit, which are "new every morning."[10] This is not metaphoric language since he insists that the ascended Jesus is just as much alive today, speaking through Scripture, worship and so forth, as he was when he lived on the earth and spoke to his first-century contemporaries. These words provide the "fixed meaning" as God speaks "new every morning" in situationally specific speech.

Lindbeck's point is that though Christianity is admittedly a text-bound faith, it is far from being made rigid with a univocal meaning determined by the reader. Rather, God—understood through the risen Jesus, the Christ-event, the privileged text (canon) and the privileged interpretation (creeds) and liturgies—is able to speak to a given community and convey the meaning of the divine reality in unique individual expressions. In this sense, a *complexio oppositorum* of multiple meanings is possible. They, however, do not originate in the mind of the individual. Instead, they originate in the mind of God who is able to convey the complex and multilayered divine reality through the flexibility of words. Such an approach, Lindbeck noted, prevents the believer from reducing the biblical text to a set of fixed doctrines with the hope of attaining a univocal (timeless and forever fixed) meaning. The Christian faith, then, is kept from ontotheology (the *Cogito*) and thereby not vulnerable to Derridá's attack.

Middle-distance. The form of theological pluralism that Lindbeck affirms has three components:

1. It reflects different dimensions of the same divine reality.

2. All of its different dimensions have their origin and are thereby grounded in the "living Word."

3. The "living Word" speaks to believers through Scripture, creeds, worship, sermons, etc.

This pluralism cannot be correctly labeled antirealism since it is anchored in the living Word. But because this pluralism does not avail a singular meta-paradigm but instead renders meanings that are "new every morning," neither can it be identified as a strict version of realism. As such, it is a hybrid, or as David Ford characterizes it, a "middle-distance realism."[11] Ford explains that

> if one moves too close and allows the dominant perspective to become, for example, one person's inner world or stream of consciousness, then the middle distance has been supplanted. Likewise, if one takes too broad an overview and substitutes the particular people, words, and actions into a generalization, a trend, or a theory, the middle distance loses its own integrity.[12]

In other words, Lindbeck's system strikes a balance between realism and antirealism. By splitting the difference between realism and antirealism, Lindbeck has attempted to avoid the triumphalism inherent within metaphysical realism *and* the problem of cultural relativization inherent within metaphysical antirealism.

Two caveats. Lindbeck's system is therefore grounded in the "privileged witnesses" of Scripture, the early church creeds, and the voice of the risen Lord Jesus who speaks to the heart of every believer with words that are new every morning. This middle-distance epistemology must be qualified by two caveats related to these sources of witnesses. In the first caveat, Lindbeck described the biblical narrative as history-like rather than historical. In the second, Lindbeck described the creeds as conditioned by time and culture.

1. The biblical narrative as history-like. Lindbeck affirmed the notion of *history-like* rather than *likely history* in reference to the historicity of the biblical narrative.[13] He explained that during the Enlightenment when modernity came to the fore in Christian theology, the focus of Scripture shifted—the narrative meaning of the biblical stories became minimized as questions related to their factualness and historicity were emphasized.[14] This preoccupation with the question of accuracy divided theology into two camps: inerrantists and historical critics. He wrote, "Both tended to think that facts (defined by the prevailing rational and empirical strands of the day) are what are important in any document, and most notably in the book of books, the Bible."[15]

Lindbeck, however, believed that this hermeneutical preoccupation was wrongheaded. It eclipsed the Bible's own worldview by preventing Scripture from revealing itself as a realistic narrative, complete with multilayered meanings, its own self-authenticating credibility and a presence of life—a perspective that provided the reader with an ever-widening and ever-deepening sense of the human and divine life. Hence, for Lindbeck, recovering the Bible as a realistic narrative required sidestepping the modernist agenda in both conservative and liberal expressions. The modern agenda tended to anchor the biblical text in questions of accuracy, a method that made the biblical narrative little more than a means to an end—the end being the acquisition of abstracted truths that are timeless and changeless.

Lindbeck's means of sidestepping this modernist preoccupation was by adopting Hans Frei's language and speaking of Scripture as "history-like." Lindbeck did not intend the term "history-like" to take the side of theological liberalism and argue for the possible fiction of Jesus, the Christ-event, etc. That would have put Lindbeck in the middle of the very debate he was attempting to avoid. Rather, the term was intended to keep the theologian off balance, rendering irrelevant the modernist agendas of the two camps. That is, he refused to enter this modernist debate on either the liberal or conservative side. He was committed to the resurrection of Jesus as a genuine event but refused to think of it in terms of conventional historical methodology, which required irrefutable and impartially presented evidence. Hence, understanding this strategy clarifies how Lindbeck can, on the one hand, speak of Scripture as history-like and, on the other hand, speak of the cross and resurrection as "the really real, the fullness of God's own identity."[16] Both are true for Lindbeck, given the specific concern that he is addressing while making each statement.[17]

2. The creeds as conditioned by time and culture. Lindbeck understands the creeds to be conditioned by time and culture, not timeless or changeless embodiments of revealed eternal truths. For him, dogmatic or confessional formulations

> are quite true within their original contexts. But when the contexts shift, the dogmas change their meaning. Consequently, to affirm the ancient truths, one must use new words, new concepts, for if one simply repeats the old, one be-

trays, rather than preserves them. In short, adherence to the historic affirmations of the faith requires reformulation.[18]

In *The Future of Roman Catholic Theology* he adds:

> Dogmas can no longer be thought of as changelessly adequate embodiments
> of revealed eternal truths, for such embodiments do not exist. Historical stud-
> ies have made Catholics as well as non-Catholics intensely aware of the time-
> conditioned and culture-conditioned character of all human language, even
> when it is used by the church. Meaning depends on the situation, and to re-
> peat abiding truths in the same old ways in radically new circumstances is not
> to preserve, but to betray them. The only way to say the same thing in a new
> context is to say it differently.[19]

In other words, though Lindbeck affirms the abiding legitimacy of the ecumenical creeds, he also affirms their historical datedness.

Such reasoning places Lindbeck's understanding of the creeds in paradoxical tension. This tension, he explains, is managed by the work of the
Holy Spirit in the lives of individual religious communities. The Spirit not
only is the revealer of the Christ-event, as reflected in Scripture and creed,
but also was engaged in its creative interpretation in the milieu of cultures
and historical settings. Take, for example, the confessions of the Reformation. Written in the shadow of the Roman Catholic Church, they were reactions against specific ecclesial abuses of that period. Though, arguably, they
were guided by the Spirit in their specific wordings, the problems that they
addressed are not the same as those of the twenty-first century. A number
of the concerns and challenges that divide Protestantism from Roman Catholicism today have undergone significant changes. As such, some of the
wordings in these confessional statements are in need of Spirit-guided revi-
sions if they are to continue to reflect the integrity of divine truth.

Yet, having said this, Lindbeck also affirmed that the rearticulations of a
creed can be perilous to orthodoxy and therefore require safeguards.[20] He
proposed three rules. Rearticulations of a creed must affirm: (a) the monotheistic principle of only one God—the God of Abraham, Isaac, Jacob and
Jesus, (b) the principle of historical specificity—the stories of Jesus as a genuine human being who was born, lived and died in a particular time and
place and (c) the principle of Christological maximalism—every possible importance to be ascribed to Jesus that is not inconsistent with the first two
rules.[21] This, he claimed, rules out such heresies as Docetism, Gnosticism,
Adoptionism, Sabellianism, Arianism, Nestorianism and Monophysitism.[22]

One may question whether these three rules satisfactorily guard against heresy. Lindbeck nevertheless believed that they did and that they pointed people to the ontological referent: the worldview within the biblical narrative centered in the Christ-event.

PLURALISM IN LINDBECK

As we have already observed, Lindbeck insists that the Christ-event is the really real; that is, it literally happened. The Scriptures and related creeds and confessions serve as privileged witnesses and interpretations to that event. Christianity, therefore, is an inescapably text-bound religion. Lindbeck, however, also insists that this does not require rigidity of that text. From an existential perspective, he asserts that Jesus—who is alive as the ascended Lord—speaks through the biblical text, worship and so forth. in order for people to hear his "present meaning."[23]

This combination generates pluralism; people are capable of "hearing God speak in many ways through Scripture."[24] In the following, we will observe what Lindbeck meant by this (a) for the individual, (b) in faith communities and (c) among larger religious traditions.

Pluralism in the individual. According to Lindbeck, the central task of the theologian as he or she approaches the biblical text is to enter into its worldview and encounter its realistic narrative complete with multilayered meanings, realism and life-giving message. It is the embrace of the worldview of the biblical text, rather than the introduction of a contemporary worldview to the biblical text that should occupy the central agenda of the individual theologian. As Lindbeck noted repeatedly in his writings, in this task "the biblical world absorbs all other worlds."[25]

This approach mitigates against a modernist approach of reducing the biblical text to universally abstracted principles. In modernism, the biblical narrative is intended to lead the reader to a cataloging of truth into formulas that are timeless, changeless and universal. When the narrative character of Scripture is replaced with the logic of such abstracted principles, the biblical worldview is eclipsed and replaced by the theologian's newly manufactured worldview that operates independently of the biblical narrative and which, accordingly, may only be "externally related to its originating [biblical] text."[26]

An appreciation of the Bible as a realistic narrative, however, causes the individual reader to understand the biblical story as the foundation on which everything else is predicated. The reader leaves his or her world and enters the world of the Bible as depicted in the form of a realistic narrative. Since the realistic narrative is complex, layered in ever-deepening and multisided meanings that generate its own pluralistic view of reality, it draws the individual reader ever deeper into its inexhaustible meaning, perspectives and dimensions. As such, the reader discovers differing understandings of the biblical text (theological pluralism) as he or she encounters and experiences its various layers.

Pluralism in faith communities. One of the more significant insights to come from Wittgenstein's postmodern theories, according to Lindbeck, is the notion of "language games." This idea recognizes that multiple meanings can legitimately emerge from the same examination of reality by differing faith communities.[27] This plurality of meanings is evident in Christian doctrine. Lindbeck draws upon the doctrine of the atonement as an illustration of this phenomenon:

> Thus in the biblical world, one word or one reality may have an indeterminate number of meanings: the sacrifice of the Passover lamb is antitypically fulfilled on the cross, which, in turn, is endlessly troped in the lives of those who follow Christ and, third, is anagogically signaled in the coming again of the Lamb slain from the foundation of the world. All three senses played a part in welding the intratextual world of the canon into a metaphorical interglossing unity of cosmic comprehensiveness, but the tropological sense is for our topic of special importance, because it is this that chiefly functioned applicatively in the embodiment of the faith in social reality by the absorbing of other worlds. By it in particular, though not to the exclusion of the other senses, each age, each culture and each individual in his or her special circumstances could be addressed directly by God speaking in and through Scripture. Yet the changing and multivocal meanings of the various scriptural words did not lead to chaos. They were all anchored in the literal sense.[28]

In other words, the biblical world expresses one reality, yet this reality can yield a wide range of meanings.

Such multiple meanings can be illustrated with Wittgenstein's famous thumbnail sketch (figure 6.1). Does this thumbnail sketch represent a duck or a rabbit? The answer depends on the angle from which the sketch is examined. Without altering a single line, different pictures emerge as one looks at the drawing from various perspec-

Figure 6.1

tives. Similarly, without violating or ignoring a single passage of Scripture, the truth of Scripture is shaped differently as the words of Scripture are examined from different perspectives and with different emphases. According to Lindbeck, such a shaping of Scripture has two sources: (a) the cultural and historical setting of the inquirer and (b) the Spirit of God who presents Scripture with a particular emphasis in mind. Lindbeck's point is that a plurality of interpretations is possible without violating the integrity of Scripture.

This phenomenon of multiple meanings—that is, hearing Jesus speak differently to different individuals—leads to an inevitable question: how does a faith community prevent theological chaos from emerging out of the multiple meanings arising among its own members or in its relationships with other faith communities? Lindbeck answers that there must be a "devout and unabashed attachment to the full range of biblical claims, however incredible they may seem to either ancient or modern man."[29] God's full revelation must be genuinely acknowledged as the norm for Christian faith as presented in the varied scriptural witness to God's revelation and the creeds that interpret them.

In other words, provided that the creeds and confessions are not violated[30]—which, according to Lindbeck, constitute "the normative status for Christian faith of the scriptural witness to God's revelation"[31]—the richness of diversity is to be understood as a plus, not a minus, for the church. He notes, for example, the great diversity of theological interpretations evident in such theologians as Barth, Pannenberg, Metz, Küng and Käsemann, yet writes approvingly that they are "genuinely united on the dogmatic level by their adherence to the common revelational center."[32] He goes on to say that these same theologians will find themselves drawing closer together, not in an impoverishing uniformity, but in an enriching diversity of perspectives within what is recognizably the same faith.

Pluralism among larger traditional bodies. We have already observed that Lindbeck understood the "cross and resurrection to define the really real, the fullness of God's own identity,"[33] Jesus as "the One in whom alone full humanness resides,"[34] and the creed "Jesus is Lord" to affirm objective truth about the unsurpassable importance of "a historically identifiable person . . . for all human beings always and everywhere."[35] How then is the Christian tradition to relate to non-Christian traditions? Lindbeck's response may be clarified by phrasing it syllogistically:

1. *Since* postmodernism has identified reason to be dependent on language, and

2. *since* non-Christian traditions and cultures *do not* possess a language predicated on Christian concepts,

3. *then* incommensurable notions of truth will tend to reside in differing traditions so that even words like *God, truth* and *faith* would possess no common framework from which to seek a foundation for mutual understanding.[36]

A second syllogism builds on the conclusions of the first:

1. *Since* incommensurable notions of truth tend to form a barrier between Christian and non-Christian traditions that impede the possibilities of a common framework for mutual understanding, and

2. *since* integral to the worldview of the biblical text is the imitation of the "Lord by selfless service to neighbors quite apart from the question of whether this promotes conversions,"[37]

3. *then* the missionary task of Christians will not be to convert non-Christians to our notions of truth, but rather "to encourage Marxists to become better Marxists, Jews and Muslims to become better Jews and Muslims, and Buddhists to become better Buddhists (although admittedly their notion of what a 'better Marxist,' etc. is will be influenced by Christian norms)."[38]

Lindbeck leaves open the possibility of the conversion of non-Christians to the Christian faith through proselytization, but argues that the more normative approach would be dialogue without the intent of producing converts.[39] As such, Lindbeck maintains the dual conceptualizations of (a) living within the singular biblical worldview and (b) honoring the pluralism of ideas in a multicultural and multireligious world.

This view, of course, would raise the eyebrows of most Protestant evangelicals. After all, is not the Great Commission part and parcel of the Christian kerygma? Lindbeck's view, however, is grounded in a Barthian prolegomena. According to this perspective, it is foolhardy to attempt to convert an individual in whose heart the Spirit of God has not first spoken the *yes* of the gospel. All one can do is present one's own worldview. Such an approach will result in helping Marxists to become better Marxists since they are now influenced by Christian norms. Conversions will take place only as the Spirit of God assists in this process.

THE QUESTION OF ANTIREALISM IN POSTLIBERALISM

My portrayal of Lindbeck as a middle-distance realist stands opposed to much of Christian scholarship that understands his system to be a Christianized version of antirealism. Since many of these same scholars find antirealism to be unacceptable to the Chrsitian faith, the postliberal paradigm has often been classified as a theological dead-end. With my portrayal of Lindbeck, I believe that insights not previously considered will come to the fore and demonstrate the possibilities of his system in advancing theology past the *Cogito* and to something that is not only genuinely post-*Cogito* but also useful to Christian theology.

This negative assessment of Lindbeck's approach centers on a particular reading of *The Nature of Doctrine*. Lindbeck wrote this book in the middle of his career, and it reflects his own theological pilgrimage at that time in his life. Published twelve years after he began his exploration of the postmodern rubric and how it may have legitimate theological application in the Christian faith, the book was a search for common ground between these two systems. The book was therefore intended to blaze a new trail for Christian theology. It was not a magnum opus—rather, it is better understood as a *terminus a quo* for Lindbeck, a new beginning from which to think. And, typical of innovative thinkers, it was sometime later that Lindbeck took note of important perspectives not considered within the book.

In the forward to the German translation, written ten years after the book's first publication, Lindbeck noted this lack, acknowledging that much was "missing from this book."[40] Among the book's deficiencies, he commented upon his failure to adequately dialogue with the theologies of Thomas Aquinas and Martin Luther.[41]

Another problem with *The Nature of Doctrine* was the unbalanced treatment Lindbeck gave to postmodernism. In the book, he gave a wide berth to Wittgenstein's postmodern epistemology, with special emphasis on the "language game" concept. Yet his critique of Derridá is absent, not to emerge in his writings until 1988, four years after the publication of *The Nature of Doctrine*. Accordingly, in *The Nature of Doctrine* one finds Lindbeck exploring the parameters from which Christian theology could positively accommodate the postmodern paradigm. Only in later writings did he move in an opposite direction, exploring the liabilities of postmodernism. Only as Lindbeck gave adequate consideration to postmodernism's strengths and weaknesses did balance appear in his "new hermeneutical setting." With this balance, Lindbeck emerged as a middle-distance realist.

The problem with much of Christian scholarship is that it critiqued *The Nature of Doctrine* on its own merits, not taking into consideration what Lindbeck wrote before and after that book. Two scholars who attended the Wheaton College Theology Conference, mentioned above, reflect this limited understanding of Lindbeck's theology. Alister E. McGrath has referenced Lindbeck in a number of his books, yet the citations are almost always limited to *The Nature of Doctrine*. Miroslav Volf's analyses are similar. By restricting their understanding of Lindbeck to *The Nature of Doctrine,* these two scholars operate on the assumption that this book is a balanced treatment of Lindbeck's postliberal paradigm—that it is his magnum opus, so to speak—rather than only a part of a theological pilgrimage that was still in progress. Hence, it is understandable why they characterized Lindbeck as an antirealist and found his thinking to be only marginally helpful in advancing theology in the current postmodern age.

SUMMARY

Unlike the other three paradigms that we have already examined in this book, post-foundational middle-distance realism is a hybrid system that has attempted to holistically reflect both the individualistic nature of truth (as we have seen in postmodernism) and its universality (as we have seen in modernism). George Lindbeck is the principal spokesperson for this system, a theology commonly known as postliberalism.

A key to understanding this theological system is the recognition that truth does not begin with abstracted principles—a system that typifies modernism—but rather in language. And since language is the product of culture in its historical setting, this recognition appears to ground truth to culture and history, causing it to become relativized to different language groups. Yet, as we have observed in this chapter, this implication would only be true if the scope of truth were limited to this world; that is, if it were a closed system. What Lindbeck has done, however, is to think in terms of an open system—by introducing God and, specifically, divine actions and language into the theological mix. Truth still begins with language, yet now God is understood as one of the speakers. As such, the problem with postmodernism is that it does not go far enough. It has failed to consider the possibility that not only do differing peoples and communities speak, but God also speaks. Truth must incorporate this wider range of language.

QUESTIONS

Basic Concepts

1. According to Lindbeck, in what respect did Derridá misrepresent the Christian religion?

2. Lindbeck argued that Derridá's system is *theologically* flawed. What was the nature of that flaw?

3. Lindbeck also argued that Derridá's system is *philosophically* flawed. What was the nature of that flaw?

4. Lindbeck explained God as interpenetrating the world with the "Word incarnate" (i.e., the Christ-event) and his authoritative witness of "a privileged text and privileged mode of interpretation." Recognizing that postmodernism argues that language precedes knowledge, how can this first move by God be understood as postmodern?

5. In Lindbeck's system, the middle-distance epistemology is further brought to light by two caveats related to these sources of witnesses. What are these two caveats?

6. How does Lindbeck understand theological pluralism for the individual believer?

7. How does Lindbeck understand theological pluralism in the religious community?

8. How does Lindbeck understand theological pluralism among religious traditions?

Further Thought

1. In this chapter, Lindbeck's epistemology is described as a middle-distanced realism. In your own words, described the nature of this epistemology.

2. What is the significance of the word of the community (little *w*) being replaced by the Word of God (big *w*) as the grounding for truth?

3. Much of Christian scholarship interprets Lindbeck's *The Nature of Doctrine* as advocating an antirealist epistemology, yet much of Lindbeck's other writings suggests a realist epistemology. Explain some of the reasons for this apparent contradiction within Lindbeck's writings and some reasons he can be seen as a realist.

4. Lindbeck also explained God interpenetrating the world through existential and always-contemporaneous divine words that possess a fixed meaning only the moment they are spoken. How can this move by God be understood as postmodern?

Absolute Truth
Revisited

In chapter one of this book, we observed that absolute truth has a dark side. Its dark side arises from the encyclopedic collection of abstracted principles understood to be universally and timelessly valid. Also in that chapter, the methodology of the Cartesian *Cogito* was clarified, noting how it has given rise to this dark side in contemporary Western culture. Finally, it was argued that this dark side of absolute truth needs redress and correction.

Nevertheless, many readers may still be troubled by this assertion. If no such encyclopedic collection of truths exists, they would say, then the whole notion of absolute truth must also not exist. Yet, from a Christian perspective, how can this be? After all, is not the following an encyclopedic collection of truths: "You shall not murder. You shall not commit adultery. You shall not steal. You shall not give false testimony against your neighbor. You shall not covet" (Ex 20:13-17a)? If these five moral declarations—located in the Ten Commandments given by God to Moses—are not universally and timelessly valid, then what are they?

This chapter will explore these concerns. We will do this by drawing from insights gleaned from the previous four chapters and, from these insights, track the direction of this theological discussion.

Our journey will require us to construct a different paradigm for conceptualizing absolute truth. Rather than thinking of absolute truth as impersonal and inanimate, we will turn this paradigm on its head, so to speak, by defining absolute truth in terms of personality and animation.[1] This, of course, will blend our definitions of God and absolute truth. Such a paradigm shift has biblical precedence. In the upper room just prior to his arrest and crucifixion, Jesus said: "I *am* the way and the truth and the life" (Jn 14:6).

This new paradigm requires us to reconsider what we have thus far considered in this book. Up until now, the four positions within the postmodern debate have been understood in a fashion depicted by figure 7.1 below. With antipostmodernism and postmodernism serving as the terminal ends of the continuum, the four positions that we examined are foundational realism, post-foundational realism, post-foundational middle-distance realism and post-foundational antirealism.

Anti-Postmodern   **Postmodern**

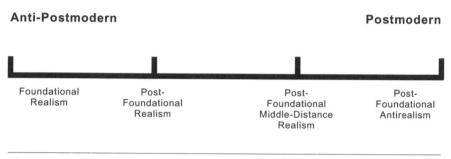

| Foundational Realism | Post-Foundational Realism | Post-Foundational Middle-Distance Realism | Post-Foundational Antirealism |

Figure 7.1

When we add the dimension of personal versus impersonal truth to the model, however, the paradigm undergoes a significant change. With this addition, two systems stand in opposition to one another. The first is labeled *personal truth* and the second *impersonal truth* (see figure 7.2). In the system of impersonal truth, antipostmodernism and postmodernism are understood as two functions located inside the same overall paradigm. Though previously we understood them to be in sharp conflict with one another (in one, truth is universalized; in the other, it is individualized), we now see a more fundamental commonality—in both absolute truth is impersonal and inanimate. In contrast, the opposing system of personal truth is more holistic in nature, capable of harmoniously incorporating both universal truth (characteristic of antipostmodernism) and individualized truth (characteristic of postmodernism) into a singular system. Personal truth is therefore plural (similar to postmodernism) and singular (similar to antipostmodernism). Because the system of personal truth is rendered synonymous with God, it carries the trinitarian implications of plurality and singularity held together in paradoxical tension.

We will explore this system of personal truth, noting its contrasts with the view of absolute truth that we examined in chapter one. As I commented in the introduction of this book, this and the following chapter draw on a number of differing voices within the Christian community that have been calling for a new system that can move theology past modernism and avoid the pitfalls of postmodernism.

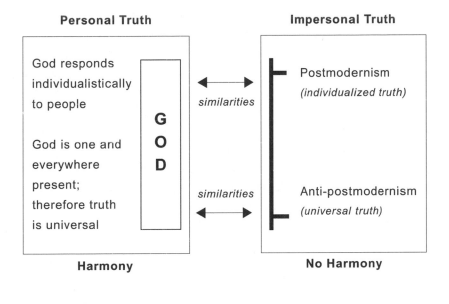

Figure 7.2

Our outline will be the following: (1) We will first look at an ancient document, the Magna Carta, noting its impact on the Western understanding of truth, particularly divine or sovereign truth. (2) We will then examine absolute truth in this new paradigm from three different perspectives: (a) with regard to God, especially the role of the Holy Spirit; (b) in light of the religious community and its doctrinal statements; (c) with respect to ecumenism. As we do so, we will draw insights from current scholarship that comments on such a paradigmatic move.

ABSOLUTE TRUTH AND THE MAGNA CARTA

Western culture holds a deep-seated assumption that law is more authoritative and fundamental than any sovereign or governmental ruler. This cultural assumption insists that *no one is—or should be—above the law.* Such thinking reaches back to the signing of the Magna Carta by King John of England in 1215.

The Magna Carta complex. With the signing of the Magna Carta, King John placed himself and all of England's future sovereigns and magistrates under the rule of law. This act was needed because of a long history of abuse by English sovereigns over their subjects. These kings tended to rule arbitrarily, enforce double standards and indulge in self-serving behaviors at the expense of their subjects. By 1215, the barons of England had taken enough of such abuse and demanded change. Codified law that resulted from the Magna Carta was designed to be impersonal and impartial, giving birth to a profound and far-reaching paradigm shift in how people of the West understood their rulers and the nature of law. Nobody, not even the king, was above the law.

The Magna Carta, however, not only impacted Western culture's approach to civil law. It also impacted its understanding of divine law. Like any other sovereign, God too was believed to be bound to a codified law that obligated him to certain behaviors. Hence, the tendency among Christians in the West has been to read the Bible in order to find a message behind the text—impersonal and impartial spiritual principles that constitute the real authority to which one must submit. That is to say, Western Christians tend to look for something behind God, something more authoritative than God, something predictable and reliable, some list of spiritual rules and regulations that will guarantee success if one only discovers them. As Larry Crabb Jr. explains in his book *Connecting: Healing for Ourselves and Our Relationships,* Christians are not seeking a relationship with God as much as they are seeking spiritual formulas by which to order their lives.

But what if there is nothing behind God? What if God does not point to some inanimate and impersonal absolute truth as the final divine arbitrator? What if, instead, when pointing to absolute truth God points to himself?[2] When we make this fundamental change in our understanding of God and absolute truth, we open the door to a peculiar form of pluralism: this truth is both singular *and* plural. It is singular since God is one. It is diverse since God's personality is multilayered, open to a wide range of responses.

The biblical record itself attests to this range of responses. The same God who said, "you shall not murder" (Ex 20:13) and "if someone strikes you on the right cheek, turn to him the other also" (Mt 5:39), and who exemplified this behavior in Jesus Christ when he refused to defend himself when struck in the face just prior to his own crucifixion (Jn 18:22), also ordered what seems to some to be equivalent to a religious *jihad* and genocide of the Hittites, Amorites, Canaanites, Perizzites, Hivites and Jebusites occupying the Promised Land (Deut 20:16-18; Josh 6:17, 21; 10:1). The same God who said that a church overseer should be the husband of one wife (1 Tim 3:2) also sanctioned polygamy as something good (Deut 21:15-17; 2 Sam 12:8). The same God who said, "you shall not covet" (Ex 20:17), also ordered the building of an ornate temple with an abundance of gold and precious stones (Ezra 1:2-5; 2:68-69). The same God who said, "you shall not make for yourself an idol in the form of anything in heaven above" (Ex 20:4), also ordered the making of a statue of two gold cherubim to be placed on the cover of the ark of the covenant (Ex 25:18). The same God who said, "you shall not give false testimony" (Ex 20:16), also blessed Rahab for giving false testimony to the leaders of the city of Jericho when she hid the two Israelite spies (Josh 6:17). And so on.

In short, God (or absolute truth) cannot be understood in the abstract— the domain of impersonal and inanimate rules. We need the context of story where truth can live and breathe. Only then can we make sense of the complexity and seeming contradictions of God's moral choices.

Narrative theology. Many scholars committed to the idea of narrative theology are calling for a paradigm shift in our understanding of truth. Brent Curtis and John Eldredge make the case for narrative theology on a devotional level. They write:

> We have lived for so long with a "propositional" approach to Christianity, we have nearly lost its true meaning. . . . Our rationalistic approach to life, which has dominated Western culture for hundreds of years, has [left us with] a faith that is barely more than mere fact-telling. Modern evangelicalism reads like an IRS 1040 form: It's true, all the data is there, but it doesn't take your breath away.[3]

In other words, it's dead. Curtis and Eldredge argue that since (a) we are a collection of our own stories and are understandable as the stories of our lives are recounted, and since (b) God—and thereby truth—is understandable in the context of his story, then (c) we will apprehend divine truth as our individual stories are seen in the broader context of God's larger story. Their argument resists propositional Christianity that is characterized, as they put it, like an IRS 1040 form, and calls instead for the personalization of truth seen in the context of interconnecting stories between God and human beings.

Stanley Grenz, a theologian that we examined earlier in this book, also argues against the notion of an impersonal message "behind the text." Grenz and coauthor John Franke write:

> The biblical message is the norming norm for theology. In saying this we must be careful not to posit a nebulous, ethereal "something" standing behind the text to which we have at best only limited access. Rather, the biblical message is in some important sense bound to the canonical text itself.[4]

And the canonical text, they maintain, is essentially a story. This is even true of the propositional statements (e.g., the Ten Commandments) located in the canonical text. Since they are presented in the context of a narrative, they tend to float aimlessly when abstracted from that narrative. Grenz and Franke's point is that the locus of revelation, and hence the biblical message, is a sacred story. God's activity is revelation—his active intervention in human life that can be recounted as a story. It reaches its height in God's action in Jesus Christ—the Christ-event.[5]

Absolute truth in stereo. When we understand truth as personal and animate, it becomes living and dynamic. It is a truth that moves, shapes and acts—one most clearly seen as the stories of our lives intersect with and are understood in the context of God's larger story. This, of course, implies that truth may be shaped differently for various people since their stories and how they are contextualized into God's larger story may be different.

Take the various theories of the atonement. Throughout church history two paradigms have dominated theological thought: liberation and sacrifice. In the first, Christ is understood as victor; in the second, as victim. Both are present in the New Testament, sometimes so close as to be taught in the same or adjacent sentences (e.g., Col 2:13-15).

Each paradigm has dominated at different points in church history. During the patristic period the liberation paradigm dominated, "with the result that the story of Christ's saving work was increasingly retold in terms of his victorious struggle unto death against demonic powers. . . . It could scarcely have been otherwise in the devil-ridden world of late antiquity."[6] Here the sacrifice motif was not denied, but neither was it emphasized. "It was not until the eleventh century and only in the West" that the liberation motif was replaced by an interpretation "for which vicarious sacrifice was central and the crucified Christ was first of all victim, not victor."[7] Anselm's *Cur Deus homo?* laid the groundwork for this paradigm shift in which the emergence of the feudal world and its system of justice offered fertile ground for this theory of the atonement to grow and eventually dominate Western thought. A generation after Anselm, Peter Abelard advanced the moral influence theory of the atonement. "When linked to a high Christology," Lindbeck comments, "This has been a powerful component of all Western atonement teaching.   . . . Without a high Christology and strong doctrine of grace, however, the moral influence view degenerates into a Pelagianism."[8]

Rather than looking at these differences in church history as evidence that in different epochs the church got the doctrine of the atonement wrong, the paradigm shift being considered in this chapter points to another possibility: different epochs ask different questions, and the Spirit of God may have responded to these questions by shaping an understanding of the Christ event differently. That is, instead of arguing that the doctrine of the atonement was lost to the church shortly after the first century and was not rediscovered until the sixteenth (as Protestants are prone to argue), we should consider the possibility that the Spirit of God offered bona fide presentations of the doctrine in intervening centuries that were not forensic (or Protestant) in orientation. Even within Protestantism today differences exist: a Reformed understanding of the atonement, for example, typically differs from a Wesleyan understanding.

In this respect, Lindbeck's words are particularly helpful: "God speaks particular words in particular settings to his people by means of the Bible."[9] This is true not only between epochs but in contemporary settings. The way in which the Spirit of God prompts a missionary to present the gospel in an animistic and aboriginal culture, for example, may differ from the way the Spirit prompts another missionary situated in a technologically oriented culture. People of animistic and aboriginal cultures, typically more sensitive to the demonic realm than technologically oriented cultures, may find the liberation motif more understandable. Similarly, the Spirit may prompt a person to present the gospel to a child one way while prompting another person to present the gospel to an adult in another way. Small children, who tend to be inclined toward the *quid pro quo,* may find the liberation model of the atonement more understandable than the forensic (legal) model. The biblical narrative can accommodate these and other variations due to the richness of the Christ-event.

ABSOLUTE TRUTH AND THE HOLY SPIRIT

This paradigm shift, however, elicits a question. By opening the door to pluralism in our understanding of absolute truth, have we not also opened the door to relativism, albeit a Christian version of it? This was the charge levied against Lindbeck following the publication of his book *The Nature of Doctrine* in 1984. The concern is that when truth is understood to take on differing shapes (or language games, as Wittgenstein explained) we are then free to shape truth as we wish, in ways that fit our own agendas, that skirt issues we may find uncomfortable or convicting. It also disallows any disagreement with other systems that we would otherwise assess as heretical (e.g., Mary as coredemptrix, redemption through good works, the nonexistence of life after death). So, by opening the door to pluralism have we not, albeit unintentionally, unleashed a pandorean cacophony of evil to spread throughout the world?

The answer to this question is *no;* in opening the door to pluralism we have not opened the door to relativism. Since truth and God are now understood to be one and the same, it is God who speaks and acts and who thereby shapes truth for us. God sets the agenda, and this is where we need to consider the role of the Holy Spirit in this process.

The reciprocal relationship of the Holy Spirit and the Word. Rather than merely being subordinated to the Word, the Holy Spirit has a reciprocal relationship with the Word, some scholars argue. D. Lyle Dabney, for example, has observed, "On the one hand, the Spirit of Christ grounds Christ and, on the other hand, is grounded by Christ."[10] Scripture gives evidence of such reciprocity.

First, Scripture demonstrates a divine priority of the Spirit over Jesus. According to the Synoptic Gospels, for example, Jesus was established by the Spirit of God from the beginning: he was incarnated by means of the Spirit (Mt 1:20; Lk 1:35), the Spirit descended upon Jesus at his baptism in the form of a dove (Mk 1:10; Lk 3:22). It was the Spirit who drove Jesus into the desert to be tempted by the devil (Mk 1:12; Lk 4:1). Moreover, the Synoptic Gospels report that after the time of temptation in the desert he returned to Galilee and performed numerous miracles through the power of the Spirit (Lk 4:14; Mt 4:23-24). Peter summarized the authenticity of Jesus' whole ministry as a unique anointing of the Spirit (Acts 10:38).

Second, Scripture also demonstrates a divine priority of Jesus over the Spirit. Here it is not so much Jesus as bearer of the Spirit but rather as the sender of the Spirit. According to Paul, the Spirit of God is first and foremost the Spirit of Jesus (Acts 16:7). Paul also observed that when a person has faith in Christ, God sends "the Spirit of his Son" into his or her heart, declaring "*Abba,* Father" (Gal. 4:6). According to the apostle John, the Father will send the Holy Spirit in the name of Christ (Jn 14:26). Furthermore, Jesus said, "But I tell you the truth: It is for your good that I am going away. Unless I go away, the Counselor will not come to you; but if I go, I will send him to you" (Jn 16:7).

Hence, neither the Word nor the Spirit is hierarchically dominant. As the Holy Spirit is elevated to a reciprocal relationship with Jesus, new horizons come into view for Western Christianity's understanding of the Holy Spirit. Here he becomes more active in the shaping of theology as he leads, anoints and empowers theological discussion and guides in its advancement. On the one hand, the activity of the Spirit remains in close coordination with the Christ-event, neither originating nor contributing any novel truth. On the other hand, in new historical contexts and in response to new challenges, the Spirit reveals the truth of Christ in ways that none of the apostolic witnesses could have anticipated, these witnesses having been limited to the culture and historical milieu of the first-century church.[11]

This understanding of the reciprocal relationship between the Spirit and Word stands opposed to the typical understanding in the Western tradition, which has emphasized the Word.[12] Here the Spirit's prime responsibility has been to remain in the shadows and validate the Word so that the Word can do his work in the mind and life of the individual believer. According to Dabney, the Western tradition has so subordinated the role of the Holy Spirit that it has resulted in his "irrelevance and speechlessness"[13] in the Christian faith. Much of the Spirit's relational dynamics has therefore been lost by such a truncated understanding of his essence and role.[14]

Plural portraits of Christ. Existing in a reciprocal relationship with the Word, the Holy Spirit's role can be recognized as much larger than is typical in the Western church. Rather than being little more than the one who endorses the Word as authoritative and divine, he is understood as the one who leads the Word into new arenas of theological expression.

Thomas Smail explains that we should think of the Spirit as an artist whose one subject is the Son, yet who paints portraits of that subject "on countless human canvases using paints and brushes provided by countless human cultures and historical situations."[15] Nevertheless, no image on any portrait, he explains, is what the Son is not, merely formed in our likeness and conforming him to our preferences and predilections. Rather, by using ever new cultural approaches and historical situations, the Spirit brings out more of the infinite variety of the saving truth that is in the Son. Smail asserts, in addition, that no portrait can ever capture the subject completely:

> Christian churches and people, sharing the concerns, the language, the questions, the achievements and the sufferings of the lands and times in which they live, are the raw materials that he uses to fashion ever new portraits of Jesus. They will all show him in his basic self-identity and continuity, but they will all make explicit something that was implicit from the first but that now the divine artist highlights and offers to our faith and love with new clarity and emphasis.[16]

These raw materials of culture and history provide ever new looks (or perspectives) on this truth. This is because the truth of Christ can be presented in an infinite variety of ways, since the Christ event itself is inexhaustible in breadth and depth. Such an understanding of the Holy Spirit gives room for religious pluralism while at the same time affirming a singular absolute truth. Jesus Christ is this singular absolute truth.

We can gain an appreciation of such breadth and depth with a casual review of church history. Beginning with the apostolic period itself, each of the four gospels presents a differing portrait of Christ. Though different, a common thread runs through all four: Christ is presented as a commoner born in the humblest of circumstances and who died an ignoble death. This contrasts sharply with the presentation of Christ in the book of Revelation, which reveals him to his servant John in great power, authority and glory. Moving closer to the present day, the way in which Christ was revealed to the Black churches in the United States during the Civil Rights Movement of the 1960s—when Christians engaged in nonviolent protest against bigotry— contrasts sharply with the way in which Christ is revealed to many of the indigenous peoples of Latin America who have chosen not to publicly protest injustices committed against them. The way in which Christ was revealed to Allied soldiers who fought Hitler during the Second World War stands in contrast to the way in which he was revealed to the Quakers and similar religious groups who chose to be conscientious objectors (pacifists) during that war. Regarding another dimension, the way in which Christ is revealed in churches with formal liturgies (e.g., Roman Catholicism, Episcopalianism, Lutheranism) differs from how he is revealed in churches typified by informal liturgies (e.g., Baptists, independents, charismatics). In each portrait, an aspect of the reality of Christ has been and is being presented, distinct from the others, yet arguably true to the integrity of the real Christ.

What is more, each portrait comes into existence through the creative power of the Holy Spirit who reveals Christ as he wishes to whom he wishes.

How do we know if the portrait we see being painted is indeed of the Holy Spirit? Of course, not all portraits should be automatically deemed legitimate. To do so would allow into our theology what is not true to the reality of God and his creation.

Distinguishing genuine from false requires the presence of some theological controls. As we have seen above, all such portraits should be Christocentric, grounded in the facticity of the Christ-event (e.g., incarnation, crucifixion, resurrection, ascension), presented in Scripture and in conformity to the early ecumenical councils (specifically First Nicaea, First Constantinople and Chalcedon). With this in mind, we would likely need three additional characteristics to accurately recognize portraits as painted by the Holy Spirit:

- A commitment to the statement "Jesus is Lord," quite likely the earliest of the apostolic creeds (cf. Rom 10:9; 1 Cor 12:3), and to the two Great Commandments (loving God and loving one's neighbor with all one's strength, heart, soul and mind), statements located in the Jewish *Shema* (Deut 6:4) and central to Jesus' *kerygma* (Mt 22:39-40).

- A well-developed awareness of the social and spiritual concerns of one's contemporary world and how they either conform to or oppose the notions of "Jesus is Lord" and the two Great Commandments.

- A recognition that the Holy Spirit does not speak singularly to an individual but rather to a whole body of believers (e.g., Acts 13:1-2).

This final characteristic carries within it an important implication: a Spirit-driven portrait of Christ will not remain restricted to an isolated group or individual but rather will resonate within a broad Christian community.

Especially noteworthy are the words of the ancient Jewish scholar Gamaliel, spoken sometime during the fourth decade of the first century. Speaking to Jewish authorities critical of the leaders of the budding Christian religion, he said, "If their purpose or activity is of human origin, it will fail. But if it is from God, you will not be able to stop these men; you will only find yourself fighting against God" (Acts 5:38-39). That is, the beliefs of a given community, if they are accompanied by the power and blessings of the Spirit of God, will naturally take root, bring forth a genuine aspect of the divine life and prevail even in a hostile environment. As such, provided that a portrait of Christ conforms to the other characteristics, this final attribute offers a compelling argument that it is indeed Spirit-driven.

ABSOLUTE TRUTH AND DOCTRINAL STATEMENTS

Having examined this paradigm shift regarding absolute truth from the perspective of the role of the Holy Spirit, we will now turn our attention to the role of individual religious communities. The question before us here asks, if absolute truth is personal and animate and, through the work of the Holy Spirit, shapes truth to the specific cultural and historical concerns of a religious community, can it be objectified in written doctrinal statements? The answer is *yes,* provided that certain conditions are met. We will consider three such conditions.

1. Doctrinal statements should avoid the sense of universality. The paradigm shift to personal and animate truth eliminates the possibility that doctrinal statements and systematic theologies have universal validity. This is because, as we already observed, the doctrinal differences among religious communities may not necessarily raise a question of false doctrine or theology. Rather, the Holy Spirit may be painting differing portraits of the Word in differing religious communities, all of which maintain the essential integrity of Jesus Christ in the process. In this respect, Stephen Toulmin is correct in his observation that in a time of

> increasing interdependence, cultural diversity and historical change, the intellectual task before natural and social scientists is not to build new, more comprehensive systems of theory with universal and timeless relevance, but to limit the scope to even the best framed theories and fight the intellectual reductionism that became entrenched during the ascendancy of rationalism.[17]

Therefore, Toulmin goes on to say, we should "pay less attention to stability and system, [and] more attention to function and adaptability."[18]

Such thinking, of course, goes against a long tradition within much of Protestant Christianity. Following the logic of the scientific method, scholars attempted to understand the essence of Scripture with scientific precision that made conclusions fixed and universal. This, of course, required these scholars to begin their analyses with the premise of radical doubt. Hence, as per the *Cogito,* all ecclesial confessions and creeds were doubted and set aside. Exegesis was limited to Scripture alone as the object of study and the scientific method as the chosen procedure. Charles P. Arand explains:

The Reformation signaled a shift in emphasis by its appeal to the Bible as the sole authority in matters of faith, but even it did not make the decisive move toward complete independence for biblical studies from the ecclesial tradition. The term "biblical theology" first came into prominence in the seventeenth century among both pietists and rationalists. The pietists wanted a theology based solely on the Bible. The rationalists called for a return to the simple and historical religion of the Bible apart from the complex dogmatics and ecclesiastical formulations.[19]

The results of the analyses of these third- and fourth-generation Protestants (seventeenth century) were doctrinal statements that they believed to be fixed and universal—carved in stone, so to speak, since they passed the rigors of scientific analysis.

Yet, when absolute truth is understood as personal and animate, studying truth with pure objectivity becomes an elusive goal. Absolute truth is not a thing to be studied, quantified and qualified. Rather, absolute truth is a person to be known (Jn 14:6), a person who has the freedom to reveal himself differently to different individuals and religious communities. In reference to the construction of doctrinal statements, two implications emerge from this insight.

A. Doctrinal statements should prioritize the biblical worldview over all other worldviews. Since God has chosen the canonical documents (Old and New Testaments) as the privileged mode of revelation and the early ecumenical councils as the authoritative interpretation of those canonical documents, the biblical/patristic worldview should be prioritized over and against the cultural norms of all other worldviews. Doctrinal statements, then, should be grounded in the biblical worldview—we are to fit our own lives into the biblical worldview rather than the other way around. Erich Auerbach explains that this move requires that we

feel ourselves to be elements in its structure of universal history. . . . Everything else that happens in the world can only be conceived as an element in that sequence; into it everything that is known about the world . . . must be fitted as an ingredient of the divine plan.[20]

And, he maintains, the divine plan has been revealed most completely in the canonical documents.

B. No singular doctrinal summation should be understood to wholly grasp the essence of the biblical worldview. This implication arises because the biblical worldview is itself enormously complex and inexhaustibly deep.

As various questions are asked, different perspectives of this same biblical reality emerge. One can no more wholly harness the message of the biblical world through theological analysis than a single psychological profile can provide an exhaustive analysis of a specific human subject. In both cases, a range of differing paradigms and summations are possible as differing questions are asked and different aspects of the life examined and experienced. Hence with intellectual humility we should bow to the limitations of finitude (creation) and recognize the impossibility of a single doctrinal summation harnessing in its entirety the reality of the biblical text and worldview. We should do this, however, not with a sense of frustration or failure but with a sense of anticipation and excitement. The juxtaposition of differing doctrinal summations offer the possibility to expand theological horizons. As was already noted, since absolute truth is a person, a level of plurality should be expected: differing summations, consequently, do not necessarily point to contradiction. As Hans W. Frei writes, "All this is to say that there are many ways of making sense of these [biblical] stories."[21]

2. Doctrinal statements should be divided into a two-tiered system where both the singularity and plurality of truth are respected. A two-tiered system is necessary to divide those articles that establish the parameters of orthodoxy (e.g., the doctrine of the Trinity, the hypostatic union) from those articles that merely distinguish the particularities of differing ecclesial bodies within the parameters of orthodoxy (e.g., the mode of baptism; the question of eternal security). These two tiers are the following:

- *The Top Tier:* The top tier corresponds to the creeds of the early church that have historically defined orthodoxy. They should be restated in the vernacular of our current culture rather than merely repeat word-for-word the original creedal statements.

- *The Bottom Tier:* The bottom tier corresponds to the particular distinctives of individual ecclesial bodies. It provides opportunity for insights that have been acquired since the first century that particular ecclesial bodies wish to emphasize and with which they want to be identified.

This division within doctrinal statements eliminates the attempts of theologians to make a claim of totality. Such claims are wrong-headed for the following reasons:

A. When one makes such a claim of totality, it assumes that the finite can contain the infinite—something that is a logical impossibility. Theologians who author such a comprehensive system are believed "to say everything, and not to leave any point unconsidered. All the statements must fit in with one another without contradiction, and the whole architecture must be harmonious, an integrated whole."[22] Moltmann elaborates:

> Because it only recognizes its own premises and only wants to have its own conclusions accepted, it comes forward with an absolute claim. In Christian theology, particularistic thinking is schismatic thinking. The divisions of the church are its premise, and it deepens these divisions through controversial "distinctive" doctrines. . . . The differences are used to stabilize our own limited identity.[23]

In other words, it reflects an unhealthy self-centeredness since the articulation of such a theology requires the theologian to assume that his or her particular system has achieved what all previous and all future systematic theologies fail to achieve.

B. When one makes the claim of totality, the theologian assumes that he or she has somehow sidestepped the influence of the *Zeitgeist* (spirit of the times), a move that many scholars believe to be impossible. The *Zeitgeist* dictates how thought is shaped in a given culture and historical moment. It provides assumptions that are so subtle and pervasive that thinkers uncritically buy into them and shape their thoughts accordingly. Paul Holmer notes, we "are victims of the '*Zeitgeist*,' not its master."[24] William Placher adds that the *Zeitgeist* "shapes the questions one asks, the assumptions one can make, and the arguments that will be persuasive."[25] Likewise, Hans-Georg Gadamer comments that our point in history composes our horizon: "The horizon is the range of vision that includes everything that can be seen from a particular vantage point. Applying this to the thinking mind, we speak of narrowness of horizon, of the possible expansion of horizon, of the opening up of new horizons, etc."[26]

In short, since theological reflection cannot escape the *Zeitgeist,* it cannot be regarded as timeless and universal. Instead each doctrine is an attempt to resolve a theological problem from a finite view located somewhere in time. It is incomplete and incompletable, since it is never capable of seeing and understanding the whole—which, of course, would imply omniscience, an attribute that will always be beyond the reach of finite human minds. Moreover, assuming that the Spirit of God has revealed himself in a unique and comprehensive way to one community over another does violence to God's personality and discretion.

Rather than attempting to formulate a comprehensive system that stands in contrast to all other theologies within the church, a two-tiered system minimizes the triumphalism on a wide range of theological arguments. Beliefs located in the bottom tier take on the form of contributions open to debate rather than as a canonical rule that divides orthodoxy from heterodoxy. Moltmann continues:

> By using the word "contributions," the writer recognizes the conditions and limitations of his own position, and the relativity of his own particular environment. He makes no claim to say everything, or to cover the whole of theology. He rather understands his own "whole" as part of a whole that is much greater. He cannot therefore aim to say what is valid for everyone, at all times and in all places. But he will set himself, with his own time and his own place, within the greater community of theology. For him this means a critical dissolution of naïve, self-centered thinking.[27]

In other words, a two-tiered system reflects the phenomenon of family resemblances within the Christian faith. The top tier establishes the overall family resemblance. The bottom tier makes room for different looks within the family. This sense of unity *plus* diversity offers the church an opportunity to love one another, as Christ prayed in his high priestly prayer, and thereby be an effective witness to an unbelieving world (Jn 17:20-23).

In addition, the top tier is understood to escape the influence of the *Zeitgeist* since, as a question of faith, the doctrines of the early ecumenical councils were superintended by the Spirit of God in a fashion that sets them apart from all other theological reflection. This, of course, implies that the bottom tier is influenced by the *Zeitgeist*. Doctrines at this lower level, then, are never final or complete.

In short, doctrinal statements, therefore, should not be too comprehensive. When a doctrinal statement is too comprehensive, it (a) runs the risk of becoming dangerously seductive, since it offers a finality of Christian thought that for some people is attractive and comforting; (b) eliminates the need to think critically; (c) mutes the Holy Spirit, who may wish to speak afresh from Scripture to a given individual or community; and (d) breeds triumphalism, which discourages rather than encourages theological conversation across denominational or ecclesiastical boundaries.

3. We should seek conversation partners with Christians who affirm differing doctrinal statements. Setting aside the scientific method and its supposed universally regnant doctrinal summations and instead recognizing the role of "the language game" upon their own religious traditions, evangelical theologians would be properly humbled so that such crossdenominational conversation is possible.

The purpose of such conversation is not to convert but rather to learn and appreciate the differences of other traditions. This, of course, runs against the underlying pressure within much of Protestant evangelicalism to a search for the all-encompassing circle of truth (which we observed in chapter three) and then encourage all peoples everywhere to affirm the rightness of that circle. Though it is possible that falsehood indeed exists within either ours or our conversation partners' doctrinal statements, we would do well to train our ears to hear how the Spirit of God may indeed be working in differing theological systems. To some extent, a different theological system cannot be rightly understood unless one enters in and examines it as an insider.

Yet this can be done with only limited success, since if one actually did become an insider one would be no longer conversing but converted. Success in this analysis will be dependent on the extent in which inquirers train their spirits to sense the presence of and shaping of truth by the Holy Spirit. This requires more than an intellectual grasp of one's personal systematic theology. It requires a knowledge of how God has moved in the past (historical theology), is moving in the present (contemporary theology) and may move in the future (prophetic thinking). In the final analysis, it requires a knowledge of God (pietistic theology), for it is in the subtleties of our personal walk with God that we hear his quiet voice prompting our spirits in one direction or another, confirming or denying what we observe in our own and differing theological communities.

Hence, the purpose of such dialogue is to gain an appreciation of and perhaps adopt certain aspects of differing traditions into one's own without the pressure to embrace another system in its entirety.

ABSOLUTE TRUTH AND ECUMENICAL DIALOGUE

The paradigm shift that we have considered thus far in this chapter provides the parameters for a new understanding of ecumenism, one that is heterogeneous rather than homogeneous in nature. It is an understanding that makes room for various portraits of Christ painted by the Spirit. In this final section we will consider insights by Lindbeck. In 1976, he was commissioned by the Rockefeller Foundation to research the theological role and contributions of seven divinity schools. His findings have special interest for the shaping of a post-*Cogito* ecumenism.

Lindbeck's proposal. The Rockefeller Foundation commissioned Lindbeck to determine the quality of the "academically and intellectually responsible transmission"[28] of theological education. This project gave him an opportunity to assess top-ranked theological schools against the backdrop of his "middle-distance realism" hermeneutic. The divinity schools evaluated were the University of Chicago Divinity School, Harvard Divinity School, Vanderbilt Divinity School, Yale Divinity School, Union Theological Seminary, the Graduate Theological Union and the University of Notre Dame Department of Theology—institutions that are "de facto ecumenical, and academically impressive."[29] The Notre Dame Department of Theology was the only school not specifically nondenominational, being part of the Roman Catholic tradition. The ensuing report authored by Lindbeck was entitled *University Divinity Schools: A Report on Ecclesiastically Independent Theological Education.*

Lindbeck's overall assessment of these divinity schools was negative. He observed that their "educational policies . . . are diffuse and ill-focused"[30] and that therefore "their *raison d'être* has become questionable."[31] He explained that the nondenominational university schools have been viewed as outdated survivors from a more religious past. In the early nineteenth century the training of ministers was so central to higher education that there was no need for the existence of separate professional schools. Now, however, theological education continues in only a handful of secularized universities where it has become so firmly institutionalized in the form of divinity schools that these universities find it difficult to drop them, though they wish they could. What is more, these theological schools are

> also marginal to the churches, even to those which originally established the universities to which they are related. The churches have not been able to rely upon them for the ministers whom they need and have therefore founded their own denominational seminaries in which the overwhelming bulk of their clergy are educated. It would seem to make little difference to either religion or the academy if ecclesiastically independent and university related theological education disappeared.[32]

Nevertheless, provided that changes were made, Lindbeck understood the nondenominational university schools to possess an important role in theological education. If they can be typified by the following three characteristics, they could make unique contributions to advance the ecumenical agenda.

First, the character of university divinity schools in a nondenominational setting "should be academic, not occupational"[33] in orientation. That is, they "should capitalize on the strengths provided by their university connections, that they should emphasize what they can do distinctively better than most denominational seminaries, and this implies a special stress on the intellectual and scholarly side of ministerial preparation."[34] Since these divinity schools were already doing this, Lindbeck's point served merely to affirm their current practice.

Second, university divinity schools in a nondenominational setting should be "self-consciously particularistic."[35] The problem that he observed in these schools was that they emphasized a universalized religious education at the expense of particular theological heritages and were therefore overly generic, abstract and impractical. He compared them to a department of linguistics in which the phenomenon of language in general is studied but with no specialized concentration on any particular tongue or literature. As Lindbeck put it, "One can no more be religious in general . . . than to speak language in general. . . . [S]tudents tend to learn a little about a multitude of religious languages without mastering any particular one."[36] Yet Lindbeck argued that a nonparticularistic (acultural) theological education is de facto impossible and that any attempt to provide such an education will produce one that is distinctively nonreligious.

According to Lindbeck, theological education that is self-consciously particularistic enhances religious understanding. It does so because it concentrates on developing competence in the specific heritages that are at the heart of religious identity. The development of such an understanding involves not only an academic immersion, but also the holistic immersion of the student within a tradition.

> Required are both the ability to speak the language of a given tradition well (which many ordinary religious people can also do, just as the native speakers of a natural tongue can often, without formal instruction, employ it with unusual skill), and also training in its intellectually and academically critical and independent use. This requires long and disciplined study of an extensive body of religious lore.[37]

For this dynamic to occur, however, a theological institution must embrace specific heritages holistically—that is, academically, liturgically and socially.

Third, university divinity schools in a nondenominational setting should be "pluralistic as well as particularistic."[38] His point was that an effective

theological education in nondenominational schools must possess a multiplicity of particularistic traditions. It is here that they have an opportunity
unavailable in denominational seminaries, which, by definition, are limited
to a singular emphasis on the teachings of their particular denomination or
tradition. Being nondenominational, such institutions could function as a
"strategically placed interchange"[39] between the church and denominational
seminaries. Moreover, they should honestly recognize differences rather
than assuming a universalist underpinning for all the differing traditions.

Lindbeck maintained that these three characteristics would position the
church to hear the Holy Spirit present the truth of the Word of God in new
and creative ways. They couple religious particularism with pluralism so that
both are viably represented and neither dominates nor overcomes the other.

The "mere Christianity" of C. S. Lewis. This conceptualization of pluralism *and* particularism in the ecumenical conversation is not original
with Lindbeck. Though writing a generation earlier, C. S. Lewis posed the
same underlying argument in *Mere Christianity*. Lewis's purpose in the
book was to present the essential elements of Christianity. In the preface
to the book, he noted, "I have thought that the best, perhaps the only, service I could do for my unbelieving neighbors was to explain and defend
the belief that has been common to nearly all Christians at all times."[40] Yet
this effort at presenting a singular understanding of the Christian faith was
not intended by Lewis to minimize the importance of particular theological
traditions. He added:

> I hope no reader will suppose that "mere" Christianity is here put forward as
> an alternative to the creeds of existing communions as if a man could adopt
> it in preference to Congregationalism or Greek Orthodoxy or anything else. It
> is more like a hall out of which doors open into several rooms. If I can bring
> anyone into that hall I shall have done what I attempted. But it is in the rooms,
> not in the hall, that there are fires and chairs and meals.[41]

The "fires and chairs and meals" are Lewis's picture of the individual ecclesial traditions. The interconnecting hall is the "mere Christianity" common
to all. Lewis's point is that both the individual rooms and the interconnecting
hall are necessary for a correct understanding of the Christian faith. Yet one
lives and finds comfort in the individual rooms, not the interconnecting hall.
The hall is necessary so that one can walk from room to room and enjoy the
"fires and chairs and meals" of differing ecclesial traditions. Hence, Lewis's
metaphor points in the direction of both particularism and plurality, a cath-

olicity that constitutes a complex unity. It was not until the generation following Lewis that the specifics of theology caught up with his broad vision.

The "vocabulary of faith" of Kathleen Norris. Reflecting on the problem of attempts to minimize differences and assume a homogenized universality, Kathleen Norris comments:

> I had learned a great deal about the nature of Christian unity when I attended an ecumenical conference with people from nearly fifty denominations. As we discussed our differences, and in particular as we tried to devise a common worship for use at the conference, I learned that the most disruptive people were those who wanted to cling to the naïve pretense that we were really all alike. Only when we had come up hard against our differences could the group discover its essential unity. We could say the Lord's Prayer together, and the Apostles' Creed. We could invoke the Trinity in our doxologies, read from the Bible, and sing glorious hymns, from ancient texts to Afro-American spirituals. We could say, "Amen" and "Alleluia," "Lord, have mercy," and "Thank you, Jesus."
>
> Tension is a creative force. But polarization, which seems an abiding sin of our age, is worse than useless. It stifles creativity, whereas a healthy dose of negative capability, the ability to hold differences in tension while both affirming and denying them, enlivens both poetry and theology. In Christian history, it has sometimes meant the difference between unity and schism, offering a synthesis that provides a third way.[42]

It is this third way that Norris affirms. Though at times we have to put our feet down and insist on certain dogma and doctrine, this third way makes room for many issues that cannot be settled with a singular certitude. Rather, the lack of such certitude reflects the multilayered character of divine reality. Articulated in multilayered language, they express theological insights in terms of mystery and paradoxical tension, where we can get at truth only partially and are therefore in need of other perspectives. Only as theologians holistically embrace their own traditions and dialectically interact with other traditions can such theological advancement take place.

SUMMARY

In this chapter, we have examined the possibilities for a post-postmodern paradigm. Its distinctive characteristic is an understanding of truth in terms of personality and animation.

This paradigmatic move defines truth in terms of *the turn to relationship*. In the quest for knowledge, the first move consists of a requisite relationship between Creator and creature, the most fundamental of all relationships. As Dabney has correctly observed, "Indeed, prior to all other questions: the question of relationship."[43] This constitutes the true prolegomenon, the first move of all theology, or as Dabney asserts, a first theology for the twenty-first century.[44] Post-postmodernism therefore agrees with the book of Proverbs and its repeated statement, "The fear of the LORD [reverential relationship] is the beginning of knowledge/wisdom" (Prov 1:7; 9:10).

When such a shift in thinking occurs, fundamental rules in the theory of hermeneutics change. The door swings open to a peculiar form of pluralism: one that is both fixed in a *singular* understanding of absolute truth, since it is grounded in the one and true God, yet *plural,* since this singular God is personal, multilayered and therefore capable of responding differently in diverse situations. Understanding history—specifically, how the story of God and our individual stories intersect—is therefore a necessary component in our pursuit of truth.

This paradoxical nature of absolute truth (singular yet plural) is possible since the Spirit of God is no longer a mere endorser of the Word. Now the Spirit is understood to also lead and shape the Word, providing various perspectives of the Word to different individuals and religious communities. As such, the Holy Spirit is understood as an artist who paints differing portraits of Christ. He uses the cultural and historical situations of diverse religious communities as his canvas, paint and choice of brushes. Each portrait is true to the integrity of the real Christ, yet none provides a singular, definitive or exhaustive depiction.

This understanding of the Spirit's role in painting diverse portraits of Christ, in turn, opens the door to a new way of looking at doctrinal statements within specific ecclesial traditions and, indeed, the whole enterprise of ecumenism. In this respect, it provides new avenues in circumventing the nagging problem of triumphalism that has plagued the church in the past and prevents its advancement in the future.

QUESTIONS

Basic Concepts

1. In contrast to the view presented in chapter one, how is absolute truth understood in this chapter?

2. In what respect are modernism and postmodernism both aspects of the same overall paradigm?

3. What has been the role of the Magna Carta in the Western understanding of absolute truth? Specifically, what is the relationship between absolute truth and sovereign rulers?

4. Explain "the Magna Carta Complex" as it applies to theology.

5. How does a dynamic understanding of truth affect our understanding of the gospel (see page 164)?

6. When the Holy Spirit is led by the Word, how do the two relate to one another?

7. When the Word is led by the Holy Spirit, how do the two relate to one another?

8. Thomas Smail claimed that no portrait of Christ is ever complete. Why is this so?

9. What was George Lindbeck's solution to the problem of Christianity drifting away from orthodoxy and into heterodoxy?

10. If absolute truth is personal and animate and, through the work of the Holy Spirit, shapes truth to the specific cultural and historical concerns of a religious community, how can it be objectified in written doctrinal statements?

11. Describe the proposed two tiers for doctrinal statements (pp. 172-74).

12. Describe Lindbeck's overall assessment of university divinity schools.

13. What are the three changes that Lindbeck proposed for university divinity schools to make them relevant to the church?

14. Explain C. S. Lewis's metaphor of the hall and rooms as a description of the church.

15. According to Kathleen Norris, in what respect is "tension a creative force" in doctrinal differences between ecclesial bodies?

Further Thought

1. Read the first two chapters of *The Sacred Romance* by Brent Curtis and John Eldredge. Then contrast propositional Christianity with narrative Christianity.

What Now?

Having examined four dominant positions in the postmodern debate in the church and considered a possible advance in the debate offered by a paradigm shift from impersonal and inanimate truth to that which is personal and animate, we have yet to address questions related to this new paradigm from a pragmatic point of view. How would such a paradigm shift affect the church in its practical life? Would it advance the church toward a deeper sense of godliness or cause it to drift into godlessness? Would such a change provide new ways of solving old and seemingly unsolvable problems or would it merely aggravate such problems? In other words, does this new paradigm shift work in the real world?

In this chapter, we will take a pragmatic look at post-postmodernism from three perspectives: (a) one's individual faith, (b) one's relationship to the church and (c) one's understanding of evangelism. These perspectives should provide the reader with an initial sense of how the church would respond under this new rubric.

FAITH

Richard Bernstein coined the term "the Cartesian anxiety"[1] to describe how the philosophical foundation of doubt rather than faith generates a corresponding visceral state of anxiety within one's soul. This anxiety is a state of mind that demands airtight solutions to the large questions of life. If no such solutions are forthcoming, it aggravates a state of anxiety, causing one to either embrace pseudo-solutions, since they are deemed better than no solutions at all, or enter a state of heightened cognitive dissonance.

This anxiety, Bernstein explained, is grounded in Descartes's *Cogito,* a methodology we have already observed, in which radical doubt serves as the foundation to knowledge. Because the purpose of the *Cogito* is to remove doubt and establish truth on a firm foundation, if one cannot follow the methodology successfully, one's foundation is therefore not firm, causing the aggravation of one's anxiety. Yet understanding absolute truth as personal and animate undercuts the premise of the Cartesian anxiety. It removes the premise because it shifts the direction of inquiry from us seeking truth to truth seeking us. Questions of scientific scrutiny are replaced with questions related to the reality of relationship.

In *The Myth of Certainty,* a book treated in an earlier chapter, Daniel Taylor offers a telling illustration of the difficulties in making a break from the *Cogito.* He asked the students in one of his classes to read a book which told of the loss a Mexican-American felt when his learning of English alienated him from his Spanish-speaking family. One of his students wrote in response:

> I thought of the struggle I have had as I read and as new things became more important. Reading theology was more important than my job, than my family at times. I would lock myself in my room and read. The more I read the harder it was to communicate with my wife about things of the Lord. The old friends I had—I know they thought that I was backsliding in my faith. I read so much and such thought-expanding books that at times my head hurt like something inside was trying to get out. I kept telling myself, and at times I still do, that I wouldn't read any more theology—only the Bible. At times I felt like Jeremiah in his work: "When I say I will not speak in His name, there is like a fire within and I cannot contain it." Still . . . there is a loss. At times, I would like to go back but I can't—there is no way to retreat.[2]

Ricoeur's wager. Paul Ricoeur formulated the notion of a wager as an epistemological move where the quest for knowledge is grounded in *faith* rather than *radical doubt.* It corresponds to the Old Testament proverb, "The fear of the LORD is the beginning of knowledge" (Prov 1:7). According to this proverb, a repeated one in the book of Proverbs, the first step in the pursuit of knowledge is a personal and humble relationship with God. This is what one would expect if truth is understood in personal and animate terms. Moreover, the fear of the Lord implies worship, and worship implies faith. We can then draw the inference that the beginning of our journey into truth is faith—not doubt. That is to say, if radical doubt (i.e., a methodology that gives rise to a hermeneutics of suspicion) no longer serves as the fundamental premise from which we seek truth, we are free to begin our journey to knowledge with faith. Ricoeur explains the essence of this wager:

> A wager is a risk, a bet. In this case . . . we are betting that a hermeneutic of belief in the Christian gospel will be more fruitful for living in the world than skeptical conclusions produced by a hermeneutic of suspicion. We will not forget our doubts. But we will press on, trying to understand ourselves and the world around us in light of the symbols of divine revelation. The wager is a form of hypothetical belief, a self-entrustment to the world of meaning created by Christian language.[3]

We no longer insist that our faith should pass the test of objectivity with rigorous scientific scrutiny. Neither do we insist that our faith be grounded in a God who is so other-worldly transcendent that faith in such a deity draws our minds away from this-worldly concerns. Rather, our faith takes on the shape of hypothetical belief. We entrust ourselves to the world of meaning created by the canonical Scriptures, the creeds and the language of faith as articulated by the Christian community.[4]

Moreover, this wager takes us into theology's hermeneutical circle. Ricoeur comments, "We must understand in order to believe, but we must believe in order to understand."[5] Yet he goes on to say that the

> circle is not a vicious circle, still less a mortal one; it is a living and stimulating circle. We must believe in order to understand: never, in fact, does the interpreter get near to what his text says unless he lives in the *aura* of the meaning he is inquiring after. As Bultmann very well says in his famous article on "the problem of hermeneutics" in *Glauben und Verstehen:* "All understanding, like all interpretation, is . . . continually oriented by the manner of posing the question and by what it aims at [by its *Woraufhin*]. Consequently, it is never without presuppositions; that is to say, it is always directed by a prior understanding of the thing about which it interrogates the text. It is only on the basis of that prior understanding that it can, in general, interrogate and interpret."[6]

The hermeneutical circle requires that we live in "the aura of meaning," which implies that we cannot understand from afar, isolated with our own thoughts, insisting that we fully comprehend before we believe. Neither can we believe with a blind faith, a naivete where our faith rests in faith, taking no interest in facts that may invalidate what we believe to be true. Rather we must step out of the role of spectator and be placed in the worldview itself before we can begin to understand it and grow in faith and knowledge.

Our pursuit of truth is therefore characterized by a circle of faith/knowledge: it neither begins with knowledge that leads to faith nor begins with faith that leads to knowledge. Being so characterized, our quest does not possess a logical or fixed starting point. Ted Peters comments:

> What we are asking here is a post-Cartesian version of Saint Anselm's definition
> of theology as faith seeking understanding. Once we have entered the belief-
> understanding circle, the process of interpreting Christian symbols begins to il-
> lumine our own life and makes it understandable in relation to divine reality.[7]

The starting point actually lies beyond us, with the Holy Spirit who sovereignly places us inside the circle of faith/knowledge. Hence, when approaching the claims of the Christian faith, we are neither objectivists nor
subjectivists—rather, we are pneumatists. We understand ourselves to be
grounded in the Holy Spirit who places us within the hermeneutical circle
as we grow in faith/knowledge.[8]

Four corollaries. Ricoeur's wager gives rise to four corollaries. First,
practice in the Christian faith precedes the maturation of faith and knowl
edge. This is because movement within the circle is not an isolated or disconnected pursuit of faith or knowledge, but rather a Holy Spirit-guided
activity in the real world where faith and knowledge are holistically integrated into our lives at a practical level. Drawing upon Michael Polanyi's
famous illustration of bicycle riding, Lindbeck explains:

> If we first had to learn what balancing skills are required for the physical action
> by mastering the complex mathematical equations that most adequately (though
> still only very partially) represent them, we would still be falling off our training
> bikes. The same is true in the sciences and other intellectual disciplines. In these
> activities also the skills required greatly surpass the grasp of the methodological
> theory. . . . [T]he theory that is relevant to practice is not first learned and then
> applied, but rather is chiefly useful as part of an ongoing process of guarding
> against and correcting errors while we are engaged in practice.[9]

Lindbeck also draws from an insight from Aristotle's *Ethics,* where he observed that "those unpracticed in virtue do not recognize even theoretically
what virtue is."[10]

The role of practice as a precursor to knowledge and faith is again what
we should expect when truth is understood in personal and animate terms.
Truth lives. As we seek truth, truth seeks us. The pursuit of truth, then, is a
participatory endeavor. Drawn into the life of truth, we are drawn into community, introspection and practical application. Such a pursuit of truth, then,
forces us to abandon the role of spectator studying in the abstract.[11] That is
to say, the study of absolute truth (i.e., God) requires that we see ourselves

as relationally connected to that which we are studying. God is no longer the object and we the subject. Rather, a crisscrossing effect makes us and God both subject and object.[12] Peters's comments are again helpful:

> This process makes theology participatory . . . because the questions we pose regarding God becomes simultaneously questions God poses to us. We ourselves become part of the questioned reality. Who am I as a finite creature looking into the abyss of infinity? Who are we as mortal human beings standing in the face of an awesome and eternal holiness? When we reflect upon biblical symbols such as God's love, God's justice, and God's grace, we can but ask ourselves: am I loving? am I just? am I gracious? Or, what is my relationship to a God who is like this? Hence, to enhance our understanding of things divine is simultaneously to enhance our self-understanding.[13]

This crisscrossing effect is forcefully presented in the writings of Helmut Thielicke. As already noted, Thielicke ministered to the spiritual needs of the German people during and after the Second World War. During the post-war years, he was entreated by the dispirited German people to respond to a recurring question about where to find a gracious God (an endeavor in which the people were the subject and God the object of inquiry). In response, Thielicke challenged the very premise of the request. He explained that God, being omniscient and omnipresent, could see everything, especially those things that the German people were concealing behind their backs. What is more, God observed that each person's hand had lost what it should have held and, in holding "so many things it cannot let go," took the shape of a fist clenched against him. Thielicke concludes:

> In monologue or in terms of self-expression the question "How can I find a gracious God?" is merely religious psychopathy. But when we see that there is another figure on the other side of the table, and that the question is only part of the conversation preceded and followed by many other things, then it is deadly serious. . . . We are at the point where God asks, "Adam, where art thou?" (Gen 3:9), "Saul, Saul, why persecutest thou me?" (Acts 9:4), "Whom seekest thou?" (Jn 18:4), and not where man asks: "Where is God?" To be sure, man does this too. He asks concerning a gracious God. But now . . . the question has a very different quality. . . . [I]t is not the scrutinizing eye of man but the seeking, transfixing, demanding eye of God, which confronts us with ourselves and leads us to hell and back again. . . . If we are to have serious dealings with God it is essential that we be quiet and first of all do nothing but simply listen and let ourselves be questioned.[14]

It is only as we first grapple with God on this practical level that our faith/knowledge is properly positioned to grow. In this respect, then, practice preceding faith/knowledge alters the Enlightenment order that understands practice as the product of knowledge.[15]

Second, *involvement in a faith community also precedes the maturation of faith and knowledge.* We cannot grow in faith/knowledge independently of active participation in a local faith community (i.e., a church). This corresponds to Derridá's definition of **signifiers** (words) and **significations** (meanings), according to which we are "always already" in the loop of understanding as members of a community. The community in which we are members presses on us language, definitions and an ordering of reality at an intuitive level that serves as a foundation from which we then think and work through its implications. It is within such communities that we learn their inner logic and paradigmatic structures. Yet such learning is neither a form of cold rationalism (objectivism) nor an irrational leap of faith (subjectivism). Rather, the faith community provides the context for application (pragmatism) and the language (signifiers and significations) from which faith and understanding (the two components of the hermeneutical circle) can holistically mature together. Trust within this community is therefore necessary

> so that we can attend to the gospel, share the gospel's realm of meaning, and let it speak to us. . . . By betting that the gospel can be meaningful, we will open ourselves to the possibility of constructing a new self-understanding and a new world-understanding. Postcritical thinking is both personally participatory and world-constructive, or better, world-reconstructive. It is integrative and holistic consciousness at work.[16]

Though every community (Christian and non-Christian alike) should be characterized by such a hermeneutical circle, what distinguishes the Christian community from all others is the intervention of God in the circle, centered in the Christ-event (specifically, the incarnation, passion and resurrection of Jesus). Yet even here we are required to make a wager. Without any means to independently verify the facticity of Jesus' incarnation and resurrection (two events without which the Christian gospel collapses), we wager that they truly took place and that they therefore have relevance for us today. These events, of course, set the Christian tradition apart from all non-Christian traditions, legitimizing its own tradition and delegitimizing all others.

Third, *the believer possesses a sense of doubt mingled with his or her decision of faith*. One has this mixture because Ricoeur's hermeneutical circle denies the possibility of objective certainty since knowledge is no longer understood to be the starting point for the development of faith.[17] This doubt, however, serves a different purpose than it did for Descartes. For Descartes, radical doubt (the *Cogito*) was merely the starting point. Through inductive reasoning, the goal was to replace it with knowledge. In post-postmodernism, doubt is never wholly resolved and must therefore exist in the shadows of one's faith.

With unusual candor, Philip Yancey describes his decision of faith in Christ in such terms:

> Examining my own periods of faithlessness, I see in them all manner of unbelief. Sometimes I shy away for lack of evidence, sometimes I slink away in hurt or disillusionment, and sometimes I turn aside in willful disobedience. Something, though, keeps drawing me back to God. What? I ask myself.
>
> "This is a hard teaching. Who can accept it?" said Jesus' disciples in words that resonate in every doubter. Jesus' listeners found themselves simultaneously attracted and repelled, like a compass needle brought close to a magnet. As his words sank in, one by one the crowd of onlookers and followers slouched away, leaving only the Twelve. "You do not want to leave too, do you?" Jesus asked them in a tone somewhere between plaintiveness and resignation. As usual, Simon Peter spoke up. "Lord, to whom shall we go?"
>
> That, for me, is the bottom-line answer to why I stick around. To my shame, I admit that one of the strongest reasons I stay in the fold is the lack of good alternatives, many of which I have tried. *Lord, to whom shall I go?* The only thing more difficult than having a relationship with an invisible God is having no such relationship.[18]

Yancey wrote this after describing the seeming absence or indifference of God at the death of a young child following a serious illness. He could have added illustrations of fatal car accidents due to drunk drivers, children born with cerebral palsy, diagnoses of cancer, tornadoes, droughts. All such events test our faith. Still lacking objective assurances, in such moments we are left with the wager: will we wager our lives and our futures on the Christian worldview and on an invisible God whose actions sometimes make no sense? Without knowing with objective certainty, will we wager our lives and our futures that the Christian worldview and our understanding of God are right and that all other worldviews and all other understandings of God are therefore wrong?[19]

To refuse to make such a wager and, instead, insist that God make sense before we move forward in faith is an act of spiritual subversion. We turn around the order of the universe and become God's master. With a tone of irony, Thielicke argues that it is only natural for the Christian to reason in such a fashion:

> Aided by my intelligence, I make up my mind about him. I know how God "must" act, in order to be really God. He "must," for instance, be wise (wise in a way that I can understand). He "must" act in a way that makes sense and is best for me. He "must" enrich my life with happiness and perhaps also with suffering (we clever human beings also know something about the uses of suffering!). He "must" preserve our nation, for our nation knows it is called to a mission in the world, and that God and providence can only exist when this mission reaches fulfillment. God "must" do all kinds of things if he is to be acclaimed as the true God. God "must" turn stones into bread. He "must" be able to leap from the pinnacle of the Temple, if he is to be acclaimed as God. It would appear, therefore, that it is we ourselves who set the conditions which God must satisfy in order that we may proclaim him God. We are God's masters.[20]

Yet, Thielicke counters, the opposite is true. God is the Master. His ways are higher than our ways (Is 55:8-11). Sometimes, in fact, they are not only higher than our ways, they are enshrouded in mystery. Most Christians agree to this in theory, but "it looks very different when we meet it in everyday life, where our practice is diametrically opposed to our theory and we aspire to be the gods of God. And so we are immediately assailed by fresh doubts."[21] Nevertheless, it is precisely here where we are called upon to set our reason aside and choose to make the wager and live by faith. That is to say, even when God is not understandable and our doubts are not altogether settled, we are faced squarely with that passage of Scripture, "the righteous will live by faith" (Rom 1:17; Gal 3:11; cf. Hab 2:4; 3:16-19; Heb 10:38) and are called on to live within that spiritual reality.

Doubt for the believer also takes on another form. James McClendon Jr. and James M. Smith describe this as the principle of fallibility. They argue that "even one's most cherished and tenuously held convictions might be false and are in principle always subject to rejection, reformulation, improvement, or reformation."[22] This, of course, corresponds to Luther's *ecclesia reformata, ecclesia semper reformada* (the reformed church is the church ever reforming itself). Hence, the believer reads the Bible and gleans insights with a tentativeness, a provisionality. This attitude contrasts with the triumphalism latent in many churches where a sense of objective finality is believed to have been achieved and all doubts removed. As Edgar V. McKnight observes, for the believer the church is "by nature provisional, subject to correction arising from further Bible reading. The church must change, for God is on the move, and the end is not yet."[23]

Fourth, *the maturation of faith and knowledge is holistically defined, grounded in the essential correctness of the Christian worldview.* This holistic definition of maturity emphasizes the role of the Holy Spirit in at least two arenas. The Holy Spirit validates the divine authorship of the canonical Scriptures, which are thus self-authenticating to the soul of the believer on an intuitive level. And the faith community—the church—validates the gospel message through the expression of *agape* love empowered by the Holy Spirit.

The Christian must again make a wager: are the canonical Scriptures of divine origin and is the gospel message preached by the church divinely superintended? Even here the believer lacks objective assurances, requiring the individual to ultimately rely upon the inner voice of the Holy Spirit to validate this claim. But as the individual observes a faith community practicing *agape* love among those inside and outside the faith, it prompts an intuitive affirmation, making the wager in favor of the Christian worldview—and against all other worldviews—more appealing.

THE CHURCH

As noted in earlier chapters, triumphalism has resulted in much fragmentation and many schisms in the church—all in the name of contending for the truth. When truth is understood as personal and animate, however, much of what used to be regarded as a question of doctrinal impurity takes on a different hue. It is possible to fellowship together without requiring a lock-step conformity in doctrine. Understanding truth as personal and animate makes room for a certain degree of theological pluralism.

Lordship salvation and the IFCA-International. In 1988, a controversy that later grew into a firestorm within the IFCA-International arose between two of its members, John F. MacArthur Jr. and Charles C. Ryrie. (We touched on this controversy earlier in this book; we will now examine it in greater detail.) That year MacArthur wrote a book that addressed the question of the gospel. The book was entitled *The Gospel According to Jesus.* The inside flyleaf of the book contains these words:

The message proclaimed today by many Christians is not the gospel according to Jesus. It is true that Jesus taught good news, but he did not teach the easy-believism that is ravaging the American evangelical movement. Many today take salvation too lightly by ignoring the warnings of Jesus that the cost of discipleship is high, the way narrow so that few find it, and that not all who call Jesus Lord will be accepted into the Kingdom. *The Gospel According to Jesus* clearly teaches that there is no eternal life without surrender to the lordship of Christ. MacArthur shows that faith without works is dead. And deadly. It is deadly because a faith without works is no faith at all. Nothing can be conceived as evidence of salvation apart from a life of obedience, a life that shows the fruit of transformed behavior. Faith is dead faith if it lacks the fruit of true righteousness. Salvation is defined not by what one does to get it but by what it produces; it is the outworking of regeneration in one's life.[24]

In the book, MacArthur argued that Protestant evangelicalism was being ravaged by a perverted gospel of easy-believism. What was needed, he insisted, was the necessary balance of lordship. Drawing on the New Testament passage, "faith without works is dead" (Jas 2:20 KJV), MacArthur insisted that the current expression of the gospel in much of Protestant evangelicalism is a dead faith (i.e., nonsalvific) since it lacks the work of a life surrendered to the lordship of Jesus Christ. It makes a mockery of the holiness of God and the gospel since it leaves the impression that a person can "believe" the gospel yet continue in a lifestyle decisively unholy. MacArthur also identified specific theologians who argued for an easy-believism and took issue with them—one notable theologian being Charles C. Ryrie, professor at Dallas Theological Seminary and also a member of the IFCA-International.

In rebuttal, Ryrie argued that lordship salvation confuses the gospel. Lordship implies works and therefore, at its essence, the gospel must be understood as distinct from it and limited to faith in the finished work of Jesus Christ upon the cross. Accordingly, Ryrie argued for the possibility that many Christians may genuinely believe the gospel yet at the same time conduct themselves in decisively carnal (unholy) lifestyles. He explained:

> That a Christian can be characterized as carnal cannot be denied, simply because the text of 1 Corinthians 3:1-3 says there were carnal believers at Corinth. Paul addresses these people as "brethren" and "babes in Christ" in verse 1; then describes them as "men of flesh" and "fleshly" in verses 1 and 3. So there were carnal or fleshly Christians in Paul's day.[25]

Like MacArthur, Ryrie insisted that every genuine Christian will manifest the spiritual fruit of a surrendered lifestyle to the lordship of Jesus Christ.[26] Yet he also placed three caveats on this assertion: (1) a believer may not always be fruitful, (2) a believer's fruit may not be outwardly evident, and (3) we must be careful not to quickly judge another since our understanding of what fruit is may be faulty and/or incomplete.[27] For Ryrie, then, the most troubling aspect of lordship salvation is that since it is impossible to qualify and quantify one's surrendered lifestyle it is equally impossible to determine if anyone is genuinely saved. Responding to MacArthur's point that a moment of spiritual failure does not invalidate a believer's credentials,[28] Ryrie asked whether "two moments" would accomplish such an invalidation. He then went on to ask:

> Or a week of defection, or a month, or a year? Or two? How serious a failure and for how long before we must conclude that such a person was in fact not saved? Lordship teaching recognizes that "no one will obey perfectly,"[29] but the crucial question is simply how imperfectly can one obey and yet be sure that he "believed" in the lordship/mastery salvation sense? If "salvation requires total transformation"[30] and I do not meet that requirement, then am I not saved? Or if my transformation is less than total at any stage of my Christian life, was I not saved in the first place?[31]

In short, Ryrie maintained that lordship salvation generates confusion within the gospel message, leaving an alleged believer in a perpetual state of uncertainty as to his or her spiritual status—not knowing whether he or she is saved or lost.

Though MacArthur and Ryrie have avoided framing their debate in terms of imputation and infusion, their arguments nevertheless fall within the classic imputation/infusion controversy. This controversy historically reaches back to the sixteenth-century Reformation and the Council of Trent (1545-1563), where Protestantism argued for imputation and Catholicism argued for infusion, and each side anathematized the other.[32] The current debate has generated a similar polarity. The MacArthur position includes the notion of infusion. The Ryrie position involves the notion of imputation. Reminiscent of the classic sixteenth-century controversy, those who align themselves with the MacArthur position have insisted that their definition of works of righteousness is to be understood as a faith *that* works. Yet, also reminiscent of the sixteenth-century controversy, those who align themselves with the Ryrie position have argued that the opposing lordship position is better understood as a salvation of faith *and* works. It is not without cause, then, that Ryrie has charged that MacArthur's position opens the door to the classic Roman Catholic understanding of salvation that Protestants have historically understood to be heretical ("works" salvation). It is also not without cause that MacArthur has charged that Ryrie's position opens a door to a version of antinomianism that Roman Catholics have historically understood to be heretical. Hence, the old adage of history repeating itself is demonstrated in this modern-day debate.

Since MacArthur and Ryrie were both members of the IFCA-International and since they adopted a heightened rhetorical argumentative style in their conversation with one another, the debate could not be contained within academia. It quickly grew in intensity and spawned a major controversy within that ecclesial body. Sides were taken as individual members aligned themselves with either MacArthur or Ryrie; some staked out positions somewhere between the two. Typically, they believed that determining the answer to this dilemma required a "common sense" approach to Scripture. That is to say, they assumed that "if everyone accepts the same theses and the same equations, they will arrive at the same answer."[33]

But such a "same answer" did not come. Attitudes of triumphalism surfaced as a sizeable number of members insisted on the absolute accuracy of their particular position. They then adopted a posture of either (a) tolerance, patiently waiting for the opposing positions to yield to the superior logic of their position or (b) confrontation and separation, demanding that the leadership of the IFCA-International endorse their position as singularly authoritative and threatening to leave that ecclesial body if no such endorsement was forthcoming. Fatigued by the presence of recurring triumphalistic attitudes within this ecclesial body, other members disengaged from the debate and either silently waited or vocally encouraged the leadership of the IFCA-International to set the issue aside and move on.

A separation did indeed take place as two sizeable multistate regionals within the IFCA-International broke away and formed their own independent ecclesial bodies.[34] Though various doctrinal disputes were cited as reasons for the ecclesial fracture, the lordship salvation debate between MacArthur and Ryrie was a centerpiece of their discontent.

Fourteen years after the initial publication of MacArthur's *The Gospel According to Jesus,* the IFCA-International chose to revisit and attempt to bring closure to this controversy during its annual convention in Kalamazoo,

Michigan, in the summer of 2002. A workshop offered at this convention attempted to find common ground between MacArthur and Ryrie. Thomas Couch led the workshop and explained that both sides operate within the Reformation paradigm, but that even in this paradigm paradoxes exist. "Much harm is done when we seize only one side of an antinomy, apparent contradiction, or mystery of truth and teach half-truth as if it were the whole truth, or bend one side of truth to confrom [sic] to another."[35]

Couch's point was that the MacArthur's and Ryrie's positions cannot be reconciled when analyzed on a rational level, yet even the Reformation doctrines of justification and sanctification cannot be wholly reconciled rationally. MacArthur and Ryrie are in essential agreement, he concluded, and their areas of apparent disagreement are due to the paradoxical Reformation doctrine of salvation. Hence, the problem was not worthy of the controversy it had spawned.

One must ask, however, whether the gospel as understood by MacArthur and Ryrie are of the same paradigm, as alleged. Though similarities between the two can be cited, profound differences nevertheless exist. For example, the way in which carnality within the church is understood is remarkably different—in the one it is a sign that the individual is not a genuine believer, in the other it is a sign that a believer is walking in disobedience. A second example pertains to Romans 10:9, where the apostle Paul states, "that if you confess with your mouth the Lord Jesus" (NKJV). In the Greek, the term "Lord" is *kyrios*. According to MacArthur, the term is a recognition that Jesus is the *sovereign master*. A failure to recognize Jesus as the sovereign master results in a nonsalvific gospel. According to Ryrie, the term is a recognition that Jesus is the *Savior*. By collapsing lordship and salvation into a singular gospel presentation, Ryrie insists, the result is a nonsalvific gospel since it has become distorted by the presence of works (cf. Eph 2:8-9). The term "obedience of the gospel" is also defined differently by the two positions. MacArthur argues that the term means the obedience of faith that results in a holy lifestyle. Ryrie argues that the term means the obedience of faith independent of a holy lifestyle. These three examples point to a mutual exclusivity between the two positions, suggesting differing paradigms.

Yet in fairness to Couch, his concept of a paradox operating within a singular paradigm is similar to my concept of dual paradigms juxtaposed against one another. In both mystery is present, since the relation of each to the other can be understood only in suprarational categories. Still the dual paradigms approach is more useful to theologians. It pushes back the notion of paradox, providing us with more room from which to examine the distinctives of each position without the pressure to (a) seek too quickly "common ground" and (b) give up too quickly in the pursuit of an understanding of their relationship.

What if . . . ? What would have been the result if the members of the IFCA-International had operated under an understanding of absolute truth that is personal and animate and applied insights generated from this paradigm shift to the lordship salvation debate?

The problem of triumphalism most likely could have been circumvented. To return to Smail's metaphoric language, which was discussed in the previous chapter, as each side of the debate recognized the legitimacy of the portrait of Christ being painted by the Holy Spirit on the other side, they could have (a) refused to define the debate as an either/or issue that threatened the theological purity of the IFCA-International and (b) seen the opposing theological position as something positive since multiple portraits have the potential of enhancing rather than detracting from a more complete understanding of Christ.

More specifically, they could have understood that different people need different portraits. For an individual raised in an extremely rigid and graceless form of Christianity, for example, Ryrie's antilordship version of soteriology may have legitimate theological currency in shaping an accurate portrait of Christ in his or her life. An individual raised in a laissez faire anything-goes form of Christianity—where, for example, a man who owns a liquor store lives with a woman outside of wedlock, regularly uses blasphemous language, yet teaches Sunday School and is affirmed by others as a genuine believer—may be led by the Holy Spirit toward a version of soteriology that is more in keeping with MacArthur's lordship definition. Admittedly, these are extremes. Yet one can articulate numerous examples that fall between these two that could, theoretically, give reason for additional Spirit-led portraits.

Two implications emerge from this illustration of the MacArthur-Ryrie debate. First, the rejection of the plurality of portraits and the affirmation of a singular soteriology yield a truncated understanding of the Christian faith. It fails to recognize that the New Testament is itself heavily contoured and that the Spirit of God should be given the freedom to creatively use the Word of God to fashion the life of Christ in a manner that reflects such contours. In other words, just as the Word of God possesses plural portraits of the life of

Christ by its biblical authors, the Spirit of God should have the freedom to paint multiple portraits of the life of Christ within the church.

Second, as we observed in the previous chapter, Christians need to learn how to honestly converse with rather than either ignore or attack differing religious traditions. William C. Placher reminds us, "Christians—like anyone else—need to know when to disagree with their conversation partners."[36] Nevertheless, he adds that Christians would perhaps progress further in their own traditions if they listened more attentively and thoughtfully to voices from other ecclesial traditions and not be so quick to reject and condemn. The purpose of such dialogue is not necessarily to resolve differences. Rather it is to learn to appreciate the rich diversity within the Christian faith— at times making changes in one's own religious tradition, at other times maintaining specific distinctives that set one's tradition apart from the others.

No doubt some subtraditions, such as extreme fundamentalists on the far Christian right, may not wish to converse with us due to an exclusivist (separatistic) perception they have of their own tradition. Yet even here we need to make ourselves available and attempt to dialogue. Sometimes those who are persistent on the absoluteness of whatever it is that has caused them to break fellowship with other ecclesial groups possess ideas worthy of serious reflection. For us to reject them could potentially result in our own spiritual impoverishment. Even if we are predisposed to think that whatever it is that has driven them to such exclusivity is essentially wrong, there still could be some elements of truth in their perspectives that warrant careful examination. Besides, a failure to communicate would demonstrate that we have become like them.

EVANGELISM

When absolute truth is understood as personal and animate, changes also occur in how the unsaved are identified and evangelized. In what follows, we will examine changes in reference to evangelism inside and outside the church.

Inside the church: the question of ecumenism. Because of the multiple portraits of Christ generated from the paradigm shift described in chapter seven, many people within the church that others do not consider genuine believers in Christ may, in fact, be believers. As we observed in chapter four, a number of differing models of the gospel exist within the New Testament—one of which is the forensic model championed by the apostle Paul, the model also championed by much of Protestant evangelicalism. There are, however, other models. In the Gospel according to John, the gospel model presented is, according to some theologians, liturgical in orientation (e.g., Jn 6:47-71). Such an understanding of the gospel is championed by much of Roman Catholicism. In the Gospel according to Matthew, it is defined in terms of relationship (e.g., Mt 7:23). With this in mind, is it not possible that many people of differing ecclesial traditions who affirm differing models of the Christ-event are nonetheless genuine believers in Christ?

In *Unbaptized God: The Basic Flaw in Ecumenical Theology,* Robert W. Jenson observed that the conventional approach to ecumenism is fundamentally flawed. In its attempt to bring about a singular doctrinal stance among differing ecclesial bodies—an attempt that is predisposed to triumphalistic thinking—doctrinal disagreements stubbornly persist, preventing any semblance of Christian unification. It is fundamentally flawed because it fails to take into consideration that which we have been observing in this and the previous chapter: namely, the possibility of multiple paradigms emerging out of the same Christ-event.

What tends to happen during ecumenical discussions, he explained, is that "as dialogues have worked down the program of controversies, and as each controversy has in the event been mitigated, its divisive power has seemed" to regenerate "and settle elsewhere." This reaction, Jenson went on to say, has occurred with "monotonous consistency."[37] Hence, the great divides in church fellowship "have come no nearer."[38]

Jenson argued that the problem is ultimately that of an undue subordination of the Holy Spirit to the Word. It has given rise to a quasi-monotheism that has resulted in a pendulum swing "between Catholic institutionalism and Protestant spiritualist individualism."[39] In both ecclesial traditions, the role of the Holy Spirit is subordinated to the Word of God in maintaining the continuity and coherence of the church, giving rise to a singular approach to church structure. In the one, the Word of God is centered in the institution. In the other, the Word of God is centered in the individual. In both, the Holy Spirit is de-centered, functioning in a mere auxiliary role as enlightener of the Word of God.

As noted in the previous chapter, the paradigm shift from impersonal and inanimate absolute truth to one that is personal and animate clearly voices the central role the Holy Spirit must play in theological development. The Holy Spirit is given his rightful place as the giver of life and community, rejuvenating the church with an unceasing action that reveals the Word of God in the ever-present here and now.

What is needed, then, is a renewed awareness that the church's continuity and coherence centers in the Word *and* the Holy Spirit. Such an awareness not only decentralizes the power structures with the church, but also gives freedom to ecclesial leaders and individual theologians to celebrate their distinct heritages as they positively relate to one another. In many cases, church members once thought to be identified with heretical ecclesial bodies will instead be understood as members of bona fide ecclesial bodies, albeit bodies whose dogma/theology/liturgy is different from one's own. A compelling illustration of this phenomenon comes from the personal testimony of Garry Wills. In his book *Why I Am a Catholic* he explains:

> I am not a Catholic because of the pope. I am a Catholic because of the [Apostles'] creed. I believe in that, and it does not mention the pope. In fact, it was formulated before there was a pope—but even to say that involves one in long arguments on the history of the papacy. Some have asked, Why not just keep the creed but forget the pope? Why not go to the Episcopal or Lutheran church, or join Eastern Orthodox Christians? But the pope is one of the reasons I stay, not a reason for going. I continually read the New Testament, after all, so wherever I find Christ I expect to find Peter close to him. But the Apostle's relationship to his savior, always close, is never quite the same from era to era, and its current form will no more be its permanent one than were any of the earlier embodiments. There have been many papacies, and reaching a reasoned relationship with the current one entails taking a long hard look at the history of the institution. It also means learning that no Christian church is perfect—not even the Episcopal or Lutheran or Orthodox. We flawed believers live with our flawed fellow believers, even with flawed brothers like the pope.[40]

Indeed! It is a breath of fresh air to hear a Christian defend his own faith—in this case Roman Catholicism—with an appeal to an early patristic creed, without arguing triumphalistically against all opposing ecclesial traditions.[41]

Outside the church: the question of evangelism. The paradigm shift that understands absolute truth as personal and animate generates a level of religious pluralism within the church. But how are we to understand such religious pluralism with those outside the church? Are we to understand non-Christian religions in a framework similar to that of John Hick (the theologian highlighted in chapter five on post-foundational antirealism)?

The answer is no. When absolute truth is understood as personal and animate, absolute truth becomes synonymous with a personal and animate God. Moreover, being personal and animate, this God possesses the wherewithal to reveal himself as he truly is. Through the power of the Spirit of God, such a self-revelation has been communicated to humankind and we know that the essence of God is trinitarian: Father, Son and Holy Spirit. He is therefore not, as John Hick insists, an unknowable God. Rather, he has broken through and manifested himself in this world so that he can be known. Though we have access to this God existentially through day-by-day experiences and encounters, our knowledge is guided through Scripture and the ecumenical (patristic) creeds.

The ecumenical creeds are the framework for reading Scripture in a distinctly orthodox way. They are summations of the essential core of the Christian faith. The apostle Paul likely had this concept in mind as he spoke about the "pattern of sound teaching" (2 Tim 1:13). Tertullian referred to the *regula fidei* (rule of faith) that should form the fundamental matrix as one studies Scripture.[42] According to Lindbeck, the ecumenical creeds of special importance are those that emerged from the first four ecumenical councils of the early church. These documents established trinitarian, christological and soteriological dogma, which, in turn, established the parameters of orthodoxy.

In their interpretation of Scripture, the sixteenth-century Protestant Reformers were committed to the creeds of the early church. Though also committed to the notion of *sola scriptura,* it was not the stark interpretation that abandoned a commitment to the creeds. Hence, they argued for the coherence of Scripture and church tradition. For Luther

> *sola scriptura* was not *nuda scriptura.* It was never simply a question of Scripture *or* tradition, Holy Writ *or* Holy Church. The sufficiency of Scripture functioned in the context where the Bible is regarded as the Book given to the church, the community of faith, which is gathered and guided by the Holy Spirit. We get a better sense of what Luther meant by this when we look at how he used church tradition. He retained the Apostles' Creed, along with the Nicene and Chalcedonian formulations.[43]

It was not that the creeds were a competing authority alongside Scripture. Rather they protected the true intention of Scripture against heretical deviations. Thus Luther argued for the coherence of Scripture and tradition, while never wavering in his commitment to the priority of the former.

With this in mind, those individuals who embrace a heterodoxical understanding of Christianity (i.e., an interpretation of Scripture that stands in opposition to the ecumenical creeds) or identify with non-Christian religions (e.g., Hinduism, Islam, Judaism) are spiritually lost and in need of salvation.

Evangelizing the lost, however, requires more than the presentation of rationalistic arguments in favor of the Christian faith. If absolute truth is understood as personal and animate, the presentation of absolute truth must also be personal and animate. This requirement has the following ramifications:

Personal: An effective gospel presentation should recognize and affect the individuality of a believer. That is, rather than speaking in the abstract, an effective gospel presentation should reach into the reality of the person of faith. In what respect has the fact of the forgiveness of sin resulted in peace deep in the believer's soul? How has repentance from sin exchanged death for life in a believer's life? Being personal, the believer needs to share from his or her own story; it is story that makes one's life known and understandable.

Animate: An effective gospel presentation should also reflect the *life* of the Christian faith. That is, rather than emphasizing its negatives (restrictions for Christians to avoid), such negatives should be placed in a broader positive context. In what respect does the knowledge of being made in the image of God, of being the bride of Christ, of the blessings of the future *eschaton* affect our lives in the here-and-now? How do the two great commandments of loving God and loving one's neighbor produce a life of intrinsic and lasting value?

In other words, evangelism that corresponds to the paradigm shift described in this and the previous chapter fashions a portrait of Christ for an unbeliever with the raw materials of one's own life. If the believer is Spirit-led in his or her presentation, the portrait's artist is ultimately the Spirit. Moreover, because the "raw materials" vary from person to person, evangelism will most likely produce a pluralism of "portraits of Christ."

Sharing absolute truth that is personal and animate must also be done in a manner that is personal and animated. This means that formula presentations (four laws, three principles, etc.) are counterproductive since they are impersonal and inanimate. Rambling and disconnected presentations from the heart—that is, rambling and disconnected presentations that are personal and animate—are preferred to ones that are more structured yet impersonal and inanimate.

SUMMARY

Having considered the theory of post-postmodernism in the previous chapter, this chapter has focused on the pragmatic outworkings of post-postmodernism in daily living. In this respect, we have observed that a central characteristic of post-postmodernism is how it undermines attitudes of triumphalism in the Christian faith and replaces them with a humble dependency upon the Word and the Spirit. We have observed this in three fundamental spheres of Christian living: faith, the church and evangelism.

Faith. In post-postmodernism, the modernist maxim of "knowledge seeking faith" is set aside and the more orthodox Anselmian maxim of "faith seeking understanding" is reintroduced. Specifically, we have observed that in post-postmodernism the Christian faith is understood in terms of a hermeneutical circle in which faith seeks knowledge *and* knowledge seeks faith. The starting point is therefore neither faith nor knowledge but instead the Holy Spirit who sovereignly places the individual believer inside the circle. This results in four corollaries: (1) practice in the Christian faith precedes the maturation of faith and knowledge, (2) involvement in a faith community also precedes the maturation of faith and knowledge, (3) the believer possesses a sense of doubt mingled with his or her decision of faith, and (4) the maturation of faith and knowledge is holistically defined, grounded in the essential correctness of the Christian worldview.

Church. In post-postmodernism, different religious traditions with diverse ways of ordering truth are recognized as legitimate within the body of Christ. This is because the Holy Spirit is given the freedom to shape truth differently for various believers without violating the essential integrity of the Word of God. In other words, the unity of the church is understood as a unity with diversity rather than a monolithic lock-step unity. It is this Spirit-driven unity with diversity that gives the body of Christ its strength.

Evangelism. With the body of Christ defined in terms of unity with diversity, ecclesial traditions previously labeled as heretical and therefore in need of salvation are now understood to be possibly within the body of Christ. Rather than evangelizing the believers of differing traditions, then, we need to learn to appreciate and learn from one another's differences. Evangelism will still be necessary within post-postmodernism, yet only among those who have veered away from or have never encountered the essential teachings of the ecumenical creeds of the early church.

QUESTIONS

Basic Concepts

1. What is "the Cartesian anxiety"?

2. When absolute truth is understood as personal and animate, in what respect does that undercut "the Cartesian anxiety"?

3. What is Ricoeur's wager?

4. According to Ricoeur's hermeneutical circle, we are neither objectivists nor subjectivists, but rather pneumatists. In what respect are we pneumatists?

5. When the Christian faith is understood in terms of Ricoeur's wager, four corollaries follow. What are they?

6. Explain Michael Polanyi's bicycle riding illustration of the Christian faith.

7. When one thinks in terms of Ricoeur's wager, how does theology become a participatory endeavor?

8. Why is there a lingering doubt in one's Christian faith when one begins with faith and then follows Ricoeur's wager?

9. Following the notion of personal and animate truth, in what respect could lordship salvation and antilordship salvation both be correct?

10. Why has the ecumenical agenda logjammed under modernism?

11. According to John Hick, religious pluralism would logically include a legitimization of non-Christian religions. How is this problem avoided when absolute truth is understood as personal and animate?

12. In light of absolute truth understood as personal and animate, how are we to understand the ecumenical creeds of the early church?

13. An effective presentation of the gospel should be personal and animate. Explain what this entails.

FURTHER THOUGHT

1. Describe the difference between *sola scriptura* and *nuda scriptura*.

2. Chapter four cites James K. A. Smith speaking approvingly of "the madness of faith." How is that to be understood in terms of Ricoeur's wager?

Postmodernism and the
Church in Context

G*ott ist tot . . . und wir haben ihn getötet!"* (God is dead . . . and we have killed him!).[1] These are the words spoken by the madman in Friedrich Nietzsche's book *The Gay Science*. The god that the madman described as dead was the god of modernism. Since the madman understood the Christian faith to be a modernist construct, the Christian faith experienced the same demise. Yet the effect of this news failed to panic his listeners as it should have. The crowd did not understand that with no God there was no longer a standard whereby people could order their lives. They did not foresee the impending gloom nor the chaos that would certainly enter their lives. "Perhaps he was hiding or was lost" they wondered, "or had simply gone on a voyage."[2] Everyone laughed. Nobody cared. Frustrated with the lack of concern by the crowd, the madman threw his lantern to the ground and broke it. "I have come too early," he said.[3]

The year Nietzsche wrote *The Gay Science*, 1882, was indeed too early. People of Western culture could not envision nor understand the death of modernism. The reason the madman threw his lantern to the ground and broke it was because the crowd did not understand the marvelous opportunity afforded them. With the death of god (that is, the god of modernism), the first step forward was to grieve his death, to let the reality that no universal standards or truths existed shake them to their bones. The second step was to enter the chaotic world of nihilism that would certainly ensue. The third step was to wait for a few brave individuals, *Übermenschen* (supermen or overlords) as Nietzsche described them, who would be the new leaders in this postmodern world and restore order. Yet because nobody seemed to care that their god had died, nor that they were the ones who killed him, they were not ready to move forward.

One hundred years later, however, things have changed. Since the closing years of the twentieth century and the outset of the twenty-first century, the epoch known as modernism has been widely believed to have died. With no universally recognized truth from which to order their lives, people have begun searching elsewhere for direction and meaning in a chaotic and undisciplined world. The *Übermenschen* have responded by picking up their own lanterns, setting out in their own ships, and charting courses for their own lives—without the constraints of an alleged absolute truth pressing upon their souls. With exhilaration, Nietzsche prophesied this event: "the sea, our sea, lies open again; perhaps there has never yet been such an open sea."[4] These are the "free spirits," the true postmoderns. The rest are followers: *Herdenmenschen,* people of the herd. Together they are shaping a new culture.

But what kind of culture is being shaped? The stated goal of many leaders in this new cultural revolution is *tolerance.* Nietzsche, however, recognized that the *will to power* would likely be a major theme. In the Nietzschean world, whoever is in power decides right and wrong.[5] This may explain the uneasiness some people have with the postmodern paradigm. With the absence of absolute truth comes a corresponding absence of absolute ethics. Sensing this, some people are wondering whether or not by killing the god of modernism and replacing it with the god of postmodernism, Western culture has essentially replaced one demon with seven others more wicked than the first (cf. Lk 11:24-26).

⸗

With the advent of postmodernism, then, Western culture has arrived at a historic crossroads. What was considered unthinkable only a few years ago is now widely regarded as normal: Nietzsche's prophecy has finally come to pass. Postmodernism has replaced modernism. The enormity of this paradigm shift is difficult to overstate. It is comparable to the paradigm shift that brought into existence the Enlightenment over two hundred years ago—and perhaps even comparable to the earlier shifts that opened the Reformation and Renaissance.

At this historic crossroads the church is called on to be a witness of Jesus Christ. And, said Jesus, part of being an effective witness requires that we understand "the signs of the times" (Mt 16:3). This requires that we understand the postmodern phenomenon so that, as Charles Colson writes, we will know how "to translate [the gospel of Jesus Christ] for today's postmoderns."[6] Colson adds that the desire for such a translation is growing in our culture. At the commencement address at Wheaton College in the spring of 2000, he said:

> This is a great moment in Christian education, for the church, and for each of you who will take away degrees today and embark upon your appointed callings. For the polls tell us that Americans are increasingly restless, dissatisfied with the moral nihilism so widespread in our culture. Increasingly numbers of Americans are discovering that what they were promised, the *summum bonum* of life—personal autonomy—not only fails to satisfy their deepest needs but has left them alone, rootless, afraid to send their kids to school. Americans can't quite articulate it yet, but they are seeking a better way to order their lives.[7]

Colson then asked, "Who will offer it?"[8] The non-Christian family, he explained, is in shambles. Public schools and the secular academy have a tiger by the tail as they struggle with the nihilistic implications of postmodernism. The answer, he concluded, is the church.

This is true, however, provided the church is equipped to move people away from the Nietzschean world of postmodernism with its penchant toward moral nihilism and into a vibrant faith centered in the absolute truth embodied in the *person* of Jesus Christ. Anything less will not work. Anything less will cause the church not only to miss this important appointment with the world at this historic crossroads, but also to veer into a cul-de-sac of its own making. In this cul-de-sac the church will find itself silenced, unable to speak God's Word with relevance and power to those who are waiting at the crossroads. That is to say, a failure to help people work through the implications of postmodernism will leave the church in its own self-imposed ghetto where it can only speak to those who are already inside its limited circle of influence.

The purpose of this book has been to bring clarity to this postmodern phenomenon, help in the equipping of Christian believers for this mission and avoid such a ghettoization. We examined the dark side of absolute truth and the imperative for ecumenical unification of the church. We then studied the four different approaches that theologians have adopted in their assessment of postmodernism. On one extreme are those who still embrace modernism, regarding its death notices as highly exaggerated. On the other extreme are those heartily in favor of postmodernism. In the middle are two additional positions. The argument of this book is that the two extreme positions are problematic and the mediating positions offer a more balanced and nuanced approach that could aid the church in its theology as it advances into this new millennium and faces the challenges and opportunities presented by postmodernism. We finally considered what the next step may be, how to move beyond postmodernism without returning to the modernist paradigm.

The dynamic observed, then, is a hermeneutical war where (a) paradigm shifts are occurring within certain quarters in the church, and (b) old paradigms are stubbornly embraced in other quarters, resisting shifts of any kind. It is the paradigm shift of postmodernism within the West that is driving this hermeneutical war in the church, where arguments favoring particularism and pluralism are pitted against one another. Yet in the midst of this war a new hybrid paradigm is emerging—one that is both particularistic and pluralistic. For lack of a better term I have called it *post-postmodernism.*

One finds parallels in post-postmodernism with trinitarian thought, which is itself a hybrid, a combination of particularism (singularity) and pluralism (multiplicity). As such, this current hermeneutical war shadows an earlier theological war that dominated the church in the third and fourth centuries, where the concern was theology proper (the nature of God). The solution was the doctrine of the Trinity established at the councils of Nicaea (325) and Constantinople (385). By working through the challenges of both modernism and postmodernism, the church may therefore find itself in a situation where history is once again repeating itself—albeit with new questions and concerns serving as the principals of the debate. The end result of this new theological war, then, may be an understanding of epistemology that is not particularistic or pluralistic but both.

Mapping Postmodernism, then, is an argument in favor of a trinitarian, or paradoxical, understanding of absolute truth. The key to unlocking this paradox is an understanding of truth where it possesses its own life. As has already been discussed in this book, such an understanding of absolute truth converges with our understanding of God: they are one and the same.

In his novel *Joshua: A Parable for Today,* Joseph P. Girzone offers a telling illustration for how God can pluralistically confront rather than accommodate culture, while still being true to himself. Girzone writes a fictional account of Jesus returning to the earth incognito in a mid-sized town in America in the latter twentieth century. He went by the name of Joshua and was a highly skilled sculptor of wood. Though curious and suspicious of him at first, the people of the town were quickly drawn to his engaging and winsome personality.

Joshua's popularity, however, did not last. Not willing to accommodate the Christians in his community who insisted that their denomination or ecclesial fellowship was the only true religion, one by one he attended all the churches in town. He also attended the local Jewish synagogue. Predictably, this behavior made him the object of much criticism and scorn. Joshua paid his critics no mind. He refused to enter into the petty triumphalistic attitudes so typical of many denominations and ecclesial bodies that make up the church.

At one point in the story, Joshua was commissioned by the leaders of the local Episcopalian and Pentecostal churches to carve two sculptures of the Apostle Peter. In the one intended for the Episcopalian church, Joshua carved a statue of Peter kneeling before a dying beggar. In the one intended for the Pentecostal church, he carved a statue of Peter in a stately authoritative pose. Then the leaders of both churches arrived at Joshua's rented home to pick up the finished works of art.

> "Gentlemen," Joshua said. "I was not expecting you to come together. It is a coincidence that both of you ordered a likeness of Peter. I tried to honor your requests and carve what I thought would be aspects of Peter's personality that would be of significance to your people."

Joshua presented each leader with his sculpture. The first to respond was the priest:

> "That is not the great Apostle Peter but some pious servant saint whom I do not even recognize," the priest said angrily.
>
> "On the contrary," Joshua said, "that is Peter at his greatest. It was not part

of Peter's personality to serve. He was born to rule, and that dominated his whole personality. As he grew spiritually to more resemble the Master, and realized his real role as the servant of God, he became much more humble in his attitude toward those he considered inferior. This figure depicts the moment in Peter's life when he had finally overcome nature and realized what Jesus meant when he washed the feet of the apostles and told them they should be the servants of God's children."

The priest was unmoved by Joshua's explanation. The Pentecostal clergyman was just as troubled by the statue intended for him, which suggested "everything about the church that Pentecostals dislike."

"Joshua," Reverend Rowland said as politely as he could, "I think, perhaps, you have made a mistake with these two figures. It seems that Father Darby would be much more happy with this statue, and I love the message in the one you did for him.

"If each of you likes the other's statue," Joshua replied, "I have no objection, you may exchange them."[9]

Contented, the two clergymen exchanged statues. Some time later, however, the priest received a phone call from the Pentecostal clergyman, who suggested they exchange statues once again. As it happened, both leaders had felt the same sense of dissatisfaction with the familiarity of the message suggested by the statues they had accepted.

The priest brought his statue to the Pentecostal church and was impressed by the spirit of humility evident in the church and the minister. As the two men exchanged statues, the priest suggested that they get together for dinner. "We would like that very much. My wife will be thrilled." The priest then returned to his church with the other statue.

They reached the church and went in to put the figure in place. When they had it positioned they stepped back and looked at it. It was a powerful and moving sculpture. It spoke with a force that would move the hardest heart. The dented tiara lying in the dust spoke powerfully of Peter's final triumph over nature and the conquest of grace. The face of the dying man Peter was attending struck Father Darby. He looked at it more closely. He looked again in disbelief. It was himself. He cringed at the thought of the great apostle on his knees caring for him. It was beneath him. And then he realized it really wasn't. Tears filled his eyes as the meaning of the statue hit him full force. The chauffeur was embarrassed and politely turned away so the priest wouldn't think he had seen. The priest knelt, not to the statue, but to offer a prayer, asking God to forgive him for his awful pride and to help him to be more like the real Apostle Peter, whom he loved so much.[10]

This vignette from Girzone's book brings to light several insights. We see God challenging rather than accommodating culture. He responds differently to different ecclesial bodies, illustrated by the two statues. We also see clerical leaders grappling and finally coming to grips with these differences, learning to appreciate the strengths of ecclesial bodies previously disdained. It was no secret that prior to Joshua's arrival the Pentecostals and Episcopalians had nothing to do with each other. It was also no secret that after Joshua's arrival they resented the fact that he attended each other's worship services rather than their own exclusively. Now, in a turn of events Father Darby has invited Reverend Rowland and his wife over for supper. And Reverend Rowland accepted the invitation. This exchange reflects the budding of a new insight, an awareness that diversity adds to rather than detracts from the Christian faith. Such are the beginnings of a new form of ecumenism in the church, one that is heterogeneous rather than homogeneous in nature.

Yet such diversity should extend far beyond the artistic expression of wooden statues. In this book we examined the controversy of the lordship salvation debate between MacArthur and Ryrie. My reason for drawing upon this issue is that it parallels the infusion/imputation debate of the sixteenth century between Roman Catholicism and Protestantism. As such, it touches upon one of the more central issues that has divided these two broad religious bodies and made ecumenical unification so difficult for Western Christendom. Just as Joshua carved different statues for differing ecclesial bodies, we need to ask whether the doctrine of salvation can be multilayered, not subject to any singular interpretation. To be sure, the gospel is one, centered in the Christ-event (i.e., incarnation, passion, ascension and parousia of Jesus). Yet, is it not possible that just as different New Testament authors interpret the meaning of the Christ-event differently (e.g., James articulates it differently than Paul), we should expect a similar range of interpretation within the contemporary church?

The post-postmodernism proposed in this book argues that the answer to this question is *yes*. Hence, it is not enough to know the Word, one must also know the Spirit—for it is the Spirit who artistically paints and gives individual expression of the Word. Ecumenical unification, then, need not require a lock-step doctrinal/liturgical/devotional conformity. We can celebrate our differences while at the same time enjoying a true sense of unity that we have in Christ.

This is where the church can offer our unbelieving friend or acquaintance the way out of the postmodern box that has left him or her with no clear exit. The answer is life—specifically, the life of God. With a personality that is inexhaustibly deep, God is able to reveal differing aspects of his life to meet the complexity of needs in this world. This is what many people are pursuing—and the church, by revealing the richness and wonders of the life of Christ, is able to offer it to them. Jesus Christ challenges both the rigidity of modernism and the relativism of postmodernism, replacing them both with life. Jesus Christ, therefore, is the way out of the box.

Jesus Christ will be revealed to a lost world as the church functions on a suprarational level where, in spite of its vast diversity of doctrine, liturgy and devotion, it can appreciate and celebrate its oneness. This combination of a oneness *and* diversity that defies rational analysis is what will catch the world's eye and cause many of them to stop, think and wonder. "See how they love and are committed to one another," they will say to themselves. And as they are watching and thinking, in the quietness of their hearts some of them will hear the Holy Spirit speak, whispering within them a single word: *Yes*.

New Questions

I mentioned in the prologue that I did not intend to be innovative in my treatment of postmodernism inside the church. Rather, I have drawn on current scholarship and systematically laid out for the reader what is being said. As such, I am not pioneering new theological territory for the church. This is true even of my treatment of post-postmodernism, to which I have, in the tradition of Adam, contributed only a name for what heretofore has been left nameless.

It is my hope that this book will cause the reader to ask new questions—specifically, where would a viable post-postmodernism take the church as it advances into the twenty-first century? The following five questions should serve as a starting point for such an inquiry.

1. By arguing for a post-postmodern paradigm for theology, one that understands the Christian faith as suprarational, that is, ultimately beyond the reach of human rationality, does this degenerate Christian theology into a fideistic system?

During the two centuries when modernism reigned in Western culture, Christian theologians attempted to circumvent fideistic thinking by anchoring the faith in the Cartesian *Cogito*. Moving from the posture of radical doubt to faith, it was believed that the Christian faith could be systematically established and recognized as such by the unbiased observer. The two broad traditions that formed through this method were liberalism and conservatism.

Yet as we dispense with the Cartesian *Cogito* and think in terms of post-postmodernism, new questions emerge. How can we convincingly state that God has indeed spoken through the Christian Scriptures, that the Christian

Scriptures are indeed the Word of God and that all other competing claims are false? Is the answer a return to **fideism?**

If this is the case, have we not, as Søren Kierkegaard advocated two centuries ago, reduced the Christian religion to a leap of faith? And, if this is true, how then do we assess (a) the claims of Christian cults that have veered away from classic orthodoxy and (b) the claims of non-Christian religions? Mormonism, for example, grounds its faith in the so-called burning in the bosom. Are we not grounding our faith similarly?

Though the charge of fideism should be a serious concern for the Christian theologian, we would be wise not to abandon fideism altogether as we work through this concern. Essential elements related to the Christ-event (the incarnation, resurrection and ascension of Jesus) are beyond the reach of independent verification. That is, since they are not open to independent verification, in these issues faith tends toward fideistic thinking. Hence, if we reject fideism in its entirety, we will likely be left with a Christian faith void of these essential elements related to the Christ-event, causing it to drift in the direction of the theological liberalism of the modern era. Working through the problem of fideism is therefore a complex endeavor.

2. In a post-postmodern context, how should we understand the doctrine of biblical inerrancy?

During the Reformation era, biblical inerrancy was juxtaposed against the traditions of the Roman Catholic Church which, according to the Reformers, did not always correspond to the biblical text. The biblical text was deemed authoritative over the traditions since, said the Reformers, it alone is inspired of God. Therefore, what is written in it is normative for the Christian believer.

During the modernist era, however, the doctrine of biblical inerrancy was framed differently. Using the radical doubt of the *Cogito* as the starting point for theological reflection, before the Christian Scriptures could be used as normative for Christian belief, they had to pass the rigors of the scientific method, with radical doubt serving as the starting point of this analysis. The means to prove Christian Scripture as inspired of God and thereby normative for the Christian believer was inerrancy. Thus, the scientific method validated the ancient historical record, showing that the large volume of prophecies have been fulfilled—with the exception of those prophecies still pointing to the future. Following the logic of the *Cogito,* only an inspired text could achieve such a high level of factual accuracy.

Yet, as explained in this book, core elements of the Christ-event stand outside the reach of the scientific method—elements that include the incarnation, resurrection and ascension of Jesus Christ (without which the Christian *kerygma,* as traditionally and historically understood, ceases to exist). This forms a major impediment to the use of the *Cogito* for establishing the Christian Scriptures as inerrant and thereby inspired of God. For one to believe in the inerrancy of the Christian Scriptures, then, one must be predisposed to believe in inerrancy. Rather than being the foundation from which Christian faith is built, inerrancy is itself a statement of faith.

How then can we frame the doctrine of inerrancy in the post-postmodern context? To repeat the argumentations of the Reformation or modernist eras will likely yield ineffective results since the challenges and corresponding concerns have changed. Since post-postmodernism emphasizes the role of suprarationality in theology, the issue of fideism that was mentioned in the previous question will likely play a role to some extent in answering this question. Also, the Anselmian formula of *faith seeking knowledge* will likely need to be revisited and rearticulated.

3. In a post-postmodern context, how are the doctrinal statements of individual ecclesial bodies to be understood?

Doctrinal statements provide the necessary framework for the reading of Scripture in a distinctly orthodox way. They are summations of the essential core of the Christian faith. The apostle Paul likely had this in mind as he spoke about the "pattern of sound teaching" (2 Tim 1:13). Tertullian referred to the *regula fidei* (rule of faith) that should form the fundamental matrix as one studies Scripture.[1]

The problem with doctrinal statements is that many ecclesial bodies have shaped their statements by means of the Cartesian *Cogito*. Working from the starting point of radical doubt, they meticulously build their doctrinal statements with an outcome, they believe, that is absolute and universally valid. The analysis is limited to (a) Scripture alone *(nuda scriptura)* as the object of study and (b) the scientific method as the chosen procedure. The outcome of their analyses are doctrinal statements believed to be universally valid—having been acquired by rigorous scientific analysis.

Yet, as postmodernism has brought to light, pure objectivity is an elusive goal. Each of our minds has been shaped by the communities in which we were nurtured. Such a shaping plays a role in how truth is organized, processed, clarified and ultimately articulated (i.e., the phenomenon of the language game). We see this, for example, in the decisively different conclusions of various theologians and the differences in doctrinal statements by those who have employed the Cartesian *Cogito*.

How then can doctrinal statements be framed in a post-postmodern framework? One possibility would be to reach back into the premodern period and look for help there. Since the early premodern period is the domain of the ecumenical creeds, one possible solution is a two-tiered doctrinal statement mentioned in chapter seven. With such a system, the essentials and the nonessentials of theology can be distinguished, opening the possibility of increased conversation and fellowship between differing ecclesial bodies who differ on the nonessentials but are in hearty agreement on those items that define orthodoxy.

4. In the post-postmodern paradigm, how does the church avoid the intrusion of contemporary insights foreign to the biblical text?

Because of post-postmodernism's penchant for differing portraits of Christ for differing ecclesial communities, the possibility exists that unbiblical insights may find their way into the warp and woof of a specific ecclesial community under the guise of being part of a unique portrait of the Spirit to that given community. An illustration is Thomas A. Harris's book *I'm OK, You're OK* as a contemporary interpretation of justification by faith. Such a book is a complete vulgarization of the doctrine. Rather than saying, "I'm okay," a more biblical response says, "I'm not okay." Hence, an ecclesial community can subtly depart from a biblical world view and embrace something decisively unbiblical in orientation. In the post-postmodern context, how can this be avoided?

The answer requires more than a rigorous study of Scripture. The subtle influences of contemporary culture color the interpretations of the most assiduous of students. Clearly, dialogue with other students of Scripture is needed.

If we believe in the doctrine of the indefectibility of the church—that is, the church will persist throughout the ages due to the guiding work of the Holy Spirit—then we should be confident that through an ecumenically structured dialogue, the Holy Spirit will guide the church as it engages in such endeavors. This approach, however, lacks the tidiness and efficiency generally desired in addressing doctrinal questions. It most likely will also

lack closure on a number of questions considered. Pressing for a more effi-
cient and expeditious approach to the settlement of doctrinal disputes without resorting to a heavy-handedness that smacks of triumphalistic (papal!)
decrees is a concern not easily resolved.

*5. Does a post-postmodern paradigm in Christian theology set into motion a
trajectory in which the Protestant denominations should reverse the schisms
and separations in their respective histories and work toward a return to the
Roman Catholic Church?*

This is the trajectory George A. Lindbeck has advocated. He believes that
the first move back to Rome should come from his own denomination, the
Evangelical Lutheran Church in America. He asserts that this denomination
is not far removed from Rome in its essential ecclesial characteristics and
therefore would be the logical first step in reversing the Protestant schism
of the sixteenth century. The Melanchthon codicil to the Schmalkald Articles,
he explains, legitimizes the view that the Lutheran separation from Rome
should only be temporary and a return to Rome should occur once Rome
ceased raging against the gospel.

The Schmalkald Articles, authored by Martin Luther in 1538, offered a defense of the Protestant understanding of the gospel and a rationalization of
the ecclesial split from Rome. The Articles were endorsed by a number of
Luther's colleagues, including close friend Philipp Melanchthon, who added
a codicil (commentary) that served as a caveat to his endorsement.

> I, Philip Milanthon, also regard the above articles as true and Christian. About
> the pope, however, I maintain that if he would allow the gospel, we might
> allow to him his superiority over the bishops which he has "by human right."
> We could make this concession for the sake of peace and general unity among
> those Christians who are now under him and might be in the future.[2]

Here Melanchthon implies that under certain theological conditions—
namely, that the Roman Catholic Church would allow a Lutheran understanding of the gospel (specifically the notion of divine imputation)—the
justification for the Protestant schism would dissolve and the interests of
"peace and general unity" would bring the vast Protestant tradition back
under the authority of the Roman pontiff. Hence the question facing the
Protestant church today is whether Rome—regardless of its understanding of divine infusion—is in general agreement with the notion of divine
imputation. If the answer is yes (and many theologians believe this to be

the case), the major impediment to a Protestant migration to Rome has been breached.[3]

Overcoming the Protestant schism, however, may not be quite that simple. Though unification of the many schisms of the Christian religion is indeed in the best interests of the church (see Jn 13:34-35; 17:20-22), one cannot simply use the rationale of the ancient Melanchthon codicil as grounds for a return of the many Protestant denominations to Rome. Much has transpired in the five hundred years since the Schmalkald Articles were written. On a negative note, during these five hundred years the Roman Catholic Church dogmatized the notion of papal infallibility at the First Vatican Council and the notion of the Assumption of Mary shortly thereafter in a papal encyclical. Such dogma strikes a negative chord to many Protestant theologians, seriously violating their theological sensibilities.[4] Moreover, many Protestant denominations have grown accustomed to their ecclesial independence, no longer seeing themselves as integrally connected to Rome as Melancthon did.

On a positive note, recent dialogue between Roman Catholic and Protestant scholars has yielded a reinterpretation of the mutual anathemas that emerged in the sixteenth century from the Protestants (e.g., the Schmalkald Articles, the Augsburg Confession) and Rome (the Council of Trent). This scholarship holds the prevailing opinion that the sixteenth-century Lutheran scholars and Roman Catholic bishops misunderstood one another in regard to the gospel, implying that the anathemas generated by this conflict are not valid since they were directed against inaccurate understandings of the opposing positions.

How then should we understand the rift between Protestantism and Catholicism in the twenty-first century? Certainly, the rift is not the same as it was in the sixteenth century. When one takes into consideration the dynamics of absolute truth as presented in the latter chapters of this book (absolute truth that is personal and animate), differing theological paradigms are possible, meaning that the differences between the two ecclesial systems do not have to generate a mutual exclusivity. Nevertheless, questions related to papal infallibility, Marian dogma, the doctrine of purgatory and so on are still sizeable in the current theological climate, generating obstacles not easily overcome.

As a result, a more practical response of the many Protestant denominations in the world today would be a reconciliation of brethren more recently separated. In this respect, we should take small bites, so to speak, rather than attempt bites so large that they cause choking and possibly even death.

The paradigm shift from modernism to postmodernism has brought about new opportunities and challenges for the church as it debates the notion of truth. Where the debate will lead Christian theology is difficult to say. As noted in this book, both modernism and postmodernism are flawed systems, meaning that the next theological step will likely move beyond these two systems to what I have described as post-postmodernism. We have also noted what this post-postmodernism might look like: a system that replaces impersonal, inanimate truth with that which is personal and animate. The strength of this move is that it identifies absolute truth with the living God. In this paradigm, truth is absolute, yet still capable of being shaped into differing portraits through the guidance of the Holy Spirit.

Finally, in the post-postmodern paradigm, absolute truth has a name: Jesus Christ. As the Creator of the heavens and the earth, Jesus Christ is the personification of truth par excellence, the One who is to be loved and known, but never mastered.

Five Major Paradigms Defined

PREMODERNISM

The premodern paradigm is a difficult concept to define due to three interconnected problems: (a) Our definition requires that we consider what premodernism is—that it is not modernism. It is the difficult task of proving a negative. (b) Our definition requires that we contrast premodernism with modernism, pitting one against the other. Yet, since premodernism had minimal historical contact with modernism, it is unclear to what extent premodernism stands opposed to modernism. A case in point is the scientific method, an important component within the modernist paradigm. Does premodernism stand opposed to or in favor of the epistemological substructure of the scientific method? Although it is true that in the Pauline epistles Hellenistic philosophy was declared to be merely vain traditions (Col 2:8), it is unclear whether Paul stood opposed to Hellenism in all its forms and expressions. All we know is that Paul's overall scheme was premodern. (c) Our definition requires that we articulate premodernism in terms of modernism and postmodernism. Modernism has been engrained in Western culture for two hundred years; postmodernism has had approximately two decades of development. We therefore cannot wholly eradicate their influences from our collective psyches. In our definition of this paradigm, we have no choice but to bring our own philosophical baggage to this definition of premodernism and shape our arguments in modernist and postmodernist categories.

A central component of modernism is that of distanciation, a perceptual scheme where the world is divided into subject and object. Like spectators watching a game from the bleachers, we assume the role of subject and examine reality with a degree of detachment (distance). It is this detachment, we believe, that enables us to study whatever happens to be our field of inquiry with objectivity and to render conclusions that are definitive and absolute. Ted Peters explains:

> We have come to assume that nature is an agglomeration of disparate things that are related to one another by impersonal laws, and the object of science is to learn what these laws are so that we can manipulate the things through technology. Social scientists over the last century have taught us even to objectify ourselves, to treat ourselves as things subject to statistical laws. The social scientists concern themselves not with persons but with concepts of persons. So now we can step out of ourselves and look at ourselves as objects. We can understand ourselves in terms of ethnic backgrounds, social location, demographic trends, or psychological principles. We can hear ourselves spoken about, even if not spoken to.[1]

This approach to truth was foreign to the premodern mind. Unaware of the notion of distanciation, premodernists never attempted to step outside of themselves and look at their own lives or particular worlds as objects. Instead, they viewed the world as an undifferentiated whole and processed data accordingly. In this respect, social relationships, personal assessments, inner motivations, external pressures and so on blended holistically into a singular perception of truth. More to the point, for premodernists the quest for knowledge was centered on an understanding of individualized agendas emerging from peoples of power (whether they be the agendas of human beings or angelic/demonic beings), and how allegiances or lack of allegiances to those agendas affected their particular worlds.

One finds this premodernist approach to truth in the Decalogue. In the prologue, God declares to the people of Israel, "I am the LORD your God, who brought you out of Egypt, out of the land of slavery" (Ex 20:2). This introductory remark places the Decalogue in historical context and serves as its grounding. The rationale for observing the Decalogue was not its alleged objective rightness (abstracted principles) but rather its historical orientation. It was grounded in the people's relationship to *Yahweh Elohim*, the One who redeemed them from the bondage of Egypt. In other words, the rationale for observing the Decalogue was based on the *quid pro quo*: "Since I did that for you, you are now obligated to do this for me." In this case, the God who redeemed the people of Israel from historical and identifiable bondage issued the commands of the Decalogue.

Such thinking is difficult for those of the modernist milieu to grasp. We instinctively insist on altruistic or impartial explanations to validate truth claims. In our estimation, the *quid pro quo* is not productive but *counterproductive* to a genuine pursuit of truth. Nevertheless, the premodernist Old and New Testaments feature repeated uses of the *quid pro quo*.

The question of allegiances and obligations (the *quid pro quo*) caused the typical premodernist to think in terms of dualisms. An individual was either allied or opposed to the agendas of a person of power. As such, these allegiances, or lack thereof, tended toward black and white thinking, with no mediating grays to address extenuating circumstances to complicated issues. In terms of the Bible,

> the paramount dualism is the antagonism between God and Satan. The other more modest dualisms are variants of this: good versus evil, obedience versus disobedience, spirit versus flesh, commitment versus self-indulgence, virtue versus sin, confession versus denial, heaven versus hell. Individualized thinking and acting have meaning because they participate in the cosmic contest between God and God's enemies. The object of religious devotion is to make a willful choice—that is, to decide to commit oneself to the divine mission and to fight against the forces of evil at work within one's own soul and the exterior world.[2]

Again, such thinking is difficult for people reared in the modernist milieu to grasp. We attempt to parse these questions with impartiality and objectivity (distanciation) in order to construct mediating principles that accommodate extenuating circumstances. Anything less is substandard—simplistic and unsophisticated thinking. Dualistic extremes become so marginalized as to be inconsequential in our overall scheme of thinking.

The *quid pro quo* also kept the typical premodernist from thinking of God and morality in altruistic and objectified terms of right and wrong. For example, the typical premodernist would never have questioned the inherent rightness of God ordering the genocide of specific people-groups (Deut 20:16-18), overlooking Rahab's lie (Josh 2:3-14; 6:25) or blessing David's deception when he feigned madness before Abimelech (Ps 34). Once again, for those of us immersed within the modernist milieu such indifference is difficult to grasp. Our preoccupation with such questions says as much about our modernist mindset (how we work through the notion of truth in our minds) as it does about the premodernist's lack of the same. In remarkable contrast, the premodernist was more concerned with questions related to loyalties and allegiances, fulfilling obligations and anticipating blessings. Jesus, speaking from within this premodernist milieu to his disciples, said it well: "You are my friends if you do what I command" (Jn 15:14).

Also essential to the premodern mind was its communal character. People did not discount the influence of tradition and culture, as is the case in modernism. Truth was bequeathed to individuals by their families and communities. Perspectives that they were challenged to either accept or reject, then, had already been explored within their communal networks. They did not face isolated questions of the rightness of alleged truth claims, but were influenced by the choices made by people they could trust. Premodern people tended to embrace what their communities affirmed, and reject what their communities denounced.

A notable exception to the premodern way of thinking is found in classic Hellenistic thought. Here, philosophers rigorously explored the exact nature of virtue—an understanding of moral rectitude independent of the *quid pro quo*. Plato's *Republic* and Aristotle's *Ethics* stand out as examples of such efforts to break free of premodern thought. It must be added, however, that the influence of such philosophy was limited to the Hellenistic upper class and should therefore be understood as a *proto*-modernism. With the collapse of the Roman Empire (an event that occurred toward the end of the first millennium), the writings of the Hellenistic philosophers were lost, not to resurface until the Renaissance (mid-fourteenth century). The intervening centuries were known as the Dark Ages of medieval Europe, primarily due to the dearth of these ancient Hellenistic writings. Nevertheless, even the Renaissance was proto-modernist, since its impact was regional in scope and limited to the upper class. Only with the advent of the Enlightenment (mid-eighteenth century) did modernist thought become widespread, reaching across the other social classes and thereby capturing an entire culture.

A significant collision between premodernism and proto-modernism occurred as the early (apostolic and patristic) church entered the world of Hellenistic thought. Premodernists responded to proto-modernism in three different ways.

Rejection. In the New Testament, Paul described proto-modernist though as "hollow and deceptive philosophy, which depends on human tradition and the basic principles of this world rather than on Christ" (Col 2:8).

Similarly, John responded to efforts to redefine Christ as an abstract principle (i.e., that which Hellenism meant by the word *spirit*) as the "spirit of antichrist" (see 1 Jn 4:1-4). This rejection tended to be articulated in generalized and sweeping condemnations (black and white thinking) with little attention given to detail.

Acceptance. The early patristic church looked for common ground between the Old and New Testament documents and Hellenistic thought. Clement of Alexandria (c. A.D. 150-211) was especially noteworthy in this respect, describing Plato and Aristotle, for example, as proto-Christians and recasting much of biblical thought in Hellenistic categories.[3]

Nuanced compromise. In the middle and latter patristic period, extreme forms of Hellenism within Christian theology were anathematized by the church (e.g., the findings of the Second Council of Constantinople, A.D. 553). A more moderated version such as that found in the writings of Augustine of Hippo (A.D. 354-430) was celebrated as an articulate expression of orthodoxy.

In the premodern mind, then, we find an absence of the scientific method that, from our modern perspective, is quite conspicuous. Without the notion of distanciation and its related notion of radical doubt, which we will consider in the next section, the assessment of truth claims operated on an entirely different rubric (allegiances and obligations, the *quid pro quo*).

MODERNISM

Central to the modernist paradigm are two epistemological moves. The first move is the notion of distanciation, which results in a subject-object split: the inquirer assumes the role of an impartial spectator. The second move is the notion of radical doubt, where the inquirer initiates the process of knowing by doubting all things, except for the fact that he or she is indeed doubting. *"Cogito ergo sum"* (I think therefore I am) was the way Descartes (1596-1650) put it in his book *Meditations*. The purpose of radical doubt was to create a blank slate, so to speak, in the inquirer's mind so that no preconceived and unevaluated notions would slip through the inductive process and thereby improperly affect conclusions rendered by this methodology. These two epistemological moves have become so ingrained within Western culture that they are not recognized "as just one form of thinking among others but rather as the only form of thinking a rational person would judge sane."[4]

Since the advent of the Enlightenment (its benchmark event being the fall of the Bastille),[5] the Western church in both its conservative and liberal traditions has been committed to this modernist agenda. Liberalism grounded its theology in intuition, with Friedrich Schleiermacher serving as its major voice. Here the inductive process (utilizing distanciation and radical doubt) was committed to the task of establishing a universalized understanding of knowledge from an intuitive perspective—a knowledge that is absolutely and universally felt to be true. Conservatism grounded its theology in rationalism with Scottish Common Sense Reason serving as its primary method. Here the inductive process (again, using distanciation and radical doubt) was committed to the task of determining absolute and universal truth from a cognitive orientation. In both cases, the human mind was elevated; the inquirer observed with the precision and altruistic, impartial rationales of God himself. This, in turn, spawned a doggedly insistent triumphalism: liberals and conservatives alike condemned all opposing positions.

By the latter decades of the twentieth century, however, the modernist paradigm lost much of its philosophical energy. Scholars could not agree on what constituted universal truth: liberals fought with liberals, conservatives fought with conservatives, and liberals and conservatives fought with each other. By the mid-twentieth century, discouragement began to set in as consensus remained an ever-elusive goal. Meanwhile, scholars identified fundamental flaws within the notions of distanciation and radical doubt. Is it really possible to separate oneself from that which one is observing? Can one truly think while truly doubting all things? A consensus began developing that the answer to these two questions was no. With such an answer, the time was ripe for a new paradigm to take the place of modernism. In the twentieth century, two major systems of thought developed in the West that were post-*Cogito* in orientation: existentialism (c. 1900-1975) and postmodernism (c. 1975-). Modernism was in decline, with its demise finally occurring, according to theologian Thomas Oden, with the collapse of the Berlin Wall in 1989.

Friedrich Nietzsche was an early critic of the modernist paradigm, arguing that the god of modernism is dead. Martin Heidegger further developed Nietzsche's insights. Other important critics of the modernist paradigm include Karl Barth, Rudolf Bultmann, Emil Brunner, Reinhold and Richard Niebuhr, Jean-Paul Sartre, Albert Camus, Ludwig Wittgenstein, Richard Rorty, Michel Foucault and Jacques Derridá.

EXISTENTIALISM

The first major philosophical system in the twentieth century to seriously challenge modernism, existentialism attempted to define truth in a context where universal/absolute truth was understood not to exist. It is, in some respects, intriguingly similar to modernism but in other respects quite opposite it. A central tenet of existentialist thought similar to modernism was the rejection of the input of culture and history in the shaping of truth. Instead, one had a blank slate in one's mind as a starting point from which to organize truth. In this sense, existentialism began where Descartes began with his famed *Cogito*. Existentialism insisted, however, that from this starting point one could not move inductively toward the acquisition of universal/absolute truth. Instead, all one could do was to experience the world as it is. Universally valid criteria (absolute truth), existentialists argued, cannot be established from a criterionless foundation (radical doubt), which rather can lead only to criterionless products: random, pragmatic decisions. Right and wrong are nonsensical notions to the existentialist, since such concepts require the existence of universal truths. Instead, decisions are based on pragmatic, criterionless considerations. This random decision-making process is existentialism's identifying mark. Alasdair MacIntyre explains:

> The existentialist individual resembles the Cartesian ego without the *cogito*. Sartre inherited from phenomenology an explicit Cartesianism. In Sartre the individual as the knowing subject is the isolated Cartesian ego; the individual as a moral being is a Kantian man for whom rational first principles have been replaced by criterionless choices. Neither God nor Nature is at hand to render the universe rational and meaningful, and there is no background of socially established and recognized criteria in either knowledge or morals. The individual of existentialism is Descartes's true heir.[6]

MacIntyre's conclusion can be explained by a syllogism. Since (a) both systems, modernism and existentialism, operate on the premise of the Cartesian ego—working through questions of truth aculturally and ahistorically with a predisposition to doubt everything, and since (b) scholars are increasingly convinced that it is impossible to achieve universalized systems of truth via the *Cogito*, therefore (c) only existentialism is consistent with the Cartesian ego, since it *rejects* the modernist path toward absolute truth and *chooses* the alternative, which consists of random, criterionless decisions. In this sense, MacIntyre explains, the existentialist is more consistent than the modernist with Descartes's philosophical methodology.

In recent years, existentialism has lost much of its momentum, for reasons similar to those given for modernism's decline: Is it truly possible to think aculturally and ahistorically (erase all influences from one's mind) and thereby think from a blank slate? Much of contemporary scholarship has concluded that the answer is no. As such, though existentialism may be Descartes' true heir, it could not withstand nor overcome the criticism that has overwhelmed the Cartesian system.

POSTMODERNISM

Postmodernism has emerged in the place of existentialism. The two have much in common, since both press in a post-*Cogito* direction, resisting the notion of universal (absolute) truth and arguing for a more localized understanding of truth. The central difference between the two is that in postmodernism truth is grounded in language/culture, whereas in existentialism truth is grounded in the emptiness of one's mind (the notion of the blank slate via radical doubt). Postmodernism insists that the emptying of one's mind is not possible. To the contrary, it insists that within one's mind is language (words, syntax, and grammar) and that people think within the context of such language, whether a language be spoken (e.g., German, Spanish, Chinese) or unspoken (e.g., hand signs, facial expressions). Language provides the framework from which thoughts are identified and organized, and therefore makes thinking possible. In this respect, one of the first endeavors of infants is the acquisition of language (in their case, basic symbols) from which thinking emerges. The implication is that since languages differ, the identification and organization of thoughts that are generated by language also differ. This phenomenon is observable in the real world, where Germans, for example, typically think differently than Spanish-speaking or Chinese-speaking people.

A central premise of postmodernism, then, is that language is prior to knowledge. One cannot think apart from vocabulary, syntax or grammar. In the context of language, thoughts give shape to systems of truth. And, since language is the product of culture and many different languages exist in the world, truth is relativized to individual cultures.

Building on the first premise, postmodernism concludes that no single metanarrative (megatruth) exists from which all other truths are organized or serves as the final arbitrator of right and wrong. Instead, specific languages/cultures serve as lenses from which reality is observed and understood. Postmodernism is therefore an antirealist system, since it insists that it is impossible to bridge the epistemological gap between phenomena (the world as it is perceived) and noumena (the world as it is).[7] Though Kantian in this respect, postmodernism presses in an anti-Kantian direction in that it is satisfied to remain on the phenomenological (perception) side, making no effort to reach across to the noumenal (reality) side. Immanuel Kant, of course, pursued ways of reaching across the gap, knowing that he would never be wholly successful—that is, he believed that a full knowledge of the thing-in-itself (reality) will always remain beyond the reach of the finite human mind. For the postmodernist, in contrast, the goal of inquiry is not a uniform understanding of knowledge (a metanarrative or megatruth) but an appreciation of differing systems of thought (an endeavor which, at times, includes the modification of one's own system) without pursuing a metanarrative.

George F. Will offers a telling (though perhaps extreme) illustration of this postmodern tendency to remain on the phenomenological (perception) side and ignore all attempts at reaching across to the noumenal (reality) side:

> Former labor secretary Robert Reich was recently found (by journalist Jonathan Rauch) to have fabricated events recounted in his book *Locked in the Cabinet*, which is loosely—*very* loosely—called a "memoir." For example, Reich recounts being bombarded by rude questions hurled at him through dense cigar smoke ("my eyes water. I feel dizzy") at an all-male ("There isn't a lady in the room") lunch of the National Association of Manufacturers.
>
> But it was a breakfast; at least a third of those attending were women; NAM rules forbid smoking; the transcript records no questions remotely like those Reich recounts. Asked about this, Reich breezily noted this—what? disclaimer?—in his book: "I claim no higher truth than my own perceptions. This is how I lived it."[8]

Will concludes, then, that for a consistent postmodernist "any proposition is true—or true enough, or as true as anything gets—if it comports with one's feelings about, or 'perceptions' of, something."[9]

This "turn to language" is believed to be more fundamental than the "turn to the subject" that characterized modernism and existentialism. And, since languages are in constant flux, even within one's own language truth is subject to change. Postmodernism, then, is not an amoral system, as is the case with existentialism. Its system of morality, however, is peculiar: (a) it is not universal, and (b) it is subject to change even on a localized level.

Postmodernism is divided into two major subcategories: constructionism and deconstructionism. Constructionism argues for the formation of systems of truth defined by the interaction of various cultures and language groups that make up our world. Ludwig Wittgenstein, with his notion of the language game phenomenon, is often considered one of the champions of this version of postmodernism. Here, truth is defined by a culture (language group).

Deconstructionism argues that within individual systems of truth, modifications to definitions are "always already" taking place, preventing truth from stabilizing even within individual systems of thought. That is, even within individual systems, definitions (and thereby understandings of truth) are in a constant state of flux, deconstructing and reshaping their societally understood meanings on the fly. Here, truth lacks definition even on a cultural level. The illustration of Robert Reich mentioned above corresponds to this more extreme form of postmodernism. Again, Will writes:

> Postmodernism [deconstructionism] is the degenerate egalitarianism of the intelligentsia. It launches a non sequitur from a truism. The truism is that because our knowledge of facts is conditioned in complex ways by the contexts in which facts are encountered, the acquisition of knowledge is not simple, immediate, and infallible. The non sequitur: Therefore all assertions are equally indeterminate—and equally respectable. All ascriptions of truth are arbitrary, so there are no standards of intellectual conscientiousness. So whoever has power shall decree the truth.[10]

This tendency to equate truth with power is rooted in the writings of Friedrich Nietzsche, a German philosopher of the second half of the nineteenth century, considered by many to be a proto-postmodernist. Jacques Derridá, an Algerian (French) philosopher of the second half of the twentieth century, is widely considered one of the champions of the deconstructionist version of postmodernism.

One of the arguments of this book is that Christians should celebrate "the turn to language" as an important contribution in the pursuit of knowledge. Not only can we see evidence that different cultures think differently (Chinese, Mexicans and Germans organize and prioritize truth differently in their minds) this epistemological move also reflects a fundamental New Testament assertion located in John's Gospel : "In the beginning was the Word" (Jn 1:1). According to the apostle John, prior to everything (including human knowledge) is language—specifically, the language (Word) of God, Jesus Christ.

Yet postmodernism is not without its problems. Clearly, the radical relativism of postmodernism that many Christian leaders are deriding is a genuine concern. Postmodernism renders absolute truth a fiction and replaces it with the less authoritative notion of points of view, opinions and impressions. When the Bible is understood within this rubric it loses its sovereign rule over our lives. Sermons become the recounting of stories. Declarative statements from the Word of God designed to confront and challenge our behavior ("Thus saith the Lord"; "You have heard . . . but I say unto you") are discouraged: "Who needs that?" the typical postmodernist asks incredulously. People are instead encouraged to prioritize experience over reason, explore their own insights and refuse to judge or be judged. Here the Bible is understood to help but not rule us. Such an understanding opens the door to insights (psychological, sociological, etc.) that have worked their way into the church from the surrounding culture. "Why not?" the postmodernist asks insistently. "Everything is a question of opinion anyway!" Alarmed by this trend, Sam Horn has correctly noted, "Postmodernism has created an environment where sin has lost its sinfulness. . . . Postmodernism's commitment to personal choice and relativism makes any choice that works for me or pleases me a right choice."[11] Charles Colson has added, "As postmoderns begin filling our pews, it becomes increasingly hard for those who think in traditional terms to communicate the biblical view of life, or even to present the gospel."[12]

Though Nietzsche is sometimes credited as one of the forefathers of the postmodern paradigm, its formal advent into Western culture did not occur until the mid-1970s or early 1980s. Important voices in the postmodern worldview include Ludwig Wittgenstein, Michel Foucault, Richard Rorty and Jacques Derridá.

POST-POSTMODERNISM

With postmodernism now center stage in Western culture, many Western people fear its lack of moral compass approaching moral nihilism. As Colson explained, "Polls tell us that Americans are increasingly restless, dissatisfied with the moral nihilism so widespread in our culture."[13] Donald Carson added that some postmodernists are themselves dissatisfied with the para digm and are therefore "casting about gamely for another worldview."[14]

It is in this atmosphere of dissatisfaction that new insights have germinated and broken ground. Common to these insights is a collection of perspectives previously considered to be mutually exclusive. On one side of the ledger, scholars insist on (a) the oneness and universality of truth, and (b) the falseness of radical relativism. On the other side of the ledger, these same scholars insist on (a) the presence of pluralism in truth, (b) a rejection of the *Cogito*, and (c) an affirmation of language games in the shaping of truth. They agree that the turn to language is fundamental to the acquisition of knowledge; yet they disagree with an unavoidable implication of this turn, that truth becomes relativized to individual language groups. These two opposing perspectives reflect trinitarian thought, which essentially exists, like these perspectives, in unrelieved tension. For lack of a better term, I have called this newly developing paradigm post-postmodernism. This paradigm can be summarized in four points.

1. Central to post-postmodernism is the notion that absolute truth does exist, yet must be understood in terms of personality and animation. Though language is prior to reason, relationship is prior to language: before someone can speak, a relationship between two individuals must exist. Hence, prior to the celebrated "turn to language" (postmodernism) is the more fundamental "turn to relationship" (post-postmodernism). And since the most fundamental relationship that exists within all of creation is the relationship between Creator and creature, post-postmodernism insists that the quest for knowledge must begin here. The role of culture (language) is governed by the more fundamental role of a personal God relating to us with actions and speech. What is more, since culture is now governed by its relation to the Creator, culture no longer has a free hand to relativize truth to cultural/historical perspectives. All truth is now grounded to the same source—God.

2. Post-postmodernism argues against the Nietzschean notion of "free spirited" individuals who see themselves liberated from absolute truth and thereby shape truth in the context of their own cultures. In the world of post-postmodernism, the correct response is centered on a different kind of individual—Jesus Christ. By faith, we are pressed upon by the Spirit of God to affirm the words of Jesus Christ as recorded in the New Testament canon: "I am the way, the truth, and the life" (Jn 14:6). Existing eternally within the Holy Trinity as the Second Person, his truth is therefore omnipresent, omnipotent and omniscient. What is more, having lived within this world in a specific culture (first century Judaism) and in a specific community (Palestinian Jews), the manifestation of his truth is observable to the human eye and thereby comprehendible. Jesus Christ has therefore breached the seemingly unbreachable Kantian noumenal/phenomenological divide, bridging eternal truth with temporal human existence. He does not shape truth, he *is* truth—truth that lives.

Post-postmodernism, then, stands opposed to the idea of multiple free-spirited individuals *(Übermenschen)*—Buddha, Confucius, Muhammad, Napoleon, Marx, Freud, Nietzsche, Heidegger, Hitler, Stalin, Derridá and even Jesus (falsely understood)—populating our world. Free spirited men and women seek to be true to themselves, attempting, as Carl Sandburg once said, to march to their own drumbeat. In contrast, Jesus (correctly understood) marches to the drumbeat of Almighty God. He is therefore much more than an individual who possesses a spark of transcendence. By faith we recognize him as the full embodiment of deity.

Jesus is only similar to the *Übermenschen* inasmuch as he stands opposed to modernism and draws people to himself. Subordinate to Jesus, therefore, are a large number of men and women used of God to present particular portraits of the divine life. It is here where differing religious communities emerge, providing finite interpretations of the divine life within the specific contexts of historical and cultural settings. Rather than competing with one another, each community with its religious, liturgical and theological distinctives exists in creative tension with the others, increasing the potential for an ever-deepening understanding of truth. It is also here where the body of Christ is most fully seen—a montage of contrasting traditions held together by Scripture and the ecumenical creeds of the patristic period.

3. Post-postmodernism is both positive and negative toward the philosophical/theological contributions of Friedrich Nietzsche. Nietzsche was correct in his assessment that Christianity had become so intertwined with the modernist paradigm—both in its liberal and conservative expressions—that the Christian faith would die with the god of modernism. Nietzsche was incorrect, however, in that Christianity need not be so characterized as a modernist construct. In its post-postmodern form, the Christian faith avoids the trappings of modernism without adopting the problematic radical relativism of postmodernism. In an odd sort of way, the death that Nietzsche's madman proclaimed has performed an important service to the church. It has motivated theologians to reassess the church's hermeneutical substructure, looking for ways to shape its theology in a decisively antimodernist fashion.

4. Post-postmodernism is dependent on Luther's *theologia crucis* (theology of the cross) and Calvin's *Deus dixit* (God speaks). Though some things can be known of God through the works of creation, it is through his intervening actions and speech in the affairs of humankind that his self-revelation is most fully known (2 Tim 3:16-17; 2 Pet 1:20-21). In this respect, God's

self-revelation is most fully disclosed at the cross, an event accurately re-corded in the canonical Scriptures. It is also the cross which grounds the Christian *kerygma*. The Spirit, then, takes that which was written (the Old and New Testaments) and shapes it to the cultural and historical milieu of the current moment, fitting it to the spiritual needs of the individual or com-munity. In this respect, the scriptural record does not remain historically dated, but is "new every morning" as God reveals himself in the contempo-rary "now" to individual cultures. This does not imply an accommodation to culture. Rather, it gives room for the Spirit of God to effectively challenge culture and draw people into the veritable life of God.

Key Terms in the
Postmodern Debate

ANTIREALISM

The distinction between realism and antirealism turns on the question of ontological referents (universals). Alvin Plantinga writes, "One speaks of realism or antirealism with respect to a given area or subject matter: universals. . . . The realist is just a person who argues that there are really such things as universals, or other minds, or propositions. . . . And of course the antirealist with respect to inferred entities denies these things."[1] Richard Rorty, an antirealist, depicts any attempt to ground a system of thought in universals as "comic": "All the Platonic or Kantian philosopher does is to take the finished first-level product, jack it up a few levels of abstraction, invent a metaphysical or epistemological or semantical vocabulary into which to translate it, and announce that he has *grounded* it."[2] Pragmatism's grounding, he argues, does not lie outside but rather inside a system; that is, it is grounded within the conversation of communities and their value systems.

In metaphysical antirealism, human constructions of reality are better understood as *lenses* from which reality is examined rather than as *bridges* from which the human inquirer attempts to acquire an objective understanding of reality. As such, the *locus* of inquiry does not reside in the object (that which is being studied), but rather in the subject (the one or ones doing the studying). Moreover, in metaphysical antirealism, differing paradigms need not be compatible with one another—as is the case with metaphysical realism—since the lenses from which reality is examined are, by definition, different.

Each lens possesses characteristics that color reality and control the focus. One's view of reality, then, is "*ours* rather than *nature's, shaped* rather than *found,* one among many which men have made."[3] Jeffrey Hensley classifies antirealism into three general subcategories.

1. Creative antirealism. This version of antirealism is related to physical objects. It asserts that "there would be nothing at all if it weren't for the creative structuring activity of persons."[4] Accordingly, objects do not exist independently of human cognition. For example, a chair that I am looking at only exists because it exists in my mind; the only reality is the reality of my mind. This is an extreme version of antirealism and is clearly an "absurd view of the history of the universe."[5] The major motion picture *Matrix* is a recent attempt to approximate and legitimize this form of antirealism. Being extreme, few antirealists are characterized by creative antirealism. Nevertheless, knowing this subcategory is valuable since it contrasts with the following two subcategories that are more mainstream within metaphysical antirealism.

2. Conceptual antirealism. Objects are distinguished and described through conceptual schemes or lenses. The actual existence of an object does not depend on human cognition, as in creative antirealism, but rather human cognition is one step removed from an object's actual existence. The differing conceptual schemes of Newtonianism and Einsteinianism in the field of physics provide an illustration. Both systems (a) are logical languages from which the scientist interprets the physical universe, (b) are effective in their interpretations within the parameters of their own respective language, yet (c) operate, as some scientists now contend, on differing fundamental assumptions that are not interchangeable. That is, Einsteinian physics does not build on the Newtonian paradigm, but rather contradicts it at key junctures. The two systems, then, are equally valid lenses within their own spheres of inquiry rather than inter-connecting bridges to a singular conceptualization of the physical universe. Accordingly, conceptual antirealism does not deny the independent reality of an object, but rather, as Donald Davidson affirms, our perception of reality "is relative to a scheme: what counts as real in one system may not in another."[6]

3. Alethic antirealism. This version of antirealism is concerned with the dynamics of truth upon human conceptual schemes. Like conceptual antirealism, it insists on the presence of lenses in front of the eyes of the seer. Truth cannot exist independently of a lens and, hence, is dependent on the conceptual interpretations of an individual's experience. Accordingly, our concepts are a screen between the world and us. As such, we "cannot as humans crawl out of our conceptual skins, as it were, but are always construing the world relative to the ways in which we represent it. What we take to be true (or false for that matter) will never be concept-free but will always depend on conceptual interpretations of our experience."[7] Advocates of alethic antirealism, then, deny the facticity of universal truth. Instead, they insist on a plurality of truths. Since the lens of each seer is culture-specific, they argue that conceptual schemes are grounded in the cultures from which they arise. As such, what one conceptual scheme may correctly render good may equally be rendered bad by another conceptual scheme emerging from a different cultural milieu. Moreover, no lenseless universals (God's eye) are believed to exist from which to adjudicate the differences of conceptual schemes among cultures.

CATHOLICITY

Catholicity is the system of doctrine, discipline and worship held in common by all denominations of the universal Christian church. Within the contemporary ecclesiastical climate, the problem with catholicity lies in the fact that a pronounced lack of consensus exists as to what is legitimate catholicity. On one extreme are the anathemas (condemnations) that have been pronounced by differing ecclesial bodies against others for having veered away from their understanding of doctrine, discipline or worship. On the other extreme is the "anonymous Christian" conceptualization that maintains that all religions everywhere affirm the same essential Christian truths, though in different words and with differing forms of discipline and worship.

Rejecting both extremes, other scholars have sought a catholicity of doctrine that honors the particularities of individual theologies while maintaining an overall continuity within the church.

COGITO

The term *Cogito* is a shortened version of the famous *Cogito ergo sum* (I think, therefore I am), authored by René Descartes in 1637 in his *First Meditations*.

The central implication of the *Cogito* is that the means to discover true knowledge requires the radical doubt of all things, and from that posture of ignorance, it begins through inductive reasoning to construct a knowledge of the universe. With this methodology, however, the one thing that cannot be doubted is the fact that one is indeed doubting. Otherwise, one could not be sure whether one was in a dreamlike stupor or actually contemplating the real world. Through this radical doubt, Descartes attempted to clear away the rubble of prejudices and preconceived opinions in his mind in order to lay down a reliable foundation for the acquisition of knowledge.

The *Cogito* launched the Enlightenment. As such, the *Cogito* lies at the heart of all modernist philosophy. Postmodernist philosophy, therefore, is necessarily post-*Cogito*. Postmodernists have attacked the *Cogito* on two fronts: (a) it is fundamentally inconsistent, since to doubt everything is to doubt even one's doubting; (b) it is overly simplistic, since one cannot escape the influence of culture no matter how rigorously one attempts to divest oneself of it. By thinking one makes use of language, which is invented and influenced by culture.

COMPLEXIO OPPOSITORUM

The Latin term *complexio oppositorum* literally means "the logic of opposites." It refers to a reality that cannot be rationally conceptualized or articulated but can nevertheless be evidenced in the unending interaction of opposites. Cardinal Nicholas of Cusa (1401-1464) described the Godhead as a *complexio oppositorum*. More recently the body of Christ (the church) has also been so described; the differing ecclesial bodies collectively manifest the reality of the body of Christ as they relate to one another in paradoxical tension.

Lindbeck used the term *complexio oppositorum* in an article published in 1960 in the context of this ecumenical dialogue. Writing approvingly of an essay by Wilhelm Stählin, Lindbeck wrote:

> Lutherans must abandon their anxious opposition to everything "Roman" and seek to appropriate the many genuinely Christian elements which the Roman Church has and we lack. In their Roman form, these elements are distorted, and so must be purified, altered and deepened. Yet the same holds true of our own distinctively Lutheran emphases. These also suffer from isolation and partiality and will gain their full significance only when brought into the *complexio oppositorum* which is the wholeness of Christian faith and life.[8]

Though Lindbeck did not continue to use this term after this early phase of his career, it nevertheless describes a trajectory that he continued to follow.

This unending dialectic—that is, *complexio oppositorum*—is not to be confused with Kantian antinomies, which suggest an unending movement toward the thing-in-itself, or with Hegelian dialectics, which suggest the unfolding of differing *Zeitgeister* through history, or with Tillichian polarities, which suggest the presence of a nonobjectifiable reality residing between the poles of symbolic utterance. Rather, it bears more resemblance to two specific postmodern constructs. (1) It is similar to Derridá's "play of the trace" with the important modification that the "play" includes the Spirit of God intervening into the affairs of humankind and communicating the mind of Christ afresh. This is a communication that is new every morning yet never violates the facticity of the Christ-event as reflected in Scripture and the creeds. (2) It is similar to Wittgenstein's "language game," where differing communities organize and order truth differently and where each community's understanding of reality is layered and cannot be wholly captured by a single "game."

Synonyms and related terms include *enantiodromia* (the running of opposites) coined by Heraclitus (c. 544-483 B.C.), eternal perichoresis (popularized by Jürgen Moltmann),[9] the perichoretic dance,[10] and the two primal concepts of "yin" and "yang" of the *I Ching*. Morrie Schwartz offered a provocative characterization of *complexio oppositorum* (what he called the tension of opposites). After describing it as a wrestling match, he was asked, "Which side wins?" His answer: "Love wins. Love always wins."[11]

FIDEISM

Fideism technically means "faith in faith." It is a faith that possesses no external referents outside itself from which to validate or falsify that which a believer affirms to be true (i.e., it possesses no apologetic analyses that ground it). Fideism is therefore a concept that turns inward on itself, grounding its system of faith in faith itself. It is often associated with that form of faith characterized by naiveté, simple-mindedness and wishful thinking.

In the final analysis, however, it is difficult to repudiate fideism. All systems of thought start with certain a priori assumptions. As such, all systems are fideistic to one degree or another. This is even true of the *Cogito,* in spite of its best efforts to stand clear of fideistic thinking.

FOUNDATIONALISM

In its broadest sense, foundationalism is merely the acknowledgement of the seemingly obvious reality that not all beliefs we hold are on the same level. Rather, some beliefs anchor others. That is, many of our beliefs receive their support from other beliefs that are more basic or foundational. Defined in this manner, nearly every thinker is in some sense a foundationalist. In philosophical circles, however, foundationalism refers to a much stronger epistemological stance than this observation about how beliefs intersect. At the heart of the foundationalist agenda is the desire to overcome the uncertainty generated by our human propensity to error and the inevitable disagreements that follow. Foundationalists are convinced that the only way to solve this problem is to find some means of grounding the entire edifice of human knowledge on invincible certainty. In its quest of invincible certainty, the foundationalist agenda operates on the premise of three maxims.

First, foundationalism asserts the existence of two classes of truth: immediate and mediate truths. Immediate truths are self-justifiable, requiring no further justification, while the justification of mediate truths is predicated upon more foundational truths.

Second, foundationalism asserts that a finite linear relationship between immediate and mediate truth exists; that is, mediate truths are not part of an infinite linear regression nor a circular regression, but rather are part of a finite linear regression that is anchored in immediate truths.

Third, when coupled with the observation that the human mind has been characterized as the "turn to the subject," foundationalism asserts that the human mind is capable of discerning *mediate* from *immediate* truths. Stanley Grenz and John Franke explain that for the foundationalist, immediate truths are "supposedly universal, context-free, and available—at least theoretically—to any rational person."[12] Being universal and context-free, these truths stand apart from culture and the historical moment and thereby establish the standards from which all cultures, regardless of their historical context, are measured. Moreover, being context-free, these truths can be articulated in the form of abstracted principles.

Derridá argues that from Plato to Hegel, Western philosophy has been a quest for foundational principles. Aristotle articulated the nature of such foundational thinking: "Spoken words are the symbols of mental experience and written words are the symbols of spoken words. Just as all men have not the same writing, so all men have not the same speech sounds, but the mental experiences, which these directly symbolize, *are the same for all,* as also are those things of which our experiences are the images"[13] (my emphasis).

Synonyms and related terms include ontotheology, metanarrative, transcendental signified, immediate knowledge, absolute consciousness, logocentrism, untraceable trace, metaphysics of presence and the God's eye perspective.

GOD'S EYE

"God's eye" describes an individual capable of viewing reality independent of cultural/historical lenses and thereby interpreting reality with the exactitude and precision of God himself. The God's eye tends to breed triumphalistic attitudes, because those who believe that they possess it are unwilling to consider other perspectives; from their estimation, their interpretations are irrefutable, and all divergent interpretations are therefore *de facto* wrong. Central to the modernist (Enlightenment) agenda was the acquisition of God's eye through a correct understanding and use of philosophy. In recent years, the God's eye has been criticized as a philosophical impossibility. Two responses have been offered.

An approximation of the God's eye. Enlightenment philosopher Immanuel Kant tempered the notion of the God's eye by arguing for a transcendental gap between phenomena (the world as it is perceived) and noumena (the world as it is). No matter how much science advances from perception to reality, a gap will always exist separating the two. Nevertheless, the gap between phenomena and noumena can be diminished and an approximation of noumena acquired if a disciplined and well-defined method is followed. In this respect, Kant's three critiques, *Critique of Reason*, *Critique of Practical Reason* and the *Critique of Judgment* (written in the late eighteenth century), have stood the test of time in that they explain the specifics of this method. This first response to the God's eye, then, falls within the scope of epistemological realism: efforts are made to bridge the transcendental gap, in spite of the fact that only approximations (a working knowledge) of reality are deemed possible. This view is modernistic in orientation and still has many followers in scholarship.

A repudiation of the God's eye. Since, as many scholars now affirm, it is impossible to shed oneself of the effects of culture and history in the way thoughts are shaped and truths articulated, efforts at bridging the transcendental gap are futile. Rather than achieving an approximation of the noumena (the world as it is)—and with it an approximation of absolute and universal truth—the influences of culture and history will result in a wide range of perspectives of truth. Hence, all we have are differing lenses (differing cultures and histories) from which we look across the transcendental gap. Differing lenses, of course, can potentially offer radically differing views of the world as it is. Because a lensless view across the transcendental gap is not possible, there does not exist any final perspective (the God's eye) that can serve as an arbitrator in critiquing the correctness of differing perspectives. This second response to the God's eye, then, falls within the scope of epistemological antirealism in that no efforts are made to bridge the transcendental gap and acquire a singularly accurate understanding of the noumena. This view is postmodern in orientation and has a growing numbers of scholars in its philosophical camp.

INDEFECTIBILITY

Indefectibility asserts that the true church will persist through the ages with an essentially accurate understanding of theology due to the guiding influence of the Holy Spirit (Jn 16:13-15). The notion of indefectibility is evident in the Augsburg Confession of 1530, which states that the Reformation "is not contrary or opposed to that of the universal Christian church, or even of the Roman Church (insofar as the latter's teaching is reflected in the writings of the fathers). . . . Therefore, those who presume to reject, avoid, and separate from our churches as if our teaching were heretical, act in an unkind and hasty fashion, contrary to all Christian unity and love, and do so without any solid basis of divine command or Scripture."[14]

The means by which indefectibility occurs is disputed by Christians today. Possibilities include the following: (a) papal or magisterial infallibility, (b) an individual theologian—or an individual theological position—to whom the church is expected to rally around and affirm, (c) the decrees rendered at legitimate ecumenical councils, the first one being the First Council of Nicaea in 325 and the seventh one being the Second Council of Nicaea in 787 and (d) the self-correction that occurs in the presence of a plurality of theologies that dialectically interact with one another with the Holy Spirit guiding the collective thinking of the church's theologians.

LANGUAGE GAME

"Language game" is a term coined by Ludwig Wittgenstein that is often associated with conceptual and alethic antirealism. Using the metaphor of a board game, the movement of the pieces on the board (individual truths) must conform to the rules of the game (the overall paradigm) in order to be valid. As such, what would be a legitimate move in one paradigm (e.g., chess) may be an illegitimate move in another paradigm (e.g., checkers). Assessing the differences in how people understand truth, then, requires a prior understanding of the paradigms (rules of the game) connected with the truth in question. Such restrictions eliminate the possibility of a truth that is universally (transculturally and ahistorically) valid.

The following syllogism explains the reason universal truth is impossible: since (a) all truths are networked and interconnected to other truths in the form of a paradigm, and since (b) there are many differing paradigms with differing rules, therefore (c) it is impossible to stand outside of a paradigm and assess the legitimacy of a truth (or truths). All such attempts to do so result in the fallacy of privileging a specific paradigm (i.e., masquerading a paradigm as supraparadigmatic) and thereby asserting an arbitrary and universal control over all other paradigms. George Weigel explains, "On this understanding, we are no longer working out the public implications of what Jefferson called 'self-evident truths'—which were, in fact, moral claims."[15] Instead, we only have truths that are self-evident from within a given paradigm of a given culture, provided that these truths correctly correspond to the conceptual framework (grammatical rules) of that particular paradigm/culture.

"Language game" is sometimes left untranslated in English texts as its original German, *Sprachspiel*.

ONTOTHEOLOGY

A cognate of foundationalism, the term *ontotheology* is attributed to Immanuel Kant, in *Critique of Pure Reason*. He explained, "Transcendental theology, again, either proposes to deduce the existence of the original being from an experience in general (without determining in any more specific fashion the nature of the world to which the experience belongs), and is then entitled *cosmo-theology;* or it believes that it can know the existence of such a being through mere concepts, without the help of any experience whatsoever, and is then entitled *onto-theology*."[16] Kant followed the Cartesian division of the subject from the essence. Thus, for Kant, it is possible to think of reality and ultimate truth as static entities (i.e., timeless and changeless). Kant nevertheless insisted that a transcendent gap exists between the noumenal and transcendental realms and that therefore the human mind can only achieve an approximation of an absolute knowledge of the thing-in-itself.

It was Martin Heidegger, however, who popularized this term in the twentieth-century conversation, arguing that from Plato to Nietzsche philosophy consisted of mere variations of ontotheological metaphysics, but the twentieth century has witnessed the eclipse of ontotheology and the emergence of post-ontotheological reflection.

PLAY OF THE TRACE

The "play of the trace" is an antonym to foundationalism. The phrase "play of the trace," coined by Jacques Derridá (1930-), expresses a dynamic that renders absolute truth (i.e., truth that is timeless, changeless, acultural and ahistorical) an impossibility.

A *trace* is the residue of a thought that influences current thinking. The play of the trace is the dynamic of the writing and erasure of traces on the inner voice of the human mind. The trace experiences its own erasure as it encounters new external influences and is thereby replaced with a new trace. The new trace, in turn, modifies the inner voice, which, in turn, modifies the paradigms from which reality is interpreted.

The play of the trace, then, is an unending process that renders knowledge incapable of reaching certainty. Since words are mere symbols of ideas, and ideas are subject to the play of the trace, words face an endless regress. For example, when one looks up the word *love* in the dictionary, one encounters a series of words arranged as a definition. Yet each of these words also possesses a definition expressed in words. As such, an endless regress is generated as ultimate meaning is pursued. Even the content of books falls under the spell of this regress and thereby fails to possess a singular fixed meaning. This is due to the fact that since the consciousness of each reader has been shaped by a unique play of the trace, each reader therefore approaches a text with a unique understanding of words and language. As such, the reader is no longer passive but active, "always already" bringing his or her own meaning of words to a text as it is read. "There is," Derridá explains, "nothing outside the text,"[17] no referent at which language is anchored.

See also "Signifiers and Significations," whose circular relationship is closely associated with the play of the trace.

REALISM

Metaphysical realists can be characterized by two statements about their understanding of reality: (1) They argue for the existence of fixed ontological referents from which to ground all thinking. (2) They argue that human constructions of reality "function as bridges between us and the world,"[18] connecting empirical data with ontological points of reference.

As such, rather than believing we interpret reality through differing lenses that can be incompatible with one another (antirealism), realists argue that differing paradigms—if they accurately reflect reality—must be compatible with one another. Accurate paradigms must be compatible because each is similarly grounded to the same ontological points of reference that can be accessed through rational analysis. For example, according to the realist, Newtonianism and Einsteinianism are not incommensurate systems—in spite of the current scientific data and arguments that suggest that they are. Rather, the realist insists that these two scientific methods, inasmuch as they accurately reflect reality, are inherently and necessarily compatible and that with time their essential compatibility will become evident. Hensley explains that metaphysical realists

> believe that reality exists "out there," independent of their minds or cognitive activity. Though we have mental and linguistic representations of the world in the form of beliefs, experiences and theories, there is a world "out there," so the realist claims, that is totally independent of these representations. For example, facts about reality such as the elliptical orbit of the planets around the sun, the atomic makeup of nitrogen, the amount of coffee in my mug and the metaphysical nature of God are "true," independent of human representations or conceptualizations or these phenomena. In short, realists claim that such objects "exist" whether or not we have a concept or cognitive grasp of them.[19]

Two noteworthy forms of metaphysical realism addressed in this book are foundational realism and Scottish Common Sense Realism.

Foundational realism. Closely associated with the Cartesian *Cogito,* foundational realism operates on the premise of radical doubt and thereby constructs an understanding of reality through the rigors of inductive reasoning. The mission of foundational realists is to acquire immediate truths in which all other truths can be grounded. In early Enlightenment thought, the means by which immediate truths were sought were empirical or rational analysis. Immanual Kant made an important contribution by combining empirical and rational analyses into a singular system which also made use of skepticism. Friedrich Schleiermacher offered an additional methodology where the pursuit of immediate truths was centered in the use of intuition.

In his book *Groundwork for the Metaphysics of Morals* Immanuel Kant offered a noteworthy example of foundational realism. Through a use of inductive reasoning Kant determined that morality can be reduced to three *a priori* (foundational) maxims: (1) "act only in accordance with that maxim through which you can at the same time will that it become a universal law," (2) "act so that you use humanity, as much in your own person as in the person of every other, always at the same time as end and never as means," and (3) "do no action in accordance with any other maxim, except one that could subsist wih its being a universal law, and hence only so that the will could through its maxim at the same time consider itself as universally legislative."[20] These three maxims, he insisted, were timeless and therefore universally applicable. Moreover, all of morality can be rightly grounded on them.

Scottish Common Sense Realism. Scottish Common Sense Realism emerged in seventeenth-century Scotland and quickly migrated to the New World, where it found a home in various schools of higher education, beginning with Princeton College and disseminating throughout the thirteen colonies. Its displacement of the dominant Puritan worldview occurred approximately one hundred years later, during the period of the American Revolution. "In this situation the Scottish philosophy proved immensely useful as an intellectually respectable way for political leaders to reestablish public virtue and for religious leaders to defend Christian truth on the basis of a science unencumbered by tradition."[21]

Closely associated with the Cartesian *Cogito,* Scottish Common Sense Realism is rightly understood as a subtle variation of foundational realism. Its distinction lies in its wider tendency to identify principles as self-evidently true—"common sense." Mark Noll comments that this system can be reduced to three distinct emphases: (1) "our perceptions reveal the world pretty much as it is and are not merely 'ideas' impressed upon our minds," (2) "just as humans know intuitively some basic realities of the physical world, so they know by the nature of their own being certain foundational principles of morality," and (3) "truths about conscience, the world, or religion must be built by a strict induction from irreducible facts of experience."[22]

In this respect Common Sense Realists are more open to the methodology of *common sense* in their pursuit of *a priori* principles than are classical foundational realists. The distinction is subtle, however, for Common Sense Realists also make use of inductive reasoning.

SEMIOTIC AND NONSEMIOTIC COMMUNICATION

The terms *semiotic* and *nonsemiotic* refer to the use and absence of symbols. Semiotic communication is that form of communication that uses symbols as a means of transferring knowledge from one individual to another. Words, for example, are symbols since they are nothing more than a string of sounds linked together intended to symbolize something else. Hand gestures and geometric shapes such as a red stop sign are also forms of semiotic communication.

In contrast, nonsemiotic communication is a form of direct communication not mediated by a symbol. The modernist philosopher Edmund Husserl believed that people think in a nonsemiotic fashion, though the only means by which to communicate such thoughts is by semiotic communication. The postmodernist philosopher Jacques Derridá has challenged this assertion, insisting that even in one's mind, one thinks in a semiotic fashion. This debate about semiotic and nonsemiotic communication serves as one of the centerpieces of the modernist-postmodernist debate.

SIGNIFIERS AND SIGNIFICATIONS

Signifiers and *significations* are terms defined by Derridá to describe the epistemological relationship between words/labels/symbols/identifiers (signifiers) and definitions/meanings/explications (significations). Unlike foundationalism, which argues for a linear relationship of knowledge (e.g., Edmund Husserl), Derridá argues for a circular relationship between signifiers and significations in which each affects the other.

Signifiers do not simply represent significations—they also precede, anticipate and produce them. This is because signifiers set the limits and establish the categories from which one observes reality. Significations must therefore conform to the limits and categories previously determined by signifiers. Significations, in turn, give rise to new interpretations of the signifiers as an individual or community undergoes new experiences or a new juxtaposition of old experiences. Therefore they have a circular relationship: (a) signifiers follow significations since they provide language for that which already exists, and (b) signifiers precede significations since they establish the categories from which reality is intuitively understood and later clarified and articulated. As James K. A. Smith observes, "The *signified* [signification] is always already a *signifier.*"[23]

Hence, gaining knowledge is not a question of starting with either a signifier or signification and arriving at a fixed understanding of reality/truth (linear logic). Rather, an individual is "always already" caught up in the circle in which each affects the other, keeping an understanding of truth in a state of constant flux. Since the dynamic is circular, neither the signifier nor the signification can be determined to be the origin or finality of meaning, and the never-ending process renders impossible an absolute meaning of either the signified or signification.

See also "play of the trace," which is closely associated with the relationship between signifiers and significations.

THEOLOGIA CRUCIS

Theologia crucis, theology of the cross, is a term coined by Martin Luther. According to Luther, to understand God, an individual must look to the cross of Jesus Christ where God has made himself most fully known. Noll explains, "The crucial element in Luther's idea of God was . . . a paradox: to understand the power that made heaven and earth, it was necessary to know the powerlessness that hung on a Roman gibbet. To conceive of moral perfection of deity, it was necessary to understand the scandal, the shame, the pain, and the sordidness of a criminal's execution."[24]

The belief that God has most completely revealed himself in the cross required an additional realization that one's sinful self needed crucifixion. *Theologia crucis,* therefore, involved "an existential awareness of how infinitely impure the sinner was before the holiness and purity of the living God. It meant, also, that the way to the one true God who revealed himself at Calvary would lead to intellectual humility and a confession of the gross ignorance of all humanity before the mystery of God's wisdom displayed at the cross."[25]

McGrath notes five components to *theologia crucis.* (1) It is a theology of divine revelation, which stands in sharp contrast to human speculation. (2) This revelation must be regarded as indirect and concealed, which means that the human mind is incapable of accessing it by means of rational analysis. (3) This revelation is to be recognized in the sufferings and the cross of Jesus Christ, rather than in human moral activity or in a study of the created order. (4) This revelation of God is accessed by means of faith and, as such, stands in sharp relief to *theologia gloriae,* theology of glory. (5) God is particularly known through suffering, whether that suffering be of Christ or of the individual.[26]

Dabney observed that Luther's emphasis on *theologia crucis* was soteriological in nature. Yet in the twentieth century, he added, new applications of this concept have emerged. In *Church Dogmatics,* Karl Barth explored ways by which *theologia crucis* would have currency in the doctrine of God. A whole cadre of theologians followed in his wake, including Jürgen Moltmann, Eberhard Jüngel, Karl Rahner, Hans Urs von Balthasar and Hans Küng. More recently, an additional application of *theologia crucis* is emerging in the arena of hermeneutical studies.

Dabney argues that *theologia crucis*, as defined by Barth, tends towards a binitarianism rather than a trinitarianism. He recommends two changes: (a) an elevation of the Holy Spirit and a deemphasis of the Word so that the two are essentially parallel to one another (anti-*filioque*) and (b) an eschatological understanding of the Trinity rather than one that is epiphanic (ahistorical and timeless). Dabney argues that with such modifications *theologia crucis* becomes more fully trinitarian and capable of speaking in the existential now rather than in fixed ahistorical categories. He coined the term *pneumatologia crucis* to describe these two changes.[27]

Finally, Dabney has noted that "each theology that has to do with the true God and true salvation must begin after Luther with the cross of Christ and turn precisely on the concept of *theologia crucis*."[28]

THING-IN-ITSELF

The thing-in-itself *(Ding an sich)* is a term coined by Immanuel Kant (1724-1804) to describe something that exists in the real world. Items such as a coffee mug, a chair or a sheet of paper, as well as people and the reality of God, are things-in-themselves. Actions or behaviors such as running, standing, smiling or frowning also fall within the parameters of this definition.

Kant insisted that the thing-in-itself is not known and cannot be known. All we have at our disposal are phenomena that emerge from the thing-in-itself and offer us clues as to its actual essence. We advance in our understanding of the thing-in-itself by means of (a) *rational analyses,* whereby we construct theories about the essence of the thing-in-itself, (b) *empirical testings,* whereby we acquire evidences of the thing-in-itself that challenge or confirm our theories, and (c) *skepticism,* whereby we always question our conclusions. This process, which Kant described as the "antinomies of pure reason," will cause us to spiral forward in knowledge without ever acquiring a final or fixed understanding of the thing-in-itself.

Accordingly, Kant described a transcendental gap as always existing between the thing-in-itself and our understanding of it. The thing-in-itself resides on the noumenological side of the gap, and our understanding of it resides on the phenomenological side. No matter how far we advance in our understanding of the thing-in-itself (a process which seemingly diminishes the width of the gap), the gap will always remain infinitely wide.

The peculiarities of the thing-in-itself have far-reaching implications for theology. No doctrine or dogma can ever possess a fixed certainty. That which we believe to be true today may be found to be false (or at least require modifications in our understanding of it) tomorrow. Progress, however, is possible as the give-and-take of the antimonies advance knowledge in the direction of the thing-in-itself.

In his book *Religion Within the Limits of Reason Alone*, Kant offers a telling illustration of this dynamic at work on the question of moral evil and its counterpart, moral rectitude.[29] On the one hand, through empirical analysis via the reading of the New Testament he ascertains that "there was once a man (of whom reason tells us nothing) who through his holiness and merit rendered satisfaction both for himself (with reference to his duty) and for all others (with their shortcomings, in light of their duty), if we are to hope that we ourselves, though in a good course of life, will be saved by virtue of that faith alone."[30] On the other hand, through rational analysis he ascertained that "with all our strength we must strive after the holy disposition of a course of life well-pleasing to God, to be able to believe that the love (already assured to us through reason) of God toward man, so far as man does endeavor with all his strength to do the will of God, will make good, in consideration of an upright disposition, the deficiency of the deed, whatever this deficiency may be."[31]

Left to themselves, each side of the antimonies is deficient. Kant observed that the empirical side was problematic since it emerged from Scripture and was therefore regional in scope; that is, it was limited to only those people within the purview of the Christian religion. Also, it cheapened grace since "it made it easy for anyone to make his peace with the Deity over the grossest vices"[32] without a corresponding changed life. Kant also observed that the rational side was problematic, since it attempted to understand the notion of absolution through inference; that is, without any direct declaration from God.

Kant believed that the two would gradually advance toward a universalized religion[33] that no longer required a written Scripture (which, as noted above, has resulted in regional religions) and which would establish "a (divine) ethical state on earth."[34] It would nonetheless be of divine origin where moral rectitude and absolution would go hand in hand. He cautioned, however, that it would advance at its own pace, since all efforts to usher it along could not be done "without damage to freedom."[35] The thing-in-itself, then, was a utopian world that we would advance toward yet never realize in its fullness.

Kant's vision of this universalized religion, however, was one where formalized worship would no longer exist, since it would be "based purely upon moral faith."[36] Regrettably, Kant failed to give consideration to an alternative possibility, Jeremiah's prophecy of a theocratic kingdom on earth:

> This is the covenant I will make with the house of Israel
>   after that time. . . .
> I will put my law in their minds
>   and write it on their hearts.
> I will be their God,
>   and they will be my people.
> No longer will a man teach his neighbor,
>   or a man his brother, saying, "Know the LORD,"
> because they will all know me,
>   from the least of them to the greatest. . . .
> For I will forgive their wickedness
>   and will remember their sins no more. (Jer 31:33-34)

Such a move requires a breach of the transcendental gap, where God moves from the noumenal side to our phenomenal side. Yet this, as noted above, is impermissible within the Kantian system.

TRIUMPHALISM

Triumphalism is an attitude that assumes that one's conceptualization or paradigm is correct and that any modification will generate a corruption or an apostasy from truth. The presence of triumphalism tends to polarize a tradition into opposing camps where either one side or the other attempts to conquer the other with arguments deemed infallible (either implicitly or explicitly). Traditions imbued with triumphalistic attitudes tend to maintain a high control on ideas permitted within their communities or fellowships as a means of maintaining doctrinal purity. Accordingly, such communities or fellowships are prone to overlegislate with detailed doctrinal statements and a plethora of official resolutions. These are designed to minimize debate and protect the communities or fellowships from schisms. They also have the adverse effect of thwarting theological creativity and innovation.

ZEITGEIST

Zeitgeist (the spirit of the times) is a term popularized by the German philosopher Georg F. W. Hegel (1770-1831). Hegel theorized that the ordering of truth could be isolated into individual epochs, all of which move in logical sequence toward the *eschaton* (the future end from which all of history is pointed). That is, as history unfolds, prevailing moods (fundamental assumptions) in societal thinking patterns undergo their own evolutionary development. This results in the phenomenon where the ordering of truth differs from epoch to epoch. Yet though different, each is nevertheless integrally related to that which precedes and replaces it—being part of a continuum that is moving systematically toward a future eschatological climax. It was unclear to Hegel, however, whether the *eschaton* constituted an ultimate or final epoch. Rather, he tended to explain it as that which always receded behind the horizon, so to speak, and was therefore never to be realized in any actual and final sense.

An important implication of a *zeitgeistlich* understanding of truth is that the locus of each new epoch is not centered in individuals who are instrumental in bringing it into existence. Rather, the locus is centered in the *Zeitgeist* itself, which carries these individuals along as they re-articulate truth in conformity to this new developing mood.

In recent years, the notion of *Zeitgeist* has been modified to where it now means little more than the prevailing intellectual mood from which a given culture thinks. In this respect, it is disassociated from the evolutionary trajectory that characterized the term in its classic definition.

Notes

Prologue: About This Book

[1] John Steinbeck, *The Log from the Sea of Cortez* (New York: Penguin, 1995), p. 62.

[2] C. S. Lewis, *God in the Dock* (Grand Rapids, Mich.: Eerdmans, 1970), p. 98.

[3] Eberhard Jüngel, *God as the Mystery of the World,* trans. Darrell L. Gruder (Grand Rapids, Mich.: Eerdmans, 1983), pp. 3, 4.

[4] Alister E. McGrath, *The Journey: A Pilgrim in the Land of the Spirit* (New York: Doubleday, 2000), p. 3.

[5] Steinbeck, *Log from the Sea of Cortez,* p. 56.

[6] Kathleen Norris, *Amazing Grace: A Vocabulary of Faith* (New York: Riverhead, 1998), p. 6.

Introduction: The Advent of Postmodernism

[1] Allan Bloom, *The Closing of the American Mind* (New York: Simon & Schuster, 1987), p. 25.

[2] Commenting on the absence of absolutes in the postmodern ethos, Stanley Grenz explains that postmoderns are not "necessarily concerned to prove themselves 'right' and others 'wrong.' They believe that beliefs are ultimately a matter of social context, and hence they are likely to conclude, 'What is right for us might not be right for you,' and 'What is wrong in our context might in your context be acceptable or even preferable'" (*A Primer on Postmodernism* [Grand Rapids, Mich.: Eerdmans, 1995], p. 15).

[3] In this respect, Robert P. Bork's book *Slouching Towards Gomorrah: Modern Liberalism and American Decline* (New York: Regan, 1996) is a veritable tour de force, cogently presented, describing many of the particulars of the postmodern paradigm in American society. The fundamental argument of this book is that the move from "classic liberalism" (modernism) to "modern liberalism" (postmodern liberalism) has resulted in a significant decline in American culture.

[4] It is the argument of this book that much of conservative Christianity falls within the modernist construct, albeit in a form that stands distinct from theological liberalism. There is an irony, then, that conservative Christianity has spent much of the twentieth century fighting modernism, while in the process affirming many of modernism's essential premises.

[5] Stanley J. Grenz and Roger E. Olson, *Twentieth-Century Theology: God & the World in a Transitional Age* (Downers Grove, Ill.: InterVarsity Press, 1993), p. 314.

[6] Gene E. Veith, "Postmodern Times: Facing a World of New Challenges and Opportunities,"

Modern Reformation 4, no. 5 (1995): 16.

[7]Edgar V. McKnight, "A Defense of a Postmodern Use of the Bible," in *A Confessing Theology for Postmodern Times,* ed. Michael S. Horton (Wheaton, Ill.: Crossway, 2000), pp. 66-67. The second internal quotation is from Rick Ritchie, "Post-Age Due: Has Anyone Noticed the Difference Between 'E.R.' and 'Marcus Welby'?" *Modern Reformation* 4, no. 5 (1995): 21.

[8]Cf. William C. Placher, *Unapologetic Theology: A Christian Voice in a Pluralistic Conversation* (Louisville, Ky.: Westminster John Knox, 1989), p. 86.

[9]See Michel Foucault's answer to the final question in "Truth and Power," interview by Allessandro Fontana and Pasquale Pasquino, trans. Colin Green, in *Power/Knowledge: Selected Interviews and Other Writings 1972-77,* ed. Colin Gordon (New York: Pantheon, 1972), pp. 131-33. In this interview, Foucault comments, "'Truth' is to be understood as a system of ordered procedures for the production, regulation, distribution, circulation and operation of statements. 'Truth' is linked in a circular relation with systems of power which produce and sustain it, and to effects of power which it induces and which extend it. A regime of truth . . . [is] not a matter of emancipating truth from every system of power (which would be a chimera, for truth is already power) but of detaching the power of truth from the forms of hegemony, social, economic and cultural, within which it operates at the present time. The political question, to sum up, is not error, illusion, alienated consciousness or ideology; it is truth itself" (p. 133). Foucault's point is that society conveys to its constituents its system of truth that ensures its own survival. The power of society, therefore, generates its own truth and, in cyclical fashion, this truth exerts its own power over society.

[10]The differences between Einsteinian and Newtonian physics, for example, are understood by many scholars as grounded in two differing paradigms that serve as lenses from which truth is examined. Hence, rather than thinking in terms of absolutes, even here truth is relativized to the paradigm or template from which one thinks.

[11]John R. W. Stott, *Christ the Controversialist* (Downers Grove, Ill.: InterVarsity Press, 1970), p. 15.

[12]C. S. Lewis, *The Abolition of Man* (New York: Macmillan, 1947), pp. 56, 57.

[13]Speaking of absolute truth's dark side, John R. W. Stott argued that evangelicalism had become complicit with modernism in its hermeneutical substructure. He then added, "Evangelical Christians could never come to terms with modernism, that is with the Enlightenment—its replacement of revelation with reason, its proclamation of the omnicompetence and autonomy of the human mind, and its glorification of objective science as the basis for its confidence in the inevitability of moral progress. It was high time this bubble burst, and we may be thankful postmodenity has pricked it" (*Evangelical Truth. A Personal Plea for Unity, Integrity & Faithfulness* [Downers Grove, Ill.: InterVarsity Press, 1999], p. 44).

[14]Alister E. McGrath, *The Journey: A Pilgrim in the Land of the Spirit* (New York: Doubleday, 2000), pp. 3-4, 11.

[15]The IFCA-International was formerly called the Independent Fundamental Churches in America. It is an ecclesial fellowship of churches and parachurch organizations, located mostly in the United States of America but also in Canada, Europe and other parts of the world. Distinctives of this fellowship include an adherence to verbal plenary inspiration, inerrancy, dispensationalism, opposition to the modern day charismatic movement and modern day ecumenism. Being fundamentalist, it also opposes theological liberalism and neo-evangelicalism, claiming that neo-evangelicalism has engaged in theological compromise with theological liberalism.

[16]Stott, *Evangelical Truth,* p. 116.

[17]Martin Luther, *The Schmalkald Articles,* trans. William R. Russell (Minneapolis: Fortress, 1996), p. 6. In the original German, this statement reads: *"und gewaltiglich wider diesen Heubtartikel strebt"* (*"Die Schmalkaldischen Artikel—Druck 1538,"* Studienausgabe [Berlin: Evangelische Verlagsanstalt, 1992], 5:359). The main article *(Heubtartikel)* is an articulation of that which constitutes the gospel: "The first and chief article is this, that Jesus Christ, our God and Lord, 'was put to death for our trespasses and raised again for our justification.' He alone is 'the Lamb of God, who takes away the sin of the world.' 'God has laid upon him the iniquities of us all.' Moreover, 'all have sinned,' and 'they are justified by his grace as a gift, through the redemption which is in Christ Jesus, by his blood.' Inasmuch as this must be believed and cannot be obtained or apprehended by any work, law, or merit, it is clear and certain that such faith alone justifies us, as St. Paul says in Romans 3, 'For we hold that a man is justified by faith apart from works of law,' and again, 'that he himself is righteous and that he justifies him who has faith in him.'"

[18]Ibid., p. 34. This quote constitutes the main portion of Melanchthon's codicil located at the end of the *Schmalkald Articles.* I am indebted to George Lindbeck for bringing this codicil to my attention. Repeatedly in his writings, Lindbeck has referenced this codicil, demonstrating its value in current ecumenical dialogue.

[19]R. C. Sproul, *Getting the Gospel Right: The Tie That Binds Evangelicals Together* (Grand Rapids, Mich.: Baker, 1999), p. 9.

[20]Helmut Thielicke, *A Thielicke Trilogy: Out of the Depths,* trans. G. W. Bromiley (Grand Rapids, Mich.: Baker, 1980), pp. 247, 248.

[21]Donald Carson, *The Gagging of God: Christianity Confronts Pluralism* (Grand Rapids, Mich.: Zondervan, 1996), p. 79.

[22]Ibid.

[23]See George Lindbeck's "A Protestant View of the Ecclesiological Status of the Roman Catholic Church" (*Journal of Ecumenical Studies* 1 [1964]), where he made this case early in his academic career. Here he wrote, "God has willed us to be men [and women] and not angels, we cannot leap back over the millennia into a direct relation to the early church. We cannot imagine an unorganized, much less a purely spiritual, continuity with the past, an ecclesiastically unorganized persistence of the faith through time and space" (p. 249).

Chapter 1: The Dark Side of Absolute Truth

[1]This, in part, explains how differing ecclesial traditions (e.g., Roman Catholicism and Protestantism) can draw upon Augustine's theological thought yet arrive at sharply differing theological positions.

[2]In other words, one can certainly find in Augustine's writings arguments that insist that the notion of finitude is good (e.g., *Eighty-three Questions* 51.2). His *Confessions,* however, argue against the blessedness of finitude. Here, a strong case is made to find a way past finitude and to the immediacy of knowledge that approximates the perfection of the beatific vision.

[3]Augustine *Confessions* 1.6.8.

[4]Ibid., 1.6.10.

[5]Augustine *De Genesi contra Manichaeos libri* 2.5.6.

[6]Augustine *Confessions* 9.10.25.

[7]Ibid., 9.10.24.

[8]See *Confessions* 11, 12, where the fallenness of temporality unfolds. For Augustine, the desire for redemption from time is simply the restoration of a previously enjoyed state of the soul in the "heaven of heaven," wherein the intellect "participates in [God's] eternity and thus "es-

capes all the revolving vicissitudes of the temporal process" (12.1.2).

[9]Ibid., 12.11.12; 12.12.15.

[10]This corresponds to Paul Tillich's notion of the abyss. According to Tillich, God is a mystery beyond and prior to all human rationality. The human mind acquires an inkling as to the nature of God, but only through divine revelation (*Systematic Theology,* vol. 1 [Chicago: University of Chicago Press, 1961], p. 174). Nevertheless, this nature is inexhaustible and therefore ultimately beyond the comprehensive reach of the finite human mind. Søren Kierkegaard agrees, observing that all finite creatures will always be limited in our knowledge of that which is historical, which, of course, includes God: "If all the angels in heaven were to put their heads together, they could still bring to pass only an approximation, because an approximation is the only certainty attainable for historical knowledge—but also an inadequate basis for eternal happiness" (Søren Kierkegaard, *Concluding Unscientific Postscript to the "Philosophical Fragments,"* ed. and trans. Howard V. Hong and Edna H. Hong (Princeton, N.J.: Princeton University Press, 1977), p. 31).

[11]James K. A. Smith, *The Fall of Interpretation: Philosophical Foundations for a Creational Hermeneutic* (Downers Grove, Ill.: InterVarsity Press, 2000), p. 146.

[12]Ibid. See Philip Yancey's assessment in which, like Smith, he argues in favor of finite knowledge and how such finitude should be regarded as good (*Reaching for the Invisible God: What Can We Expect to Find?* [Grand Rapids, Mich.: Zondervan, 2000], pp. 43-44).

[13]René Descartes, *Discourse,* in *Oeuvres de Descartes,* ed. C. Adam and P. Tannery (Paris: Vrin/CNRS, 1964-1976), part 4.

[14]René Descartes, *First Meditations,* in *Oeuvres de Descartes,* ed. C. Adam and P. Tannery (Paris: Vrin/CNRS, 1964-1976), 7:17; *The Philosophical Writings of Descartes,* ed. J. Cottingham, R. Stoothoff and D. Murdoch (Cambridge: Cambridge University Press, 1985), 1:12.

[15]Descartes *Discourse* 6:31; *Philosophical Writings of Descartes* 1:126.

[16]Descartes *First Meditations* 1:12.

[17]Ibid., 10:389; *Philosophical Writings of Descartes,* 1:26.

[18]Descartes *Philosophical Writings of Descartes* 1:27.

[19]In the sixth of Descartes's *Meditations* he exhorted the reader to be thankful for the manner in which God has devised the human mind and body. Nevertheless, the *Cogito* was a methodology that a finite human being could utilize to transcend the limitations of finitude and arrive at universalized (absolute) truth. As such, he respectfully tips his hat to finitude and then proceeds to overcome it.

[20]See Eberhard Jüngel, *God as the Mystery of the World,* trans. Darrell L. Gruder (Grand Rapids, Mich.: Eerdmans, 1983), pp. 105-52. Jüngel also positioned Nietzsche at the end of this same trajectory. That is, Jüngel claimed that Nietzsche brought the notion of the *Cogito* to its conclusion.

[21]See Thomas C. Oden, *Two Worlds: Notes on the Death of Modernity in America & Russia* (Downers Grove, Ill.: InterVarsity Press, 1992), p. 32.

[22]Alasdair MacIntyre, "Epistemological Crises, Dramatic Narrative, and the Philosophy of Science," in *Why Narrative? Readings in Narrative Theology,* ed. Stanley Hauerwas and L. Gregory Jones (Grand Rapids, Mich.: Eerdmans, 1989), p. 143.

[23]Ibid., p. 144.

[24]Ibid. MacIntyre credits Etienne Gilson for this insight (see Etienne Gilson and Thomas Langan, eds., *A History of Philosophy* [New York: Random House, 1963], p. 90). Cf. C. S. Pierce, who wrote in 1868, "We must begin with all the prejudices which we actually have when we enter upon the study of philosophy. These prejudices are not to be dispelled by a maxim, for they

are things which it does not occur to us can be questioned. . . . Let us not pretend to doubt in philosophy what we do not doubt in our hearts" (cited in William C. Placher, *Unapologetic Theology: A Christian Voice in a Pluralistic Conversation* [Louisville, Ky.: Westminster John Knox, 1989], p. 26).

[25]This phrase "always already," of course, is a Derridean term denoting that one does not begin at the beginning in one's quest for knowledge. Rather, the influences of one's culture set the stage, so to speak, for all thought. As thinking commences, therefore, one is in the middle, carrying with oneself much cultural baggage.

[26]Stanley J. Grenz and John R. Franke, *Beyond Foundationalism: Shaping Theology in a Postmodern Context* (Louisville, Ky.: Westminster John Knox, 2001), p. 10.

[27]George Lindbeck, "Barth and Textuality," *Theology Today* 43 (1986): 365.

[28]Ted Peters, *God—The World's Future: Systematic Theology for a Postmodern Era* (Minneapolis: Fortress, 1992), p. 9.

[29]This attitude is well reflected in the words of Michael Shermer: "Scientism is a scientific worldview that encompasses natural explanations to all phenomena, eschews supernatural and paranormal speculations, and embraces empiricism and reason as the twin pillars of a philosophy of life appropriate for an age of Science. . . . We follow . . . the dictates of our shamans; . . . it is scientism's shamans who command our veneration . . . with scientism as the foundational stratum of our story and scientists as the premier mythmakers of our time" ("The Shamans of Scientism," *Scientific American,* June 2002, p. 35).

[30]Friedrich Schleiermacher, *On Religion: Speeches to Its Cultured Despisers,* trans. Richard Crouter (Cambridge: Cambridge University Press, 1992), p. 117.

[31]See Friedrich Schleiermacher, *The Christian Faith,* ed. H. R. Mackintosh and J. S. Stewart (Edinburgh: T & T Clark, 1989), pp. 371-524, 723-37; and *On Religion,* p. 219.

[32]Schleiermacher did recognize that the manner in which one experienced God-consciousness was determined by one's religion, culture and experiences (designated at one point in *The Christian Faith* by his use of the term "moment"). At first glance, this sounds postmodern. That which distinguishes it from the postmodern paradigm, however, is that all these temporal influences are to be resisted as one pursues the true God located, said Schleiermacher, in the Christian faith.

[33]Richard Crouter, "From Kant to Romanticism," in the introduction to Schleiermacher, *On Religion,* p. 38.

[34]See George A. Lindbeck, *The Nature of Doctrine: Religion and Theology in a Postliberal Age* (London: SPCK, 1984), pp. 55-58, where he further develops his objection to "anonymous Christianity." Also see Peters, *God—The World's Future,* p. 351.

[35]This concept, of course, comes from the third thesis in Rahner's *Theological Investigations,* trans. Karl H. Kruger (London: Darton, Longman & Todd, 1966), 5:131.

[36]Grenz and Franke, *Beyond Foundationalism,* p. 62.

[37]See, for example, George M. Marsden, *Fundamentalism and American Culture: The Shaping of Twentieth Century Evangelicalism 1870-1925* (Oxford: Oxford University Press, 1980); *Understanding Fundamentalism and Evangelicalism* (Grand Rapids, Mich.: Eerdmans, 1991); *The Evangelical Mind and the New School Presbyterian Experience* (New Haven, Conn.: Yale University Press, 1970), pp. 47-52; Mark A. Noll, "Common Sense Traditions and American Evangelical Thought," *American Quarterly* 37, no. 2 (1985): 216-38. Also see Sydney E. Ahlstrom, "The Scottish Philosophy and American Theology," *Church History* 24 (1955): 257-72; Theodore Dwight Bozeman, *Protestants in an Age of Science: The Baconian Ideal and Antebellum American Religious Thought* (Chapel Hill: University of North Carolina Press, 1977);

E. Brooks Holifield, *The Gentlemen Theologians: American Theology in Southern Culture 1795-1860* (Durham, N.C.: Duke University Press, 1978), pp. 72-154; Henry F. May, *The Enlightenment in America* (New York: Oxford University Press, 1976), pp. 307-62; and Elizabeth Flower and Murray G. Murphey, *A History of Philosophy in America,* 2 vols. (New York: G. P. Putnam's Sons, 1977), 1:203-393.

[38]Noll, "Common Sense Traditions," p. 223.

[39]R. A. Torrey, *What the Bible Teaches* (New York: Revell, 1898), p. 1.

[40]Lewis Sperry Chafer, *Systematic Theology* (Dallas: Dallas Seminary Press, 1947), 1:5.

[41]Noll, "Common Sense Traditions," pp. 223-24.

[42]Grenz and Franke, *Beyond Foundationalism,* p. 13. James K. A. Smith offers a telling illustration of this propensity within conservative Christianity: "This general 'interpretation of interpretation' was captured very well by a recent advertisement in a leading evangelical periodical: 'God's Word. Today's Bible translation that says what it means,' the dust cover boldly proclaimed. Underneath the photograph, in large bold letters the publishers heralded 'NO INTERPRETATION NEEDED'" (*Fall of Interpretation,* p. 39).

[43]Charles Hodge, *Systematic Theology* (Grand Rapids, Mich.: Eerdmans, 1946), 1:10.

[44]Charles Finney, *Lectures on Revivals of Religion* (New York: Leavitt, Lord, 1835), p. 29. In this and the following illustrations on evidentialist apologetics, I am indebted to Noll, "Common Sense Traditions." This quote from Finney is cited in Noll, p. 224.

[45]Interview with Jerry Falwell, *Penthouse,* March 1981, p. 150, as cited in Noll, "Common Sense Traditions," p. 225.

[46]See Larry Crabb Jr., *Connecting: A Radical New Vision* (Nashville: Word, 1997), where he makes a strong case against the notion of spiritual formulas.

[47]Noll, "Common Sense Traditions," p. 227.

[48]On theological reactions to Paine, see Gary B. Nash, "The American Clergy and the French Revolution," *William and Mary Quarterly* 22 (1965): 402-4; and James H. Smylie, "Clerical Perspectives on Deism: Paine's *The Age of Reason* in Virginia," *Eighteenth-Century Studies* 6 (1972-1973): 203-20.

[49]Noll, "Common Sense Traditions," p. 227. On Carnell, see Gordon R. Lewis, *Testing Christianity's Truth-Claims: Approaches to Christian Apologetics* (Chicago: Moody Press, 1976), pp. 176-284. Josh McDowell, *Evidence That Demands a Verdict: Historical Evidence for the Christian Faith* (San Bernardino, Calif.: Campus Crusade for Christ, 1972); *More Evidence That Demands a Verdict: Historical Evidence for the Christian Scriptures* (San Bernardino, Calif.: Campus Crusade for Christ, 1975); *Daniel in the Critics' Den: Historical Evidence for the Authenticity of the Book of Daniel* (San Bernardino, Calif.: Here's Life, 1979).

[50]Philip Yancey, *Soul Survivor: How My Faith Survived the Church* (New York: Doubleday, 2001), p. 1.

[51]John D. Caputo, "How to Avoid Speaking of God: The Violence of Natural Theology," in *Prospects for Natural Theology,* ed. Eugene Thomas Long (Washington, D.C.: Catholic University Press, 1992), pp. 129-30.

[52]Rex Koivisto, *One Lord, One Faith: A Theology for Cross-Denominational Renewal* (Wheaton, Ill.: Bridgepoint/Victor, 1993), p. 162.

[53]Smith, *Fall of Interpretation,* p. 44.

[54]As of 1980, David B. Barrett identified 2,050 organized churches and denominations in the United States. This number includes thirty-two archdioses and one hundred thirty-four dioces of the Roman Catholic Church ("Denominationalism," in *Dictionary of Christianity in America,* ed. Daniel G. Reid, Robert D. Linder, Bruce L. Shelley and Harry S. Stout [Downers Grove,

Ill.: InterVarsity Press, 1990], p. 351). Also see Tom W. Smith, "Classifying Protestant Denominations," *GSS Methodological Report No. 43,* revised July 1987, for a detailed statistical analysis of the differing Protestant denominations.

[55]Anthony C. Thiselton, *New Horizons in Hermeneutics: The Theory and Practice of Transforming Biblical Reading* (Grand Rapids, Mich.: Zondervan, 1992), p. 143.

[56]Timothy George, *Theology of the Reformers* (Nashville: Broadman, 1987), pp. 81-82. Also see Mark A. Noll, *Turning Points: Decisive Moments in the History of Christianity* (Grand Rapids, Mich.: Baker, 1997), p. 155, where he offers an argument similar to that of George.

[57]See Hans W. Frei, "Response to 'Narrative Theology': An Evangelical Appraisal," *Trinity Journal,* summer 1987, pp. 21-22, where he debated Carl F. H. Henry.

[58]Grenz and Franke, *Beyond Foundationalism,* p. 13.

Chapter 2: The Ecumenical Imperative

[1]See George Lindbeck, "A Protestant View of the Ecclesiological Status of the Roman Catholic Church," *Journal of Ecumenical Studies* 1 (1964): 265-66, where he argues similarly.

[2]John R. W. Stott, *Christ the Controversialist* (Downers Grove, Ill.: InterVarsity Press, 1970), p. 20.

[3]Ibid.

[4]Ibid.

[5]Marshall McLuhan, *Understanding Media: The Extension of Man* (New York: McGraw Hill, 1964), pp. 7-21.

[6]George Lindbeck, "Ecumenism and World Mission: Foundations, Principles and Policies," *Lutheran World* 17, no. 1 (1970): 71.

[7]Those who insist on a paradoxical embrace of both reject the notion that God must be understood in terms of an either/or proposition. Would it not be more correct, they ask, to understand God in terms of both/and, though the human mind cannot adequately grasp the interconnectedness of this paradox? Such a question takes us back to the dual notion of the Trinity, where it is understood as immanent reality (a timeless essence) and as an economic reality (a time-oriented essence). Karl Rahner challenged such duality, however, insisting that "the 'economic' Trinity is the 'immanent' Trinity and the 'immanent' Trinity is the 'economic' Trinity" (*The Trinity,* trans. Joseph Donceel [New York: Herder & Herder, 1970], p. 22). The implication of this assertion is that what one sees in the outworking of the Trinity inside of time is the essence of God. Rahner continues, "We are no longer embarrassed by the simple fact that in reality the Scriptures do *not explicitly* present a doctrine of the 'immanent' Trinity (even St. John's prologue is no such doctrine)."

[8]John F. MacArthur Jr., *The Gospel According to Jesus* (Grand Rapids, Mich.: Zondervan, 1988), p. 59.

[9]Dallas Willard, *The Divine Conspiracy: Rediscovering Our Hidden Life in God* (San Francisco: HarperSanFrancisco, 1998), p. 75.

[10]Jürgen Moltmann, *Theology of Hope: On the Ground and the Implications of a Christian Eschatology* (Minneapolis: Fortress, 1993), p. 49.

[11]MacArthur, *Gospel According to Jesus,* p. 15. MacArthur footnotes his claim, stating: "Lewis Sperry Chafer, whose teachings helped generate the popularized gospel of today, held that 'to impose a need to surrender the life to God as an added condition of salvation is most unreasonable. God's call to the unsaved is never said to be unto the Lordship of Christ'" (*Systematic Theology* [Dallas: Dallas Seminary, 1948], 3:385). Cf. Rich Wager, "This So-Called Lordship Salvation," *Confident Living,* July-August 1987, pp. 54-55. Wager comes to the astonishing con-

clusion that it is a perversion of the gospel to invite an unsaved person to receive Jesus Christ as Savior and Lord. To present Christ as Lord to a non-Christian is 'to add to scriptural teachings concerning salvation,' he declares" (MacArthur, *Gospel According to Jesus,* p. 15).

[12]Willard, *Divine Conspiracy,* p. 49.

[13]See Karl Rahner, *The Church and the Sacraments,* trans. W. J. O'Hara (New York: Herder, 1963), p. 14.

[14]See Moltmann, *Theology of Hope,* pp. 40-41. Moreover, Moltmann argues that the *logos* of the epiphany corresponds to the pagan religions of the world to which Israel was situated near and from which God called Israel to be separated.

[15]Jürgen Moltmann, *The Trinity and the Kingdom* (Minneapolis: Fortress, 1993), pp. 151-52. Moltmann goes on to say that the distinction between the immanent (timeless) and economic (time-centered) trinities are more theoretical than real; that is, "the two form a continuity and merge into one another. . . . The triune God can only appear in history as he is in himself, and in no other way" (ibid., pp. 152, 153). See note 7 of chapter 2.

[16]This insight, of course, is borrowed from a famous quote from Supreme Court Justice Potter Stewart who, in reference to pornography, wrote, "I shall not today attempt further to define the kinds of material I understand to be embraced within that shorthand description; and perhaps I could never succeed in intelligibly doing so. But I know it when I see it" (Jacobellis *v.* Ohio, 378 U.S. 184 [1964]). What Stewart said of pornography is equally true of *agape* love: though difficult to define, one nevertheless knows it when one sees it.

[17]George Lindbeck, "The Marks of the Church and Roman Catholicism: A Lutheran Views the Roman Catholic Church," *Una Sancta* 22 (1965): 4. I am indebted to Lindbeck for this perspective.

[18]Ibid.

[19]Francis A. Schaeffer, *The Church Before the Watching World* (Downers Grove, Ill.: InterVarsity Press, 1971), p. 76, italics added.

[20]Ibid., p. 87 n. 1.

[21]Robert W. Jenson, *Unbaptized God: The Basic Flaw in Ecumenical Theology* (Minneapolis: Fortress, 1992), p. 3.

[22]Ibid., p. 1.

[23]Lindbeck, "Marks of the Church and Roman Catholicism," p. 20. Also see Moltmann, *Theology of Hope,* p. 326, where Moltmann makes the same essential argument.

[24]George Lindbeck, *The Future of Roman Catholic Theology* (Philadelphia: Fortress, 1970), p. 47 n. 34.

[25]Much of what follows is based upon the insights by George Lindbeck, who first proposed such an understanding of the church in 1965 in his essay "The Marks of the Church and Roman Catholicism: A Lutheran Views the Roman Catholic Church," published in *Una Sancta* 22.

[26]Lindbeck, "Marks of the Church and Roman Catholicism," p. 14.

[27]Ibid., p. 15.

[28]George Lindbeck, "The Church," in *Keeping the Faith: Essays to Mark the Centenary of* Lux Mundi, ed. Geoffrey Wainwright (Philadelphia: Fortress, 1988), p. 193.

[29]Lindbeck, "Marks of the Church and Roman Catholicism," p. 21.

[30]John R. W. Stott, *Evangelical Truth: A Personal Plea for Unity, Integrity & Faithfulness* (Downers Grove, Ill.: InterVarsity Press, 1999), p. 20.

[31]Moltmann, *Theology of Hope,* p. 40.

[32]Ibid., pp. 40-41.

[33]Ibid., p. 41.

[34]Gabriel Fackre, *Restoring the Center: Essays Evangelical & Ecumenical* (Downers Grove, Ill.: InterVarsity Press, 1998), p. 22. In his *Ecumenical Faith in Evangelical Perspective* (Grand Rapids, Mich.: Eerdmans, 1993), Fackre adds, "Theological tribalism happens in the Christian community when fundamental Christian identity is associated with loyalty to the subcommunity of common stock with its attendant customs and traditions" (p. 74).

[35]Fackre, *Restoring the Center,* p. 22.

[36]Ibid., p. 23.

[37]Karl Rahner, *Theological Investigations,* trans. Karl H. Kruger (Baltimore: Helicon, 1966), 5:131.

[38]Fackre, *Ecumenical Faith in Evangelical Perspective,* p. 74.

[39]Jean-François Lyotard, *The Postmodern Condition: A Report on Knowledge* (Minneapolis: University of Minnesota Press, 1984), p. 82.

[40]Stanley J. Grenz, *A Primer on Postmodernism* (Grand Rapids, Mich.: Eerdmans, 1995), pp. 45-46.

[41]Steven Conner, *Postmodernist Culture* (Oxford: Basil Blackwell, 1989), p. 9.

[42]John Hick, *Problems of Religious Pluralism* (New York: St. Martin's, 1985), p. 73.

[43]Grenz, *Primer on Postmodernism,* p. 41.

[44]This is part of Luther's rejoinder to Erasmus in *De servio arbitrio* (*LW* 33:21). It is found in Lindbeck's writings in *Infallibility* (Milwaukee: Marquette University Press, 1972), pp. 48, 61; "A Battle for Theology," in *Against the World for the World: The Hartford Appeal and the Future of American Religion,* ed. Peter L. Berger and Richard John Neuhaus (New York: Seabury Press, 1976), p. 43 n. 3; and "Problems on the Road to Unity: Infallibility," in *Unitatis Redintegratio 1964-1974—The Impact of the Decree on Ecumenism,* ed. Gerard Bekés and Vilmos Vajta (Frankfurt am Main: Verlag Lembeck, 1977), p. 101.

[45]George Lindbeck, "Confession and Community: An Israel-like View of the Church," *The Christian Century* 107 (May 9, 1990): 492.

[46]George Lindbeck, "Pope John's Council: First Session," in *Dialogue on the Way: Protestants report from Rome on the Vatican Council* (Minneapolis: Augsburg, 1965), p. 18.

[47]George Lindbeck, "Theologische Methode und Wissenschaftstheorie," *Theologische Revue* 4 (1978): 269; the original German reads, *"So fungiert der Rahmen als alles umgreifendes funktionales Apriori, als eine Brille, durch die alles gesehen wird."* All translations of this article are mine.

[48]Ibid., p. 268.

[49]Ibid.

[50]Ibid., pp. 270-71.

Chapter 3: Foundational Realism

[1]William A. Dembski and Jay Wesley Richards describe theological liberalism today as "post-Enlightenment liberalism." They note, for example, that the subject of apologetics, one of the staples of classic Enlightenment liberalism, has fallen on hard times: "indeed, a person would be hard-pressed to find a denominational seminary that includes it today" (*Unapologetic Apologetics* [Downers Grove, Ill.: InterVarsity Press, 2000], p. 11).

[2]See the appendix for a better understanding of distinctions and similarities in modernism, existentialism and postmodernism.

[3]Millard J. Erickson, *Postmodernizing the Faith: Evangelical Responses to the Challenge of Postmodernism* (Grand Rapids, Mich.: Baker, 1998), p. 63. Erickson is not correct, however, in that the word *postmodernism* reaches back into the 1930s, yet did not achieve the status it has today as the label for a major epistemological system until the 1980s.

[4]Ibid., pp. 63, 64.

[5]It is no accident that Charles Colson titled his book that addresses the problems related with postmodernism *How Now Shall We Live?* (Wheaton, Ill.: Tyndale, 1999), a book whose title closely approximates a previously written book by Schaeffer, *How Should We Then Live?* (Old Tappan, N.J.: Revell, 1976). On the dedicatory page, Colson writes, "We dedicate this book to the memory of Francis A. Schaeffer, whose ministry at L'Abri was instrumental in Nancy's conversion [i.e., Nancy Pearcey, coauthor of the book] and whose works have had a profound influence on my own understanding of Christianity as a total worldview." Similarly, the dedicatory page to Douglas Groothuis's book *Truth Decay: Defending Christianity Against the Challenges of Postmodernism* (Downers Grove, Ill.: InterVarsity Press, 2000), reads, "To Francis A. Schaeffer (1912-1984) and Carl F. H. Henry, intellectual mentors who taught me to love the truth and understand the times."

[6]Francis A. Schaeffer, *The God Who Is There* (Downers Grove, Ill.: InterVarsity Press, 1968), p. 13. Schaeffer adds, "These dates are arbitrary as the change came, in Europe at least, fairly gradually. In America the crucial years of change were from 1913 to 1940, and during these relatively few years the whole way of thinking underwent a revolution" (ibid.).

[7]Ibid., p. 14.

[8]Ibid.

[9]Ibid., p. 17.

[10]In this respect, Martin Heidegger comments, "Nietzsche, the thinker of the thought of will to power, is the last metaphysician of the West. The age whose consummation unfolds in his thought, the modern age, is a final age. This means an age in which at some point and in some way the historical decision arises as to whether this final age is the conclusion of Western history or the counterpart to another beginning" (*Nietzsche,* trans. David Farrell Krell [San Francisco: HarperSanFrancisco, 1991], 3:8). Heidegger's point is that the modernist trajectory that has governed philosophy of the West has its origin in Plato and ends with Nietzsche. Laurence Lampert adds, "Heidegger agrees with Nietzsche on the basic matter: all previous philosophy is governed by Platonism and what is needed is the overcoming of Platonism" ("Heidegger's Nietzsche Interpretation," *Man and World* 7 [1974]: 357).

[11]Schaeffer, *The God Who Is There,* p. 22.

[12]Ibid.

[13]Ibid., p. 68.

[14]Ibid., p. 52.

[15]Ibid., p. 38.

[16]Ibid., p. 42.

[17]Ibid., p. 73.

[18]*The Complete Works of Francis A. Schaeffer* (Wheaton, Ill.: Crossway, 1982), 1:37.

[19]Ravi Zacharias, *Can Man Live Without God?* (Dallas: Word, 1994), pp. 128-29.

[20]Schaeffer, *The God Who Is There,* p. 127.

[21]Charles Colson argues similarly. In his address at Cambridge University in August 1998, he said, "Although apologetics and reason will not lead someone to God, they will at least set the stage whereby that person can understand what is happening in his or her heart when God is moving in that life. Apologetic is necessary to set the framework for us to understand the reality of the Christian experience. This is particularly so in this age when all truths are considered equal, when there is no truth, when there is nothing to base it upon, when the Christian memory is being erased from our culture" ("C. S. Lewis: The Prophet of the Twentieth Century," reprinted in *Chuck Colson Speaks: Twelve Key Messages from Today's Leading*

Defender of the Christian Faith [Uhrichsville, Ohio: Promise Press, 2000], pp. 105-6).

In chapter four, where post-foundational realism will be presented, the notion of an un-apologetic theology will be advanced. This is a major line of demarcation. In foundationalism, faith is grounded in a Spirit-guided reason. In post-foundationalism, faith is grounded in a Spirit-guided intuition. In the post-postmodernism that I will present later in this book, I will suggest that both intuition and reason should operate in a circular relationship in which neither has the upper hand.

[22]Schaeffer, *The God Who Is There,* p. 88.

[23]Ibid., p. 92.

[24]Ibid., p. 87.

[25]Ibid., p. 94.

[26]A common criticism of Schaeffer has been that his writings are reductionistic in orientation; that is, they overly simplify with exaggerations, distortions and noteworthy omissions that typically follow such a genre.

[27]Kevin J. Vanhoozer, "Exploring the World; Following the Word: The Credibility of Evangelical Theology in an Incredulous Age," *Trinity Journal* 16 (1995): 8.

[28]Alister E. McGrath, "Evangelicals and Postliberals: Pitfalls and Possibilities," keynote address to Wheaton College, April 21, 1995, cassette tape 9505-1304, Wheaton College archives.

[29]René Descartes, *Discourse,* in *Oeuvres de Descartes,* ed. C. Adam and P. Tannery (Paris: Vrin/CNRS, 1964-1976), 6:31; *The Philosophical Writings of Descartes,* ed. J. Cottingham, R. Stoothoff and D. Murdoch (Cambridge: Cambridge University Press, 1985), 1:126.

[30]René Descartes, *First Meditations,* in *Oeuvres de Descartes,* ed. C. Adam and P. Tannery (Paris: Vrin/CNRS, 1964-1976), 1:12.

[31]Located in Roger R. Nicole and J. Ramsey Michaels, eds. *Inerrancy and Common Sense* (Grand Rapids, Mich.: Baker, 1980), pp. 7-8. The line regarding the Bible "as originally written," however, requires comment: Those who affirm the position commonly called *King James Version Only* have taken the question of inerrancy to another level. In their estimation, it is not sufficient to affirm inerrancy in the original autographs. Instead, some version of the Bible in the church's current possession must be inerrant. Their argument can be shaped as two syllogisms: First, (a) if inerrancy is limited to the original autographs, and (b) if the church no longer possesses the original autographs, then (c) the church is left with an errant Bible from which to know God and study theology. Second, (a) if God desires that we know him, and (b) we can only have confidence in his message if the Word given to us is inerrant, then (c) some Bible in the church's possession must be inerrant. The second syllogism, of course, means that inerrancy cannot be limited to the original autographs, a conclusion that strikes out the first clause of the first syllogism. Through historical-critical research, proponents of the *KJV Only* position have concluded that the version of the Bible endowed with inerrancy is the King James Version. In their estimation, this is the Word of God. All other versions of the Bible are therefore errant and not to be confused with the Word of God.

[32]This is how Harold John Ockenga, former president of Gordon-Conwell Theological Seminary, understood this definition (see the preface to Nicole and Michaels, *Inerrancy and Common Sense,* pp. 7-8).

[33]Harold Lindsell, for example, has written, "Once limited inerrancy is accepted, it places the Bible in the same category with every other book that has ever been written. Every book contains in it some things that are true. And what is true is inerrant. . . . [Limited inerrancy] leaves us in a vacuum without any basis for determining what parts of the Bible tell the truth and what parts do not. For the evangelical, the genius of inspiration lies in the fact that it disposes

of those problems and provides for us a book that we can trust so that when we come to it, we do not need to do so with suspicion nor do we need to ask the question: 'Is this part to be trusted?'. . . [O]nce inerrancy goes, it leads, however, slowly, to a further denial of other biblical truths. . . . How is it that when errancy begins to creep in among evangelicals it always is accompanied by ethical deceit and moral failure?" *The Battle for the Bible* (Grand Rapids, Mich.: Zondervan, 1976), pp. 203, 207.

[34]Ted Peters, *God—The World's Future: Systematic Theology for a Postmodern Era* (Minneapolis: Fortress, 1992), p. 26.

[35]The *veritable facteur* is a Derridean term that literally means the "true postman." Derridá counters, insisting that all postmen deliver information from a historical and cultural reference point, eliminating the possibility of one single *facteur* (postman) being the final arbitrator of right and wrong.

[36]R. C. Sproul, "The Case for Inerrancy: A Methodological Approach," in *God's Inerrant Word: An International Symposium on the Trustworthiness of Scripture,* ed. John Warwick Montgomery (Minneapolis: Bethany Fellowship, 1973), pp. 242-61. See Jeffrey L. Sheler, *Is the Bible True? How Modern Debates and Discoveries Affirm the Essence of the Scriptures* (Grand Rapids, Mich.: Zondervan, 1999), for a rounded presentation of this third method.

[37]This is true notwithstanding such apologetic efforts by authors such as Josh McDowell. In his bestselling books *Evidence That Demands a Verdict* and *More Evidence That Demands a Verdict,* circumstantial evidence is offered to demonstrate the veracity of the New Testament claims of the incarnation, resurrection, etc. He claims to use judicial rather than scientific arguments to support his case, yet even here, his argument falls short since these first-century witnesses that he cites for support are not open to cross-examination.

[38]George Lindbeck, "Review Symposium," *Theology Today* 46 (1989): 59. Bernard Ramm characterizes the doctrine of inerrancy to be a version of bibliolatry: "Bibliolatry is the unusually high veneration of sacred Scripture. Many contemporary theologians believe that the fundamentalists' view of the Bible as verbally inspired, inerrant, on all matters, and infallible in all its teachings is a case of bibliolatry" (*A Handbook of Contemporary Theology* [Grand Rapids, Mich.: Eerdmans, 1966], p. 23).

[39]George Lindbeck, "The Story-Shaped Church: Critical Exegesis and Theological Interpretation," in *Scriptural Authority and Narrative Interpretation,* ed. Garret Green (Philadelphia: Fortress, 1987), p. 165.

[40]Groothuis, *Truth Decay,* p. 12.

[41]Ibid.

[42]Schaeffer, *The Church Before the Watching World* (Downers Grove, Ill.: InterVarsity Press, 1971), p. 76.

[43]Rex Koivisto, *One Lord, One Faith: A Theology for Cross-Denominational Renewal* (Wheaton, Ill.: Bridgepoint/Victor, 1993), p. 123.

[44]Ibid., p. 136. Here James K. A. Smith agrees with Koivisto, observing that "much of what evangelicals of differing stripes consider to be a divine imperative is actually a highly mediated interpretation" (Smith, *The Fall of Interpretation: Philosophical Foundations for a Creational Hermeneutic* [Downers Grove, Ill.: InterVarsity Press, 2000], p. 41).

[45]Koivisto, *One Lord, One Faith,* p. 140.

[46]Smith, *Fall of Interpretation,* p. 42.

[47]Ibid., p. 197; italics in original. Cf. Koivisto, *One Lord, One Faith,* pp. 123, 140-47, 182.

[48]Schaeffer, *How Should We Then Live?* p. 145.

[49]Josh McDowell and Bob Hostetler, *The New Tolerance* (Wheaton, Ill.: Tyndale House, 1998), p. 50.

[50]Ibid., p. 9.

[51]See ibid., pp. 53-68.

[52]Michael S. Rose has offered a compelling example within the seminaries of the American Catholic Church of how bizarre one's behavior and thinking patterns can descend once the negative side of postmodern thought takes hold (*Goodbye, Good Men: How Liberals Brought Corruption into the Catholic Church* [Washington, D.C.: Regnery, 2002]). Though the entire book is worth reading, special attention should be given to chapters 5 and 6.

[53]Thomas C. Oden, "The Death of Modernity and Postmodern Evangelical Spirituality," in *The Challenge of Postmodernism,* ed. David S. Dockery (Grand Rapids, Mich.: Baker, 1995), p. 26.

[54]Ibid. Oden's criticism of "those in it" is an apparent exaggeration since some postmodern scholars are now going on record and questioning whether a distinguishable paradigm of postmodernism even exists. Patricia Waugh, for example, asks, "Has there been a break with modernity or Modernism or are we still in a condition of Late rather than Post-modernity?" (*Postmodernism: A Reader* [London: E. Arnold, 1992], p. 113). Jean-François Lyotard also affirms that postmodernism "is undoubtedly a part of the modern" (*The Postmodern Condition: A Report on Knowledge* [Minneapolis: University of Minnesota Press, 1984], pp. 71-82). Yet, interestingly, he reverses the order, noting, "A work can only become modern if it is first postmodern. Postmodernism thus understood is not modernism at its end but in the nascent state, and this state is constant" (ibid.).

[55]Donald Carson, *The Gagging of God: Christianity Confronts Pluralism* (Grand Rapids, Mich.: Zondervan, 1996), p. 78.

[56]Ibid. These are also the arguments in William D. Watkins, *The New Absolutes* (Minneapolis: Bethany House, 1996); James Davison Hunter, *Culture Wars: The Struggle to Define America* (New York: Harper Collins, 1991), p. 246; S. D. Gaede, *When Tolerance Is No Virtue: Political Correctness, Multiculturalism, & the Future of Truth and Justice* (Downers Grove, Ill.: InterVarsity Press, 1993), p. 45.

[57]Carson, *Gagging of God,* p. 78.

[58]Ibid., p. 79.

[59]Alister E. McGrath, *Evangelicalism & the Future of Christianity* (Downers Grove, Ill.: InterVarsity Press, 1994), p. 17.

[60]Ibid., pp. 53-87.

[61]McGrath points the reader to a number of scholastic studies: Wade Clark Roof and William McKinney, *American Mainline Religion: Its Changing Shape and Future* (Princeton, N.J.: Rutgers University Press, 1987); Robert Wuthnow, *The Restructuring of American Religion: Society and Faith Since World War II* (Princeton, N.J.: Princeton University Press, 1988).

[62]McGrath, "Evangelicals and Postliberals: Pitfalls and Possibilities."

[63]Ibid. Also see Vanhoozer, "Exploring the World; Following the Word," 8-9, where the same observation is made by another evangelical scholar.

[64]Timothy Phillips and Dennis Okholm, introduction to *The Nature of Confession: Evangelicals & Postliberals in Conversation* (Downers Grove, Ill.: InterVarsity Press, 1996), p. 8.

[65]Ibid.

[66]Daniel Taylor, *The Myth of Certainty* (Dallas: Word, 1986), pp. 14-15. This book is good in helping people work out the problems of the Cartesian anxiety from their understanding of the Christian faith.

[67]Søren Kierkegaard, *The Point of View of My Work as an Author,* in *The Modern Tradition: Backgrounds of Modern Literature,* ed. Richard Ellmann and Charles Feidelson Jr. (New York: Oxford University Press, 1965), p. 751; cited in Taylor, *Myth of Certainty,* pp. 25-26.

[68]Schaeffer, *The God Who Is There*, p. 127.

[69]Taylor, *Myth of Certainty*, p. 26.

[70]Ibid., p. 71.

Chapter 4: Post-Foundational Realism

[1]See Stanley J. Grenz and John Franke, *Beyond Foundationalism: Shaping Theology in a Postmodern Context* (Louisville, Ky.: Westminster John Knox, 2001), pp. 67-68.

[2]Karl Barth, *The Word of God and the Word of Man*, trans. Douglas Horton (Boston: Pilgrim Press, 1928), p. 43.

[3]Karl Barth, *The Epistle to the Romans*, trans. Edwyn C. Hoskyns (London: Oxford University Press, 1960), p. 1.

[4]Ibid.

[5]Ibid., p. 10.

[6]See Kierkegaard, *Philosophical Fragments*, eds. and trans. Howard V. Hong and Edna H. Hong (Princeton, N.J.: Princeton University Press, 1985), p. 35, where he argues similarly. Here he insists that human reason encounters God as the Unknown God precisely because the Unknown "is different, the absolutely different" from human reason. Reinhold Niebuhr has similarly observed, "The Other" meets us "at the limits of our consciousness" (*The Nature and Destiny of Man* [New York: Charles Scribner's Sons, 1964], 1:130). Barth adds, "Between God and man and between God and the creature in general, there consists an irrevocable otherness" (*Church Dogmatics*, trans. G. T. Thomson [Edinburgh: T & T Clark, 1969], 2/1:189).

[7]Stanley J. Grenz and Roger E. Olson, *Twentieth Century Theology: God & the World in a Transitional Age* (Downers Grove, Ill.: InterVarsity Press, 1992), p. 67.

[8]Barth, *Church Dogmatics* (Edinburgh: T & T Clark, 1975), 1/1:42.

[9]See John Calvin, *Institutes of the Christian Religion*, ed. John T. McNeill, trans. Ford Lewis Battles (Philadelphia: Westminster Press, 1960), 1.1.3.

[10]Barth, *Church Dogmatics*, 1:345.

[11]Ibid.,1:397.

[12]Ibid., 1:439.

[13]Ibid., 1:465.

[14]Barth, *Epistle to the Romans*, p. 314

[15]Here Barth draws upon Kierkegaard who insisted that at the existential moment, time is touched by eternity (see Kierkegaard, *The Concept of Dread*, trans. Walter Lowrie [Princeton, N.J.: Princeton University Press, 1957], p. 79). Barth writes, "Eternity is simultaneity of beginning, middle and end, and to that extent it is pure duration. . . . Eternity is not, then, an infinite extension of time both backwards and forwards. Time can have nothing to do with God" (*Church Dogmatics*, 2/1:608). When a person encounters God, then, he or she encounters God in a timeless now.

[16]Jürgen Moltmann, *Theology of Hope: On the Ground and the Implications of a Christian Eschatology* (Minneapolis: Fortress, 1993), pp. 39-40.

[17]Eberhard Jüngel, *Karl Barth: A Theological Legacy*, trans. Garrett E. Paul (Philadelphia: Westminster Press, 1986), p. 22.

[18]See Miroslav Volf, *After Our Likeness: The Church as the Image of the Trinity* (Grand Rapids, Mich.: Eerdmans, 1998), pp. x-xi. Further in the book, Volf offers the following characterization of the Free Churches: "The various Free Churches are growing most rapidly among Protestants, particularly among the Pentecostals and the charismatic groups, who are characterized not only by the notion of religious immediacy, but also by a high degree of participation

and flexibility with respect to filling leadership roles (but which at the same time are often populist-authoritarian). . . . Today's global developments seem to imply that Protestant Christendom of the future will exhibit largely a Free Christian form. Although the Episcopal churches will probably not surrender their own hierarchical structures, they, too, will increasingly have to integrate these Free Church elements into the mainstream of their own lives both theologically and practically" (ibid., pp. 12, 13). Also see Volf, "Catholicity of 'Two and Three': A Free Church Reflection on the Catholicity of the Local Church," *The Jurist* 52 (1992): 525-46.

[19]See Kevin D. Miller, "The Clumsy Embrace," *Christianity Today,* October 26, 1998, pp. 65-69.

[20]Miroslav Volf, "Theology, Meaning & Power," in *The Future of Theology: Essays in Honor of Jürgen Moltmann* (Grand Rapids, Mich.: Eerdmans, 1996), p. 105.

[21]Miroslav Volf, "Theology, Meaning & Power: A Conversation with George Lindbeck on Theology & the Nature of Christian Difference," in *The Nature of Confession,* ed. Timothy Phillips and Dennis Okholm (Downers Grove, Ill.: InterVarsity Press, 1996), p. 57.

[22]Ibid.

[23]Ibid., pp. 47-48.

[24]Ibid.

[25]Ibid., p. 52.

[26]Ibid., p. 63.

[27]James K. A. Smith, *The Fall of Interpretation: Philosophical Foundations for a Creational Hermeneutic* (Downers Grove, Ill.: InterVarsity Press, 2000), p. 96.

[28]Ibid., p. 99.

[29]Similar to his criticism of Heidegger, Smith argues that the ghost of the *Cogito* inhabits Derridá's writings. Derridá's understanding of postmodernism is predicated on the *Cogito* and thereby in a clandestine and perhaps unconscious fashion has reintroduced it into system. The following is a summary of Smith's critique of Derridá.

First, Derridá argued for the universal domination of culture upon human thought. He insisted that "the pure voice"—that is, a voice unencumbered by the influences of culture—is a myth. In its stead, within the mind of each individual exists the traces of meanings from the community in which he or she is located, and therefore one's voice is "always already" tainted by their influences. Stated otherwise, a signifier (a word) points back to a signified (a meaning); yet every signified is itself made up of other signifiers, which in turn points back to more signifieds. Rather than being a form of linear logic that reaches back to primal meanings articulated in primal words, the dynamic of signifiers and signifieds is a form of circular logic, one where knowledge possesses no beginning or endpoint. As Derridá put it, "There is nothing outside the text"—no external reference at which language stops (*Of Grammatology,* trans. Gayatri Chakravorty Spivak [Baltimore, Md.: Johns Hopkins University Press, 1976], p. 158). Since there are no primal meanings, neither can there be primal (or absolute) knowledge. Instead, all words and their meanings are in constant flux since they are constantly being modified by the other.

Second, since all knowledge is in a state of flux, Derridá argued that not only is nothing known with certainty, all communication contains a distancing ("the harsh law of spacing" [Ibid.]) between speaker and hearer. This results in inevitable miscommunication. To interpret, then, is to do violence against true knowledge since what is interpreted is never the same as what was originally intended by the communicator.

Third, Derridá observed that in all communities distortions in communication are inevitable, which are acts of violence against truth. "Affecting oneself by another presence, one corrupts oneself (makes oneself other) by oneself" (ibid., p. 153).

Fourth, similar to Heidegger, Derridá argued that finding one's own identity requires a pulling away from community and its cultural influences. Resisting the intersubjectivity of community, Derridá yearned for that which he insisted was truly beyond the reach of the individual—a Cartesian solipsism of pure knowledge. Still, by reaching for it, the individual is able to rise above the general status quo of society and achieve a greater validation of his or her own life.

[30]Smith, *Fall of Interpretation,* p. 100.

[31]Ibid.

[32]Ibid., p. 102.

[33]Ibid., p. 180.

[34]Ibid., p. 181.

[35]Ibid., p. 183. Bernard Ramm has written similarly, "Christianity has a specific absurdity. . . . The Christian faith is . . . not a rational philosophy that man perceives in terms of rational structures. To the contrary, the Christian faith at its center repels the mind because its central thesis is absurd. It is paradoxical" (*A Handbook of Contemporary Theology* [Grand Rapids, Mich.: Eerdmans, 1966], p. 7). Also, Reinhold Niebuhr has written, "The final truth about life is always an absurdity but it cannot be an absolute absurdity. It is an absurdity inasfar as it must transcend the 'system' of meaning which the human mind always prematurely constructs with itself as the center. But it cannot be a complete absurdity or it would not achieve any credence" (*Nature and Destiny of Man,* 2:38 n. 1). Emil Brunner has added that the decisive event of all history took place on Golgotha, an event that is "unintelligible, absurd. . . . For the cross and its meaning . . . is unique, never to be repeated, and therefore far above all human analogies; it can never be understood along the lines of intellectual argument" (*Revelation and Reason: The Christian doctrine of Faith and Knowledge,* trans. Olive Wyon [London: Student Movement Press, 1947], p. 166).

[36]Smith, *Fall of Interpretation,* p. 169. Alan Sokal ("A Physicist Experiments with Culture Studies," *Linguafranca,* May-June 1996, p. 62, cited in Robert H. Bork, *Slouching Towards Gomorrah* [New York: Regan, 1996], p. 269) made a similar observation about the testings of reality: "Anyone who believes that the laws of physics are mere social conventions is invited to try transgressing those conventions from the windows of my apartment. (I live on the twenty-first floor.)"

[37]See Charles Colson and Richard John Neuhaus, eds., *Evangelicals and Catholics Together: Toward a Common Mission* (Dallas: Word, 1995).

[38]See, for example, Richard Lints, "A Chasm of Difference: Understanding the Protestant and Roman Views of Salvation," *Tabletalk,* December 1994; also see R. C. Sproul, *Getting the Gospel Right: The Tie That Binds Evangelicals Together* (Grand Rapids, Mich.: Baker, 1999).

[39]The Johannine interpretation of the gospel tends to turn on liturgical themes, evidenced, for example, by the statement of Jesus in John 6 where the eating of the flesh and the drinking of his blood (reminiscent of the Eucharist) is a stated requirement for the acquisition of eternal life. Protestant evangelicals, whose tradition tends to minimize liturgical themes, has typically interpreted this passage of Scripture metaphorically. Roman Catholics, on the other hand, maximize liturgical themes and interpret this passage of Scripture as clearly a reference to the importance of divinely mandated liturgy. They buttress their case with the observation that the Gospel According to John was written towards the end of the first century, several decades after the church had come into existence and the practice of the Eucharist initiated. Hence, the immediate audience of John's Gospel would have naturally made a liturgical con-

nection to Jesus' words unless John had added a caution not to do so somewhere in his text. The fact that he did not do so is evidence that John himself saw a connection between these words of Jesus (c. early 30s) and the practice of the first century church (c. 90s).

[40]Protestant evangelicals have long recognized the differing lenses of the four Gospels (Matthew, Mark, Luke, John) in presenting the life of Christ. Smith is arguing for a similar recognition of differing lenses within the New Testament, from which the gospel itself is articulated and defined.

[41]What Smith is arguing for roughly corresponds to Lindbeck's assertion in his seminal *The Nature of Doctrine: Religion and Theology in a Postliberal Age* (London: SPCK, 1984): "As is generally true in debates between fundamentally different outlooks, there is no neutral point of view from which to adjudicate differences. The outlooks themselves shape the criteria and skew the evidence in their own favor. . . . To say that doctrines are rules is not to deny that they involve propositions. The rules formulated by the linguist or the logician, for example, express propositional convictions about how language or thought actually work. These are, however, second-order rather than first-order propositions and affirm nothing about extra-linguistic or extra-human reality. For a rule theory, in short, doctrines qua doctrines are not first-order propositions, but are to be construed as second-order ones: they make . . . intra-systematic rather than ontological true claims" (pp. 73-80). Smith would insist, however, that though intrasystematic, these truth claims are pointed at the thing-in-itself (that is, ontologically defined reality) and therefore draw their doctrines from a given perspective of the thing-in-itself. These doctrines, then, do not float in midair like a blimp, oblivious to any relevance to reality (as Volf criticizes, noted earlier in this chapter) but instead are focused on reality and are to be assessed based on empirical testing and analysis. Lindbeck argues similarly in many of his writings, though regrettably not clearly so in *The Nature of Doctrine*.

[42]Grenz and Franke, *Beyond Foundationalism,* p. 54.

[43]Ibid., p. 65.

[44]Ibid., p. 94.

[45]Stanley J. Grenz, *Theology for the Community of God* (Nashville: Broadman & Holman, 1994), p. x.

[46]Ibid., p. 11.

[47]Ibid., p. 7.

[48]Grenz and Franke, *Beyond Foundationalism,* p. 84.

[49]Ibid.

[50]Ibid., pp. 62-63.

[51]See Hans W. Frei, *The Eclipse of Biblical Narrative: A Study in Eighteenth and Nineteenth Century Hermeneutics* (New Haven, Conn.: Yale University Press, 1974), where this same insight regarding the realistic narrative is presented.

Chapter 5: Post-Foundational Antirealism

[1]Keith E. Johnson, "John Hick's Pluralistic Hypothesis and the Problem of Conflicting Truth-Claims," in *World Religions Index* <wri.lcadcru.com/theology/hick.html>.

[2]John Hick, "A Pluralist View," in *Four Views on Salvation in a Pluralistic World,* ed. Dennis L. Okholm and Timothy R. Phillips (Grand Rapids, Mich.: Zondervan, 1996), p. 29.

[3]Ibid., p. 30.

[4]Ibid.

[5]John Hick, *God Has Many Names* (London: Macmillan, 1980), p. 2.

[6]Hick was a Presbyterian minister at Northumberland, England (1953-1956); served as an as-

sistant professor of philosophy at Cornell University in Ithaca, New York (1956-1959), the Stuart Professor of Christian Philosophy at Princeton Theological Seminary in Princeton, New Jersey (1959-1964), and lecturer in divinity at Cambridge University in Cambridge, England (1964-1967).

[7]Hick, for example, noted, "I do not think that it is possible to settle theological issues with 'The Bible says . . .' The Bible is a collection of documents written during a period of about a thousand years by different people in different historical and cultural situations. The writings are of a variety of kinds, including court records, heavily edited and slanted history, prophetic utterances, hymns, letters, diary fragments, memories of the historical Jesus, faith-created pictures of his religious significance, apocalyptic visions, etc. The human authorship and historical setting must always be taken into account in using the Scriptures. We do not, for example, need today to take over the prescientific beliefs and cultural assumptions of people living in the remote past in a much different human world. If they thought that the earth is flat and that physical diseases are caused by demons, we do not have to follow them in that" (*God Has Many Names*, p. 33).

[8]Ibid., p. 5.

[9]John Hick, *God and the Universe of Faiths* (New York: St. Martin's Press, 1973), p. 143.

[10]It would be incorrect, however, to identify Hick as faithfully incorporating the Kantian thing-in-itself into his own system in a fashion agreeable to Kant. For Kant, though the thing-in-itself is unknowable by means of the methodology of the *antinomies of pure reason,* one can draw near and approximate an understanding (always, of course, subject to modification). Accordingly, as the inquirer faithfully made use of the antinomies, a similarity of knowledge would develop with other inquirers who also made use of the antinomies. In other words, a sense of convergence would result. For Hick, however, no such convergence would result, since he made no use of the antinomies. In making reference to the Kantian system, Hick's only purpose was to validate the existence of the transcendental gap between reality and perception by referencing an esteemed Enlightenment philosopher.

[11]Gregory of Nyssa *Against Eunomius* 1.42; as cited in Hick, "A Pluralist View," p. 48.

[12]Hick, "A Pluralist View," p. 48.

[13]Ibid., pp. 44-45.

[14]Ibid., p. 46.

[15]Hick, *God Has Many Names*, pp. 18-19.

[16]John Hick and Brian Hebblethwaite, eds., *Christianity and Other Religions* (Glasgow: Collins, Fount Paperbacks, 1980), p. 182.

[17]John Hick, *Problems of Religious Pluralism* (New York: St. Martin's Press, 1985), p. 56. Neo-Nazism and the Ku Klux Klan, for example, would undoubtedly be two of those religions/philosophies that, according to Hick, were not authentically in orbit around the true God.

[18]Ibid. I am indebted to Ward J. Fellows for this insight, as presented in his Ph.D. dissertation, *The Dilemma of Universalism and Particularism in Four Christian Theological Views of the Relation of Christianity to Other Religions* (New York: Union Theological Seminary Press, 1988).

[19]Fellows, *Dilemma of Universalism and Particularism*, p. 157. McGrath argues similarly, "Professor Hick claims that all religions are different responses to or embodiments of the Real. Can he show me that 'Real'? Is it publicly observable, or is it the only conclusion forced on us by such public observation? And if it is unknown, why does he make such strong claims on its basis? Nobody can 'show' me a quark; but scientists can show me the experimental and theoretical considerations that lead to it being postulated and accepted. Can Professor Hick

demonstrate that 'the Real' is responded to or embodied in this way? He has often written of a 'Copernican Revolution' in theology. But that Revolution took place by discrediting the older view by public empirical observation, which ultimately forced the rightness (or may I say 'superiority'?) of that view on all" ("Response by McGrath," in *Four Views on Salvation in a Pluralistic World,* ed. Dennis L. Okholm and Timothy R. Phillips [Grand Rapids, Mich.: Zondervan, 1996], p. 70). McGrath's point is that by failing to identify the Real in even a rudimentary form, Hick has no legitimate means by which to assess which religions are in true orbit around the center. Without a means to make such an assessment, his system collapses into meaninglessness.

[20]Hick, "A Pluralist View," pp. 34-35.

[21]Ibid., p. 35.

[22]Ibid.

[23]Ibid., pp. 35-36.

[24]In his book *Slouching Towards Gomorrah: Modern Liberalism and American Decline* (New York: Regan, 1996), Robert Bork recognizes this dichotomy or metamorphosis within liberalism. He describes what I call New Liberalism as "modern liberalism": " 'Modern liberalism' may not be quite the correct name for what I have in mind. I use the phrase merely to mean the latest stage of the liberalism that has been growing in the West for at least two and a half centuries, and probably longer. Nor does this suggest that I think liberalism was always a bad idea. So long as it was tempered by opposing authorities and traditions, it was a splendid idea. It is the collapse of those tempering forces that has brought us to a triumphant modern liberalism with all the cultural and social degradations that follows in its wake. If you do not think 'modern liberalism' an appropriate name, substitute 'radical liberalism' or 'sentimental liberalism' or even, save us, 'post-modern liberalism.' Whatever name is used, most readers will recognize the species" (pp. 4-5). Bork's book is a compelling presentation of the distinctions between the classic liberalism of past decades with the modern liberalism that has taken over the social sciences in the West and left its mark on the political landscape, particularly those politicians who identify themselves as liberals.

[25]Friedrich Schleiermacher, *On Religion: Speeches to Its Cultured Despisers,* trans. from the third German edition by John Oman (New York: Harper, 1958), p. 39.

[26]Nicola Hoggard Creegan, "Schleiermacher as Apologist: Reclaiming the Father of Modern Theology," in *Christian Apologetics in the Postmodern World,* ed. Timothy R. Phillips and Dennis L. Okholm (Downers Grove, Ill.: InterVarsity Press, 1995), p. 60.

[27]Ibid., p. 62.

[28]Friedrich Schleiermacher, *The Christian Faith,* ed. H. R. Mackintosh and J. S. Stewart (Edinburgh: T & T Clark, 1989) p. 16, italics added.

[29]Joseph C. Hough Jr., "Acknowledging that God Is Not Limited to Christians," *New York Times,* late edition, January 12, 2002, B9.

[30]See George A. Lindbeck, *The Nature of Doctrine: Religion and Theology in a Postliberal Age* (London: SPCK, 1984), pp. 55-58, where he further develops his objection to "anonymous Christianity."

[31]Ted Peters, *God—The World's Future: Systematic Theology for a Postmodern Era* (Minneapolis: Fortress, 1992), p. 351.

[32]Hough, "Acknowledging That God Is Not Limited to Christians," B9.

[33]Ibid.

[34]Clark H. Pinnock, "Response to John Hick," in *Four Views on Salvation in a Pluralistic World,* ed. Dennis L. Okholm and Timothy R. Phillips (Grand Rapids, Mich.: Zondervan, 1996), p. 62.

[35]Ibid.

[36]John Hick, *An Interpretation of Religion: Human Responses to the Transcendent* (New Haven, Conn.: Yale University Press, 1989), p. 246.

[37]R. Douglas Geivett and W. Gary Phillips, "A Response to Hick," in *Four Views on Salvation in a Pluralistic World,* ed. Dennis L. Okholm and Timothy R. Phillips (Grand Rapids, Mich.: Zondervan, 1996), pp. 77-78.

[38]Ibid., p. 73.

[39]Ibid., p. 74.

[40]Hick writes, "We are not speaking of something that is in principle unique, but of an interaction of the divine and human which occurs in many different ways and degrees in all human openness to God's presence" (*The Metaphor of God Incarnate: Christology in a Pluralistic Age* [Louisville, Ky.: Westminster John Knox, 1993], p. 109).

[41]Hick, *Metaphor of God,* p. ix.

[42]Ibid., p. 7.

[43]Geivett and Phillips, "A Response to Hick," p. 76.

[44]McGrath comments, "Professor Hick argues that it is 'not possible to establish the unique moral superiority of any one of the great world religions.' That is true, in part because no universal moral framework exists by which such a public and universal judgment can be made; the collapse of the credibility of the Enlightenment worldview has seen to that" ("Response by McGrath," p. 69).

[45]William D. Watkins, *The New Absolutes* (Minneapolis: Bethany House, 1996), pp. 22-23.

[46]John Leo, *Washington Times,* as quoted in "That's Outrageous! (It's All Relative)," *Reader's Digest* 152, no. 910 (1998): 75.

Chapter 6: Post-Foundational Middle-Distance Realism

[1]Noteworthy books by Frei that should be considered part of the postmodern debate include *The Eclipse of Biblical Narrative: A Study in Eighteenth and Nineteenth Century Hermeneutics* (New Haven, Conn.: Yale University Press, 1974); *The Identity of Jesus Christ: The Hermeneutical Bases of Dogmatic Theology* (Philadelphia: Fortress, 1967); *Theology and Narrative* (New York: Oxford University Press, 1993); (with Garrett Green) *Scripture Authority and Narrative Interpretation* (Philadelphia: Fortress, 1987); *Theological Reflections on the Accounts of Jesus' Death and Resurrection* (New York: National Council of Churches of Christ in the United States of America, 1966); *Narrative Theology* (cassette with Carl F. H. Henry; New Haven, Conn.: Vieth Resource Center, 1986). For the other names, see David H. Kelsy, *The Use of Scripture in Recent Theology* (New York: Fortress, 1975).William C. Placher, *Unapologetic Theology: A Christian Voice in a Pluralistic Conversation* (Louisville, Ky.: Westminster John Knox, 1989). Ronald F. Thiemann, *Constructing a Public Theology* (New York: Westminster John Knox, 1991).

[2]George Lindbeck, "Review Essay," *Pro Ecclesia* 3 (1994): 235.

[3]"A Panel Discussion: Lindbeck, Hunsinger, McGrath & Fackre," in *The Nature of Confession,* ed. Timothy Phillips and Dennis Okholm (Downers Grove, Ill.: InterVarsity Press, 1996), p. 247.

[4]Yale News Release, "Five Alumni to Receive Wilbur Lucius Cross Medals," Office of Public Affairs at Yale, May 25, 1998.

[5]James J. Buckley, "Doctrine in the Diaspora," *Thomist* 49 (1985): 7.

[6]Lindbeck, "Review Essay," p. 235.

[7]George Lindbeck, "Scripture, Consensus, and Community," *This World* 23 (1988): 21.

[8]Douglas Groothuis describes this as the "intellectual suicide" of postmodernism (*Truth Decay:*

Defending Christianity Against the Challenges of Postmodernism [Downers Grove, Ill.: Inter-Varsity Press, 2000], p. 106).

[9]See Peter L. Berger's similar observation in *The Precarious Vision: A Sociologist Looks at Social Fictions and Christian Faith* (Garden City, N.Y.: Doubleday, 1961), p. 166.

[10]Lindbeck, "Scripture, Consensus, and Community," p. 20. It is noteworthy that Luther emphasized the priority of oral proclamation over the written deposit: "So it is not all in keeping with the New Testament to write books on Christian doctrine. Rather in all places there should be fine, goodly, learned, spiritual, diligent preachers without books, who extract the living Word from the old Scripture and unceasingly inculcate it into the people, just as the apostles did. For before they wrote, they first of all preached to the people by word of mouth and converted them" (*The Gospel for the Festival of the Epiphany,* in *Luther's Works, Sermon 2,* trans. S. P. Hebart, ed. Hans J. Hillerbrand [Philadelphia: Fortress, 1974], 52:206). Luther also wrote, "The gospel signifies nothing else but a sermon, a report concerning the grace and mercy of God merited and acquired through the Lord Jesus Christ with his death. Actually, the gospel is not what one finds in books and what is written in letters of the alphabet. It is rather an oral sermon and a living Word, a voice that resounds throughout the world and is proclaimed publicly, so that one hears it everywhere" (*Luther's Works, Catholic Epistles,* trans. Martin H. Bertram, ed. Jaroslav Pelikan [St. Louis: Concordia Publishing, 1967]).

[11]David F. Ford has described the postliberal project, specifically Lindbeck's contribution to the project, as a "middle-distance realism" ("'The Best Apologetics Is Good Systematics': A Proposal about the Place of Narrative in Christian Systematic Theology," *Anglican Theological Review* 67 (1985): 247. Jeffrey Hensley is also not convinced that Lindbeck is an antirealist and presses for the possibility that "Lindbeck's postliberalism is, in principle, compatible with metaphysical realism" ("Are Postliberals Necessarily Antirealists? Reexamining the Metaphysics of Lindbeck's Postliberal Theology," in *The Nature of Confession,* ed. Timothy Phillips and Dennis Okholm [Downers Grove, Ill.: InterVarsity Press, 1996], p. 71).

[12]Ford, "Best Apologetics," pp. 235-36.

[13]George Lindbeck, "Theologische Methode und Wissenschaftstheorie," *Theologische Revue* 4 (1978): 278.

[14]See Lindbeck, "Scripture, Consensus, and Community," p. 11.

[15]Ibid. Also see James J. Buckley, "Beyond the Hermeneutical Deadlock," in *Theology After Liberalism: A Reader,* ed. John Webster and George Schner (Malden, Mass.: Blackwell, 2000), pp. 196-97.

[16]George Lindbeck, "Barth and Textuality," *Theology Today* 43 (1986): 362.

[17]Consider, for example, the following from Lindbeck: "Historical criticism when rightly used is the main bulwark against the ravages of fundamentalism, on the one hand, and the allegorizing individualism of pietistic and existentialist reading, on the other. . . . Without the use of historical critical tools, there could be no retrieval of classic hermeneutics. Yet, to return to the obvious, critical history is constructively helpless. In the absence of any functional equivalents to the classic canonical, grammatical (or doctrinal), narrational, and figural interpretive strategies . . . it possesses no means of its own to move from what texts meant in the past to what they can and should mean now for believers. It is thus incapable of providing communally persuasive guidance in the present for Christian faith and life, and the hermeneutical supplements devised to repair its failures (most brilliantly, perhaps, by Bultmann) is also unsuccessful. Nonfundamentalist mainline churches are now reaping the bitter fruits of this interpretive paralysis" ("The Gospel's Uniqueness: Election and Untranslatability," *Modern Theology* 13 [1997]: 438, 439).

[18]George Lindbeck, "The Reformation in an Ecumenical Age," *Princeton Seminary Bulletin* 61 (1967): 22.

[19]George Lindbeck, *The Future of Roman Catholic Theology* (Philadelphia: Fortress, 1970), p. 99. Walter Kasper has written similarly, "Heresy is possible . . . not merely through the denial of already fixed formulae of faith, but also through the rigid clinging to these formulae in a new confessional situation" ("The Relationship Between Gospel and Dogma," in *Man as Man and Believer,* trans. Theodore L. Westow, ed. Edward Schillebeeckx and Boniface Willems [New York: Paulist], p. 157).

[20]George A. Lindbeck, *The Nature of Doctrine: Religion and Theology in a Postliberal Age* (London: SPCK, 1984), p. 95.

[21]Ibid., p. 94.

[22]Ibid., p. 95.

[23]Lindbeck, "Scripture, Consensus, and Community," p. 20.

[24]Ibid., p. 21.

[25]George Lindbeck, "Atonement & the Hermeneutics of Intratextual Social Embodiment," in *The Nature of Confession,* ed. Timothy Phillips and Dennis Okholm (Downers Grove, Ill.: Inter-Varsity Press, 1996), p. 226. For a detailed description of Lindbeck's understanding of absorption, see also his *The Nature of Doctrine,* pp. 32-41, and idem, "The Gospel's Uniqueness," pp. 432-33. In "What It Means to Me," Walt Russell provides helpful illustrations of the problems related to Bible study when the contemporary world is permitted to absorb the biblical world (*Christianity Today,* October 26, 1992, pp. 30-32).

[26]Ibid.

[27]Lindbeck, "Theologische Methode," pp. 270-71. In *The Nature of Doctrine,* Lindbeck makes the same point, addressing the differences in Aristotelian, Newtonian and Einsteinian physics, all of which bear a semblance of accuracy in their own domain (pp. 10-11).

[28]Lindbeck, "Atonement & the Hermeneutics," pp. 228-29.

[29]Lindbeck, *Future of Roman Catholic Theology,* p. 113.

[30]See George Lindbeck, "The Reformation Heritage and Christian Unity," *Lutheran Quarterly* NS 2 (1988): 497.

[31]Lindbeck, *Future of Roman Catholic Theology,* p. 113.

[32]Ibid. Also consider Lindbeck's words in "The Gospel's Uniqueness," where he writes, "The Bible is thus its own interpreter, not as bare text, but in its classic construal. Although it was the Reformers who first formulated this dictum in opposition to late medieval claims, it was implicit in catholic practice from patristic times. The heretics erred, so it was regularly argued, not because they failed to submit to ecclesiastical authority, but because they ignored the *scopus* of scripture as the communally edifying and canonically unified word from God" (p. 433).

[33]Lindbeck, "Barth and Textuality," p. 362. Also see Lindbeck, "The Gospel's Uniqueness," pp. 423-50.

[34]Lindbeck, "Barth and Textuality," p. 362.

[35]George Lindbeck, *Infallibility* (Milwaukee: Marquette University Press, 1972), p. 62.

[36]See Lindbeck, *Nature of Doctrine,* p. 48.

[37]Ibid., p. 54.

[38]Ibid. See George Lindbeck, "Modernity and Luther's Understanding of Freedom of the Christian," in *Martin Luther and the Modern Mind: Freedom, Conscience, Toleration, Rights,* ed. Manfred Hoffmann (Lewiston, N.Y.: Edward Mellen, 1985), p. 16, where Lindbeck further develops this thought. Also see J. Augustine DiNoia, "Theology in Dialogue," in *Theology After*

Liberalism: A Reader, ed. John Webster and George Schner (Malden, Mass.: Blackwell, 2000), pp. 152-183.

[39]Lindbeck, *Nature of Doctrine,* pp. 54-55.

[40]George A. Lindbeck, "Vortwort zur deutschen Ausgabe," in *Christliche Lehre als Grammatik des Glaubens* (Gütersloh: Chr. Kaiser/Gütersloher Verlagshaus, 1994), p. 20, my translation.

[41]Ibid.

Chapter 7: Absolute Truth Revisited

[1]This paradigm corresponds to Martin Buber's notion of the "I-Thou" described in his book *I and Thou.* His point is that all real theology is a personal encounter between God and the self. Drawing upon Buber's insights, Emil Brunner has written, "In the New Testament faith is the relation between person and person, the obedient trust of man in God who graciously stoops to meet him. Here revelation is truth as encounter, and faith is knowledge as encounter" (*Revelation and Reason: The Christian Doctrine of Faith and Knowledge,* trans. Olive Wyon (Philadelphia: Westminster Press, 1946), p. 9).

[2]Two centuries ago, Kierkegaard (1813-1855) pushed theology in this direction arguing that truth is ultimately found, not in reason, but in passion—for it is in one's passion that God is encountered and understood (see Kierkegaard, *Concluding Unscientific Postscript to the "Philosophical Fragments,"* ed. and trans. Howard V. Hong and Edna H. Hong [Princeton, N.J.: Princeton University Press, 1977], where he developed this argument). Similarly, Karl Barth has written, "The subject of revelation is the Subject that remains indissolubly Subject. We cannot get behind this Subject. It cannot become an object" (*Church Dogmatics,* trans. G. T. Thomson [Edinburgh: T & T Clark, 1975], 1:438). He also noted that to see divine revelation as a series of propositions is to "de-personalize revelation" (*Church Dogmatics,* 1:310).

[3]Brent Curtis and John Eldredge, *The Sacred Romance: Drawing Close to the Heart of God* (Nashville: Thomas Nelson, 1997), pp. 44, 45.

[4]Stanley J. Grenz and John R. Franke, *Beyond Foundationalism: Shaping Theology in a Postmodern Context* (Louisville, Ky.: Westminster John Knox, 2001), p. 72.

[5]Grenz and Franke argue that understanding divine truth requires an interaction between the history of the church and the story framed in our own historical-cultural milieu: "In appropriating the biblical text, the Spirit speaks, but the Spirit's speaking does not come through the text in isolation. Rather, we read the text cognizant of the fact that we are the contemporary embodiment of a centuries-long interpretive tradition within the Christian community (and hence we must take seriously the theological tradition of the church). And we read realizing that we are embedded in a specific historical-cultural context (and hence we must pay attention to our culture)" (ibid., p. 75).

[6]George Lindbeck, "Atonement & the Hermeneutics of Intratextual Social Embodiment," in *The Nature of Confession,* ed. Timothy Phillips and Dennis Okholm (Downers Grove, Ill.: InterVarsity Press, 1996), p. 233.

[7]Ibid. It was this version of the atonement that Barth was particularly fond of. He wrote, "Because it was the Son of God, i.e., God Himself who took our place on Good Friday, the substitution could be effectual and procure our reconciliation with the righteousness of God, and therefore the victory of God's righteousness, and therefore our own righteousness in His sight" (*Church Dogmatics,* trans. G. T. Thomson [Edinburgh: T & T Clark, 1969], 2/1:403; cf. 4/1:253).

[8]Lindbeck, "Atonement & the Hermeneutics," p. 234. Lindbeck goes on to say that without a

high Christology, Jesus is "important chiefly as an example of self-sacrificing love, which human beings have a strength and goodness to imitate if only they will do so" (ibid.). This, of course, spawns a self-righteousness foreign to the New Testament documents.

[9]Ibid.

[10]D. Lyle Dabney, *Die Kenosis des Geistes: Kontinuität zwischen Schöpfung und Erlösung im Werk des Heiligen Geistes* (Neukirchen-Vluyn: Neukirchener Verlag, 1997), p. 123, my translation. Literally, *"zweifache Beziehung zwischen dem Geist und Christus, in der einerseits der Geist Christus bestimmt und andererseits von Christus bestimmt wird."* In this section, I am indebted to Dabney's insights of this reciprocal relationship between Spirit and Word as noted in his book *Die Kenosis des Geistes*.

[11]See D. Lyle Dabney, "A First Theology for a Twenty-first Century," in *The Future of Theology: Essays in Honor of Jürgen Moltmann* (Grand Rapids, Mich.: Eerdmans, 1996), p. 159.

[12]This, of course, suggests that the *filioque* clause of the Western church (which includes Roman Catholicism and Protestantism) needs to be seriously reconsidered. The Niceno-Constantinopolitan Creed of 381 originally stated that the Holy Spirit "proceeds from the Father." An important implication of this statement is that Spirit does not proceed from the Son and is therefore not subordinate to the Son. Rather, the Spirit and Son are in a parallel relationship with one another. The Western church, however, unofficially (that is, without the authority of an ecumenical council) began adding the word *filioque* ("and the Son") to the Niceno-Constantinopolitan Creed. Hence, the creed was modified to read that the Holy Spirit "proceeds from the Father *and the Son*." With this move, the Spirit became subordinate to both the Father and the Son. Current theological discussion is engaged in this question (e.g., Jürgen Moltmann, *The Trinity and the Kingdom* [Minneapolis: Fortress, 1993]; Dabny, *Die Kenosis des Geistes;* Robert W. Jenson, *Unbaptized God: The Basic Flaw in Ecumenical Theology* [Minneapolis: Fortress, 1992]; and Thomas Smail, *The Giving Spirit: The Holy Spirit in Person* [London: Hodder & Stoughton, 1988]). In this discussion, either a repudiation of the *filioque* clause or its serious modification is being argued as a means of freeing the Western's church's limited understanding of the role of the Holy Spirit.

[13]Dabney, *Die Kenosis des Geistes,* p. 117, my translation. Bernard Ramm has argued similarly, "Liberalism had no means of doing justice to this doctrine [of the Spirit], for it denied the supernatural revelation and redemption upon which it rests. Fundamentalism was only a step removed from liberalism, for in so emphasizing the verbal inspiration of Scripture and the inerrancy of Scripture it also embarrassed the role of the witness of the Spirit" (*A Handbook of Contemporary Theology* [Grand Rapids, Mich.: Eerdmans, 1966], p. 121).

[14]The phenomenon of the three waves of the Holy Spirit of the twentieth century (the Pentecostal movement of the early twentieth century, the charismatic movement of the mid twentieth century, and manifestation of charismatic gifts in traditionally noncharismatic churches in the latter twentieth century) may be understood as an attempt to overcome the seeming irrelevance afforded the Holy Spirit in Western Christianity. Having said this, I am not endorsing all the phenomena associated with the three waves of the Spirit that have occurred in the twentieth century. It is merely a recognition that Western theology and the activity of the Spirit have been at odds with one another and in need of significant reassessment in the systematic theology of Western Christianity.

[15]Smail, *The Giving Spirit,* p. 77.

[16]Ibid., pp. 77-78.

[17]Stephen Toulmin, *Cosmopolis: The Hidden Agenda of Modernity* (New York: Free Press, 1990), p. 193.

[18]Ibid., p. 192.

[19]Charles P. Arand, "The Church's Dogma and Biblical Theology," in *A Confessing Theology for Postmodern Times,* ed. Michael Horton (Wheaton: Crossway, 2000), pp. 15-16.

[20]Erich Auerbach, *Mimesis* (Princeton, N.J.: Princeton University Press, 1968), p. 15.

[21]Hans W. Frei, *The Eclipse of Biblical Narrative: A Study in Eighteenth and Nineteenth Century Hermeneutics* (New Haven, Conn.: Yale University Press, 1974), p. 12.

[22]Moltmann, *Trinity and the Kingdom,* p. xi.

[23]Ibid., p. xiv.

[24]Paul L. Holmer, *The Grammar of Faith* (San Francisco: Harper & Row, 1978), p. 12.

[25]William C. Placher, *Unapologetic Theology: A Christian Voice in a Pluralistic Conversation* (Louisville, Ky.: Westminster John Knox, 1989), p. 107.

[26]Hans-Georg Gadamer, *Truth and Method,* trans. Garrett Barden and John Cumming (New York: Seabury Press, 1975), p. 269.

[27]Moltmann, *Trinity and the Kingdom,* p. xii.

[28]George Lindbeck, *University Divinity Schools: A Report on Ecclesiastically Independent Theological Education* ([New York]: The Rockefeller Foundation, 1976), p. 2.

[29]Ibid., p. vi.

[30]Ibid., p. 33.

[31]Ibid., p. 24.

[32]Ibid., p. 21. Christopher Jencks and David Reisman argue similarly, commenting thus on the Union Theological Seminary-Columbia University affiliation: "The advantages of such an arrangement for Columbia are less clear, but presumably a theological affiliation helps protect the University against charges of godlessness and helps appease trustees who are worried about the University's failure to teach morality and wisdom. Having a 'token' seminary tool is this respect rather like admitting a handful of 'token' Negroes, who quiet the conscience and whose presence can be emphasized when hostile questions are tasked by critics." Then, turning to Harvard, they add, "When, for example, President Nathan Pusey of Harvard decided to launch his first major fund drive in behalf of the Divinity School [in 1953], he acted primarily not out of personal conviction, but his decision had a benign political effect too. While it antagonized the many faculty who thought religion in rather bad taste, it also consolidated alumni support by assuring them that Harvard was not quite the center of godless radicalism that its critics assumed" (*The Academic Revolution* [New York: Doubleday, 1968], pp. 211-12).

[33]Lindbeck, *University Divinity Schools,* p. 14.

[34]Ibid.

[35]Ibid.

[36]Ibid., pp. 9, 39. See Lindbeck, "Theological Education in North America Today," *The Council on the Study of Religions* 8, no. 4 (1977): 87, where Lindbeck offers a similar argument.

[37]Lindbeck, *University Divinity Schools,* pp. 53-54.

[38]Ibid., p. 14.

[39]Ibid., p. 22. Also see Talcott Parsons and Gerald M. Platt, *The American University* (Cambridge: Harvard University Press, 1973), where a similar argument is made (pp. 49-50).

[40]C. S. Lewis, *Mere Christianity* (London: Collins, 1956), p. vi.

[41]Ibid., p. xi.

[42]Kathleen Norris, *Amazing Grace: A Vocabulary of Faith* (New York: Riverhead, 1998), pp. 289-90.

[43]Dabney, "A First Theology for a Twenty-first Century," p. 158.

[44]Ibid.

Chapter 8: What Now?

[1]See Richard J. Bernstein, *Beyond Objectivism and Relativism: Science, Hermeneutics, and Praxis* (Philadelphia: University of Pennsylvania Press, 1983), pp. 16-20.

[2]Daniel Taylor, *The Myth of Certainty* (Downers Grove, Ill.: InterVarsity Press, 2000), p. 28.

[3]Ted Peters, *God—The World's Future: Systematic Theology for a Postmodern Era* (Minneapolis: Fortress, 1992), p. 28.

[4]Describing Kierkegaard in this respect, Bernard Ramm notes, "Kierkegaard introduced the term risk into theology. According to Kierkegaard, the intellect may be followed up to a point, but it eventually comes to juncture where it no longer can serve. If we are to proceed in the existential territory, it must be by faith, passion, and paradox. The paradox cannot be relieved but remains in force. The self accepts the paradox in the passion of faith, but the intellect views the acceptance of the paradox as a risk" (*A Handbook of Contemporary Theology* [Grand Rapids, Mich.: Eerdmans, 1966], p. 114). Kierkegaard wrote, "Without risk there is no faith. Faith is precisely the contradiction between the infinite passion of the individual's inwardness and the objective uncertainty" (Søren Kierkegaard, *Concluding Unscientific Postscript to the "Philosophical Fragments,"* ed. and trans. Howard V. Hong and Edna H. Hong (Princeton, N.J.: Princeton University Press, 1977), p. 182). "For without risk there is no faith, and the greater the risk the greater the faith" (ibid., p. 188). Also see Emil Brunner, *Revelation and Reason,* trans. Olive Wyon (Philadelphia: Westminster Press, 1946), pp. 46ff.

[5]Paul Ricoeur, *The Symbolism of Evil,* trans. Emerson Buchanan (New York: Harper & Row, 1967), p. 351. It is my assertion that Ricoeur does not sufficiently distance himself from the antirealism that I addressed in chapter five of this book. I therefore agree with Kevin Vanhoozer, who observed that "Ricoeur has merely transposed subjectivity into a new key" and that ultimately the object of "reference" remains only the human self (*Biblical Narrative in the Philosophy of Paul Ricoeur: A Study in Hermeneutics and Theology* [Cambridge: Cambridge University Press, 1990], p. 140). What is missing in Ricoeur is the epistemology of *theologia crucis,* which shifts the center of knowledge away from the self or community and to God. See Edgar V. McKnight, "A Defense of a Postmodern Use of the Bible," in *A Confessing Theology for Postmodern Times,* ed. Michael S. Horton (Wheaton, Ill.: Crossway, 2000), pp. 76-80, where he develops the notion of the hermeneutical circle from an evangelical perspective.

[6]Ricoeur, *Symbolism of Evil,* p. 351. Bernard Ramm comments, "If Christianity is a paradox, an absurdity, a possibility, then a person does not assent to Christianity; he can only decide for Christianity" (*Handbook of Contemporary Theology,* p. 31). Here is where Kierkegaard's leap of faith comes into play.

[7]Peters, *God—The World's Future,* p. 28.

[8]From our perspective, however, entrance into the circle requires a decision, an act of our will.

[9]George A. Lindbeck, "Atonement and the Hermeneutics of Intratextual Social Embodiment," in *The Nature of Confession,* ed. Timothy R. Phillips and Dennis L. Okholm (Downers Grove, Ill.: InterVarsity Press, 1996), p. 225.

[10]Ibid.

[11]This is true even in the hard sciences. Brunner's comments are helpful: "Every multiplication table already implies man's relation with God, for we cannot count at all without the implicit presupposition of infinite number. We cannot say, 'That is true,' without appealing to absolute Truth" (*Revelation and Reason,* p. 56).

[12]Bernard Ramm adds, "The notion that God is Subject and not Object is suggested by Pascal's thought. His belief that God was not open to natural theology nor to the approach of the

philosophical way suggests as much. God known by the intuition of the heart means that God is Subject, who only discloses Himself from His side when man makes the proper motions of faith. It is in Kierkegaard that the idea is broached more explicitly. Kierkegaard states that there is an objective way of knowing something and a way of subjectivity. Because of the very nature of God the objective way can never serve for the knowledge of God. Corresponding to God as Subject is our subjectivity, and only as our subjectivity is excited do we encounter God, the Subject" (*Handbook of Contemporary Theology*, p. 54). Also see Barth, *Church Dogmatics* (trans. G. T. Thomson [Edinburgh: T & T Clark, 1969], 2/1:26), where he offers a similar argument against the spectator stance as one studies theology.

[13]Peters, *God—The World's Future*, p. 29.

[14]Helmut Thielicke, *A Thielicke Trilogy: Out of the Depths*, trans. G. W. Bromiley (Grand Rapids, Mich.: Baker, 1980), pp. 249-51.

[15]Edgar McKnight offers a telling illustration of this reversal in the quest of knowledge. He explains that Third World Christians "are teaching us that understanding of the Bible doesn't always move in a logical fashion from theory to praxis. Bernard Lategan has studied the interpretation of Romans 13 in the South African context, highlighting reading strategies affirming or resisting what appears to be a requirement of Christians to obey the state. Some of the interpretations that Lategan studied were the work of groups of South African biblical scholars who had seen the effects of official practices of apartheid upon their fellow South Africans. They were concerned with the text of Romans that declares Christians are to be subject to governing authorities, because the Dutch Reformed Church had used that text to support the system of apartheid. The scholars, many of them Reformed, wanted to challenge the interpretation of the Dutch Reformed Church. They often organized their arguments in logical fashion, moving from questions of language, to questions of history, to questions of praxis. But in fact they began with praxis. They knew that apartheid was wrong and needed to be abolished. They began with praxis and developed theory adequate to praxis" (McKnight, "A Defense of a Postmodern Use of the Bible," pp. 77-78).

[16]Peters, *God—The World's Future*, p. 28.

[17]This corresponds to that which Kierkegaard once wrote in his journal: "It is really Christianity that has brought this doubt into the world, for in Christianity this self received its meaning. Doubt is conquered not by the system [of rationality] but by faith, just as it is faith that has brought doubt into the world" (*Philosophical Fragments/Johannes Climacus*, ed. and trans. Howard V. Hong and Edna H. Hong [Princeton, N.J.: Princeton University Press, 1985], p. 256).

[18]Philip Yancey, *Reaching for the Invisible God: What Can We Expect to Find?* (Grand Rapids, Mich.: Zondervan, 2000), p. 38.

[19]Kierkegaard describes this as "the eternal decision" (*Concluding Unscientific Postscript*, p. 199). A person does not assent to Christianity based upon the irrefutable conclusions of rational analysis; rather, he or she can only decide for Christianity based upon a faith that still has many unanswered questions. Emil Brunner has similarly observed that becoming a Christian "cannot therefore be appropriated in one act of objective perception of truth, but only in an act of personal surrender and decision" (*Revelation and Reason*, p. 371).

[20]Helmut Thielicke, *A Thielicke Trilogy: Between God and Satan*, trans. C. C. Barber (Grand Rapids, Mich.: Baker, 1980), p. 18.

[21]Ibid.

[22]James McClendon Jr. and James M. Smith, *Convictions: Defusing Religious Relativism* (Valley Forge, Penn.: Trinity Press International, 1994), p. 112.

[23]McKnight, "A Defense of a Postmodern Use of the Bible," p. 74.

[24]John F. MacArthur Jr., *The Gospel According to Jesus* (Grand Rapids, Mich.: Zondervan, 1988), flyleaf.

[25]Charles Ryrie, *So Great Salvation* (Wheaton, Ill.: Victor, 1988), pp. 30-31.

[26]See, for example, ibid., p. 45.

[27]Ibid., pp. 45-46.

[28]MacArthur, *Gospel According to Jesus,* p. 199.

[29]Ibid., p. 174.

[30]Ibid., p. 183.

[31]Ryrie, *So Great Salvation,* p. 48.

[32]In recent ecumenical dialogues between the Roman Catholic Church and the Lutheran World Federation, it has been determined that a level of misunderstanding had occurred between the two positions in the sixteenth century and that their mutual anathemas were attacking phantom constructs of the other side. More correctly, the Reformers, though emphasizing imputation, also recognized the role of infusion; and the Catholic scholars at the Council of Trent, though emphasizing infusion, also recognized the role of imputation. Moreover, each side characterized the other in extreme language that gave a false presentation of their true positions. This is not to say that genuine differences did not exist between the two sides, but that these differences were not as stark as originally articulated. The recent acknowledgement of such misunderstandings is of particular note when considering the lordship salvation debate between MacArthur and Ryrie.

[33]Interview with Jerry Falwell, *Penthouse,* March 1981, p. 150, as cited in Mark A. Noll, "Common Sense Traditions and American Evangelical Thought," *American Quarterly* 37, no. 2 (1985): 225.

[34]Those two regionals were the New England Regional (Connecticut, Maine, Massachusetts, New Hampshire, Rhode Island, Vermont) and the Del-Mar-Va Regional (Delaware, Maryland, Virginia). These ecclesial fractures occurred in the early 1990s. Even in the late 1990s, I noted through personal experience and interviews that the membership within the IFCA-International was still polarized and thereby troubled by the effects of this debate.

[35]Thomas Couch, "Finding 'Common Ground' in the Lordship Salvation Controversy," unpublished paper presented at the IFCA-International Convention, Kalamazoo, Michigan, June 28, 2002.

[36]William C. Placher, *Unapologetic Theology: A Christian Voice in a Pluralistic Conversation* (Louisville, Ky.: Westminster John Knox, 1989), p. 117.

[37]Robert W. Jenson, *Unbaptized God: The Basic Flaw in Ecumenical Theology* (Minneapolis: Fortress, 1992), p. 3.

[38]Ibid., p. 1.

[39]Ibid., p. 134.

[40]Garry Wills, *Why I Am a Catholic* (Boston: Houghton Mifflin, 2002), p. 6.

[41]Whether the pope is a "flawed believer" is an open question to many opposing (anti-Catholic) ecclesial traditions.

[42]See Irenaeus *Against Heresies* 1.9.4; 1.22.1; 1.27.1; 3.11.1; and Tertullian *On the Pallium* 3.1; 6.2; 8.1.

[43]Timothy George, *Theology of the Reformers* (Nashville: Broadman, 1987), pp. 81-82. Also see Jaroslav Pelikan, *The Riddle of Roman Catholicism* (New York: Abingdon, 1959), pp. 47-48.

Conclusion: Postmodernism and the Church in Context

[1]Friedrich Nietzsche, *The Gay Science,* trans. Walter Kaufman (New York: Vintage, 1974), §125.

[2]Ibid.

[3]Ibid.

[4]Ibid., §343.

[5]Charles Colson has written similarly. In his commencement address at Wheaton College in 2000, entitled "The Cultivation of Conscience," he said, "In postmodernism there is only one ultimate certainty: power" (reprinted in *Chuck Colson Speaks: Twelve Key Messages from Today's Leading Defender of the Christian Faith* [Uhrichsville, Ohio: Promise Press, 2000], p. 74).

[6]Charles Colson, "More Doctrine, Not Less," *Christianity Today,* April 22, 2002, p. 96.

[7]Colson, "Cultivation of Conscience," p. 79.

[8]Ibid.

[9]Joseph F. Girzone, *Joshua: A Parable for Today* (New York: Collier, 1987), pp. 154-55.

[10]Ibid., pp. 175-76.

Epilogue: New Questions

[1]See Irenaeus *Against Heresies* 1.9.4; 1.22.1; 1.27.1; 3.11.1; and Tertullian *On the Pallium* 3.1; 6.2; 8.1.

[2]Martin Luther, *The Schmalkald Articles,* trans. William R. Russell (Minneapolis: Fortress, 1996), p. 34. Melanchthon began referring to himself as "Melanthon" in 1531.

[3]In this respect I recommend Lindbeck's "A Question of Compatibility: A Lutheran Reflects on Trent," in *Justification by Faith: Lutherans and Catholics in Dialogue,* ed. H. George Anderson, T. Austin Murphy and Joseph A. Burgess (Minneapolis: Augsburg, 1985), pp. 230-40. Here Lindbeck argues forcefully that the differences between sixteenth century Lutheran theologians and the Roman Catholic theologians at the Council of Trent amounted to a misunderstanding on the question of the gospel. Polemical attacks on the extremities of either position mitigated the similarities between the more reasoned theologians on either side. Many contemporary Roman Catholic theologians, he explains, insist that Trent "combined *assensus* and *fiducia* [an *assent* to the *faith:* two Lutheran terms associated with infused righteousness] in its concept of faith" (p. 233), although they did not specifically embrace these terms. "If something like this is the case," Lindbeck adds, "then a doctrinal reconciliation which was practically impossible in the sixteenth century may be possible today" (p. 232). He cites a number of Catholic and Protestant theologians who are of the same theological opinion: Carl Peter, Edmund Schlink, Otto Pesch, Reinhard Koesters and Michael Schmaus.

Another theologian of note, Richard John Neuhaus, has made a similar observation of the Roman Catholic Church and responded with a dramatic change of his own ecclesiological identification. Having migrated from the Missouri Synod to the Evangelical Lutheran Church in America, Neuhaus left Lutheranism altogether in 1990 to join the Roman Catholic Church, insisting that the Reformation schism was no longer necessary, due to Rome's reforming itself.

[4]It has also struck a negative note for some Catholic theologians. See, for example, Garry Wills, *Papal Sin: Structures of Deceit* (New York: Doubleday, 2000).

Appendix: Five Major Paradigms Defined

[1]Ted Peters, *God—The World's Future: Systematic Theology for a Postmodern Era* (Minneapolis: Fortress, 1992), p. 12.

[2]Ibid., p. 24.

[3]For example, Clement writes, "Plato too was a follower of our system of law, and it is obvious that he had spent a lot of time on each of its precepts. . . . What is Plato but Moses speaking Greek?" (*Stromateis* 1.22.150, in *Fathers of the Church,* trans. John Ferguson, vol. 85 [Wash-

ington, D.C.: Catholic University of America Press, 1991]).

[4]Peters, *God—The World's Future,* p. 11.

[5]This date, of course, is somewhat arbitrary. My choosing 1789 is due to the fact that the fall of the Bastille was enormously significant in the historical development of philosophical thought. With the success of the French Revolution, Enlightenment philosophy, which heretofore was restricted to a limited cadre of scholars, now became the staple of an entire culture. Therefore, though Descartes (1696-1650) predates the Enlightenment's official advent by over one hundred years, he can still be identified as its essential founder. Such is always the case with major paradigmatic shifts in philosophy: founders and important early thinkers always predate the time when paradigms make their seismic shifts and rearrange the way in which entire cultures think.

[6]Alasdair MacIntyre, "Existentialism," in *The Encyclopedia of Philosophy,* vol. 3 (New York: Macmillan, 1967), p. 153.

[7]Central to the Kantian system, of course, is to explore ways to lessen the distance of this gap so that, though the gap cannot be breached, approximations can be acquired that can provide us with a working knowledge of reality. This working knowledge was enhanced, for example, through the Kantian antinomies where empirical and rational knowledge competed with one another in the exploration of truth. Knowledge, then, was always subject to revision as further information was uncovered. The Kantian system, then, pressed in anti-postmodern direction in that, though recognizing the presence of a gap between phenomena (perception) and noumena (reality), it was never satisfied with the gap and always pressed towards an accurate understanding of reality where phenomena was increasingly minimized.

[8]George F. Will, *With a Happy Eye But . . .* (New York: Free Press, 2002), p. 35.

[9]Ibid.

[10]Ibid., pp. 35-36.

[11]Samuel Horn, "Ministering in a Postmodern World: How Shall We Then Live?" *Integrity of Heart* 6, no. 1 (2001-2002): 12.

[12]Charles Colson, "More Doctrine, Not Less," *Christianity Today,* April 22, 2002, p. 96.

[13]Charles Colson, "Cultivation of Conscience," in *Chuck Colson Speaks: Twelve Key Messages from Today's Leading Defender of the Christian Faith* [Uhrichsville, Ohio: Promise Press, 2000], p. 79.

[14]Donald Carson, *The Gagging of God: Christianity Confronts Pluralism* (Grand Rapids, Mich.: Zondervan, 1996), p. 79.

Glossary: Key Terms in the Postmodern Debate

[1]Alvin Plantinga, "How to Be an Anti-Realist," *Proceedings and Addresses of the American Philosophical Association* 56, no. 1 (1982): 48. Also see Alvin Plantinga, "Reason and Belief in God," in *Faith, Rationality, Reason, and Belief in God,* ed. Alvin Plantinga and Nicholas Wolterstorff (Notre Dame: Notre Dame University Press, 1983), pp. 16-93; Jeffrey Hensley, "Are Postliberals Necessarily Antirealists? Reexamining the Metaphysics of Lindbeck's Postliberal Theology," in *The Nature of Confession,* ed. Timothy Phillips and Dennis Okholm (Downers Grove, Ill.: InterVarsity Press, 1996), pp. 69-80; Raymond Dennehy, "Unreal Realism," *Thomist* 55 (1991): 631-55; Donald Davidson, "On the Very Idea of a Conceptual Scheme," *Proceedings and Addresses of the American Philosophical Association* 47 (1973-1974); and Hilary Putnam, *Reason, Truth and History* (Cambridge: Cambridge University Press, 1981), *Realism and Reason* (Cambridge: Cambridge University Press, 1983), and *The Many Faces of Realism* (La Salle, Ill.: Open Court, 1987).

[2]Richard Rorty, *The Consequences of Pragmatism* (Minneapolis: University of Minnesota Press, 1982), p. 168.

[3]Ibid., p. 166, italics in original.

[4]Plantinga, "How to Be an Anti-Realist," p. 48.

[5]Hensley, "Are Postliberals Necessarily Antirealists?" p. 73.

[6]Donald Davidson, "On the Very Idea of a Conceptual Scheme," p. 5.

[7]Hensley, "Are Postliberals Necessarily Antirealists?" p. 74.

[8]Lindbeck, "Book Reviews," *Lutheran World* 6 (1959-1960): 317. The essay by Stählin is located in *Die Katholizität der Kirche,* ed. Hans Asmussen and Wilhelm Stählin (Stuttgart: Evangelisches Verlagswerk, 1957).

[9]See Jürgen Moltmann, *The Trinity and the Kingdom* (Minneapolis: Fortress, 1993), pp. 157-58.

[10]Stanley Grenz and John R. Franke, *Beyond Foundationalism: Shaping Theology in a Postmodern Context* (Louisville, Ky.: Westminster John Knox, 2001), p. 24.

[11]Mitch Albom, *Tuesdays with Morrie* (New York: Doubleday, 1997), p. 40.

[12]Grenz and Franke, *Beyond Foundationalism,* p. 30.

[13]Aristotle, *De interpretatione* 16a3-8; in *The Basic Works of Aristotle,* ed. Richard McKeon (New York: Random House, 1941).

[14]The Augsburg Confession §21, *Confessions and Catechisms of the Reformation,* ed. Mark A. Noll (Grand Rapids, Mich.: Baker, 1991), p. 97.

[15]George Weigel, "Faith, Freedom, and Responsibility," in *Evangelicals and Catholics Together: Towards a Common Mission,* ed. Charles Colson and Richard John Neuhaus (Dallas: Word, 1995), p. 61.

[16]Immanuel Kant, *Critique of Pure Reason,* trans. Norman Kemp Smith (New York: St. Martin's Press, 1929), A632/B660.

[17]Jacques Derridá, *Of Grammatology,* trans. Gayatri Chakravorty Spivak (Baltimore, Md.: Johns Hopkins University Press, 1976), p. 158.

[18]Hensley, "Are Postliberals Necessarily Antirealists?" 77.

[19]Ibid., p. 70.

[20]Immanuel Kant, *Groundwork for the Metaphysics of Morals,* trans. Allen W. Wood (New Haven, Conn.: Yale University Press, 2002), pp. 37, 47, 52.

[21]Mark Noll, "Common Sense Traditions and American Evangelical Thought," *American Quarterly* 37, no. 2 (1985): 218.

[22]Ibid., pp. 220-23.

[23]James K. A. Smith, *The Fall of Interpretation: Philosophical Foundations for a Creational Hermeneutic* (Downers Grove, Ill.: InterVarsity Press, 2000), p. 118.

[24]Mark A. Noll, *Turning Points: Decisive Moments in the History of Christianity* (Grand Rapids, Mich.: Baker, 1997), p. 167.

[25]Ibid., p. 169.

[26]See Alister McGrath, *Luther's Theology of the Cross: Martin Luther's Theological Breakthrough* (Grand Rapids, Mich.: Baker, 1990), pp. 148-75, with special emphasis on pp. 149-50.

[27]D. Lyle Dabney, *Die Kenosis des Geistes: Kontinuität zwischen Schöpfung und Erlösung im Werk des Heiligen Geistes* (Neukirchen-Vluyn: Neukirchener Verlag, 1997), pp. 109-21, my translation.

[28]Ibid., p. 110, my translation.

[29]See Immanuel Kant, *Religion Within the Limits of Reason Alone* (New York: Harper, 1960).

[30]Ibid., p. 110.

[31]Ibid.

[32]Ibid., p. 111.
[33]Ibid., p. 113.
[34]Ibid.
[35]Ibid.
[36]Ibid., p. 115.

Author Index

Abelard, Peter, 165
Ahlstrom, Sydney E., 254
Albom, Mitch, 280
Anselm, 164, 185, 213
Aquinas, Thomas. See Thomas Aquinas
Arand, Charles P., 170, 273
Aristotle, 73, 185, 280
Auerbach, Erich, 274
Augustine of Hippo, 26-30, 33, 45, 127, 252
Balthasar, Hans Urs von, 246
Barrett, David B., 255
Barth, Karl, 23, 75, 80, 97-104, 116-17, 119,
    121-22, 127, 153-54, 223, 245-46, 263, 272
Berger, Peter L., 270
Bernstein, Richard, 182, 275
Bloom, Allan, 13, 250
Bork, Robert P., 250, 265, 268
Bozeman, Theodore Dwight, 254
Brunner, Emil, 223, 265, 275-76
Buber, Martin, 272
Buckley, James J., 143, 269
Bultmann, Rudolf, 184, 223
Cage, John, 76
Calvin, John, 38, 230, 263
Camus, Albert, 223
Capote, Truman, 76
Caputo, John D., 41, 255
Carnell, Edward J., 40
Carson, Donald, 22, 90, 91, 252, 262, 279
Chafer, Lewis Sperry, 39, 255-56
Clement of Alexandria, 278
Colson, Charles, 205, 228, 259, 265, 278-79
Conner, Steven, 258
Copernicus, Nicolaus, 128-29
Couch, Thomas, 194, 277
Crabb, Lawrence, Jr., 40, 162, 255
Creegan, Nicola Hoggard, 132, 268
Crouter, Richard, 254
Curtis, Brent, 163, 181, 272
Dabney, D. Lyle, 5, 166-67, 180, 245-46,
    273-74, 280

Davidson, Donald, 233, 279-80
Dembski, William A., 258
Derridá, Jacques, 4, 110, 139, 143-47, 157, 187,
    223, 227, 230, 241, 244, 261, 264-65, 280
Descartes, René, 3, 26, 30, 34, 38, 45-46, 73,
    182, 188, 253, 260, 279
Dionysius the Areopagite, 127
Eckhart, Meister, 127
Eldredge, John, 163, 181, 272
Erickson, Millard, 71, 258
Erigena, John Scotus, 127
Fackre, Gabriel, 258
Falwell, Jerry, 40, 255, 277
Fellows, Ward J., 130, 141, 267
Finney, Charles, 39-40, 255
Flower, Elizabeth, 255
Ford, David F., 148, 270
Foucault, Michel, 4, 15-16, 88, 223, 228, 251
Franke, John R., 45, 116, 164, 237, 254-56,
    263, 266, 272, 280
Frei, Hans W., 44, 142, 149, 172, 256, 266,
    269, 274
Gadamer, Hans-Georg, 173, 274
Gaede, S. D., 262
Geivett, R. Douglas, 136-38, 141, 268
George, Timothy, 43, 256, 277
Gilson, Etienne, 253
Girzone, Joseph, 207, 209, 278
Gregory of Nyssa, 267
Grenz, Stanley J., 14, 45, 62-63, 101, 116-22,
    164, 237, 250, 254-56, 258, 263, 266, 272,
    280
Groothuis, Douglas, 86, 259, 261
Harris, Thomas, 214
Hegel, Georg W. F., 74, 237, 249
Heidegger, Martin, 4, 75, 110, 139, 230, 240,
    259, 264-65
Henry, Carl F. H., 259
Hensley, Jeffrey, 233, 270, 279-80
Heraclitus, 236
Herrmann, Wilhelm, 98
Hick, John, 23, 68, 124-41, 198-99, 202, 258,
    266-68
Hodge, Charles, 39, 255
Holmer, Paul, 173, 274
Horn, Samuel, 279
Hostetler, Robert, 89, 261-62

Subject Index

anonymous Christianity, 37, 62, 133-34, 234
antirealism, 97, 126-28, 141, 155, 158, 232-34
apophatic theology, 127
biblical (realistic) narrative, the, 39, 43-45, 148, 151-52, 163-64
Cartesian anxiety, the, 182, 202, 262
catholicity, 59, 66, 86, 234
Chalcedonian formulation, the, 137-38
charismatic movement, the, 251
Cogito, the, 3-4, 6, 30-34, 38, 43-45, 71-72, 78, 80, 85, 91-95, 97-101, 103, 109-12, 117, 120, 122, 124, 142, 155, 159, 170, 182-83, 188, 211-14, 222, 224-25, 234-36, 253, 264
complexio oppositorum, 147, 235
conservatism, theological, 5, 34-35, 37-38, 44-45, 71-72, 98, 107, 120, 211, 250
Copernican revolution, the, 22, 126, 128-30, 139-41, 268
correlational theology, 37, 62
creeds and confessions, the, 39, 42, 45, 118, 147, 149-51, 153, 199, 214
cultural-linguisticism, 144
dispensationalism, 39, 251
ecumenism, 5, 18-20, 24, 47-70, 175-79, 197, 209, 251
Einsteinian physics, 233, 251
epiphanic model of God, the, 50-53, 55-60, 70, 104, 117
eschatological model of God, the, 50, 53-55, 57-61, 70
existentialism, 2, 24, 71-72, 74-80, 94, 224, 225, 258, 270
evangelism, 182, 196-202
evidentialist apologetics, 39-40, 45
fideism, 112, 211-13, 236
fides quaerens intellectum (faith seeking knowledge), 85, 95, 185, 213
filioque, 5, 246, 273
foundationalism, 23, 236-37
God's eye, the, 25, 34, 64, 237-39

Heilsgeschichte (salvation history), 65-66
hermeneutical circle, the, 184-88
hermeneutics of creation, the, 109-10, 112, 122-23
hermeneutics of suspicion, the, 15, 88, 183-84, 251
higher critical methodology, the, 99-101, 125
hyperfundamentalism, 93
imputation, the doctrine of, 54, 192, 209, 215
indefectibility, the doctrine of, 42, 214, 239
inerrancy, the doctrine of, 38, 80-84, 95-96, 212-13, 251, 260, 273
infusion, the doctrine of, 192, 209, 215
intratextuality and extratextuality, 106-9, 122-23
King James Only controversy, the, 260
language game theory, 7, 68, 127, 152, 155, 236, 239-40
leap of faith, the, 74, 212
liberalism, theological, 3, 5, 34-37, 44-45, 71, 97-98, 104-6, 109-11, 115, 131-35, 138, 141, 211, 250-51, 258, 268, 273
lordship salvation controversy, the, 190-96
Magna Carta, the, 161-62
Melanchthon codicil, the, 19, 215-16, 252
metanarrative, 116, 119-21
modernism, 1, 3-4, 6-7, 9, 13, 18, 21, 23-24, 34-35, 61-62, 64, 80, 90, 92, 95, 113, 132, 148, 203-4, 210, 217, 222-23, 238, 250-51, 258
neo-evangelicalism, 251
neo-orthodoxy, 75, 97-98, 119
neo-Platonism, 30
Newtonian physics, 233, 251
nuda scriptura, 43, 199, 202, 213
ontotheology, 144, 237, 240
papal infallibility, 66, 216, 239
pietism, 21, 91-92
play of the trace, the, 236, 241
postliberalism, 142-43, 270
postmodernism, 1, 3-7, 9, 13-18, 20, 22-26, 47, 62-64, 67, 70-72, 75-80, 82, 88-91, 96, 133-35, 138-40, 143-44, 146, 152, 156-58, 160-61, 204-6, 210, 217, 225, 235, 250, 254, 258-59, 262, 268-69